Mathematical
Foundations
of
Programming

Mathematical Foundations of Programming

FRANK S. BECKMAN
Brooklyn College of the City University of New York

 ADDISON-WESLEY PUBLISHING COMPANY
Reading, Massachusetts • Menlo Park, California
London • Amsterdam • Don Mills, Ontario • Sydney

Library of Congress Cataloging in Publication Data

Beckman, Frank S.
    Mathematical foundations of programming.

    (Systems programming series)
    Includes bibliographies and index.
    1. Logic, symbolic and mathematical.   2.   Formal languages.   I.   Title.
    QA9.B36   519.4   79-1453
    ISBN 0-201-14462-X

For Shirley, and Susan,
Denise, Jonathan, Howard, and Michael

THE SYSTEMS PROGRAMMING SERIES

*The Program Development Process Part I—The Individual Programmer	Joel D. Aron
The Program Development Process Part II—The Programming Team	Joel D. Aron
*The Structure and Design of Programming Languages	John E. Nicholls
*Mathematical Foundations of Programming	Frank Beckman
Structured Programming: Theory and Practice	Richard C. Linger Harlan D. Mills Bernard I. Witt
*The Environment for Systems Programs	Frederic G. Withington
*Coded Character Sets; History and Development	Charles E. Mackenzie
*An Introduction To Database Systems, Second Edition	C. J. Date
Interactive Computer Graphics	James Foley Andries Van Dam
*Sorting and Sort Systems	Harold Lorin
*Compiler Design Theory	Philip M. Lewis II Daniel J. Rosenkrantz Richard E. Stearns
*Communications Architecture for Distributed Systems	R. J. Cypser
*Recursive Programming Techniques	William Burge
Conceptual Structures: Information Processing in Mind and Machines	John F. Sowa
*Modeling and Analysis: An Introduction to System Performance Evaluation Methodology	Hisashi Kobayashi

*Published

IBM EDITORIAL BOARD

Preface

The author's intent in writing this book is to cover in descriptive terms a good part of the mathematics that bears upon computer programming and, in some cases, upon computer design. We are not concerned with the substantial body of mathematics relevant to the uses of the computer but restrict the discussion to those subjects that have implications to the fundamental nature of the computing process.

The appropriate subject areas—mathematical logic and foundations, computability and recursive function theory, formal linguistics, and automata theory—are vast, with a rapidly growing body of literature that has been undoubtedly stimulated by the sweeping role of the computer. This book does not provide a treatment of these topics with mathematical depth. It is not suitable for serious students of mathematics in undergraduate or graduate courses devoted to these subjects, where a more formal and complete development might be desirable. It is possible, however, that in some cases such students may find in the sequel a perspective or an emphasis that is different from that which might appear in a more rigorous coverage of these topics.

Relaxing the need to be rigorous, concise, and complete has allowed us to be more expository than might be tolerable in a work of greater mathematical sophistication. We are more concerned with telling what these subjects are about than with giving self-contained expositions of them.

The hundreds of thousands of persons who work in computer programming or who are in training for this profession have very diverse mathematical backgrounds. Many who entered the field before the general availability of formal computer science programs in the colleges are emigrants from liberal arts or commercial backgrounds and often have very meager backgrounds in mathematics. There are even some with undergraduate majors in the sciences or in mathematics who are not comfortable with a strong mathematical treatment that is conducted with high standards. Yet it seems that those who will spend their working lives in computing should have some curiosity about, and acquire some understanding of, what mathematics has to offer in providing a greater insight into the phenomena surrounding the computer—even when this insight has no apparent immediate utility. It is this group, as well as undergraduate students in computer science, for which this "intelligent layman's" treatment of these subjects is intended. There is, however, a great risk in attempting something of this kind. There is, on the one hand, the danger of being superficial, imprecise, and distorting of the subject matter so that it loses intellectual appeal, and, on the other hand, of not succeeding in reaching the audience for which the work is intended. We hope we have been able to navigate successfully between these two perils.

With several small exceptions that can be ignored, no knowledge of the calculus or of college level mathematics is assumed on the part of the reader. However, this material is far from being mathematically trivial, and after teaching it to a number of undergraduate classes, the author believes that the student should have a level of mathematical maturity that is normally associated with the completion of a year of the elementary calculus or, perhaps, with the completion of a year of finite mathematics. Some mathematical talent is required, and a number of exercises of varying difficulty are included in the text with, in some cases, part of the mathematical exposition being relegated to the exercises. The reader is also expected to have significant familiarity with the art of programming.

We have emphasized mathematical concepts and results that relate to computer programming in several different ways. Some fundamental ideas and techniques should routinely be part of the arsenal of every programmer. Some topics provide a cultural background, in part, to the programming art. Some are finding application in the design of programming systems and compilers as programming evolves from an art to a science, and some topics have no significant utility at present but are relevant to emerging theories that may lead to important applications in the future.

We suggest that this material is suitable for a one-year course for undergraduate majors in computer science or in computational mathematics. For many students this course might be considered in place of a set of undergraduate courses currently bearing titles such as: Discrete Structures, Theory of Computability, Formal Languages and Automata, Sequential Machines. The author believes that handling this subject matter in this manner will enable a more appropriate and better-defined separation between undergraduate and graduate offerings in these mathematical areas of computer science.

Chapter 1 emphasizes the fundamental nature of effective procedures— those procedures that can be executed on a digital computer with no restrictions on time or on size of storage. In an appendix some provocative questions concerning the roles of effectiveness in mathematics and in physics are briefly mentioned. For most, but not all, classes it would be wise not to discuss this appendix in the early part of the course. It should be omitted or, perhaps, reviewed near the end of the course. Chapters 2 and 3 touch on a miscellany of topics that bear upon programming. These are rather loosely lumped together as being within the foundations of mathematics, and they include the concept of a function, some of its generalizations and methods of definition, Boolean algebra and some of its models, including the propositional calculus, the use of "genetic" methods in mathematics and in computing theory, formal systems, the technique of arithmetization, some fundamental notions of set theory, a very brief introduction to transfinite numbers, and, as an appendix, a description of the rudiments of graph theory.

In Chapter 4 the fundamental ideas of the theory of recursive, or computable, functions and some implications to the definition of procedures and to structured programming are very briefly considered. The elaboration of the concept of a computable function through the use of Turing machines is considered in Chapter 5, culminating in the notion of Turing's "shortcode" that some have seen as an anticipation of the use of higher level programming languages. Chapter 6 emphasizes the universal Turing machine as a theoretical model of the digital computer, gives some additional implications of Turing machine theory to the "real" world of computing, and looks at other models of the computing process.

Chapter 7 includes some general remarks about automata, emphasizing the notions of "state" and "state transition," and including a general classification of automata. Chapter 8 is devoted to the very important class of finite state automata, an area that is of great importance in the theory of compiling and of programming systems design. Chapter 9 concerns symbol manipulation systems and presents an introduction to formal linguistics. It includes discussions of syntax and semantics, Chomsky's methods for defining grammars, and implications of these concepts to techniques for defining programming languages and for writing their compilers.

Chapter 10 covers some of the significant relationships between formal languages and automata and between formal languages and programming systems. Brief mention is made of some ongoing work on program verification and on methods for defining the semantics of programming languages.

We cite, as an addendum, some provocative work, marginally related to this last point, on the design of a formal language that has been suggested for communication with remote civilizations within the galaxy. Chapter 11 provides a look at the newly developing, and somewhat chaotic, theory of computational complexity. A number of diverse results that have been obtained to date are briefly described in order to give the reader an appreciation of the kinds of problems that are studied in this area. Chapter 12 offers some summarizing remarks on the evolution of key ideas and new fields during the last several decades and refers to the interesting injection, in the last few years, of some unifying notions of modern algebra and the possible influence of these ideas on the future development of a number of these subjects. Almost all of this book concerns the contributions of mathematics to computing; however, it is noted as well that mathematics has a debt to computing (which cannot be fully assessed at present). An appendix to Chapter 12 is intended to give the reader some taste of the abstract approach of algebra in the study of some of the problems of automata, languages, and machines.

It is a pleasure to acknowledge the assistance I have received from a number of people. First, it was my good fortune that the IBM Corporation assigned Mrs. Joanne Bennett to type the manuscript. She is an extremely efficient and fast technical typist whose work conforms to the highest standards. The need to supply her periodically with quantities of manuscript sufficient to satisfy her voracious appetite for work counteracted my usual compulsion to procrastinate, and encouraged me to complete the book.

I am very grateful to the following individuals who have read the manuscript and made many constructive comments: the members of the IBM Editorial Board, especially Gerhard Chroust; Keith Harrow of Brooklyn College, and Daniel Moore of The Ohio State University.

Gordon Bassen, Jacob Brandler, and Rochelle Goldsmith of the Brooklyn College staff have taught classes based upon the manuscript and have given me much valuable feedback.

Gail Goodell, Bill Gruener, and Rima Zolina of the Addison-Wesley Publishing Company have each taken a personal interest in preparing the book for publication and have been very helpful. My daughter Susan Feller has furnished drawings which appear in Chapters 7 and 9, and my daughter Denise Beckman has critically read the manuscript.

Brooklyn College   F.S.B.
City University of New York
January 1980

Contents

CHAPTER 3
FOUNDATIONS OF MATHEMATICS II (APPLICATIONS)

CHAPTER 4
RECURSIVE FUNCTIONS

CHAPTER 9
FORMAL LANGUAGES—INTRODUCTION

CHAPTER 10
FORMAL LANGUAGES—FURTHER RELATIONSHIPS WITH
AUTOMATA AND PROGRAMMING LANGUAGES

1
The Effective

Several reviewers of this work have been irritated by the title of this chapter, taking the awkward construction to be an affectation of the author, and perhaps a word in defense is desirable. The ungrammatical title was chosen as an attention-getter to signal the pervasive occurrence and fundamental importance of effective, or computable, procedures—those procedures that can be stated completely in numeric terms and executed in finite time on a digital computer that has as much storage capacity as may be needed. Such procedures can more loosely be characterized as those based on the manipulation of symbols using rules that are simple, unambiguous, finite in length and finite in number. In a sense "the effective" is the same as "the completely precise," and we do not know what the limits are in mirroring the real world within the computer. If we had simply called this discussion "effective procedures," implying that we were looking at one particular class of procedures within some general classification, this might not convey the vital role that such procedures play. The emphasis in these computable procedures on finite methods and on constructing results—"one *can find* a number such that . . ." and not merely "*there exists* a number such that . . ."—is one that relates to the underlying structures of mathematics, physics, and philosophy. Much of mathematics has been cast in these (computable) terms and there are those who feel that *all* of mathematics should have this constructive orientation. We include in an appendix to this chapter, in a brief discussion of *constructive mathematics,* one example of a kind of mathematical argument from the elementary calculus that some mathematicians believe should be avoided. This example may be somewhat more technical than desirable for our announced intended reader, "the intelligent layman," but such instances will occur infrequently throughout the text.

1.1   DEFINITION OF EFFECTIVENESS

The notion in the computer sciences that a procedure is "effective" has a quite specific meaning which extends beyond the usual definition of this word as "producing a desired and definite effect." Loosely equivalent terms, frequently used, are "mechanical," "constructive," "finitistic," and "algorithmic." In programming digital computers we are always concerned with such procedures—with exhibiting concrete results which can always be expressed in numeric form. These procedures lead to these results in an unequivocal fashion. If they are repeated without change they yield the same results. It is the actual results that are of interest to us; we want to reach the point where we can display them, and we are not satisfied merely by knowledge of their existence. Such procedures are defined by the following characteristics:

1. They are *deterministic*—implied by the fact that we expect to obtain the same results from identical starting conditions.

2. They are executable in *finite time* and using some *finite facility*. We usually assume, however, that if it becomes necessary to increase this facility during the execution of the procedure, such as by increasing the quantity of paper available for a computation, this will be done. That is, the amount of "intermediate storage" needed is not necessarily known beforehand.

There is a considerable element of unreality in requiring only that our resources be finite without stating some limit on their size. This allows, for example, procedures that might take more time than the reputed age of the universe or that might require a storage capacity that exceeds the size of a finite universe. We shall, however, in several of the following chapters, consider procedures or machines that are restricted in their scope.

3. The execution of each such procedure is *"mechanical"* or *"constructive"* and can be precisely described so that another intelligence, or perhaps a device, could receive this description and use it to apply the procedure and obtain identical results.

4. These procedures can be *cast in numeric terms*—perhaps as a consequence of (3). They involve objects that can be represented by the natural numbers (i.e., the positive integers $1, 2, 3, \ldots$), and we can always interpret

the operations within such procedures as arithmetic operations. The numeric results obtained are possible values of things which are significant in our applications. Further, even the statements of these procedures are finite and can, themselves, be represented as natural numbers. (This last point will be made clearer in Chapter 5.)

The emphasis on procedures of this kind is, perhaps, the most distinctive characteristic of the study of the theory underlying digital computing. The broader consideration of them has significant implications to mathematics, physics, and philosophy. In discussing some aspects of effective procedures we shall touch briefly on several questions of profound character, and still not completely resolved to the satisfaction of all workers in the field, regarding the fundamental nature of mathematics. Our purpose is not to provide a complete description of these questions but merely to show that the things we are concerned with in digital computing form part of a great tableau of intellectual activities that are strongly related in spirit.

In other areas of discourse we often use terms or concepts or make analyses or classifications where we lack a completely clear understanding of the things we are talking about. Notions may be used that are vague and somewhat confused, and these may be used by different people with somewhat different meanings. Such subjective concepts as "soul," "happiness," "beauty," and "love" provide obvious examples of this. Usually, this vagueness is not avoidable, but we are able to tolerate the situation as long as the one who hears these words can translate them into seemingly compatible concepts in his or her own mind. Even in considering apparently objective qualifiers, we often lack the exactitude required to base effective procedures upon them. Consider, as a somewhat homely example, the procedure implicit in determining if a man is "bald." The usual determination of such a fact involves some subjective judgment and would hardly constitute an "effective" procedure. But we can easily define such a procedure that is, necessarily, somewhat absurd. We might, for example, say that he is "bald" if he has fewer than 15,000 hairs on the "top" (which would have to be clarified) of his head; otherwise, he is not. In this form we can conceive of an automaton making this decision. Note that we might modify the procedure and allow three responses to the question of his baldness—yes, no, undetermined. But here, too, in order to obtain a procedure which always yields the same answer for the same subject (that is, it is deterministic) we would have to supply a similarly preposterous definition. In our dealings with computers it is, of course, this kind of complete precision that is required.

Some parts of our implied definition of effective procedures are, however, subject to some very severe criticism. What, for example, do we mean by the procedures' being mechanical or constructive? Constructive by what?

As remarked by Rosser [10], the ancient Greeks, in considering the construction problems of elementary plane geometry, had a quite restricted notion of geometric constructibility in mind. When they considered the problem of trisecting the angle, or dividing an arbitrary angle into three equal parts, the tools that could be used were limited to the ruler and the compass. With such restrictions (familiar, of course, to all who have studied high school geometry) this famous problem, which had defied solution for over 2000 years, was finally proven in the nineteenth century to be impossible of solution in the general case. However, by use of some very simple additional devices, such as a paper strip, the problem can be easily solved (see Fig. 1.1). Similarly, implicit in any constructive or finitely performable procedure is an inventory of allowable fundamental steps.

In considering these weaknesses in our definition, two recourses are open to us. First, we can leave undefined the notion of finitely performable operations and depend upon an intuitive understanding of what we mean by such operations, perhaps limiting ourselves to certain standard arithmetic operations but without specifying these. This approach may seem imprecise, but if we recall that in any logically developed subject it is necessary to start the development with some undefined elements (in order to be able to make a beginning), then this approach does not seem so unreasonable. It may be as proper to begin with such undefined notions as, say, to accept the integers as the basic building blocks of mathematics, without attempting to define the integers in terms of still more fundamental concepts. Such an approach of not specifying the basic finitely performable operations is taken in the exposition of constructive mathematical analysis given by Bishop [2].

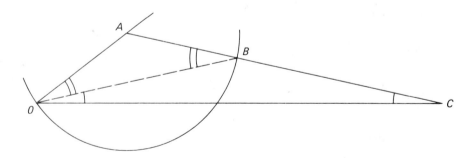

Fig. 1.1   Trisection of the angle AOC. Pick an arbitrary point A on one side and with it as center draw the circle passing through O. Slide a ruler, or straight edge, passing through A until the segment BC is equal to OB. We then have $\angle ACO = \angle BOC$, $\angle AOB = \angle ABO = 2\angle BOC$ and, therefore, $\angle BOC = (1/3)\angle AOC$.

We may, on the other hand, introduce some particular device, or class of devices, and define the "mechanical" or "constructive" procedures to be those which can be executed on these devices. Similarly, we may describe certain manipulations on strings of symbols, including perhaps arithmetic operations on strings of digits, and then define the permissible basic operations in terms of these string manipulations. We would then consider only those operations which fit within this framework. We shall discuss at length in the following chapters the implementation of the first approach by the use of Turing machines, and we shall also consider equivalent symbol manipulation schemes. In any case, a major assumption is implicit in the assertion that these "formal" systems are adequate to provide suitably broad definitions of "effective" procedures. For, once we define an effective or constructive procedure to be one that can be executed by a particular kind of apparatus or, perhaps, by a schema involving symbol manipulations, there can be no guarantee that we shall not encounter at some time a procedure that will be intuitively acceptable to us as constructive without our being able to execute it using the permissible means. We can verify only that all constructive procedures that we can conceive of at the time are executable within the allowable framework. Our statement of the permanent validity of this tenet will constitute an act of faith, incapable of proof, or as it is generally called, a "thesis" (see the discussions of Church's and Turing's theses in Chapters 4 and 5). Given a system for the formal definition of effective procedures to, say, compute functions, we can argue that it is sufficiently general if we are unable to conceive of any procedure that our intuition tells us is effective without such a procedure being executable within the assumed framework. However, any assumed framework, no matter how simply or elegantly it may be stated, includes some artificial restrictions, and it is not difficult to understand the attitude of those who prefer to leave undefined the notion of "finitely performable procedures."

1.2 THE MODERN AGE OF PYTHAGORAS

Returning to property (4) of effective procedures we observe that in digital computing we can always restrict, with no loss of generality, the objects of discussion to be the natural numbers—or, if we include zero as well, the nonnegative integers: $0, 1, 2, \ldots$. (In the literature it seems that the *natural numbers* are defined about half the time to be the positive integers and about half the time to include zero as well. We prefer the former definition, zero being in our view a more abstract notion, not quite as "natural" as $1, 2, \ldots$.) That we can dispense with such things as the negative integers or with alphabetic information comes as no surprise, for in practice we encode these other forms of information so that their representations look like natural numbers. For example, the minus sign in the representation of a negative integer may be identified by the "1" of a binary code, and we employ such encodings as the ASCII or EBCDIC codes to represent alphameric information.

The decimal or binary point is similarly handled by encoding. A number written in decimal floating point notation $A \cdot 10^{\alpha}$, or in binary floating point form $B \cdot 2^{\beta}$, can be represented in the machine by the pair of integers (A, α) or (B, β). Programming languages include facilities for users to tell the compiler through declarative statements what data formats should be assumed in the representation of variables. This information is needed to encode the internally stored strings of bits that represent the data, to determine how these stored data should be interpreted when used in calculation, and how they should be translated to readable strings of output characters. When we write

DECLARE M2 FIXED DECIMAL (8, 2);

in PL/I we are telling the compiler that when the variable M2 is to be printed it should be as an eight-digit decimal field with the decimal point two places from the right. The decimal point does not appear as a separate symbol in the internal representation of M2. Whether the representation of the decimal point in any system is by an EBCDIC or ASCII character or it is determined, as in our PL/I example, by a separately recorded scale factor, the internally stored data is a string of bits—a natural number.

Further, the steps in our procedures are expressible as arithmetic operations—or they involve making a choice from among several possible courses of action. We can conceive of procedures which have some of the characteristics of effective procedures but which operate on quite different objects than numbers—such as following a recipe to bake a cake or the mechanical procedure for adjusting the mixture setting on a four-barrel carburetor. However, unless we can describe these procedures with complete precision in symbolic terms or, equivalently, in terms of numbers and operations on these numbers, we shall not regard them as "effective." If we make completely precise the cake-making recipe and the carburetor adjustment procedure, they will lend themselves to this expression in arithmetic terms.

We have come, in our enormously varied use of computers, to appreciate how surprisingly nonrestrictive this limitation to the natural numbers may be. Our ever-widening span of applications, including the use of modeling and simulation, lend considerable credence to the notion attributed to Pythagoras (and cited in Aristotle's *Metaphysics*) that "the being of all things is number." (Bertrand Russell conveys this in poetic fashion in the prologue to his autobiography [14], where he briefly refers to the key passions, including the quest for knowledge, that dominated his life, "... I have tried to apprehend the Pythagorean power by which number holds sway above the flux.") This idea was the philosophical kernel of Pythagoreanism, and numbers were considered the elements of everything. Even such things as reason, justice, and marriage were identified with distinct numbers. The primacy of number, unlike some of the other principles of this school of philosophy, such as its emphasis on the transmigration of souls and the strict prohibition against eating beans, has a continuing validity that is far reaching indeed. Our modern emphasis on the computer is quite in line with these supposed beliefs of Pythagoras.

The fundamental role played by the natural numbers in mathematics is given a striking emphasis by the remark of the nineteenth century German mathematician, L. Kronecker, on the historical development of mathematics: "The natural numbers have been made by God; everything else is the work of man."

We are always doing arithmetic in using computers even when our applications seem far removed from it. Any data-processing operation can always be viewed as a computation of a *function* defined on the natural numbers (the input can always be regarded as an encoding of an integer) which assumes values (the output) that are interpretable as natural numbers. We shall discuss functions in more detail in Chapter 2, but a few brief remarks are appropriate here. Mathematically, a function is a *map* that associates a value with each of a set of admissible values, called its *domain*. The totality of assumed, or output, values is called its *range*. It is understood that, unless otherwise qualified, a function is single valued, that is, it takes on

Fig. 1.2 Pythagoras and Euclid as shown in the painting *The School of Athens* by Raphael. Pythagoras on the left is holding a book and the youth holds a tablet containing the Pythagorean harmonic scale. Euclid on the right is bending over to explain a problem to his pupils.

a unique value for each element in its domain of definition. If a function is defined on all the natural numbers we say it is *total*. We call it *partial* if its domain is not necessarily all the natural numbers, allowing it to be undefined for some arguments. Thus the partial functions include as a proper subset the total functions. (If every member of a set *B* is a member of the set *A* and there are some members of *A* that are not in *B*, then *B* is said to be a *proper* subset of *A*.) In view of the above remarks we are concerned only with functions that have their domains and ranges within the set of natural numbers and, usually, the word "function" will be used only in this restricted sense. Also, "number" will usually mean "natural number."

Our definitions imply, for example, that the domain of the function $\phi(x) = \sqrt{x + 4}$ is the set $\{0, 5, 12, 21, ...\}$, while its range is the set $\{2, 3, 4, 5, ...\}$.

The domain (and then, necessarily, the range) of a function might be the null set, or the set having no members, as, for example, in the case of the function defined by $\phi(x) = \sqrt{2(x + 1)^2}$. Since $\phi(x) = (x + 1)\sqrt{2}$, it is seen that $\phi(x)$ is not a natural number for any integral value of *x*.

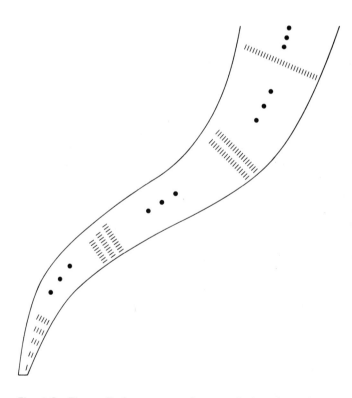

Fig. 1.3   The stuff of computer science and of mathematics.

When we simulate some process on a computer or examine computationally the workings of a mathematical model we not only are providing additional evidence for the principle espoused by the Pythagoreans, but we are also applying a technique that is important in mathematical logic—that of *arithmetization*. As used in logic, the expressions and statements of some logical system (see the discussion of *formal* systems in Chapter 2) are translated into numbers. Further, the proofs or derivations that lead from one or more statements to a new statement are translatable into functions that operate on the numbers corresponding to the given statements and yield as result the number corresponding to the new statement. We then can describe much of what takes place within a logical or formal system in terms of *arithmetic* and operations on *numbers*. This technique is illustrated by the arithmetization of Turing machines, which is described in Chapter 5.

1.3 ALGORITHMS

By an *algorithm* we mean an effective procedure that may be used to compute a function or to determine the truth or falsity of each statement within some class of statements concerning the natural numbers. The second case may also be viewed as the computation of a function if we identify "truth" and "falsity" by, say, 1 and 0 and consider as input those parameter values which serve to identify a particular statement within the given class of statements. As we have indicated above, we shall in later chapters make precise the notion of an effective procedure by assuming the equivalence of this vague notion and of procedures within certain well-defined formal frameworks. This will also make exact the notion of an algorithm. However, the term has been used for centuries without this usage being very much hampered by the vagueness implicit in the notion of finite, mechanical procedures. In the Middle Ages the word was used to refer to the execution of the arithmetic operations, as these are now universally taught in elementary schools, by the use of the Indo-Arabic numerals as opposed to the use of the abacus. The term is derived from the work on arithmetic of the Arab mathematician, al-Khwarizmi [1], who wrote his "Liber algorism" (the book of al-Khwarizmi) in Baghdad about 825 A.D.

If a function can be computed by some algorithm or effective procedure, we say that the function is *effectively calculable,* or *effectively computable.* (Sometimes "computable" is used in the literature with the special meaning of being computable by a machine, especially, Turing machine; cf. Chapter 5. We shall, however, not distinguish between "calculable" and "computable.") If an effective procedure exists to compute a partial function at those values of its arguments where it is defined, the function is a "partial effectively computable function."

As an example of an algorithm, we could give the mechanical procedure that obtains the sum or product of two numbers written in decimal notation. We prefer, however, to cite the less trivial classical "Euclidean algorithm" that is used to determine the greatest common divisor (GCD) of two numbers. We denote by $GCD(a, b)$ the greatest common divisor of two numbers a, b, that is, the largest number that divides both a and b exactly.

Given two numbers a, b, we determine $GCD(a, b)$ by applying the following procedure to obtain a sequence of quotients $q_1, q_2, \ldots, q_N$ and of remainders $r_1, r_2, \ldots, r_{N-1}$.

Suppose b is the smaller of a, b. We divide a by b giving a quotient q_1 and a remainder r_1. We next divide b by r_1 to get a quotient q_2 and a remainder r_2. Continue dividing repeatedly to obtain a sequence of q's and of r's as follows:

$$
\begin{aligned}
a &= q_1 b + r_1 \\
b &= q_2 r_1 + r_2 \\
r_1 &= q_3 r_2 + r_3 \\
&\ \ \vdots \qquad \vdots \\
r_{N-2} &= q_N r_{N-1} + r_N \\
r_{N-1} &= q_{N+1} r_N
\end{aligned}
\tag{1.1}
$$

The procedure terminates when the last division is exact, i.e., when, with reference to the above notation, $r_{N+1} = 0$. When this occurs, we conclude that r_N is $GCD(a, b)$.

It is a simple matter to see that the procedure must always terminate eventually since the successive remainders $r_1, r_2, \ldots$ are nonnegative and strictly decreasing and must, therefore, eventually vanish. We can show that r_N is a divisor of both a and b by first observing that from the last equation of (1.1) it divides r_{N-1}. Then, from the next to the last equation it must divide r_{N-2} and, repeating the argument, it must divide $\ldots r_2, r_1, b, a$.

To see that r_N is the *greatest* common divisor of a, b we note that, from the first equation of (1.1), any divisor of a, b is also a divisor of r_1. From the second equation we note that it must also be a divisor of r_2 and, by repetition, it must be a divisor of each of $\ldots r_{N-3}, r_{N-2}, r_{N-1}$.

Hence, r_N has been shown to be a divisor of a, b and any divisor of a, b is a divisor of r_N. These two facts imply that r_N is $GCD(a, b)$.

To illustrate the execution of this algorithm we determine $GCD(90, 924)$

$$
\begin{aligned}
924 &= 10 \cdot 90 + 24 \\
90 &= 3 \cdot 24 + 18 \\
24 &= 1 \cdot 18 + 6 \\
18 &= 3 \cdot 6.
\end{aligned}
$$

Therefore, $GCD(90, 924) = 6$.

The Euclidean algorithm, then, can also be said to be a *decision procedure* to determine the truth or falsity of the statement which, for given numbers x, y, asserts that "x and y are relatively prime" (i.e., x, y have no common divisors except 1).

We recognize in this algorithm all the distinctive characteristics we have cited for effective procedures.

Often, the completeness of our understanding of some situation is reflected by the extent to which we can define such procedures. For example, J. A. Moorer [9] writes, in a discussion of computer-aided musical composition:

> Some of the things Schoenberg does not give us that are essential for computer composition are functions to evaluate musical fragments. For instance, he defines "cadence" as a "progression of harmonies selected and arranged to produce a movement towards an ending on a definite degree." He illustrates this concept with many examples from Beethoven and Mozart, but he does not give us an algorithmic formula for determining whether a given fragment is a cadence. He also does not specify what elements contribute toward "movement," or even how one tells what a passage is moving toward. The programmer is then forced to use his own ingenuity to fill in the missing information. ... The degree to which Schoenberg is specific is the degree to which I believe we understand human composition.

Every systems analyst of experience has encountered such situations where existing procedures are described that are vague, imprecise, dependent upon an ill-defined exercise of judgment, and possibly employing incomplete information and poor communications—procedures that in their original form cannot be executed by a machine. In these situations we have examples either of procedures that are not effective or, at best, of procedures that can be made effective. The work of the analyst consists of recognizing the feasibility of doing this and of proving their effectiveness, after clarifying and refining the procedures, by defining them well enough to be able to program them. It is the actual programmed implementation of the procedures that conclusively demonstrates their effectiveness.

1.4 BERRY'S PARADOX

To illustrate difficulties that may lie behind an uncritical acceptance of some notions about effectively defined procedures, we consider a paradox given early in this century by G. G. Berry which is discussed, but not with all its implications, in a 1906 paper of Bertrand Russell [12]. The paradox is a variation of another and slightly older paradox due to Jules Richard.

Consider the defining phrase Q:

"the least integer not nameable in fewer than nineteen syllables."

This appears to denote a definite integer which, after very little checking, would seem to be the number $111,777$. (Count the syllables in "one hundred and eleven thousand, seven hundred and seventy seven.") However, the phrase Q can then be considered a name for this number *and* it involves only eighteen syllables. Thus it appears that the least integer not nameable in fewer than nineteen syllables can be named in eighteen syllables. Even if we were wrong in identifying $111,777$ as the number apparently defined by Q and the correct choice were another (necessarily larger) number, μ, the contradiction would still apply.

A little reflection makes plausible the idea that the difficulty must lie in our understanding of being "nameable." It seems that Q itself should not be considered an acceptable name for an integer. What, then, do we mean when we say that a particular string of words identifies or names a number? There are at least two possibilities to consider; we may mean that (1) the string of words provides sufficient information to enable us to write down (perhaps after an extended period of time) a unique number that satisfies the given description, i.e., it denotes an effective procedure to find a number—or we may take the weaker position that (2) the string of words provides information that implies that a unique number exists which possesses a stated property, *but* we are not necessarily able to find it. Even if we take (2), the less demanding alternative (for if (1) holds, then (2) necessarily follows), as the meaning of being "nameable," we may attempt to explain our paradox along the lines that no such integer as that defined by Q exists. We may, in fact, recall and seek analogies with the more familiar paradox concerning "the barber (male) who shaves those men in town, and only those men, who do not shave themselves." The apparent contradiction in this well-known verbal trickery then shows up in considering the question of whether the barber cited shaves himself. If he does, then he does not, and if he does not, then he does. This paradox is easily explained by noting that no such barber can exist. The contradictory self-reference implicit in the definition prevents any person from satisfying the description. Our paradox in this case is no deeper than if we postulated the existence of a man who is two inches taller than himself and thereby concluded that $2 = 0$.

In Berry's paradox, then, we may similarly conclude, because of the contradictory self-referential character of our definition, that no integer defined by the phrase Q exists since among the possible names implicit in the expression "nameable in fewer than nineteen syllables" of Q is Q itself. If, therefore, the number μ were named by the phrase Q it would not be nameable by Q, and thus Q is not the name of any number.

However, this is not the whole story. Let us persist in trying to view Q as a legitimate name of an integer, temporarily disregarding its self-contradictory character. Further, let us in the following assume the "stronger" meaning of "name" as in (1). Let us try to describe a procedure which will actually yield a number that has the requisite property. We first write down all the possible strings of nineteen or less English syllables. There are only a finite number of these, and once we determine the syllables that appear in the vocabulary of a standard English dictionary it is clear that we can go about compiling such a list. We may, for example, prepare our list in alphabetic order. It will be quite long, perhaps of the order of 10^{80} items, assuming something like 10,000 syllables. However, remember that we are assuming no restraints on the length of a procedure or on the amount of scratch paper that may be required to implement it (even if this exceeds the mass of a possibly finite universe). Therefore, the enormity of the process we are describing does not rule against its feasibility.

Let us, then, take this list, denoting the successive strings as $S_1, S_2, \ldots, S_M$, where M is the length of the list, and attempt to determine μ, the integer defined by Q. Starting with the number 1 we shall go through the list, most of the entries of which are gibberish, and attempt to find a string of syllables which defines the number selected. Thus, for the number 1 we may find (among others)

$$1 \leftrightarrow \text{ONE}$$

We do the same for 2, searching for a phrase that names or identifies 2. We perform this search repeatedly, our goal each time being the number which is one more than the number sought in the preceding search. In order to be able to carry this out *we assume that for an arbitrary number* N *we are able to determine if a given string of words provides a name for* N. Continuing, it seems that we must eventually come across a number for which our search fails, for there are only a finite number of strings in our list and, therefore, only a finite number of positive integers that these can represent. Thus, we arrive at the number μ, the first positive integer which is not "nameable" by any string in the list. The phrase Q itself is in our list, but this does not offer any particular difficulties, with the key assumption we have made. That is, we suppose, as with all other strings, that for a particular number N we can determine whether or not Q is a name for N. If we accept our earlier conclusion about Q, then for all numbers N we decide negatively about Q being a possible name for N.

It then seems that we have an effective procedure which must culminate in finding a number μ which is not named by any string of less than nineteen syllables, and this seems to refute our earlier proof that the phrase Q does not identify an integer, i.e., Q is not the name of a number and it is the name of a number. Where is the flaw in our argument? A review of our procedure shows that only one step can be seriously questioned, that being our ability to determine whether or not an arbitrary given string of words S is a name for an arbitrary integer N. We have here a heuristic argument which antici- pates some of the more rigorously obtained results of the theory of compu- tability and leads to the conclusion that *there is no effective procedure that will always enable us to determine if a purported name of an arbitrary number actually represents that number.*

Some vagueness is implicit in our discussion because we have dealt with strings of words drawn from a natural language, like English. However, we could assume a much more precise language, such as a programming lan- guage, to put together the defining expressions for the natural numbers and we could carry through our argument within such a more formal linguistic structure. The basic steps in our argument and conclusion would remain the same. The result in this case would take the form of the assertion that *there is no effective procedure to determine if an arbitrary given program com- putes a number* (cf. the discussion of the "halting problem" in Section 6.2).

We may ask how the "weaker" usage of "name" implicit in (2) might affect our argument, but this provides only a trivial variation of our discus- sion. For, let us assume now that we are able to examine an arbitrary string of syllables and determine (effectively) if it is a bonafide name in this other sense—that is, there exists some number which possesses the property it indicates, but we cannot necessarily find that number. Then, as before, we might go through the list of strings $S_1, S_2, \ldots, S_M$ and make this determina- tion about each string. We could then cull our list to include only those strings which are, in this looser sense, the names of numbers. Let us call this reduced list $S_1', S_2', \ldots, S_P'$. We consider the set of numbers named by these strings. We do not necessarily know them, but they exist. Now, consider all other natural numbers except these numbers (i.e., the *complement* of this set of numbers). This subset of the natural numbers has some smallest member (one says in mathematics that the natural numbers are "well ordered" to mean they possess the property that *every* subset of them includes a smallest member), and this smallest number is named by Q.

As before, the flaw resides in the assumption that we are able to deter- mine (effectively) of a given string whether or not it is a name, even in this relaxed sense, of some number. This cannot be done.

EXERCISES

1.1 Assume a binary computer with a word size of 25 bits. Consider the problem of encoding floating point numbers as binary words. Show how to map the first 2^{25} nonnegative integers, represented in binary notation by a full word, into floating point numbers of the form $A \cdot 10^\alpha$ where $-300 < \alpha < +300$ and $0.1 \leq |A| < 1$. Do it in such a way as to have the greatest possible precision in the representation of A. That is, how many bits should be allocated to the representation of A, how many to the representation of α?

Give a bound on the relative error in representing numbers in the range $-10^{300} < x < +10^{300}$ by this notational scheme.

1.2 Write a segment of code in some programming language that includes facilities to handle I/O interrupts (e.g., PL/I) to define a procedure that terminates but is not deterministic (and, therefore, not effective). Explain briefly why it is not deterministic. (*Hint:* Tolerances on I/O unit operations for such devices as card readers, tapes, and printers substantially exceed instruction cycle times.)

1.3 Describe an effective procedure to map all books that might ever be written into the natural numbers so that every book can be "recovered" by an effective procedure from its integer representation. (Ignore the handling of diagrams, pictures, etc.; they represent a special, but solvable, problem.)

1.4 Give what might, perhaps, be viewed as evidence in support of the Pythagoreans by showing how the following may be mapped into the natural numbers (i.e., digitized, cf. Exercise 1.5) so that the object being mapped can be recovered (in some cases only approximately) from its image, i.e., the map is invertible:

    a. the pressure at various ocean depths

    b. for a portion of an electrical circuit—the potential drop, current intensity, resistance

    c. pictures of Jupiter from Pioneer 10

    d. the symphonies of Beethoven

    e. the intensity of pain experienced by human subjects in some physiological experiment

    f. the odors of chemical solutions produced in a laboratory.

1.5 Give three examples of things that you do not see how to digitize. (To *digitize* something is to express it as a finite decimal number.)

1.6 Give two examples of a method that is *not* effective for determining a total function that maps the natural numbers into the natural numbers. Explain briefly in each case why the procedure is not effective.

1.7 Find by the Euclidean algorithm the greatest common divisor of 195 and 884. Determine, using this algorithm, if 924 and 2,275 are relatively prime.

1.8 Prove that it is not possible to write a program for any computer, no matter how big or how much time is allowed for its execution, that will serve as an oracle capable of receiving as input an arbitrary English statement and eventually giving as printed output the word TRUE or the word FALSE as it is correctly applicable to the input statement.

1.9 Comment on the constructive or nonconstructive aspects of existence in each of the following assertions (i.e., in each case consider if "exists" means "can be determined"):

  a. A solution to the equation $x^2 = 4$ exists.
  b. A solution to the equation $x^2 = 5$ exists.
  c. A number exists that is not the solution to any polynomial equation.
  d. A number exists that indicates how many raindrops fell on New York City on June 29, 1975.
  e. There exist five consecutive 7's in the infinite decimal representation of π.

1.10 Show that the function that maps each number n from 1 to 365 into the world population at midnight of the nth day during the year 1995 is effectively computable even though the program to compute it cannot now be written.

1.11 Write a program in some suitable programming language that will compose from the letters A, E, I, O, U all possible strings that contain each letter precisely once. Print these 120 strings in lexicographic, or alphabetic, order.

1.12 Does the phrase "the greatest integer nameable in twenty-two or fewer syllables" constitute a meaningful definition of some number?

1.13 One of Zeno's paradoxes (c. 500 B.C.) is the following. The hare and the tortoise (originally stated in terms of Achilles and the tortoise) engage in a race. The overconfident hare, after establishing an overwhelming lead, takes time out to go to sleep, in his disdain for the tortoise. When he awakens he sees that the tortoise has overtaken him and is some distance ahead. Now, Zeno argues, it is not possible for the hare to catch up to the tortoise. For, let the position of the tortoise when the hare first observes him after awakening be P_1. The hare runs to position P_1, but by the time he reaches it the tortoise has reached a new position P_2. This situation recurs. Since (1) the hare must always reach the position, say P_n, where the tortoise has been before he can pass him, (2) the tortoise will have moved on ahead by this time to P_{n+1}, and (3) there are an infinitude of such situations, the hare can never pass the tortoise.

  Analyze this paradox. A refutation does not consist of another and different argument showing that the hare *can* pass the tortoise. Seek, rather, the flaw in Zeno's argument. The analysis involves in part the properties of time and space considered in looking at the possible effectiveness of physical processes, as well as the possible convergence of infinite mathematical processes. (Cf. Section 1.7.)

1.14 (More on the difficulty of dealing with the infinite.) Let us consider the following "gedanken" experiment (literally "thought" experiment). Suppose that every natural number is written on a card. We shall place these cards in a bag of unlimited capacity in accordance with the following scheme. At the first time step t_0, we put the numbers 1, 2 into the bag. At each subsequent time step t_k $(k > 0)$ we shall remove the biggest number in the bag and then insert the next pair of numbers.

  Thus, at t_0 we put 1, 2 into the bag; at t_1 we remove 2 and put in 3, 4; at t_2 we remove 4 and put in 5, 6, ...; in general, at time step t_k $(k > 0)$ we remove the number $2k$ and put in $2k + 1$, $2k + 2$.

Suppose, next, that these time steps are selected as $t_0 = 0$, $t_1 = 1$, $t_2 = 1\frac{1}{2}$, $t_3 = 1\frac{3}{4}, \ldots, t_k = 2 - (1/2^k)$, ... in terms of some appropriate unit of time.

At time $t = 2$, what is in the bag? It seems reasonable to conclude that all the odd integers remain, since every even integer was removed at some prior time step.

Next, modify the procedure so that at each time step t_k ($k > 0$) we remove not the biggest number $2k$ but, rather, the smallest number k that is in the bag. As before, there is at each step a net gain of one in the number of cards in the bag. Now, what remains in the bag at time $t = 2$? Can you, in fact, name even one number that is left in the bag? If not, how can this be when we have continually been increasing the contents of the bag at every step before $t = 2$? (Suggested by A. Bomberault.)

1.15 Oliver Wendell Holmes wrote the following in *The Autocrat of the Breakfast Table,* 1857: The calculating power alone should seem to be the least human of qualities, and to have the smallest amount of reason in it, since a machine can be made to do the work of three or four calculators, and better than any one of them. Criticize this comment.

APPENDIX
EFFECTIVENESS IN THE ROOTS OF MATHEMATICS

In the natural sciences of physics, chemistry, and biology every student learns of the continual replacement of antiquated, flawed theories by newer ones that represent nature more accurately. Our progress in these fields hopefully indicates a convergence to some ultimate truth. Mathematics is rarely described in these terms, especially at the elementary level. There *is* a continual reappraisal of mathematical theories and a search for more elegant, unifying, and powerful systems, but the underlying principles are often seen to be as rigorous and secure as it is possible to be. Mathematicians do make mistakes, but these are generally taken to be human errors, often correctable, in applying the fundamental and universal laws of the subject. Such errors do not lead to the rejection of basic notions and of whole fields that rest on these notions such as, say, the repudiation of spontaneous generation in biology or of myriad notions of the alchemists. Observations of nature have never caused us to reject a part of mathematics. We might, it is true, find that Euclidean geometry does not accurately portray the physical world, but this in no way casts doubt on Euclidean geometry as a mathematical system. *If* we accept the axioms of the system, the theorems of the subject are taken to be inescapable. We may decide that nature does not adhere to these axioms (e.g., the shortest distance between two points may not in reality be a straight line), but this does not impair the logical structure of the subject. The basic laws of mathematics are usually taken to be inviolate.

This is not a correct picture of the situation. The handling of the infinite in mathematics and the nature of proofs that employ, in a sense, infinite arguments have troubled a number of mathematicians and in some cases led to paradoxes that are very difficult to explain.

It is felt by some that a suitable restriction to effective procedures will put mathematics on safer ground. We have included a very brief discussion of some of these fundamental issues because of their great importance. We recognize that it is difficult for a student to appreciate the subtleties of the situation without a substantial knowledge of mathematics. In fact, comparatively few students of advanced mathematics are exposed to these ideas. These questions are generally considered in the study of mathematical logic, an area often viewed as peripheral to modern mathematics.

For these reasons, we have included this material in an appendix. It can be omitted by the reader whose interests do not extend beyond that material which is directly applicable to the computer.

We have also included, in passing, some brief and relevant remarks pertaining to the nature of effective processes in physics.

1.5 FOUNDATIONS OF MATHEMATICS AND TROUBLES WITH THE INFINITE

R. Wilder, in his book *Evolution of Mathematical Concepts* [18], argues that our progress in mathematics is in large measure influenced by the stresses of our culture—intellectual as well as physical. For example, the environmental needs to achieve a better understanding of mechanics and physics led to the development of the differential and integral calculus and to the analysis of real functions. These theories led, in turn, to "hereditary stresses," in Wilder's terminology, that demanded a mathematics of the infinite for better understanding and development.

It is, on first consideration, remarkable that those theoretical developments in mathematics which bear most closely on digital computing began, to a large extent, within the several decades preceding the advent of the modern digital computer. While the first electromechanical and electronic computers do not seem to be directly attributable to these studies in mathematical logic, computability, and automata theory, it seems clear that the intellectual climate created by these investigations encouraged those engineering developments that have led to the modern computer. Reciprocally, these mathematical subjects have received considerable stimulation from the remarkable developments in digital computing.

The concern with the effective is far from being peculiar to digital computing. Quite related developments have occurred in the study of the foundations of mathematics. To many, mathematics appears to be that area of intellectual activity where we seem to be on firmest ground. Toward the end of the nineteenth century it began to appear reasonable from the work of such mathematicians as Frege and Peano, among others, that all of mathematics might be developed with a convincing clarity of structure and of procedural rules similar to the model afforded by Euclidean geometry. With its set of "self-evident" truths, or axioms, and its rules for inferring new statements from old ones, elementary plane geometry provides a prototype of what we now call a *formal* system (cf. Chapter 2). It seemed plausible that we could hope to describe all of mathematics by starting with the natural numbers, enunciating a small number of axioms and rules of inference, and then weaving a grand web of definitions and results which, mathematically speaking, would be all-encompassing.

However, the discovery of certain paradoxes (such as Russell's paradox of 1901, which is described below) caused mathematicians and logicians to become more suspicious and cautious in their dealings with infinite sets and infinite processes. As long as we deal with finite objects, or finite collections of objects, and finite proof procedures we are on safe ground, but this is not true when we make indiscriminate use of the infinite. As Hilbert has written [6], "Just think: in mathematics, this paragon of reliability and truth, the very notions and inferences, as everyone learns, teaches, and uses them, lead to absurdities. And where else would reliability and truth be found, if even mathematical thinking fails?"

Some possible pitfalls in using the infinite have been brought to the attention of every student of elementary mathematical analysis in the study of infinite series. If, for example, we ignore the fact that infinite series are very different from finite ones we might go through the following well-known "proof" that $2 = 1$.

Consider the infinite series, $S = 1 - 1/2 + 1/3 - 1/4 + \ldots$. One learns in the elementary calculus that this series sums to (i.e., the sum of an increasing number of terms approaches arbitrarily closely to) the natural logarithm of 2, but it is not necessary to know this to understand the following argument.

By reordering the terms in S and following each positive term by two negative terms we write

$$
\begin{aligned}
S &= (1 - 1/2 - 1/4) + (1/3 - 1/6 - 1/8) + (1/5 - 1/10 - 1/12) + \ldots \\
&= (1/2 - 1/4) + (1/6 - 1/8) + (1/10 - 1/12) + \ldots \\
&= [(1 - 1/2) + (1/3 - 1/4) + (1/5 - 1/6) + \ldots]/2 \\
&= S/2
\end{aligned}
$$

Dividing both sides by S, we arrive at the disturbing conclusion that $2 = 1$! The flaw in our argument resides, of course, in the assumption that we can rearrange the terms in S without affecting the limiting value of this sum. This is a legitimate operation in manipulating finite series, but it is not, in general, true for infinite series. The careless handling of these infinite operations led to the fallacious result.

A good part of the mathematical development of the first part of the nineteenth century was devoted to putting the earlier, partly heuristic, mathematics (which sometimes led to false conclusions and, therefore, could not be trusted) on a firmer basis. In particular, the more careful consideration of infinite series led to a clearer understanding of the kinds of operations that can be performed legitimately on them, and errors of the kind we have illustrated were avoided.

That we had best proceed with great caution when dealing with the infinite is a lesson that has been given in several forms, starting perhaps with the paradoxes of the ancient Greek philosopher Zeno [11,13]. Around the beginning of the twentieth century it became clear that even after several centuries of the development of mathematics beyond the differential and integral calculus our approaches to the foundations of the subject were in trouble—that, in particular, the handling of infinite sets left much to be desired. A number of paradoxes were discovered which brought this out. The properties of finite sets and rules for working with them could not be blindly applied to infinite sets. In particular we consider briefly the famous paradox discovered in 1901 by Bertrand Russell.

Russell's paradox involves infinite classes and can be described as follows. Classes, or aggregates, of things may be divided into two categories: those classes which are members of themselves and those classes which are not members of themselves. For example, the class of all classes is a member of itself (since a class is a class), or the somewhat restricted class of all classes having more than 7 members is a member of itself, since there are more than 7 classes having more than 7 members. On the other hand, the class of all tables in New Jersey is not a table (although it is in New Jersey) and, therefore, is not a member of itself. So, it seems that we can characterize every class according to whether or not it possesses this property of self-membership. Now, consider the class W of all classes which are not members of themselves. We then ask if W is a member of itself. If W is a member of W then, by the definition of W, it must not be a member of itself. On the other hand, if W is not a member of itself then it must be a member of itself. Thus, either of the two possibilities implies its contradiction.

The paradox sounds trivial, but its implications are profound. As Russell remarked in his autobiography [14], "It seemed unworthy of a grown man to spend his time on such trivialities, but what was I to do? There was something wrong, since such contradictions were unavoidable on ordinary premises. Trivial or not, the matter was a challenge. Throughout the latter half of 1901 I supposed the solution would be easy, but by the end of that time I had concluded that it was a big job."

Such difficulties seemed to justify the attitudes of a few mathematicians who, earlier, had been very wary of arguments that dealt with the infinite. It is of interest to note that the German mathematician L. Kronecker, in the late nineteenth century, had in some respects anticipated these frailties of mathematics even before the appearance of such disturbing paradoxes. Kronecker refused to accept any glib handling of the infinite. A definition of a mathematical entity or property was acceptable to him only in case it could be exhibited or verified in a finite number of steps. He coped with the difficulty of the actually infinite by refusing to accept it [16]. Not only did he reject the work of George Cantor on transfinite numbers (briefly mentioned in Section 3.7), but he even rejected such uses of the infinite as those necessary to the extension of the number system from the rational numbers to the irrationals, since the definitions of the irrational numbers depend upon the performance of infinite processes.

For example, the number $\sqrt{2}$ might be defined (following some work of the nineteenth century German mathematician Dedekind) as the following partition of the rational numbers into two disjoint classes—those rational numbers (S_1) which when squared give a result that is less than 2 and those rational numbers (S_2) which when squared give a result that is greater than 2. It is, then, this partition of the rational numbers, or this "cut," separating them into S_1 and S_2, that can be interpreted as the number $\sqrt{2}$. Note, however, that in this kind of definition we do not hesitate to introduce these infinite subsets of the rational numbers, assuming that we can freely refer to them as though they were completed entities [6].

When in 1882 Lindemann proved that π could not be the root of any polynomial equation with integral coefficients (such as $5x^3 - 3x^2 + 17x - 6 = 0$) and thus proved the impossibility of a solution to the ancient problem of constructing with ruler and compass a square having the same area as a given circle, Kronecker said to him "Of what use is your beautiful investigation regarding π? Why study such problems since irrational numbers are non-existent?" [17].

More generally, Kronecker, in the 1880s, rejected the methods of such great mathematicians of the period as Weierstrass, Dedekind, and Cantor, arguing that their fundamental definitions were only words, since they did not enable one in general to decide whether a given object satisfies the definition [8].

However, Kronecker's rejection of the infinite was too sweeping. The solution was not to play it safe by discarding the sickness of mathematics but, rather, to see how much of its beauty and power could be preserved while avoiding falsity.

What has all this to do with computing? We shall see next that one approach to mathematics, which some believe will provide a more secure and more meaningful foundation, is based upon the principle that a mathematical statement is meaningful only insofar as it describes or predicts the results of computations performed on the natural numbers. That is, not only do the natural numbers comprise the basic building blocks of mathematics, but "even the most abstract mathematical statement has a computational basis" [2].

1.6   CONSTRUCTIVE MATHEMATICS

After the discovery of the paradoxes, including that of Russell, it became clear that in order to avoid such seeming contradictions it would be necessary to qualify some of our working procedures in the development of mathematics. It is true that we can apparently avoid the paradoxes by introducing additional restraints which, even though they may seem a bit unnatural, will keep us away from arguments that lead to false conclusions. Russell's theory of types has this character, and it considers a class which has classes among its members as something intrinsically different from a class of objects which are not themselves classes. On the other hand, and in keeping with the significance of the notion of effectiveness, one may take the approach of modern constructive mathematics and base everything on only finitely performable, or on effective, procedures.

A developing skepticism concerning the unthinking application of ideas that are valid for finite sets to infinite sets led around 1910 to that approach to the foundations of mathematics which is called intuitionism. This is primarily due to the work of L. E. J. Brouwer, a Dutch mathematician. It is not difficult to understand some of the principal objections which were made by Brouwer to the existing practices in mathematics, and we shall try, without being unduly formal, to convey the flavor of a few of these objections. In essence, these are quite similar to Kronecker's. The fundamental tenet is that a mathematical statement is acceptable only if it lends itself to verification by some finite process.

In classical mathematics the assertion that "there exists a number such that ..." is often made without, however, knowing how to go about finding or constructing the number whose existence is asserted. Of what meaning, then, is such a statement which does not lend itself to direct verification? To the intuitionists, at least, such a statement is meaningless. As A. Heyting has written in his book on intuitionism [5], "If 'to exist' does not mean 'to be constructed' it must have some metaphysical meaning. It cannot be the task of mathematics to investigate this meaning or to decide whether it is tenable or not." In this respect mathematical truth has a timeless quality, quite different from assertions of ordinary discourse. We are never concerned with "there existed" or "there will exist" but always "there exists." Few of us, except those with a literal acceptance of Genesis, would doubt the past

existence of at least two 1000th generation ancestors, even though we cannot display these forebears. It is, however, reasonable to believe that a mathematical object does not exist unless it can be constructed.

The rejection of the assertion of an existence, unaccompanied by a method for finding, then must lead to a rejection of the "law of the excluded middle" in classical logic. This law, or axiom, asserts that every statement is either true or false. If the law of the excluded middle were always valid, we would have to say that the statement Q, given below, is always true. Here, D represents a domain containing a number n, and $P(n)$ is some statement about n. The law of the excluded middle then implies that Q is a true statement, no matter what D and $P(n)$ are assumed to be.

Q: Either there exists a number n in a domain D such that $P(n)$, or there does not exist a number n in a domain D such that $P(n)$.

The statement Q, in turn, is equivalent to:

Q': Either there exists a number n in a domain D such that $P(n)$ or, for all n in D, n does not satisfy $P(n)$.

Now, if "there exists" is equated to "we can find or construct" and if "n does not satisfy $P(n)$" is taken to mean "we can show that n does not satisfy $P(n)$," then the following statement must be universally true if we accept the principle of the excluded middle.

R: Either we can find a number n in the domain D such that $P(n)$ or, for all n in D we can show that n does not satisfy $P(n)$.

If D is a finite set, this last assertion is clearly true, for we can then, in some finite time, examine every element of this set and either find a number n that satisfies $P(n)$ or we shall, by exhausting the set D, show that every element in it does not satisfy $P(n)$.

However, for infinite sets we cannot in general do this—certainly not by searching—for our search may be interminable. This is true in spite of the fact that we may very well be able to solve a particular problem, either by succeeding in finding a number in D that satisfies $P(n)$ or by being able to give a proof that every element in D does not have this property. Thus, R is not acceptable to the intuitionists as a universal law, for there is no assurance that we can *prove* it for every possible problem that can be put in these terms.

For example, we might take $P(n)$ to be the statement that "n is not expressible as the sum of two prime numbers" and take as D the set of even numbers. The famous "Goldbach conjecture" in the elementary theory of numbers states that every even number can be written as the sum of two primes. Although so simply stated, it has defied proof for several centuries.

R, for these choices of D and $P(n)$, then becomes:

> Either we can find an even number n such that n is not expressible as the sum of two primes or, for all even numbers, we can show that n is the sum of two primes.

We know of no general principle, such as the exhaustive search through finite sets, that can be used to verify this statement by demonstrating which of the two given alternatives is correct. To be acceptable to the intuitionists, such a principle would have to exist and be generally applicable, even to this statement, in order to justify the law of the excluded middle. Hence, the intuitionists do not accept the assertion that for every statement S either S is true or S is false.

To repeat, then, we see the significance in a constructive approach to mathematics of distinguishing between:

> A: *There exists* a number n that has some given property $P(n)$, and
>
> B: *We can construct* a number n that has the given property $P(n)$.

In considering a given function $f(x)$ we might write A, B in the form:

> A': For given x, *there exists* a number n such that $n = f(x)$ and
>
> B': For given x, *we can construct* a number n such that $n = f(x)$.

In this case we might also consider the following statement which is, in a sense, intermediate between A' and B':

> C: *There exists some effective procedure* (but we do not necessarily know it) which for given x will yield a number n such that $n = f(x)$.

This last statement is intermediate in the sense that B' implies C, and C implies A'. B' is the "strongest" statement of the three and A' is the "weakest." Sometimes, in the development of the associated theory, C has been taken to be the meaning of the constructibility of the function $f(x)$. However, a strict constructionist (nothing to do with some American presidents' Supreme Court choices) will only take B' to be the proper meaning. Consider, as an example, the function $f(x)$ defined as being equal to 1 for all values of x if there are intelligent beings in the universe other than humans (assuming humans to be such beings) and, otherwise, $f(x)$ is 0 for all values of x. It is immediately seen that this function is constructible in the sense of C. However, no one knows if $f(x)$ should be taken as identically equal to 0 or to 1, and we cannot, therefore, assert B'.

We shall illustrate, by example, an argument of classical mathematics that employs the infinite and is highly suspect from the intuitionist point of view because of its nonconstructive character. We consider the fundamental

theorem (Bolzano-Weierstrass) of elementary analysis which asserts that every bounded infinite set of points has a limit point. This theorem is essential to the classical development of the differential and integral calculus. We shall review certain aspects of a proof of this theorem as it might be given for a set of points on a finite line segment. The theorem states then that if we are given any infinite set of points S on a finite line segment l there exists a point P in l which is a limit point of S, i.e., there are points in S that are arbitrarily close to P.

The crux of the weakness in the proof is that an infinite sequence of decisions must be made, and there is no way beforehand to give a finitely stated procedure for making this infinitude of decisions.

The usual argument proceeds as follows. Divide l into two equal parts $l_1^{(1)}, l_2^{(1)}$. Since S includes an infinite number of points, at least one of these two segments $l_1^{(1)}, l_2^{(1)}$ must contain an infinite number of points of S (for if both segments contained only a finite number then l would contain only a finite number). We assume we can then identify one of the two segments as containing an infinite number of points of S, and we then make the further dubious (from the point of view of the intuitionists) assumption that the process can be repeated indefinitely. This leads to an infinite sequence of nested intervals $l, l_i^{(1)}, l_i^{(2)}, l_i^{(3)}, \ldots$ (where i at each occurrence is either 1 or 2), each segment in this list being contained in the preceding one and having half the length of the preceding one. Further, by our selection process each segment contains an infinite number of points of S. We then argue that there is one (and only one) point P that is common to all these shrinking intervals and that it has the stated property of being a limit point of S.

To return now to the questionable point, the claimed existence of the sequence of shrinking intervals is denied in a constructive approach to mathematics. We are not able, for an arbitrary set S, to indicate beforehand which of the two halves of the line segment $l_i^{(k)}$ that arises at the kth stage of this process will contain an infinite number of points of S. Our claim at each step is that "there exists" one of the two halves of $l_i^{(k)}$ which contains an infinite number of points of S, but no statement about how "to find" this half is given. We might very well be able to do this for a particular set S, but nothing can be said of an arbitrary set S. Our proof, then, lacks a constructive character. The existence of the infinite nested sequence of intervals which identifies a limit point is asserted, but there is no effective (therefore finite) procedure to yield this sequence of intervals. Our proof depends on the assumption that the infinite set of decisions necessary to the determination of this sequence can be made, in its totality, even though we cannot in general make the determination at the kth stage without having made all of the k-1 earlier determinations. This would be acceptable if we could state some finite procedure that could be used to make the determination for all k, but again this is not feasible for an arbitrary set S. We can, in fact, show within classical mathematics that the number of possible finite procedures that one might write down to accomplish the construction of the infinite sequence of nested intervals is in a sense much smaller than the number of infinite point sets. There are, then, an infinite number of sets for which no construction of a limit point along these lines can be given in finite form. It is possible, however, to modify the statement of this theorem and its proof so that it is constructively valid (see Bishop [2]).

When S. Kleene, the well-known mathematical logician, gave a talk some years ago on the fundamentals of intuitionism he was asked how he, in view of these misgivings about classical mathematical methods, taught the elementary calculus. He responded that he taught it with his fingers crossed.

We have by no means given here a complete picture of constructive mathematics or of intuitionism (the two are not quite the same), but we have wanted only to emphasize the most significant aspects of a constructive orientation. Certain assumptions which Brouwer made because he felt them to be necessary to understand the continuum of real numbers seem in retrospect to have clouded this particular approach to constructive mathematics. In 1927, the great German mathematician David Hilbert, contemplating the small portions of mathematics that the intuitionists had obtained after having restricted the logical apparatus of the classical mathematician along the lines we have implied, wrote, "For, compared with the immense expanse of modern mathematics what would the wretched remnants mean, the few isolated results, incomplete and unrelated, that the Intuitionists have obtained..." and also, "Taking the principle of the excluded middle from the mathematician would be the same, say, as proscribing the telescope to the astronomer or to the boxer the use of his fists. To prohibit existence statements and the principle of excluded middle is tantamount to relinquishing the science of mathematics altogether."

It now appears that this most illustrious mathematician was probably wrong. The recent work of E. Bishop [2] provides a straightforward, but nevertheless rich, development of mathematical analysis from a constructive point of view. It seems clear that the story is far from being finished as of this writing, and it is still premature to assess the full implication to mathematics of a restriction to effective methods in its development.

1.7   EFFECTIVE PROCESSES IN PHYSICS

We have stated that one approach to making precise the notion of an effective computation is to describe some physical device and to define effective computations in terms of the procedures that can be accomplished on it.

Turing machines, and in particular the universal Turing machine which will be described in Chapters 5 and 6, are examples of this, but of course we are not restricted to such theoretical constructs for examples of such devices. Any real computer, subject to the condition that we provide it with as much in the way of storage facilities as it may need during the course of a computation (see property (2) under the definition of effective procedures), is such a device. The initial configuration of the computer includes a representation of the input data as well as the program defining the procedure that it is to execute. The successive changes in its configuration (observed at discrete moments like the successive frames of a motion picture film) lead to a terminal configuration that includes a representation of the output. (The "configuration" is here understood to include all input and output facilities, including any tapes, disks, paper, cards, and so forth that may be used during the computation.) The behavior of the computer, in terms of this sequence of configurations, is then a physical realization of the effective computation being executed.

It seems reasonable to look more generally at physical processes and ask whether these are in all cases examples of effective procedures. Any physical experiment can be viewed as a form of a "computation" where the initial observed data are the values of the input arguments, and the observed physical variables at the completion of the experiment are the results. If we neglect errors of observation, are these processes always examples of effective computations? It is plausible that the answer to this question is negative because of some of the remarks that appear below, but, in our view, the reasons given that may lead to this conclusion are not completely convincing.

We consider the salient properties of effective procedures and make some brief observations on how these may apply to physical processes in general.

Determinism.   There seems to be a prevailing attitude that the Heisenberg principle of indeterminism or uncertainty, in particular, rules out the possibility of determinism in nature. Both it and the theory of relativity imply that the very act of observation affects that which is being observed. The Heisenberg principle asserts that one cannot specify or determine simultaneously both the position and velocity of a particle with full accuracy—the more accurately that an experiment will determine the position of a particle the less accurately will it yield its velocity. Therefore, since we can never determine with complete accuracy the initial state of a physical system, we cannot predict its future course. To quote Schrödinger [15], "Nature is supposed to be such that a knowledge of state sufficiently accurate for sharp prediction of the future is not only unobtainable but also unthinkable."

That this implies the indeterminism of nature is not clear, for the question has been raised of whether such indeterminacy is in the experimenter rather than in nature.

In this discussion of determinism a criterion of verifiability is implicit. We have in the preceding section defined a procedure to be deterministic if it always yields the same result starting with the same input. However, more is usually implied, usage often being such that determinism implies predictability and included in this is the tacit assumption that the future can be *computed* from the past.

Further, the assertion that identical starting configurations lead to identical terminal configurations is meaningless unless we can observe these configurations. This brings to mind the verifiability criteria of constructive mathematics, but here, of course, verifiability is by idealized physical experimentation rather than by "finite processes."

Our ability to simulate alleged nondeterministic processes by the use of random number generation and Monte Carlo methods (see Chapter 7) on deterministic devices (computers) seems to justify in some respects the hesitancy that Einstein indicated in accepting the notion of random processes in nature ("God does not throw dice."). That is, since we are able to mimic nondeterminism with deterministic devices, can we be certain that nature is not doing the same thing in those instances where our observations appear to indicate some nondeterministic physical behavior.

Another reported comment of Einstein is quite relevant to this matter and seems to weaken the case for determinism in nature, or at least for the theories we develop to explain nature. We quote from a letter from Wolfgang Pauli to Max Born that appears in Born [3].

> ... Einstein does not consider the concept of "determinism" to be as fundamental as it is frequently held to be and he denied energetically that he had ever put up a postulate such as "the sequence of such conditions must also be objective and real, that is, automatic, machine-like, deterministic." In the same way he disputes that he uses as criterion for the admissibility of a theory the question "Is it rigorously deterministic?"
>
> Einstein's point of departure is "realistic" rather than "deterministic," ...

Finiteness.   The property of being finite in space and time is probably not to be questioned for all physical processes. At least, nothing in our observations or theories denies finiteness.

Representation by natural numbers.   Can we represent as integers the physical variables that enter into a physical configuration? In other words, do all these variables take on only discrete values? While, perhaps, mass, because of the elementary particles which may be the building blocks of matter, and energy, because of the quantum theory, can be so represented, it would seem that space and time at least defy such representation ("natura non facit saltus"). However, recent speculation on the possibility of elemental lengths and indivisible time intervals may mean that it is premature to cite the continuity of space and time as reasons for deciding against these possibilities.

The "mechanical" character of procedures.   The question we have asked concerning physical processes can, it seems, be interpreted as asking if mechanical models exist to explain all physical processes. If the answer to this is negative for some physical processes, but these are nevertheless deterministic and involve only physical variables that can be represented by the natural numbers, then we should probably want to revise our notion of effectiveness. Or, rather, the theses that equate our intuitive notion of effective computations to precise formal schemes will have to be changed.

We shall say no more about these provocative and profound questions. It suffices to note that the physical devices of automata theory (see Chapter 7) that may be assumed in defining effective procedures, or subclasses of such procedures, will be idealized and perfect machines whose operation will not depend upon the unresolved questions we have raised.

1.8   THE ARITHMETIZATION OF PHYSICS

We look briefly at a question somewhat different from the preceding but closely related to it. We ask not if all physical processes are examples of effective processes but, rather, if these physical processes can be approximated arbitrarily closely by effective processes. In Chapter 6 we define a "decimally approximable number" to be a real number for which we can compute, to any desired closeness, a decimal number that approximates this given number. We can ask a similar question for physical processes. Is it possible to describe arithmetic procedures (effective procedures) that will mimic to any desired accuracy (as confirmed by our observations) real physical processes?

In recent years a great deal of computational experience has been obtained that makes for a convincing argument that the answer to this question is affirmative. Much, if not all, of the mathematics of physics can be reformulated in terms of arithmetic (cf. D. Greenspan [4]).

The differential and integral calculus was introduced by Newton and Leibnitz in order to cope with physical problems involving continuous variables and functions of continuous, not discrete, arguments. The fundamental operations that lead to such mathematical constructs as the derivative or the definite integral involve the passage to the limit of some sequence of operations that is assumed to continue indefinitely.

Consider, for example, the problem of assigning a meaning to an instantaneous velocity. This leads to the definition of the derivative. Given a particle moving in a straight line, its average velocity over some time interval is the distance through which it moves divided by the length of the time interval. If we then let the time interval shrink to zero, the limit of this average velocity provides the definition of the instantaneous velocity, or of the derivative.

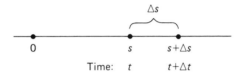

The particle moves from s at time t to $s + \Delta s$ at time $t + \Delta t$. Its average velocity during this interval is $\Delta s / \Delta t$. The instantaneous velocity ds / dt at s is then defined as the limit as $\Delta t \to 0$ of $\Delta s / \Delta t$.

However, a computational approach to this problem can proceed without taking the passage to the limit. We can compute the average velocity over a very small interval or over a sequence of successively shrinking intervals using only arithmetical methods. With certain assumptions we can approximate to any desired accuracy the "instantaneous velocity."

We have earlier cited Kronecker's remark concerning the evolution of all mathematics starting with the natural numbers. The computational approach represents a reversal of this development, going back to the natural numbers. Many of the processes of analysis, the use of the continuous and of infinite procedures, can be approximated in terms of arithmetical operations.

Beyond this approximation of the continuous by the discrete, there are many places in nature where the discrete is closer to reality, where the physical theory uses a continuous model that does *not* conform to nature, situations where there are in reality a collection of discrete objects, but where analysis can only deal with this collection by assuming that it is a mathematically continuous structure. For example, matter is made up of individual molecules. A gas is not a continuous medium but consists of a set of randomly moving molecules. With the computer we can often study the behavior of such a structure by treating it as a collection of discrete objects rather than as a continuous medium. That is, the behavior of a gas can be studied by computing the behavior of a large number of individual molecules of the gas and then averaging this behavior. Using "Monte Carlo" techniques (cf.

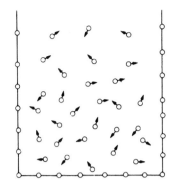 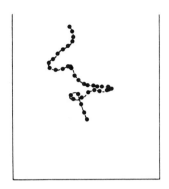

Fig. 1.4 Computer generated model of molecules in a heavy gas. Diagram at right shows motion of a light molecule introduced to the gas, illustrating buoyancy (from Greenspan [4]).

Chapter 7), it is possible to assign characteristics descriptive of a set of random particles (their velocity, distribution, etc.) and then to follow in the computer the motions of these individual particles (Fig. 1.4).

1.9 SOME ANALOGIES

At the risk of being overly simplistic we point out a pervading "show me" attitude that extends through the following subjects. This is, in our view, reminiscent of a salient characteristic of effective processes.

Constructive mathematics—"a number exists only if we know how to go about finding it."

Operational philosophy of physics—"physical concepts are meaningful only insofar as their effects can be observed."

Philosophy of pragmatism—"all our conceptions derive their meaning only from things we can observe."

The reader may, influenced by the analogies we have made and the seemingly universal occurrence of the computable, tend to see everything in these terms. At this point, it may be worth recalling the words of Justice Oliver Wendell Homes, Jr., "Life is painting a picture, not doing a sum."

REFERENCES

1. al-Khwarizmi, *Kitab al jabr w'al-muqabala,* c. AD 825.

2. Bishop, E., *Foundations of Constructive Analysis.* New York: McGraw-Hill, 1967.

3. Born, M., *The Born–Einstein Letters, Correspondence Between Albert Einstein and Max and Hedwig Born from 1916 to 1955 with Commentaries by Max Born.* Translated by Irene Born. New York: Walker and Co., 1971.

4. Greenspan, D., "Arithmetic Applied Mathematics." *Comp. and Math. with Appl.,* **3,** 4 (1977). Pergamon Press, Ltd. Reprinted by permission.

5. Heyting, A., *Intuitionism; an Introduction.* Amsterdam: North-Holland Publishing Co., 1966.

6. Hilbert, D., "On the Infinite," 1925. Translated by Stefan Bauer-Mengelberg in *From Frege to Gödel,* ed. by Jean van Heijenoort. Cambridge: Harvard University Press, 1966.

7. Hilbert, D., "The Foundations of Mathematics," 1927. Translated by Stefan Bauer-Mengelberg in [6].

8. Kleene, S. C., "Foundations of Mathematics." *Encyclopaedia Brittanica,* 1971.

9. Moorer, J. A., Letter in *Comm. Assn. Comp. Mach.,* **15,** 11 (November 1972).

10. Rosser, J. B., "Constructibility as a Criterion for Existence." *J. Symbolic Logic,* **1** (1936).

11. Russell, B., *Principles of Mathematics.* London, 1903.

12. Russell, B., "Les Paradoxes de la Logique." *Revue de Métaphysique et de la Morale* **14** (1906).

13. Russell, B., *Our Knowledge of the External World.* London, 1914.

14. Russell, B., *Autobiography* (1872–1914). Boston: Little, Brown and Company, 1967.

15. Schrodinger, E., "Indeterminism and Free Will." *Nature,* **138** (1936).

16. Struik, D. J., *A Concise History of Mathematics.* New York: Dover, 1948.

17. Turnbull, H. W., "The Great Mathematicians," in *The World of Mathematics.* Vol. 1. Ed. by J. R. Newman. New York: Simon and Schuster, 1954.

18. Wilder, R. L., *Evolution of Mathematical Concepts; an Elementary Study.* New York: Wiley, 1968.

2
Foundations
of
Mathematics I

This chapter and the next comprise a potpourri of introductory topics drawn from the foundations of mathematics. These topics, largely chosen from mathematical logic and from the study of formal systems, are particularly important in putting the study of the computer on a more scientific basis. In fact, the salient mathematical ideas set the stage historically for the development and utilization of the electronic digital computer.

The notion of a function, or a mapping of objects of some "domain" into objects of some "range," underlies programming. Programs define algorithms for computing functions, and the methods for defining functions have implications to the design of programming languages; well-designed languages include features to facilitate the computation of functions. A hierarchy of functions exists, with functions of functions being at a higher level, and these notions have led to some specialized programming features in some advanced languages.

Formal systems are systems representing mathematical structures and in which symbols are manipulated in game-like fashion. These symbols denote elements of the structure being represented, and the results of these manipulations are translatable into properties of that structure. Once defined, a formal system concerns form rather than meaning. These ideas relate to the use of a computer in simulation. Also, the technique of *arithmetization* in logic, of casting a mathematical structure in terms of numbers and arithmetic operations, is in the same vein as the application of the computer to a multitude of situations where useful results are obtained by working within the domain of numbers.

The same "laws of thought" that were studied by Boole in his development of Boolean algebra are at the root of computer processes. This area of logic is essential both to the design of computer hardware and to the design of computer languages.

2.1 INTRODUCTION

The foundations of mathematics concern the recognition and study of the fundamental objects of mathematics (such as numbers, sets, points, lines, etc.), their basic properties and the use and limitations of the logical and mathematical methods we employ in building theories about them. The subject matter appropriate to these studies is vast, and we shall only touch very lightly on some aspects of it that are particularly relevant to the computer sciences. As we have indicated earlier, digital computers are mathematical machines. In any use of a computer at all we are computing some mathematical function—that which maps the input, interpreted as a number, or perhaps, as a string of numbers, into the output, similarly interpreted. It is, therefore, not surprising that the foundations of mathematics play a role in the study in depth of these devices.

2.2 THE MEANING AND EXTENSIONS OF FUNCTION

We have briefly discussed in Chapter 1 the notion of a function and shall now give a somewhat amplified treatment of this concept because it plays such a vital role in computer-related, and indeed in all, mathematics.

Let us consider, first, a situation where we are interested in the relationship between two things that have magnitude and can, therefore, assume numeric values. It is often convenient, although not necessary, to think of one of these things as being allowed to vary independently of the other and of the second as being determined, perhaps in some unknown way, by this independent variable. For example, consider the question of describing the volume of a sphere in terms of the radius. It is natural to think of the radius as the independent variable, or the *argument*, and of the volume as being the dependent variable. The correspondence between the radius and the volume is expressed by the equation

$$V = \tfrac{4}{3}\pi r^3.$$

The format of the equation clearly signals the independent variable r, on the right, and the dependent variable V, on the left of the equal sign, and it defines V as a function of r. A function then is a *correspondence* between two variables that associates with each given admissible value of one of the variables a unique value of the second variable. Using our earlier terminology (Chapter 1), it is a *map* relating these variables (just as an ordinary map relates some part of the earth's surface to a configuration on a sheet of paper).

If we had used other names for the variables involved, say W for the volume and s for the radius, and written

$$W = \tfrac{4}{3}\pi s^3,$$

the function or correspondence between these two variables would be the same. As we learn in high school algebra this correspondence is often shown graphically, and the picture in Fig. 2.1 might be used to depict the correspondence between r and V.

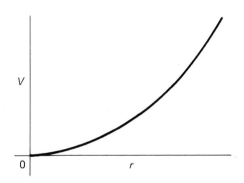

Fig. 2.1   The graph of $V = \tfrac{4}{3}\pi r^3$.

The function may not be defined for some values of the independent variable. For example, the volume of a sphere is not defined for negative values of the radius.

As an illustration of such a restriction in a commerical computation we might write the deduction due to personal exemptions in a tax collection as:

DEDUCTION = 750 ∗ EXEMPTIONS;

It is usually the intent that this function DEDUCTION not be defined for fractional or negative values of EXEMPTIONS, and later uses of DEDUCTION in the program may be based on the assumption that it is always a nonnegative integer. If, however, fractional exemptions are allowed for, say, the elderly or blind, then it must be a nonnegative integral multiple of some fixed fraction.

We call the set of values of the independent variable for which the function is defined the *domain* of definition of the function. The set of values that the function can assume is called its *range*. Every function then is a mapping from its domain of definition to its range.

The notion of a function can be extended in several ways. First, the dependent variable may depend on several arguments, not just one. Perhaps this is a sophisticated concept, for the author recalls what in retrospect seems to have been interminable discussions in high school of whether human intelligence depended on heredity or environment. The idea that it might depend on both (even ignoring the relative weights of the two factors) seemed to be an elusive notion, difficult to comprehend. As a less controversial example, the pressure of a confined gas depends on both the volume and the temperature of the gas. Even if we do not know the exact nature of this dependence on two variables we can express the fact that such a dependence exists by writing

$$P = f(V, t),$$

indicating that the pressure P is some unspecified function of both the volume V and the temperature t.

In this case the functional correspondence is that between the pressure P and the *pair* of independent variables (V, t). To each pair of admissible values of V and t there corresponds some value of the pressure P. We might regard the pair of values (V, t) as a single object, or for that matter more generally regard an n-tuple (i.e., a list of n elements, sometimes called a "tuple" if n is unspecified) of arguments as a single object, and the domain as a collection of such objects. We can then still consider the function as associating some value in its range with each (single) object in its domain. The objects in the range can equally well be tuples of numbers rather than single values.

2.3   A FUNCTION CONSIDERED AS A MAPPING FROM ONE SET INTO ANOTHER

In all cases, then, a function is a mapping defined on the elements of a domain D and assuming as values the elements of a range R, and we might write for a function f with domain D and range R,

$$f : D \to R.$$

The important condition is that for each object x in the domain D there be one, and only one, object y in the range R. Sometimes y is called the "image" of x under f. The definition does permit two objects x_1, x_2 in D to have the same image y in R. Thus, if we consider the correspondence that to each argument x in the domain of positive real numbers associates a positive *or* negative square root of x (that is, one or the other but not the pair or 2-tuple of square roots),

$$y = \pm \sqrt{x},$$

this is *not* an example of a function. However, usage in the literature has not always been consistent, and at times the phrase "single-valued function" has been used in the sense we have given for "function," with references to a "multivalued function" as something which violates the condition that the function's image in the range be unique for each element in the domain.

As noted earlier, if a function on the natural numbers is defined for all natural numbers it is said to be a *total* function; if it is defined for some, possibly not all, natural numbers it is a *partial* function. A total function, then, is also an example of a partial function (since "some" includes "all").

If the domain D of a function f is a subset of some set X (possibly all of X), we may say that f is partial on X. We can still write

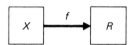

or $f: X \rightarrow R$, even when f is not defined for all members of X.

We may also write

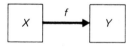

or $f: X \rightarrow Y$ even if the range of f is not all of Y. That is, f maps some of the elements of X into Y.

We say that the map f has the property of being "one-to-one" (sometimes called "injective") if to every element x in its domain D there corresponds a distinct element y in its range R. That is, no two elements in D are mapped into the same element in R. In this case we can invert the mapping, and we say that the "inverse" map from R to D, designated as "f^{-1}," exists. If $f(x) = y$, we can write $f^{-1}(y) = x$

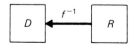

where $f^{-1}: R \to D$. If $f: X \to Y$ is total on X, $f^{-1}: Y \to X$ is not necessarily total on Y.

If we have $f: X \to Y$, and the range of f is *all* of Y, i.e., the images of f "cover" Y, then the mapping f is said to be "onto" (sometimes called "surjective"), and f maps X "onto" Y. If f is a one-to-one onto mapping from X to Y, then f^{-1} exists and is total on Y.

Example.   Consider the function $f: X \to Y$ where $X = \{0, 1, 2, 3, 4, 5, 6, 7, 8, 9\}$, $Y = \{$I, II, III, IV, V, VI, VII, VIII, IX$\}$, that maps a given decimal digit d into the Roman numeral representation of $d/2$.

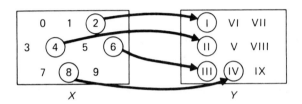

We see that f is partial on X, into Y. The domain D of f is $\{2, 4, 6, 8\}$; the range R is $\{$I, II, III, IV$\}$. f is one-to-one, and f^{-1} exists. f^{-1} is partial on Y. Its domain is $\{$I, II, III, IV$\}$; its range is $\{2, 4, 6, 8\}$.

Example.   Let X be the set of nonnegative integers. Consider the function $f: X \to X$ defined by $y = f(x) = x^2 - 3$. The domain D of f, or the set of values of x for which $f(x)$ is defined, is the set $\{2, 3, 4, 5, ...\}$. The range R of f, or the set of possible values of y, is the set $\{1, 6, 13, 22, ...\}$. $f(x)$ is one-to-one, for no two distinct numbers x_1, x_2 are mapped into the same number. The mapping f is not onto X since, for example, $f(x)$ never assumes the value 2.

The inverse map $f^{-1}: X \to X$ is defined by $x = f^{-1}(y) = \sqrt{y+3}$ (obtained by solving $y = x^2 - 3$ for x). The domain of f^{-1} is $\{1, 6, 13, 22, ...\}$, or, that is, it is the same as the range of f. The range of f^{-1} is $\{2, 3, 4, 5, ...\}$, the same as the domain of f.

2.4 ON SOME WAYS OF DEFINING FUNCTIONAL RELATIONSHIPS

There are several ways of *defining* functions mathematically. A function can be given *explicitly*, such as by the equation

$$Y = 3 * (X ** 3) - 2 * (X ** 2) + 5.$$

This equation describes Y as a function of X. A function may also be defined *implicitly*, such as by the equation

$$3 * X * (Y ** 2) - (X ** 2) * Y = 180.$$

In this latter case, one would have to solve the given equation for a given value of X to find the corresponding value of Y. This corresponding Y would not in this instance be unique (which means Y would not be a function of X) unless we impose some further condition such as taking the larger (in absolute value) of the roots when there are two real roots.

In considering functions on the natural numbers, a definition may involve a *recursion* (cf. Chapter 4), where the defining expressions for the function may involve the function itself.

Consider, for example, the function defined by the two equations:

$$\begin{cases} f(0) = 1 \\ f(n) = n * f(n-1) \text{ for } n > 0. \end{cases}$$

These equations enable us to obtain $f(n)$ at $n = 0, 1, 2, \dots$. We see that $f(1) = 1 * f(0) = 1, f(2) = 2 * f(1) = 2 * 1, f(3) = 3 * f(2) = 3 * 2 * 1, \dots$, and, in general, $f(n) = n * (n-1) * (n-2) * \dots * 1 = n!$

We shall see later the key role that this technique for the definition of functions plays in computing. The example we have given involves, more precisely, the use of the operation called *primitive recursion* for defining a function $\phi(x)$. Two equations are given which enable us, first, to compute the function $\phi(x)$ at the starting value of zero and, second, to step along through the natural numbers, computing the function at any argument in terms of its value at the preceding argument. The notion is closely related to that of iteration, or the repeated application, of some procedure. We shall elaborate on these matters in Chapter 4.

Some programming languages include facilities for defining functions recursively. The following fragment of PL/1 code shows the above function defined recursively. Within the body of the procedure being defined, a reference is made to the procedure itself.

```
FACTORIAL: PROCEDURE (N) RECURSIVE RETURNS (FIXED);
           IF N = 0 THEN RETURN (1);
           ELSE RETURN (N * FACTORIAL (N - 1));
END FACTORIAL;
```

In computer applications, functions are frequently defined by storing tables. This is feasible if the domain includes only a finite, and not too large, set of values. In this case, the function $f(x)$ can be represented by storing in the machine, in some form, all pairs of values $(x, f(x))$ for all values of x that might appear in the course of the computation. (This set of pairs is called the *graph* of the function, cf. below.) A table lookup is required, rather than an arithmetic computation, to determine the value of $f(x)$ for a given x. Income tax tables for the lower range of incomes provide an obvious example of such functional representation.

Example.   The graph of the function $f(x) = x^2 - 3$ is the set of pairs $\{(2, 1),$ $(3, 6), (4, 13), (5, 22), \ldots\}$, where we consider f to be defined on the natural numbers.

The reader should recognize that our brief mention of these several ways to define functional relationships is given only to stress a few important notions; it is by no means complete. After all, every program provides a definition of a function, that which maps the input into the output, and in a superficial sense all of computer science is concerned with effective means to define functions.

2.5 FUNCTIONS DEFINED ON OBJECTS OTHER THAN THE NATURAL NUMBERS

In considering functions as mappings from one set into another there is no reason to restrict these sets to be sets of natural numbers, or even of n-tuples of natural numbers, and we have frequent occasion in computer science to deal with functions defined on other kinds of objects. We may, for example, consider collections of strings of symbols and mappings of these strings into other strings. For example, let Σ^* be the set of all finite strings formed from the symbols in the English alphabet (Σ is often used to designate the alphabet of some language). Consider the mapping HEAD that associates with each string its leading character, HEAD: $\Sigma^* \to \Sigma$. We have:

$$\text{HEAD(ABRACADABRA)} = \text{A}$$

The function, JOIN, defined on pairs of such strings is another example. This function maps each ordered pair (i.e., there is a *first* and a *second* member of each pair) of strings into the string formed by concatenating them.

$$\text{JOIN(CAR, FARE)} = \text{CARFARE}$$

We shall, in the sequel, use the words "map" or "mapping" and "function" interchangeably, and we shall consider mappings whose domains and ranges seem very different from the natural numbers. For example, we might take as the domain of a mapping a set of arithmetic statements about particular integers such as:

1. $2 + 3 = 4$ 4. $6 < 4 - 5$
2. $7 < 10$ 5. $6 \div 2 = 7 - 4$
3. $5 - 3 < 12$ 6. $3 ** 3 = 9$

Each of these statements is either true (T or 1) or false (F or 0). We can then consider the mapping which associates to each such statement a value of 1 (or T) or 0 (or F). The given statements would then have the following values:

$$(1)\ 0, (2)\ 1, (3)\ 1, (4)\ 0, (5)\ 1, (6)\ 0.$$

In all cases the functions that arise in computer science involve domains and ranges that are *countable* sets (cf. the discussion in Section 3.7).

2.6   FUNCTIONS OF FUNCTIONS

We might even take *functions* themselves as objects of the domain of some mapping. Such a mapping might associate with each function in its domain some object such as a natural number or, possibly, some other function. We thus can consider a hierarchy of such mappings, starting with functions that map natural numbers into natural numbers

$$f : N \rightarrow N.$$

Then at a second level we would have mappings of functions into functions

$$F : f \rightarrow f$$

and perhaps, at a still higher level, mappings like

$$\phi : F \rightarrow F,$$

and so forth.

Examples of this sort of thing abound in mathematics and are fundamental to its development. A host of names including operator, transformation, morphism, functional, functor, etc., are used to refer to various situations of this kind.

In computing we can consider a program—a procedure—a routine—as providing a definition of some mapping of its input into its output. We may indicate symbolically that a particular program P designates such a mapping by writing

$$P : I \rightarrow O.$$

A compiler, then, would be an example in our hierarchy of a mapping of higher order, for it maps programs into programs

$$\text{compiler} : \text{programs} \rightarrow \text{programs}.$$

A "compiler-compiler" would be at a still higher, or a third, level, for it maps the specifications of a programming language into a compiler for that language.

Higher level mappings arise in the evolution of mathematics as we study sets, sets of sets, sets of sets of sets, and so forth. Perhaps comparable to this occurrence, an increasing sophistication is recognizable in some of the more advanced programming languages that provide features to deal with situations of this sort. PL/1 possesses this capability in a rudimentary way [3], ALGOL 68 has still more capability [6, 10], and SETL has considerable flexibility along these lines [8, 9]. For example, ALGOL 68 takes advantage of the fact that programs, routines, and procedures are themselves values and can therefore be parameters of other routines in calling statements.

Example. (ALGOL 68): An identity declaration like

$$\mathrm{PROC(PROC)} f = (\mathrm{PROC}\ a) : \mathrm{E}$$

causes the calling statement

$$\mathrm{CALL}\ f(x \bigstar y)$$

to result in the definition of a as a *procedure.* It is elaborated as

$$\mathrm{PROC}\ a = x \bigstar y : \mathrm{E}$$

Therefore, the value possessed by 'a' is a routine. Whenever the identifier 'a' appears in the elaboration of E, it results in this routine for the computation of the expression '$x \bigstar y$', and it is compiled in this way. Thus, the original procedure definition for f involves a higher level of definition. It does not define f as an ordinary function; it defines f as a function of a function. In our example, f associates the function $x \bigstar y$ with the function name a. Thus, f is a map from the domain of functions to the range of functions, $f : a \rightarrow x \bigstar y$.

The words "data type" are used with different meanings in the literature. The more common one, of course, refers to such entities as: integers, floating point numbers, fixed point numbers, complex numbers, alphabetic strings, bit strings, etc. However, some authors have defined data types of higher order to refer to the hierarchical situation we have described.

2.7   RELATIONS

If we abandon the requirement that a function associate a *unique* object in its range with every object in its domain, we are led to the notion of a relation. A function can be considered as being equivalent to its *graph.* Even when we cannot draw a picture such as Fig. 2.1, the graph of a function can still be regarded as the collection of all pairs (x, y) where x is an object in its domain and y is the associated object in its range (either or both objects may be n-tuples, $n > 1$, not just single numbers). From the requirement that there be a unique y for each x, it follows that if (x_1, y_1) and (x_1, y_2) are in the graph of a function f, then y_1 must necessarily be the same as y_2. This condition does not hold for a *relation*, which is defined to be *any* subset of pairs (x, y) without this restriction that no two different pairs have the same first component. The *domain* of a given relation is the set of all x's or first members of the pairs that constitute the relation; the *range* is the set of all y's or second members of these pairs.

We can describe a relation either by listing the pairs (x, y) that comprise it or, equivalently, by indicating that property which is satisfied by precisely these pairs. (See the definition of "predicate" in Section 2.12). The reasonableness of the name "relation" becomes apparent when we consider that "A is a brother of B" is an example of a relation. It involves as domain some human beings, and the pairs (A, B) that satisfy this stated relation are not restricted to having a unique B for given A. Examples of relations on the integers include: $x < y, x > y, x + 2 \neq y$. We note that an infinite number of pairs (x, y) with, say, $x = 7$ satisfy the relation $x < y$.

If the pair (x, y) is in the graph of a relation R we may write xRy to denote this fact. Equating the relation to its graph we can then say that "R is the set of pairs (x, y) such that xRy." This can be written, using conventional notation (cf. Section 3.4), as

$$R = \{(x, y) \mid xRy\}.$$

A relation R is said to be *reflexive* if for every element x in its domain we have xRx. It is *symmetric* if whenever xRy holds so does yRx. It is *transitive* if whenever we have both xRy and yRz it follows that xRz. The relation "A is a brother of B" is not transitive nor is it reflexive or symmetric (why not?).

A relation that possesses all three properties of being reflexive, symmetric, and transitive is called an *equivalence*, e.g., if $R = \{(x, y) \mid x - y$ is a multiple of $7\}$, then R is an equivalence.

Note that the ordinary equality of numbers, $x = y$, is a relation that is reflexive ($x = x$), symmetric (if $x = y$ then $y = x$), and transitive (if $x = y$ and $y = z$, then $x = z$). Equality is thus an equivalence.

As another example, consider the following relation S defined on the domain consisting of all words in the English language. Let xSy if and only if the two words x, y both end in the same last three letters. It is quickly seen that S is an equivalence. Other examples appear in the exercises.

2.8 THE DESIGNATION OF FUNCTIONS AND
THE LAMBDA NOTATION

We have used the conventional means of designating functions in writing defining expressions such as

$$f(x) = x^2$$

to indicate that function which maps every value of the variable x into the number x^2. There are, however, some disquieting aspects of this notation. We cannot take the "=" sign as meaning that the right-hand side is a complete description of the function f, that it is in a sense equivalent to the map $x \to x^2$, because some essential information is missing from it. To see this, suppose that we write what should be an equivalent designation if f is defined on all the integers:

$$f(x + 1) = x^2 + 2x + 1.$$

The right-hand side, viewed alone, does not tell us whether it is intended to designate the function

$$x + 1 \to x^2 + 2x + 1,$$

which is a rewriting of $x \to x^2$, or perhaps,

$$x \to x^2 + 2x + 1,$$

which is a quite different function. The missing information, the argument of f, appears only on the left-hand side.

Or, again, if we write

$$f(x) = 3x + y,$$

where y is some arbitrary quantity whose value is to be assigned (a parameter), we cannot tell from the right-hand side $3x + y$ (which is an example in mathematics of a "form") whether the intent is that x or that y be the independent variable. Also, if we write $g(s, r) = 2r + 3s$ and ask for the value of g at $(4, 1)$, it is not clear, without further convention, whether the intent be that $r = 4$ and $s = 1$ or vice versa.

The point is that the function f is not quite the same as that which is denoted by the expression "$f(x)$." The latter, which is an abbreviation for "the value of the function f at x," indicates the value or object into which x is mapped by the function f. As we have seen, this omits some information necessary to a complete specification of f. This slight defect of notation is in most usage not very serious, but an indiscriminate use of the notation in considering *operators*, or functions of functions, may lead to some confusion. Suppose, for example, that G is an operator which maps functions into functions and we write

$$Gf(x + 1). \tag{2.1}$$

Two interpretations of this expression can be considered, corresponding to the two possible meanings we might give the product abc in elementary algebra. In this latter case, in the absence of any rule such as scanning from left to right, the expression may mean (1) the result of obtaining $a(b)$ followed by $(a(b))c$, or it may mean (2) the result of obtaining $b(c)$ followed by

$a(b(c))$. The statement that these two results are the same, or that the order does not matter in performing this continued multiplication is, of course, known as the associative law of multiplication. This law holds in multiplication, but there is no reason to think that it is true in all other situations.

In the case of (2.1), we can similarly take it to mean (1) determine the function into which G maps f and then determine the value of this function for the argument $x + 1$, or it may mean (2) take the value of $f(x + 1)$, considered as a function of x, and determine the function into which this is mapped by G.

These two interpretations correspond to writing (1) $(G(f))(x + 1)$ or (2) $G(f(x + 1))$. Unlike ordinary multiplication they may give quite different results. Suppose, for example, that G is the operator that maps the arbitrary function f into the function ϕ, $G(f) = \phi$, where $\phi(x) = xf(x)$. If, then, f is the constant function $f(x) = 1$ (i.e., $f(x)$ is 1 for all values of x), we have $\phi(x) = x$. We thus can write $G(f(x)) = \phi(x)$ or, alternatively, since $\phi(x) = x$ and $f(x) = 1$, write $G(1) = x$.

We then have

$$(G(f))(x + 1) = \phi(x + 1) = x + 1,$$

while on the other hand,

$$G(f(x + 1)) = G(1) = x.$$

A more precise notation, called the lambda [λ] notation, removes the ambiguity present in the usual functional notation by clearly signaling the independent variables in a function definition.

The function $x \rightarrow f(x)$ is denoted by $\lambda\, xf(x)$. Thus $\lambda x(x^2)$ represents the function defined by the equation $f(x) = x^2$; $\lambda x(3x + y)$ specifies that x is the independent argument in the function $g(x) = 3x + y$, and $\lambda x(x^2 + 2x + 1)$ shows clearly that the map $x \rightarrow x^2 + 2x + 1$ is intended and not the map $x + 1 \rightarrow x^2 + 2x + 1$.

To write an expression like $f(x + 1)$, the result of applying the map f to $x + 1$, where $f(x) = x^2$, we would write

$$(\lambda x(x^2))(x + 1).$$

In so doing, the kind of confusion that, was implicit in the standard notation is removed. This last expression denotes the value of the function $f : x \rightarrow x^2$ when x is $x + 1$, and not the function $x \rightarrow x^2 + 2x + 1$.

A function of several variables $(x_1, x_2, \ldots, x_n) \rightarrow f(x_1, x_2, \ldots, x_n)$ is represented by $\lambda x_1 \lambda x_2 \ldots \lambda x_n f(x_1, x_2, \ldots, x_n)$. The sum function for three arguments is then written $\lambda x_1 \lambda x_2 \lambda x_3 (x_1 + x_2 + x_3)$.

A calculus for the manipulation of expressions employing this notation has been developed [2] and is called the "lambda calculus." It is used in one of the several methods of defining the class of computable functions. Some investigations into the design of computing machines that operate on such lambda expressions have been made [1,5], with proponents advocating significant advantages to such an approach to machine design.

Perhaps a key point of the lambda notation is implicit in the programmed definition of functions. If we consider the definition of a function by a subroutine, the subroutine alone does not constitute the complete definition of the function. The missing ingredient is, of course, the argument or arguments to be used in the computation. Thus in using, say PL/I, we might write

$$\text{CALL FUNCTION}(X1, X2);$$

to cause the execution of the subroutine labeled FUNCTION that will use the arguments $X1, X2$. The subroutine that performs the computation must be given the locations of the arguments that it is to use before it can be executed.

2.9   GENETIC METHODS IN DEFINING SETS

Many of the sets, or collections of objects, that arise within mathematics and the computer sciences have a generative character. That is, in defining a set we may be given certain fundamental objects in the set and, in addition, be given rules for forming new objects from old ones, or from objects already known to be in the set. The defined set then consists of all objects that can be formed by starting with the fundamental objects and repeatedly applying the rules for forming new objects.

The class of all human beings (from the past, present, and future) would probably be, if we accept the theory of evolution, impossible to define sharply. However, as with most beliefs based on orthodoxy, things are considerably simplified if we take Genesis literally. With this hypothesis we can define the class of human beings by writing

$$\text{HUMAN} :: = \text{ADAM} \mid \text{EVE} \mid \text{CHILD(HUMAN, HUMAN)}$$

In words, understanding that the symbol "$\mid$" is to be interpreted as "OR," this notation is to be taken as meaning that a member of the class of human beings is either Adam or Eve or the child of any two human beings. Only Adam and Eve are seen to be humans from a first application. A second application of the rule yields Cain and Abel and their brothers and sisters and then, by repetition, all generations until Armageddon. This particular definition is recursive in that the class of humans is defined in terms of itself with the word HUMAN appearing on both sides of the defining expression.

Such methods of defining collections of objects have been called "genetic" by Hilbert [4], and our example shows the appropriateness of the name. Perhaps the most obvious example of their use in mathematics appears in the definition of the natural numbers. These can be obtained by starting with the number 1 and repeatedly applying a rule that furnishes the successor of a number when we are given that number (see Section 12.2, "Peano's Axioms"). Here, each new member has just one "parent," unlike our biblical example. More generally, the method may presume any number of "parents" in generating new members.

As we shall see, examples of the use of the method abound in the study of programming languages and in computer science in general.

2.10 FORMAL SYSTEMS

During the last 100 years there has been a notable attempt to use mathematical logic to put mathematics on a firmer foundation and thus minimize the risks in the use of intuition by our fallible intellects (cf. Appendix to Chapter 1). A frequent device has been the use of *formal systems*—systems where we manipulate symbolic expressions without regard to their possible meaning. The methods used have either motivated or been rediscovered in the employment of techniques useful for the study of programming languages and their compilers.

By way of example, we briefly describe the first steps in a formal approach to the study of the game of checkers, a game familiar to all readers. We shall do this only in the most superficial manner and shall not at all consider the substantive problem of what constitutes good strategy in playing this game.

Let us first consider the elements, or *objects*, in the game of checkers to be board positions. We designate the two contestants as White and Black where each uses pieces of the corresponding color. Starting with the configuration of Fig. 2.2, Black makes the first move and a game is a sequence of board positions, each of which is obtained from the preceding one as a result of a legitimate move. There are 32 squares on a checkerboard where a piece can be situated (Fig. 2.2). Each such square can contain no piece, a black checker, a black king, a white checker, or a white king. We can then represent each board position P by a string of 33 digits, $P = A_1 A_2 \ldots A_{32} B$, where each digit A_i $(i = 1, 2, \ldots, 32)$ corresponds to one of the 32 labeled squares of Fig. 2.2 and can be taken to be, say, 0, 1, 2, 3, or 4 according to the five listed possibilities. B is defined to be 0 or 1 according to whether White or Black is to make the next move. There are a finite number, $2 \cdot 5^{32}$, of such configurations for P, not all of which are *feasible* board positions, that is, positions that can be reached in playing a game. For example, there cannot be 13 black pieces in play. These configurations are the "objects" of our system. The rules of the game imply that if $P = A_1 A_2 \ldots A_{32} B$ is a particular board position, then there is a small set of possible board positions that can result from

	1		2		3		4
5		6		7		8	
	9		10		11		12
13		14		15		16	
	17		18		19		20
21		22		23		24	
	25		26		27		28
29		30		31		32	

Fig. 2.2   Checkerboard notation. The numbered squares are usually dark-colored and the others are light-colored. Initially, Black occupies squares 1 to 12, and White 21 to 32.

a legitimate move by White or by Black. We can indicate that the position $P' = A_1'A_2'\ldots A_{32}'B'$ is a successor position to P as a result of a legitimate move by writing

$$P \rightarrow P'.$$

If a sequence of moves alternately made by Black and White (i.e., a feasible game fragment) leads from position P to position Q, we can write

$$P \rightarrow * \, Q.$$

It is possible in these terms to play checkers on a computer, in the sense merely of playing a legal game, without pursuing the goal of winning. The *formalization* of the game includes the symbolic representations of board positions, and we can consider "well-formed formulas" of this system to be expressions of the form $P \rightarrow * \, Q$ where P, Q are board positions. Suppose P_0 is the initial board position

$$11111111111100000000003333333333331$$

(Black makes the first move). A "game" is then a sequence of board positions $P_0 \rightarrow P_1 \rightarrow P_2 \rightarrow \ldots \rightarrow P_n$ leading to a position P_n that has no successor. (Because, for example, there remain checkers of only one color, or there is no feasible move for the player who is to make the next move; we omit the complicating conditions under which a draw can be reached.)

It is not likely that the game has ever been described in these pseudo-mathematical terms, but we can consider the "axioms" of the system to be the rules that determine when a position P can have a successor position P' ($P \rightarrow P'$). These rules are easy to describe with reference to the two-dimensional array, as just about everyone in the Western world has learned as a child, but rather clumsy to describe in terms of the one-dimensional strings that represent board positions. A "theorem" of the system might be taken to be a statement of the form $P_0 \rightarrow * Q$, indicating that position Q is a feasible board position, one that can be reached in a game.

Having defined this rudimentary prototype of a formal system, we turn to a more detailed description of such a system, appropriate to its use in mathematics. In general, a formal system for the study of some mathematical structure is defined by taking the following steps (1) through (4). We shall illustrate this in a following discussion of Boolean algebra.

1. Identify the basic elements of the structure. For example, in geometry these might be points, lines, and planes; in logic they might be statements (assertions that are either true or false); in the study of the integers they might be the objects zero and one; in programming languages they might be the basic words and symbols that can appear within program statements. Introduce, if necessary, symbols or primitive terms to represent these basic elements and also, as needed, symbols to denote the essential attributes, operations, relations, and so forth that may involve these terms and are of special significance. These symbols can be any identifiers we please—single letters or marks, words, sentences, anything that will serve as a name for that which is being represented. For example, as part of the description of decimal data in a particular programming language, we might (as in the description of ALGOL [7]) describe the formation of the decimal integers by using as primitive terms the symbols that represent the ten digits. We might write

$$< \text{digit} > :: = 0 \mid 1 \mid 2 \mid 3 \mid 4 \mid 5 \mid 6 \mid 7 \mid 8 \mid 9.$$

Here, the brackets "$< >$" are taken to mean "the symbolic expressions for the members of the class" named within the brackets. In this case, the class is the class of decimal digits.

The formal notational scheme here illustrated is an example of the "Backus-Naur form," also called the "Backus normal form" (BNF), introduced in the report on ALGOL [7] as a technique for defining programming languages.

2. Describe, as in the discussion of genetic methods, how to form new objects in terms of objects already known to be in the system. Specify this by indicating how to form new strings of symbols, or new terms, that represent these new objects. For example, we might define the representations of all members of the class of nonnegative integers K, where the fundamental objects are the decimal digits, by writing

$$< K > :: = \; < \text{digit} > \; \mid \; < K > < \text{digit}>.$$

This means that the symbolic strings representing the nonnegative integers are formed by taking any digit or any symbolic string representing a nonnegative integer and appending a digit to it. These rules admit strings of arbitrary length and with possible leading zeros as representors of the nonnegative integers. We leave to the reader (cf. Exercise 2.15) the changes that would be needed to admit only strings that do not have a leading zero.

As a part of the description of elementary algebra we might let the letters of the alphabet denote variables, which are some of the primitive terms of the system. After introducing the operation symbol $+$ we can specify that if x, y are two terms then $(x + y)$ is a term or, in the BNF notation, we might write

$$<\text{term}> :: = (<\text{term}> + <\text{term}>) \mid <\text{primitive term}>.$$

3. Describe how statements or "formulas" involving the terms and special symbols of the system are formed. These, also, have a genetic or constructive character. Our prescriptions may include recursive rules showing how the symbolic strings representing new formulas can be formed from those representing earlier obtained formulas.

Thus, if the symbols $2, 3, 5, (,), >$ are included among the primitive symbols in a discussion of elementary algebra, $5 > (2 + 3)$ would be a properly formed string of symbols identifying a statement (which happens to be false), but $> 5)23 (+$ would be an ill-formed, meaningless string of these same symbols. The rules describing the formation of well-formed strings comprise the "syntax" of the system. The properly formed strings representing formulas are often called "well-formed formulas" or "wff's." The term is also used to refer to those properly formed strings that represent the objects of the system.

This is analogous to the construction of properly formed statements within a programming language. The syntax of the language specifies how well-formed statements are formed from the basic symbols and words of the language (cf. Chapter 9).

4. Specify certain fundamental statements, or formulas, that are assumed to be true. These are called the "axioms" or "postulates" of the system. Further, specify how from one or more true statements others can be obtained by using principles of logic and special rules that may be peculiar to the system being defined. The true statements so generated are the "theorems" of the system.

A formal system then consists of all these components—a set of admissible symbols, rules for composing wff's, axioms which are the fundamental wff's assumed to be true, and rules for generating new true statements (or theorems) from previously obtained ones.

The Euclidean plane geometry studied in secondary school has some characteristics of such systems, but our dependence on diagrams in the usual exposition of this subject is a serious violation of the specifications for formal systems. Carelessly drawn inferences from diagrams are, in fact, the bases for a number of fallacies of plane geometry that are occasionally seen in works on mathematical recreations.

In studying a mathematical structure by the device of a formal system, the system must, in a sense, mirror that structure. The most crucial step is perhaps the enunciation of the axioms. Once the system is laid down, the derivation of the theorems within it can proceed through symbolic manipulation and in game-like fashion with no further reference to the structure it is designed to emulate.

The formal description of a programming language has, as we have indicated, some of the aspects of a formal system. Steps (1), (2), (3) are followed in describing properly formed statements and programs within the language (cf. Chapter 9).

2.11 ARITHMETIZATION

We referred briefly in Chapter 1 to the technique of arithmetization that is used in mathematical logic. We shall elaborate somewhat upon these ideas because of their great significance in computing as well as in logic.

We have noted, in reference to the Pythagoreans, the primacy of number. When, in the very varied applications of the computer, we map many different classes of objects into the natural numbers we are, perhaps, giving further evidence of the primary significance of number in the order of things. In these applications many differing kinds of objects or situations ranging from checks to checkers, from formulas to forests, from payrolls to poems are mapped into the class of natural numbers N (or, perhaps, into sequences of natural numbers).

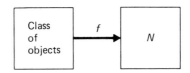

Since we shall want to be able to "recover" each object from its representation—for example, it would certainly not do to map all of the objects into zero—it is necessary to have our map one-to-one so that no two objects are mapped into the same number. The map is then, as we have noted, invertible.

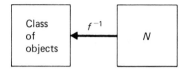

In the study of a formal system, the technique of arithmetization, when applied, includes the mapping of the terms and formulas of the system into the natural numbers by such invertible functions. Further, (1) the generating operations that yield new terms from existing terms, (2) those operations that obtain new wff's from existing terms and wff's and (3) those operations that yield new theorems from existing theorems can all be replaced by *arithmetic functions* that map the numbers corresponding to the existing terms, wff's, theorems into the numbers corresponding to the new terms, wff's, theorems which are derivable from these existing objects.

This is shown schematically in part in Fig. 2.3, which shows the arithmetization of the derivation of theorems in a formal system.

A similar diagram will show the arithmetization of the derivation of wff's from the terms of the system.

In the arithmetization of the system, on the right-hand side of Fig. 2.3, we work with *numbers* and arithmetic *operations* performed on these numbers. The arithmetization is a *simulation* of the formal system in which the original objects of the system and the operations performed on these objects have been replaced by numbers and arithmetic operations performed on these numbers. The operations that can be performed within the system, shown on the left-hand side of Fig. 2.3, are mirrored by the arithmetic operations that occur on the right-hand side of Fig. 2.3. The arithmetized processes mimic the symbolic manipulations within the system. This is said in the sense that if we perform the mappings in the order $A \rightarrow B$ fol-

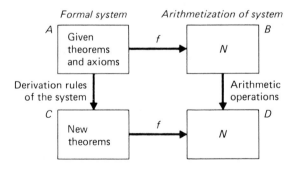

Fig. 2.3   The arithmetization of a formal system.

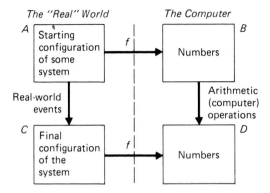

Fig. 2.4 Simulation—mirroring a real world situation in the computer. The simulation is correct if the two paths from A to D lead to the same results.

lowed by $B \rightarrow D$, or in the order $A \rightarrow C$ followed by $C \rightarrow D$ (corresponding to the two paths from A to D), the results are the same. (In mathematics we say that the diagram "commutes.")

The technique is significant in our survey because in a larger sense it is the essence of what is meant by simulation in many applications of computing (see Fig. 2.4). The programmed operations in a simulation process can, although there may be no point to doing it, always be expressed as arithmetic operations. This will follow from the discussion in Chapter 4 where the computer-defined functions are claimed to be the same as a class called the "partial recursive functions."

2.12   BOOLEAN ALGEBRA

In 1854, the English mathematician George Boole published his magnum opus, *An Investigation of the Laws of Thought*. In this work he applied mathematical methods to the study of logic as it apparently guides our thinking (even when we are not aware of using it), and he introduced an algebra for the manipulation of symbols that represent statements. The formulation of this work that we shall give adheres to modern usage and differs somewhat from Boole's original schema, but the basic ideas are the same.

A "statement" (or "proposition") in logic, unlike its use as an equivalent of "instruction" in many programming languages, is a verbal or symbolic (or both) expression that we can assert to be either true or false. Thus: "some roses are red," "$2 + 3 = 4$," "computers can be used for either good or evil,"

" 'VENUS' follows 'ADONIS' in alphabetic ordering," are examples of statements. Every statement has a "truth value" of either TRUE or FALSE. Or, as in many of those programming languages that include facilities for the handling of such expressions, we shall say that the value of the statement is 1 if it is true, 0 if it is false.

Such expressions as "5 + 6 $*$ 7," "thou shalt not follow a multitude to do evil," "twas brillig and the slithy toves did tyre and gimble in the wabe," "who is Sylvia, what is she?", are not statements for it is not meaningful to speak of their being either true or false.

In some cases it may be extremely difficult, or perhaps impossible, to determine if a given statement is true or false, although we may concede that one or the other possibility must hold. Such statements as "there are no positive whole numbers x, y, z, n with $n > 2$ that satisfy the equation $x^n + y^n = z^n$," or "there are five consecutive 7's somewhere in the infinite decimal representation of π" are of this kind.

In still other instances it may be quite questionable as to whether an apparent statement can even be said to have truth value, even if we ignore the matter of determining whether it be true or false. Such declarations as "life has purpose," "God exists," "there exist real numbers that can not be individually described or individually characterized or referred to in any manner whatsoever,"[1] may be in this category. We leave to the reader the adjudication of this matter for each of our sample declarations. In fact, Niels Bohr has noted that often a statement that appears to be "profound" is characterized by the fact that both the statement *and* its contradiction seem to possess some deep validity. Our last examples may be in this category.

The conditional statements we use in writing programs, however, involve arithmetic operations and are finitely verifiable, not subject to any uncertainty because of a possibly clouded meaning of truth or falsity.

Relations become mathematical statements when particular numbers are substituted for the arguments. Thus, the relation "$y \geq x + 2$" becomes for $x = 6$, $y = 3$ the false statement "$3 \geq 8$." Such relations on the natural numbers are also known as *predicates*.

We shall now take the first steps toward defining a formal system for the study and manipulation of statements.

1. We denote arbitrary statements, or propositions, by the letters A, B, $C, \ldots$. Each such symbol represents a "Boolean variable" which can take on the value 0 for FALSE or 1 for TRUE—just as in elementary algebra we let

---

[1]   In fact, there is a general belief by mathematicians that in a certain sense more of these surprisingly unapproachable numbers exist than of the other kind. See the discussion of transfinite numbers in Section 3.7.

symbols like x, y, z represent variables that can take on values that are real numbers.

We shall also use the symbols "$\neg$" for NOT, "$|$" for OR, and "$\&$" for AND. If A is the statement "$\ldots$," then "$\neg A$" shall denote the statement "it is not true that '$\ldots$'," or "'$\ldots$' is false," or simply "NOT A." $\neg A$ is also called "the negation of A." The symbol "$\neg$" is a *unary* connective, for it applies to a single statement. $\neg A$ is TRUE (or 1) if A is FALSE (0), and FALSE if A is TRUE. Table 2.1 shows the values of $\neg A$ for the two possible values of A.

TABLE 2.1.   TRUTH TABLE FOR $\neg A$

A	$\neg A$
0	1
1	0

If B is the statement "xxx" then "$A \mid B$" shall denote the statement "either '$\ldots$' or 'xxx' is true (and perhaps both are true)." $A \mid B$ is also known as the "disjunction" of A and B. Again, we can tablulate the values of $A \mid B$ (giving rise to a "truth table") for each of the four possible combinations of values of A and B.

TABLE 2.2.   TRUTH TABLE FOR $A \mid B$

A	B	$A \mid B$
0	0	0
0	1	1
1	0	1
1	1	1

"$A \& B$" shall denote the statement "both '$\ldots$' and 'xxx' are true." $A \& B$ may also be called the "conjunction of A and B." Both "$|$" and "$\&$" are binary connectives.

TABLE 2.3.   TRUTH TABLE FOR $A \& B$

A	B	$A \& B$
0	0	0
0	1	0
1	0	0
1	1	1

Other symbols that àre sometimes used for these same connectives are as follows:

$$\neg A: \quad -A, \overline{A}, \sim A, A', \text{NOT } A$$
$$A \mid B: \quad A \vee B, A + B, A \oplus B, A \text{ OR } B$$
$$A \& B: \quad A \wedge B, A \cdot B, AB, A \star B, A \text{ AND } B.$$

2. The wff's, or "statements" of our system are those expressions or symbolic strings that we can form using the symbols for Boolean variables and applying any number of times the three connectives. To avoid ambiguity, we shall also have to use the left and right parentheses (,) just as in elementary algebra we use parentheses to make clear the interpretation of complex expressions. Let *"BE"* represent this class of wff's or Boolean expressions. We can now define, using the BNF notation, how the symbolic strings that represent the members of this class are formed.

$$<\text{Boolean variable}> :: = A \mid B \mid C \mid ... \mid Z$$

(We can assume an alphabet of any size.)

$$<BE> :: = <\text{Boolean variable}> \mid (<BE> \mid <BE>) \mid \neg <BE> \mid$$
$$(<BE> \& <BE>).$$

Every Boolean expression defines a Boolean function that yields a value of 0 or 1 for every possible set of truth values assigned to the Boolean variables of which it is composed. The value for each combination of arguments can be computed by repeated reference to the truth tables for $\neg A, A \mid B, A \& B$.

Thus, the truth table for the Boolean expression

$$((A \& (B \mid C)) \mid \neg B)$$

can be computed as shown in Table 2.4.

TABLE 2.4.   TRUTH TABLE FOR $((A \& (B \mid C)) \mid \neg B)$

A	B	C	$(B \mid C)$	$(A \& (B \mid C))$	$\neg B$	$((A \& (B \mid C)) \mid \neg B)$
0	0	0	0	0	1	1
0	0	1	1	0	1	1
0	1	0	1	0	0	0
0	1	1	1	0	0	0
1	0	0	0	0	1	1
1	0	1	1	1	1	1
1	1	0	1	1	0	1
1	1	1	1	1	0	1

We note that $((A \& (B \mid C)) \mid \neg B)$ takes on the same truth values for different combinations of arguments as the much simpler expression $(A \mid \neg B)$.

3. In this particular formal system, the wff's, or the statements about propositions or statements are themselves statements, as we shall see, and there-

fore do not comprise new objects in the system. We shall introduce two new symbols involved in making statements about statements.

The symbol "$=$" appearing between two Boolean expressions as in $(A \mid \neg B) = ((A \,\&\, (B \mid C)) \mid \neg B)$ shall mean not that the two expressions appearing on both sides of the "$=$" are identical but, rather, that for given values of the Boolean variables which appear in them they have the same truth value—one is not true while the other is false. (In mathematics, the symbol "$\equiv$" is often used for "is identical with," as opposed to the "$=$" that is usually used in a sense similar to that we have just given.) This is consistent with our use of the "$=$" in elementary algebra. For example, when we write

$$x^2 - y^2 - 2x + 1 = (x + y - 1)(x - y - 1),$$

we mean that the two forms on both sides of the "$=$" take on the same values for all admissible values of x, y.

We note, however, that the "$=$" is expressible in terms of the other connectives; the truth table for $A = B$ is identical with that for $(\neg A \,\&\, \neg B \mid (A \,\&\, B))$.

TABLE 2.5

A	B	$A = B$	$(\neg A \,\&\, \neg B) \mid (A \,\&\, B)$
0	0	1	1
0	1	0	0
1	0	0	0
1	1	1	1

Therefore, $A = B$ can always be replaced by this other expression which involves the connectives $\neg, \&, \mid$.

The symbol "$\supset$" between two expressions, as in $A \supset B$, denotes "implies," and this expression is read as "A implies B" or "if '...' then 'xxx'." The arrow "$\rightarrow$" is often used for this purpose as well, $A \rightarrow B$ having the same meaning as $A \supset B$. By definition, $A \supset B$ has the same meaning as $(\neg A \mid B)$ or "either A is false or B is true" (to see the reasonableness of this definition, note that if "either A is false or B is true" then "if A is true, B must be true," and conversely). From this definition, the truth table for $A \supset B$ is as shown in Table 2.6.

TABLE 2.6   TRUTH TABLE FOR $A \supset B$

A	B	$A \supset B$
0	0	1
0	1	1
1	0	0
1	1	1

What we have done so far constitutes the definition of the *syntax* of this formal language, the rules for forming those well-formed symbolic strings that represent the objects and formulas of the system. It remains to attach "meaning" to, or to define the *semantics* of, these expressions (cf. the discussion of the syntax and semantics of formal languages in Chapter 9). This can be done through our use of truth tables. Every Boolean expression defines a truth table and this table implies the meaning of that expression. For example, if we keep in mind the association of "1" with TRUE and "0" with FALSE, we see that the table for "$A \mid B$" indicates that this expression denotes a statement that is TRUE when either A or B (possibly both) is TRUE. Similarly, "$A \rightarrow B$" is an expression that represents a statement which is TRUE if A is FALSE or if B is TRUE.

If we are given the "double implication," both $A \rightarrow B$ and $B \rightarrow A$ (i.e., $(A \rightarrow B)$ & $(B \rightarrow A)$), this is often written $A \leftrightarrow B$. This is then the same as $A = B$, for it is quickly seen that the truth table for this conjunction is identical with that for $A = B$. In other words, we can say that two statements are "equivalent" if each implies the other. We note from the table that $A \supset B$ is true when A is false, independently of the value of B. Or, in terms of the verbal interpretation of these logical symbols, a false statement implies any statement, whether that statement be true or false. It may not be clear at this point in our discussion that this means we can "prove" the truth of any statement at all if we accept as hypothesis a false statement, but such is the case. Some years ago, Bertrand Russell, after having mentioned this fact in a lecture, was challenged by a member of the audience to deduce from the false statement "$2 + 2 = 3$" that he was the Pope. "That is easy," Russell immediately replied. "From $2 + 2 = 3$ we conclude, subtracting 2 from both sides, that $2 = 1$. I and the Pope are two; therefore, we are one." However, this theorem that a false hypothesis implies any conclusion whatsoever has probably been used more widely by politicians than by mathematicians.

If we have $A \rightarrow B$, we often say that "B is a necessary condition for A." That is, A cannot be true unless B is true. We also say that "A is a sufficient condition for B." That is, it suffices for A to be true in order for B to be true.

Thus, if A is the statement "Mary is a good programmer," and B is the statement "Mary includes ample comments in her program documentation," A is a sufficient condition for B, and B is a necessary condition for A.

Tautologies.   Some Boolean expressions take on the constant value 1 for all possible assignments of values to the Boolean variables of which they are composed (they are always true). Consider the following expression S,

$$(A \supset B) \supset ((C \mid A) \supset (C \mid B)).$$

The truth table for this expression is computed as in Table 2.7.

TABLE 2.7

A	B	C	$(A \supset B)$	$(C \mid A)$	$(C \mid B)$	$((C \mid A) \supset (C \mid B))$	S
0	0	0	1	0	0	1	1
0	0	1	1	1	1	1	1
0	1	0	1	0	1	1	1
0	1	1	1	1	1	1	1
1	0	0	0	1	0	0	1
1	0	1	0	1	1	1	1
1	1	0	1	1	1	1	1
1	1	1	1	1	1	1	1

We see that S is identically 1; that is, it is always true, no matter what the truth values of the statements A, B, C may be. Such statements are called "tautologies." They comprise the theorems of our system.

The method of truth tables can be used to verify quickly that the following are tautologies:

$$\text{i. } (A \& B) = (B \& A)$$
$$((A \& B) \& C) = (A \& (B \& C)),$$

i.e., the connective AND is commutative and associative. Thus, we can write $A \& B \& C$ without parentheses.

$$\text{ii. } (A \mid B) = (B \mid A)$$
$$((A \mid B) \mid C) = (A \mid (B \mid C)),$$

i.e., the connective OR is commutative and associative. Thus, we can write $A \mid B \mid C$ without parentheses.

$$\text{iii. } (A \& (B \mid C)) = (A \& B) \mid (A \& C),$$

i.e., AND is distributive over OR.

$$\text{iv. } (A \mid (B \& C)) = (A \mid B) \& (A \mid C),$$

i.e., OR is distributive over AND.

We note the analogy with the laws of elementary algebra if the "&" is thought of as ordinary multiplication and the "|" as addition (with the exception of the last tautology, for addition is not distributive over multiplication). This explains the use of the symbols $\ast$, $\cdot$ for AND and of $+$ for OR.

4. The technique of using truth tables to determine if a given Boolean statement is a tautology makes it unnecessary in this exposition to postulate a set of basic axioms of the system and to describe how theorems are to be

derived from these axioms. It is quite possible to do this, to enunciate a set of one, two, three, four, or more axioms and to define rules for deducing theorems (modus ponens, substitution, cf. below and the exercises), but the truth tables enable us to determine by a straightforward computation (an effective procedure) if a given statement is always true, i.e., is a tautology. However, while the truth table technique provides an algorithm to verify that a given statement is a theorem, it provides at best a very awkward mechanism to *discover* new theorems or tautologies. A formulation employing axioms and rules of inference would be better for this purpose.

2.13   AN AXIOMATIC FORMULATION OF THE PROPOSITIONAL CALCULUS

One particular axiomatic formulation for a calculus of propositions, or for the "propositional calculus," is the following:

Axioms:

1. $(P \mid P) \rightarrow P$

2. $P \rightarrow (P \mid Q)$

3. $(P \mid Q) \rightarrow (Q \mid P)$

4. $(P \rightarrow Q) \rightarrow ((R \mid P) \rightarrow (R \mid Q))$

Rules:

1. *Substitution.* If a given Boolean expression is true (a tautology), it will remain true if any Boolean variable appearing within it is replaced in all its occurrences by an arbitrary Boolean expression.

2. *Modus ponens.* If $X \rightarrow Y$ is a tautology, where X, Y are arbitrary Boolean expressions and X is a tautology, then Y is a tautology.

Definitions: Note that the symbols $\neg$, $=$, and $\&$ do not appear in the axioms. Meaning is assigned to expressions containing these symbols in accordance with the following definitions, which are consistent with our earlier usage. We shall write "$\overset{\text{Df}}{=}$" between two expressions to mean that the expression to its left "is equal by definition to" the expression to its right.

1. $(P = Q) \overset{\text{Df}}{=} (P \rightarrow Q) \& (Q \rightarrow P)$

2. $(\neg P \mid Q) \overset{\text{Df}}{=} (P \rightarrow Q)$

3. $(P \& Q) \overset{\text{Df}}{=} \neg (\neg P \mid \neg Q)$

In this formulation, the tautologies include the axioms and all additional tautologies, or theorems, that can be obtained from the axioms by repeated application of the rules of substitution and modus ponens.

We illustrate the use of these methods to prove several propositions. We shall follow a format similar to that used for proofs in elementary Euclidean geometry. Parentheses are omitted in several places where no confusion results from such omission.

Example 1.   Prove the theorem $T_1 : (Q \to R) \to ((P \to Q) \to (P \to R))$.

Step	Reason
(1) $(Q \to R) \to ((\neg P \mid Q) \to (\neg P \mid R))$	Use rule (1) in axiom (4). Replace P by Q, Q by R, R by $\neg P$.
(2) $(Q \to R) \to ((P \to Q) \to (P \to R))$ QED	Definition (2) used in step (1).

Example 2.   Prove the law of the excluded middle $T_2 : \neg P \mid P$.

Step	Reason
(1) $P \to (P \mid P)$	Use rule (1) in axiom (2). Replace Q by P.
(2) $(P \to (P \mid P)) \to (P \to P)$	Use rule (1) in T_1. Replace Q by $(P \mid P)$, R by P. Then use axiom (1) and rule (2) to assert the right-hand side as a theorem.
(3) $P \to P$	Step (2) and rule (2).
(4) $\neg P \mid P$ QED	Definition (2).

All the theorems of this calculus of statements can be proven in this manner. Some of the proofs may be rather difficult to formulate, unlike the straightforward use of the method of truth tables. The latter is an effective, easily programmable, "decision procedure" for determining the truth or falsity of statements in the propositional calculus.

2.14   THE METHOD OF "REDUCTIO AD ABSURDUM"

Every student of high school plane geometry has seen the use of this method, which is used widely in all of mathematics, to prove propositions. It is applied in the following way to prove a statement P. We assume that P is false (i.e., we assume $\neg P$). Then, under this hypothesis we proceed to prove some absurdity; usually we prove the self-contradicting conclusion that the hypothesis is false. That is, we prove P to be true after having assumed its contradiction $\neg P$. We then conclude that $\neg P$ cannot be true, the assumption of $\neg P$ having been "reduced to the absurd." Therefore, P must be true, for by the "law of the excluded middle" either P or $\neg P$ must be true.

Using the language of the Boolean algebra of logical propositions we are, in applying this method, using the following theorem of logic:

$$(\neg P \to P) \leftrightarrow P.$$

This theorem is readily proven by the method of truth tables.

We illustrate use of the method by giving the proof, attributed to Euclid, that $\sqrt{2}$ *is* not a rational number, that is, it cannot be expressed in the form p/q where p, q are natural numbers. Assume the contradiction of this proposition, that is, assume $\sqrt{2}$ *is* a rational number p/q. We can further assume that p/q is written in lowest terms or that any common factor has been canceled from numerator and denominator. We then have $\sqrt{2} = p/q$ or, squaring both sides and clearing of fractions, $p^2 = 2q^2$. Hence p^2 is an even number and so must p also be even, say $p = 2m$. Therefore, $(2m)^2 = 2q^2$ or, dividing through by 2, $2m^2 = q^2$ and q is also seen to be an even number.

But now we have arrived at the conclusion that *both* p and q are even, contradicting our hypothesis that they have no common factors. We therefore conclude that our hypothesis must be false and $\sqrt{2}$ can*not* be expressed in the form p/q.

2.15   FORMING A BOOLEAN EXPRESSION
WHOSE TRUTH TABLE IS GIVEN

The truth table for a given Boolean expression is, using our earlier terminology, the graph of the function defined by that expression. We have seen that more than one Boolean expression can correspond to a given truth table, there being, in fact, an infinite number of such Boolean expressions.

It is a simple matter to write a particular Boolean expression having a given truth table as its graph. We show this in the following by describing the "disjunctive normal form" of a Boolean function.

Suppose, for example, we are given Table 2.8 for a Boolean function that we tentatively call F.

TABLE 2.8

A	B	C	F
0	0	0	0
0	0	1	1
0	1	0	1
0	1	1	0
1	0	0	0
1	0	1	0
1	1	0	1
1	1	1	0

We seek a Boolean expression for F with this given truth table. We note that F is true if and only if (1) A is false, B is false, C is true, or if (2) A is false, B is true, C is false, or if (3) A is true, B is true, C if false. That is, F is true if (1) $(\neg A \;\&\; \neg B \;\&\; C)$, or if (2) $(\neg A \;\&\; B \;\&\; \neg C)$, or if (3) $(A \;\&\; B \;\&\; \neg C)$. Using the connector "$|$" we can write this last statement as

$$F = (\neg A \;\&\; \neg B \;\&\; C) \mid (\neg A \;\&\; B \;\&\; \neg C) \mid (A \;\&\; B \;\&\; \neg C).$$

This is now a Boolean expression for F formed directly from the truth table. It is called the disjunctive normal form since F is written as a disjunction of terms. Every Boolean function can thus be written as a disjunction of conjunctions of Boolean variables and their negations.

2.16   ON "POLISH NOTATION"

The original use of the parenthesis-free notation bearing the surprisingly nationalistic name that is in common use today was in the propositional calculus. The Polish mathematician, J. Lukasiewicz, a member of the pre-World War II "Great Polish School of Mathematics" (a school closed largely through the efforts of A. Hitler and his followers) introduced the scheme of writing $p \rightarrow q$, or $p \supset q$, as Cpq. With this writing of the implication symbol as a prefix, no parentheses are needed in writing complex expressions. For example, the statement

$$(p \supset q) \supset ((q \supset r) \supset (p \supset r))$$

becomes in Polish notation:

$$CCpqCCqrCpr.$$

More generally, any binary operator can be written in front of its two operands. If we have an arithmetic expression involving several different operations such as

1. $((a + b) \div (c \times d)) - (e - f)$

this becomes, in "Polish notation"

2. $- \div + ab \times cd - ef.$

This prefix notation has wide application in compiling. It is a comparatively straightforward task to scan a string like (2) and compile the program that computes it. The handling of (1) is a more complicated affair.

The compelling advantage of the prefix notation is that it is completely unambiguous, requiring no parentheses or additional conventions. An expression like $a + b * c$ is not well-defined unless parentheses are inserted or some precedence relationship is stated about the arithmetic operations (such as, do multiplications before additions). However, when written in prefix notation, no such conventions are needed. Thus, the two possible interpretations of this expression would be in prefix notation the two different strings, $+ a \star bc$ and $\star + abc$, according respectively to whether the multiplication or the addition is done first.

A slight variant of this notation is "postfix" notation in which the operator is written directly after its two operands. A number of hand calculator models are designed to handle arithmetic in this manner.

EXERCISES

2.1 If $f(x) = x^2 - 3x + 2$ then $f(2y + z - 1) = ?$

2.2 Let $A = \{1, 2, 3,\}$, $B = \{8, 9\}$, $C = \{2, 3\}$. The graph of $f: A \to B$ is given as $f = \{(1, 9), (2, 9), (3, 8)\}$.

    a. What are the domain and the range of f?

    b. Is f a one-to-one mapping of A to B?

    c. Is f an onto mapping?

    d. Is f invertible?

2.3 Let $f(x) = x + 2$, $g(x) = 2x + 3$ be functions defined on the integers (positive, negative, zero).

    a. What is $f(g(x))$? $g(f(x))$?

    b. Give the values of: $f(4)$, $g(0)$, $f^{-1}(6)$, $g^{-1}(7)$. Is $g^{-1}(8)$ defined?

    c. Is f a one-to-one mapping from the integers into the integers? Is g?

    d. Are f and g total functions on the integers?

2.4 If N is the set of nonnegative integers, give an example of a total function $f: N \to N$ which is invertible and whose inverse is total, but do not use as an example $f(x) = x$.

2.5 Do the following equations provide enough information to define a function $f(x)$ on the nonnegative integers? Compute $f(4)$, $f(5)$.

$$\begin{cases} f(0) = 2 \\ f(1) = 4 \\ f(x + 2) = x \cdot f(x). \end{cases}$$

2.6 Do the following equations provide a proper definition of a function $f(m, n)$ of two arguments? The arguments are assumed to be nonnegative integers.

$$\begin{cases} f(0, n) = n + 1 \\ f(m, 0) = f(m - 1, 1) \\ f(m, n) = f(m - 1, f(m, n - 1)). \end{cases}$$

Find $f(2, 2)$.

2.7 Let a relation xRy be defined by $x \le y + 2$. Is R reflexive? symmetric? transitive?

2.8 Define a relation R on the set $\{a, b, c, d, e\}$ as follows. $R = \{(a, a), (b, b), (c, c),$

$(d, d), (b, c), (c, d)\}$. R is not an equivalence. Why not? What ordered pairs should be added to make it one, using the smallest possible number of additional pairs?

2.9 A relation R is defined by: xRy if x and y are positive integers, and x divides y, and $x^2 + y^2 < 25$. Write the graph of R.

2.10 Is the relation "x divides y" reflexive? symmetric? transitive?

2.11 How many functions $f: S \rightarrow S$ with domain equal to S (f if total on S) and range in S are there if S has n elements? How many such one-to-one functions are there?

2.12 Let f be a function that maps each n–bit binary word into either 0 or 1. How many such functions are there?

2.13 Write a PL/I recursive procedure (or use any other programming language with this capability) to compute the nth Fibonacci number. These numbers $\{F_k, k = 0, 1, 2, 3, \ldots\}$ are defined by the equations:

$$\begin{cases} F_0 = 0 \\ F_1 = 1 \\ F_k = F_{k-1} + F_{k-2} \quad (k \geq 2). \end{cases}$$

2.14 What is the value of $(\lambda x(3 + x^2))(3 + y)$?

2.15 Describe, using the BNF, the symbolic strings that represent the nonnegative binary integers written with no leading zeros (except for 0 itself) and no $+$ sign.

2.16 Consider all finite strings formed from the letters of the alphabet A, B, ..., Z. Letting this class of strings be denoted by $<$STRING$>$, define $<$STRING$>$ using the BNF. Extend this and define, with the BNF, all strings (call these $<$WORD$>$) that contain the substring CAT.

2.17 Which of the following are logical statements? (Those readers unfamiliar with the notation of (c), (d), (e) should look at Section 3.4, Miscellaneous Special Nota-tion.)

   a. $2x + 3y$
   b. GO TO 1000
   c. $\exists\, x, y(x + y = 5)$
   d. $\forall\, x, y(y > x + 2)$
   e. $\exists\, x(\forall z(2x + 3z))$

2.18 The relation on the natural numbers x, y $\{((x + y) \leq 10) \,\&\, (y \leq 4x)\}$ becomes a true statement for which pairs of natural numbers?

2.19 Show that $A \mid (B \,\&\, C) = (A \mid B) \,\&\, (A \mid C)$ is a theorem by computing the truth tables of the Boolean expressions on either side of the "$=$" sign.

2.20 Compute the truth tables for the following statements and indicate which are tautologies:

$$(A \,\&\, B) \rightarrow (A \mid B)$$
$$(A \mid B) \rightarrow (A \,\&\, B)$$
$$((A \,\&\, B) \,\&\, (\neg A)) \rightarrow B$$
$$(A \rightarrow \neg B) \rightarrow (A \rightarrow B).$$

2.21 The Boolean algebra of statements or propositions has been defined in terms of three basic operations: $\neg, \&, |$. Show that $A \& B$ can be expressed in terms of $\neg, |$ and, therefore, that these two operations $\neg, |$ are sufficient for all Boolean expressions. Show, similarly, that $\neg, \&$ are adequate to replace the symbols $\neg, \&, |$.

2.22 Determine by truth table if

$$(P \to Q) \to ((\neg R \to \neg Q) \to (P \to R))$$

is a tautology.

2.23 Let us write $A \, ! \, B$ to denote the "exclusive OR" of A, B; i.e., $A \, ! \, B$ is true if and only if precisely one of A, B is true. Write the truth table for $A \, ! \, B$ and express it in terms of $\&, |, \neg$.

2.24 We define "A NOR B" written as "$A \uparrow B$" to mean the statement, "neither A nor B is true." Write the truth table for $A \uparrow B$. Express $A \uparrow B$ in terms of $\&, |, \neg$. Also, express $\neg A, A \& B, A \mid B$ using only the symbol "$\uparrow$" as a connector.

2.25 Write a PL/I program (or use any other appropriate programming language) that will test whether

$$(P \to Q) \to ((Q \to R) \to (P \to R))$$

is a tautology.

2.26 Prove, by truth tables, DeMorgan's laws:

$$(A \mid B) = \neg(\neg A \& \neg B)$$
$$(A \& B) = \neg(\neg A \mid \neg B).$$

State the generalizations of these laws for n statements $A_1, A_2, \ldots, A_n$.

2.27 Show that there are an infinite number of Boolean expressions equivalent to any given one.

2.28 Write a segment of PL/I code using the BOOL operation[1] (or use any other appropriate programming language) that will, from two given bit strings

$$X: 0111010101, \, Y: 1101010010,$$

form a string Z of the same length as X, Y where each bit Z_i ($i = 1, 2, \ldots, 10$) is the NAND ("not and") of the corresponding bits in X, Y (i.e., $Z_i = \neg(X_i \& Y_i)$).

---

[1] In PL/I the BOOL operation is used as follows. The statement $Z = \mathrm{BOOL}(X, Y, W)$; where X, Y are bit strings of the same length and W is a four-bit binary string, results in the computation of a bit string Z of the same length as X, Y. Each bit Z_i in the string Z is obtained from the corresponding bits X_i, Y_i in X, Y by applying a binary Boolean operation whose truth table is defined by W; e.g., if we write $Z = \mathrm{BOOL}(X, Y, W)$, where $X = 10111011$, $Y = 11011101$, $W = 1010$, then W defines the following truth table

X_i	Y_i	Z_i
0	0	1
0	1	0
1	0	1
1	1	0

The word W read from top to bottom 1010

The result of this operation will be, then, $Z = 00100010$.

2.29 Given the PL/I statement

$$Z = \text{BOOL}(X, Y, W);$$

where $W = '1011'B$, each bit Z_i in Z is equal to what Boolean function of the corresponding bits X_i, Y_i in X, Y? (Use the disjunctive normal form.)

2.30 Another standard form for Boolean functions is the "conjunctive normal form" in which a Boolean function is expressed as a conjunction of disjunctions; e.g., $F = (A \mid \neg B) \& (\neg A \mid B)$. Show that such a form can be given for any statement F by (i) writing $\neg F$ in disjunctive normal form; (ii) taking the negation of the result of (i) by using DeMorgan's laws (Exercise 2.26).

2.31 Prove the tautologies:

    a. $(P \to Q) \to ((R \to P) \to (R \to Q))$

    b. $P \mid (Q \& R) = (P \mid Q) \& (P \mid R)$

    c. $P \to (\neg P \to Q)$.

Do not use truth tables. Give deductive proofs, based upon the given axioms for the propositional calculus, by applying the rules of substitution and of modus ponens.

REFERENCES

1. Berkling, K., "A Compiling Machine Based on Tree Structures and the Lambda Calculus." *IEEE Transactions on Computers,* **C-20,** 4 (April 1971).

2. Church, A., "The Calculi of Lambda Conversion," in *Annals of Mathematics Studies,* Vol. 6. Princeton, New Jersey: Princeton University Press, 1941.

3. IBM Corporation. *OS PL/I Optimizing and Checkout Compilers: Language Reference Manual.* Order No. GC 33-0009.

4. Kleene, S. C., Foundations of Mathematics." *Encyclopedia Britannica,* 1971.

5. *Lambda Calculus and Computer Science Theory,* Proceedings of the Symposium held in Rome, March 25–27, 1975. IAC–CNR Istituto per la Applicazioni del Calcolo "Mauro Picone," Consiglio Nazionale delle Richercho. Edited by C. Boehm. New York: Springer, 1975 (Lecture Notes in Computer Science, Vol. 37).

6. Lindsey, C. H., and S. G. Van Der Meulen, *Informal Introduction to ALGOL 68.* Amsterdam: North-Holland Publishing Company, 1973.

7. Naur, P., ed. "Revised Report on the Algorithmic Language ALGOL 60." *Comm. Assn. Comp. Mach.,* **6,** 1 (January 1963).

8. Schwartz, J. T., *Set Theory as a Language for Program Specification and Programming.* New York: Courant Institute of Mathematical Sciences, Lecture Notes.

9. Schwartz, J. T., *An Interim Report on the SETL Project, Installment 1: Generalities.* New York: Courant Institute of Mathematical Sciences, Lecture Notes, February 1973.

10. Van Wijngaarden, A., B. Mailloux, J. Peck, and C. Koster, "Report on the Algorithmic Language ALGOL 68." *Numer. Math.,* **14,** 2 (1969).

3
Foundations of Mathematics II (Applications)

In the last chapter we introduced Boole's calculus for reckoning with propositions expressed in symbolic form. We elaborated this as a formal system. Once this is done, a symbolic structure exists which can be used in other domains, or *models* of the theory, where the elements are not propositions but do have the same fundamental properties as propositions. In this chapter we describe Peirce's fundamental idea of looking at switching circuits as a model for Boolean algebra. It is this simple but powerful notion together with the use of bistate devices for the representation of binary digits that underlies the circuit design of electronic computers. In order to illustrate the application of these ideas, we look at some details of the execution of binary arithmetic.

We briefly introduce rudimentary set theory as still another model of Boolean algebra. Mathematical set theory plays a fundamental role in the development of mathematics, and some of the key ideas have greatly influenced the design of some programming languages and the design of new data base systems. Infinite sets have numbers associated with them as do finite sets, and this is explored in the theory of *transfinite* numbers. We sketch only the basic ideas of this theory, but these are sufficient to enable us to conclude that there exist functions that cannot be computed by any program whatsoever.

3.1   REALIZATIONS OF BOOLEAN ALGEBRA

The Boolean algebra we have described as a formal system in the preceding chapter resulted from our attempt, following Boole's work, to set up a mathematical model with which to study the properties of statements. Once this algebra is established in purely formal terms that include rules for forming symbolic expressions for statements and rules for determining whether a given expression represents a true statement, a machinery exists whose application to quite different domains can be considered. The situation may perhaps be likened to the use of Hollerith's punched card machines, which were originally designed with the restricted goal of analyzing the 1890 census data. However, later, these machines were widely used for a great variety of commercial data-processing applications. We look briefly at some other interpretations or *models* of Boolean algebra that are of special importance in computing.

First, as noted by the nineteenth century American philosopher and logician, C. S. Peirce (see Fig. 3.1), a Boolean variable $A, B, C, \ldots$ can designate the transfer property of a part of an electric circuit with one input and one output.

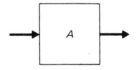

That is, we shall consider only if the "black box" A (implying that we have no idea of what is inside the box) conducts or does not conduct electricity. We ignore questions of the resistance of A and the intensity or other properties of a possible current; we only ask if an electrical current can flow or not, and we assume the conductive property to be an "all or nothing" one.

If the box, or switch, A transmits a current, we shall say that the value of A is 1; if it does not transmit, its value is taken to be 0.

The interior of A could be a switch that is either open or closed, as determined by its UP or DOWN position.

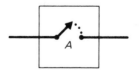

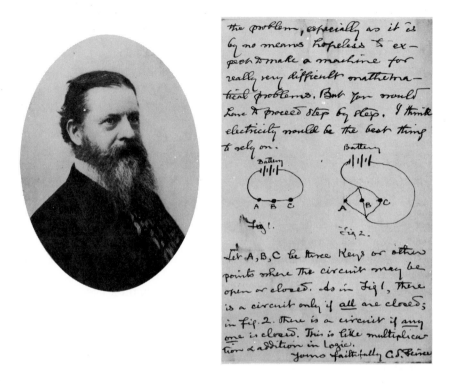

Fig. 3.1 A letter from Charles S. Peirce to his former student Allan Marquand contains the first known description of a switching circuit designed to perform logic.

With this simple notion, we are now able to give interpretations to expressions formed from the Boolean variables $A, B, C, \ldots$ by using the connectives $\neg, |, \&$. If we use switches for $A, B, C, \ldots$, then we have the following physical realizations of the fundamental Boolean expressions.

$\neg A$

The output is connected to the UP or OPEN position of the switch A, i.e., this box conducts when switch A is UP.

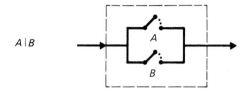

$A \mid B$

The two switches A, B are connected in parallel. The box conducts if either switch is closed or in the DOWN position.

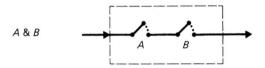

$A \& B$

The two switches are connected in series. The box conducts only if both switches are closed or in the DOWN position.

Any Boolean expression or function, built up from these elemental ones, now becomes a description of a circuit diagram. The Boolean variables appearing in the expression will be represented by different switches set at 0 or 1 according to their UP or DOWN positions. There is one slight encumbrance in this interpretation. When the same variable appears in different parts of the expression, copies of the switch representing that variable, with these all having the same setting at any given time, will have to appear in the circuit realization. (We leave it to the reader to design somewhat more complicated circuits where no replication of the switches caused by repeated appearances of the same Boolean variable in the expression would be necessary.)

For example, Fig. 3.2 gives the realization of the Boolean expression $(A \& (B \mid C)) \mid (\neg B)$.

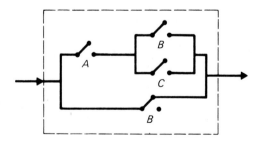

Figure 3.2

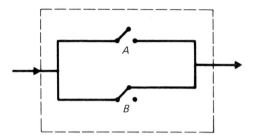

Figure 3.3

We consider any circuit that functions in identical manner for a given setting of the switches A, B, C to be equivalent to this circuit. From our earlier remark about the equivalence of this given Boolean expression and the expression $A \mid \neg B$, an equivalent circuit would be that in Fig. 3.3.

We shall give a simple example of an application of these ideas to a practical circuit design. Consider the problem of designing a circuit so that a light bulb can be controlled from either one of two switches. Letting A, B denote the two switches, we can describe the closed (light ON) or open (light OFF) state of the circuit L for all possible positions of the switches by the table below. An UP position of either switch will be represented by 0, a DOWN position by 1, and we assume that the light is off when both switches are DOWN. If the circuit is closed, we shall say $L = 1$, if open then $L = 0$. The following table lists the state of L for all possible settings of the switches A, B.

A	B	L
0	0	0
0	1	1
1	1	0
1	0	1

We can consider this table to be a truth table and write a Boolean expression involving A, B that defines L as a Boolean function of A, B. We can do this in many ways, but by using the disjunctive normal form we obtain

$$L = (A \& (\neg B)) \mid ((\neg A) \& B).$$

This expression now provides a description of a circuit that will accomplish the desired task. We leave it to the reader to observe that the circuit of

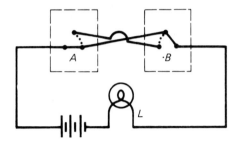

Fig. 3.4 Circuit diagram to control a light from either of two switches.

Fig. 3.4 is a realization of this expression. It is shown with switch *A* DOWN (1) and switch *B* UP (0). The light is on.

3.2 THE HAPPY MARRIAGE OF BINARY ARITHMETIC AND BOOLEAN ALGEBRA

The two values that can be assumed by a Boolean variable, TRUE, FALSE, or 1, 0, can equally well be considered to be the two digits needed for the binary representation of numbers. A sequence of k Boolean variables will then represent a k-place binary number. A Boolean function defined on these k variables can be considered in *numeric* terms as a function defined for arguments that are k-place binary numbers and whose value for each such given number is the number 0 or 1. A sequence of m such Boolean functions could be used to define a function that maps a k-place binary number into an m-place binary number. It is this simple notion that makes possible the practical design and construction, using electronic components, of calculating devices.

A slight variant of the realization of Boolean algebra that we have described in the preceding section will be more useful to us in exploiting these ideas. Instead of letting switches denote Boolean variables, we consider the states of designated electric leads (which could, of course, be determined by the setting of switches) to represent Boolean variables. We suppose that each such lead can assume two distinct states. It may carry an electrical signal or not carry one—or it may be either at an electric potential that exceeds some specified threshold value or, alternatively, it may be at a potential that is below some smaller critical value. In any event, the two possible states are in practice clearly differentiated and sufficiently distinct to avoid any possible confusion in their recognition.

The realization of the primitive Boolean functions can then be easily described. The AND will be an organ with two inputs and one output.

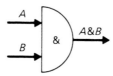

The output lead carries a 1 signal only when both inputs A, B carry such signals. (Such organs are called *gates* since they control the flow of electrical signals through the circuit.) Note that, in arithmetic terms, the output signal is the ordinary product of the two input bits.

The OR gate will be similar.

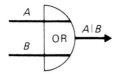

Its output is a 1 if either A or B is 1. This is the same as the ordinary sum of A and B, except when $A = 1$ and $B = 1$.

The negation of A, or $\neg A$, will be realized by a gate with one input.

Its output is in numeric terms equal to $1 - A$. This gate is called an *inverter.* It is often in practice simply denoted by drawing a small circle in the line. Thus in the following circuit the signal for A is inverted *before* entering the box.

We shall in the following assume the availability of gates to perform the AND, OR, NOT functions in composing more complex circuits and shall illustrate the use of these concepts by considering the problem of adding two binary numbers. First, we consider the addition of two one-digit numbers, or bits. The sum will, of course, be a two-bit number if both operands are 1. We content ourselves initially with the design of a circuit that will compute only the right-most bit of the sum in all cases. The following table describes this output bit H for two input bits, A, B.

A	B	H
0	0	0
0	1	1
1	0	1
1	1	0

We note that H is the same as the "exclusive OR" (Exercise 2.23, Chapter 2) of A, B. It is equal to 1 if and only if precisely one of the two variables A, B is 1. A Boolean expression for H can be written, using the disjunctive normal form, as

$$H = (A \mathbin{\&} \neg B) \mid (\neg A \mathbin{\&} B).$$

A circuit to compute H is shown in Fig. 3.5. It is called a "half-adder," for it computes only one of the two possible bits in the sum of A and B; it computes the right bit of the sum. Note that we allow lines to split, as signals "flow" through the box, but we shall not allow here, or in other applications, the ambiguous situation where lines merge.

In the addition of two one-bit numbers the left-most bit of the possible two-bit sum $(0 + 0 = \underline{0}0, 0 + 1 = \underline{0}1, 1 + 1 = \underline{1}0)$ is called the *carry bit*. The

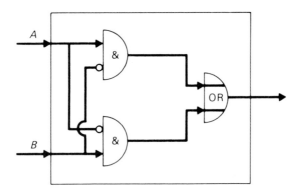

Figure 3.5

addition of two m-place binary numbers, $A_m A_{m-1} \ldots A_1$ and $B_m B_{m-1} \ldots B_1$ (where each A_i, B_i is either 0 or 1), can be accomplished if we add the corresponding bits A_i, B_i in each of the m positions together with, except for the sum of the two right-most bits, the carry bit (0 or 1) resulting from the addition in the preceding position (called the *carry in* bit). The result of this addition will then be a *sum bit* and a *carry out bit* to the next position. That is, we require a box that can receive three inputs and will yield two outputs. In the following diagram, C_I denotes the carry in bit from the preceding position, and C_O is the carry out bit to the succeeding position.

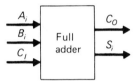

The addition of two m-place numbers, $A_m A_{m-1} \ldots A_1$ and $B_m B_{m-1} \ldots B_1$, using such components, is illustrated in Fig. 3.6. The inputs of each full adder are shown on its right. The result $S_{m+1} S_m S_{m-1} \ldots S_1$ can contain $m + 1$ bits, the left-most, or $m + 1$'st, bit being called the "overflow bit." The right-most full adder has 0, not shown, as its third input.

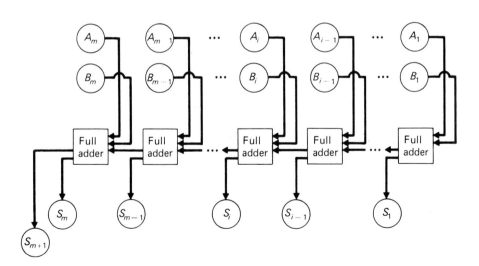

Figure 3.6

The table describing the behavior of the full adder is shown below.

A	B	C_I	C_O	S
0	0	0	0	0
0	0	1	0	1
0	1	0	0	1
0	1	1	1	0
1	0	0	0	1
1	0	1	1	0
1	1	0	1	0
1	1	1	1	1

The right-most bit S of the sum can be obtained by finding the right bit H in the sum of A, B and then determining the right bit in the sum of H and C_I. (S is the right-most bit in $(A + B) + C_I$.) We thus have

$$S = (C_I \,\&\, \neg H) \mid (\neg C_I \,\&\, H).$$

Using the disjunctive normal form we can write the carry out bit C_O as

$$C_O = (\neg A \,\&\, B \,\&\, C_I) \mid (A \,\&\, \neg B \,\&\, C_I) \mid (A \,\&\, B).$$

(N.B.: $A \,\&\, B$ is the equivalent of $(A \,\&\, B \,\&\, C) \mid (A \,\&\, B \,\&\, \neg C)$.)

These equations imply the circuit diagram (Fig. 3.7) for a full adder.
In the actual physical implementation of such a circuit the electrical signals being transmitted appear as pulses rather than as continuous electrical flows. This then makes it necessary to include signal delaying devices, shown as D in the circuit diagram, to assure the synchronization of signals that should arrive as input to some organ at the same time.

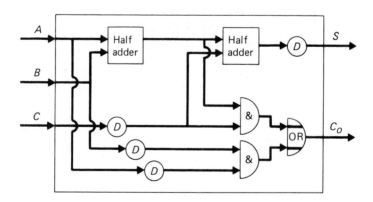

Figure 3.7

Shannon's thesis, published in the *Transactions of the American Institute of Electrical Engineers,* pro provided a theoretical basis for the entire set of operations that would be designed into electronic digital computers.

Figure 3.8

Electric Adder To The Base Two

A circuit is to be designed that will automatically add two numbers, using only relays and switchs. Although any numbering base could be used the circuit is greatly simplified by using the scale of two.

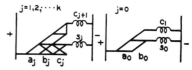

Figure 35. Circuits for electric adder

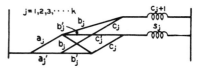

Figure 36. Simplification of figure 35

The Switch to Base Two

In 1937 Claude E. Shannon, for his master's thesis at M.I.T., described a way of using symbolic logic to improve electrical switching circuits. In one example, he showed how to simplity an "Electric Adder to the Base Two."

3.3   THE BOOLEAN ALGEBRA OF SETS

We look at still another realization, or model, of Boolean algebra, its very important application to the study of sets.

A *set* is a collection (finite or infinite) of objects or elements, and these elements may themselves be sets composed of still other elements. If x is an element of the set S, we write $x \in S$, the contradiction of this fact being written $x \notin S$. The ideas of set and of set membership are fundamental to the development of mathematics and are usually taken to be primitive notions, not subject to definition in terms of still more basic concepts.

We begin by considering some "universe" from which the elements that can appear as members of sets can be drawn. We shall not, in this brief introduction, deal with the hierarchy obtained by introducing sets of sets. As

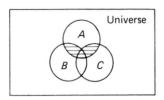

Figure 3.9

has been widely studied in the introduction to the "new math" that has been offered in recent years at the elementary school level, it is convenient to think of the picture in Fig. 3.9.

Consider all the points in some region (possibly infinite) of the plane to be the totality of possible objects, or elements, with which we can form sets. This region will be the universe U in our example, and U itself is one of the possible sets of points we can consider. The subregions A, B, C in Fig. 3.9 are some of the infinite number, in this case, of sets made up of some of the elements of the universe. Associated with each well-defined set S is its *characteristic function* $C_S(x)$, that function defined for every element x of the universe, which is equal to 0 if $x \in S$ and is equal to 1 if $x \notin S$. ($C_S(x)$ is just as often defined to be 1 if $x \in S$ and 0 if $x \notin S$.) The characteristic function, in a sense, "decides" about the possible membership in S of every element in the universe.

Given a set S we can consider that set S' which consists of all elements in U that are *not* in S. S' is called the *complement* of S and we can write

$$S' = \{x \mid (x \in U) \,\&\, (x \notin S)\},$$

where the expression within braces denotes "the set of all objects x such that x is in the universe U and x is not in S."

From the definition of the characteristic function, we have $C_{S'}(x) = 1 - C_S(x)$.

We also provide U with a complementary set. From the given definition, $U' = \{x \mid (x \in U) \,\&\, (x \notin U)\}$, and, therefore, this complement of U has no members. It is called the *null set* and is denoted by Φ. Sometimes, the null, or vacuous, set is written as $\{\ \}$.

The *union* of two sets A, B, which are subsets of U, is written $A \cup B$ and is defined as that set whose members are elements of either A or B.

$$A \cup B = \{x \mid (x \in A) \,\text{OR}\, (x \in B)\}.$$

(We have used OR here to avoid confusion with the vertical bar representing "such that.")

It is easily verified that $C_{A \cup B}(x) = C_A(x) \cdot C_B(x)$.

The *intersection* of two subsets A, B, written $A \cap B$, is defined to be that set whose members are elements of both A and B.

$$A \cap B = \{x \mid (x \in A) \,\&\, (x \in B)\}.$$

Two sets are said to be *disjoint* if they have no elements in common. If A, B are disjoint, we have $A \cap B = \Phi$.

The characteristic function for the intersection of A, B is given by $C_{A \cap B}(x) = C_A(x) + C_B(x) - C_A(x) \cdot C_B(x)$.

We leave it to the reader to recognize those regions of Fig. 3.9 which represent $A \cup B$ and $A \cap B$, where A, B are the indicated circular disks.

The relation of inclusion between two sets A, B, written $A \supseteq B$ or equivalently $B \subseteq A$, denotes that the set B is contained in the set A, or, in other words, that if x is an element of B, then x is an element of A:

$$(A \supseteq B) \leftrightarrow ((x \in B) \rightarrow (x \in A))$$

From the definition, we see that A includes A, or $A \supseteq A$. If we have both $A \supseteq B$ and $A \subseteq B$ it follows that A and B contain the same elements and are therefore equal. We write $A = B$ to denote this fact. If $A \supseteq B$, but $A \neq B$, we may write $A \supset B$. B is then said to be a *proper* subset of A.

We can now enunciate a number of theorems, or true statements, about sets. These follow directly from the given definitions by applying basic logic. Each of these statements asserts the equality of two sets. The left- and right-hand expressions on either side of the "$=$" sign denote sets formed from the sets A, B, C by using the operations of intersection, union, and complementation.

Commutativity of intersection: $A \cap B = B \cap A$

Commutativity of union: $A \cup B = B \cup A$

Associative laws: $A \cap (B \cap C) = (A \cap B) \cap C$
$A \cup (B \cup C) = (A \cup B) \cup C$

Distributive laws: $A \cap (B \cup C) = (A \cap B) \cup (A \cap C)$
$A \cup (B \cap C) = (A \cup B) \cap (A \cup C)$

Properties of complementation: $(A \cap B)' = A' \cup B'$
$(A \cup B)' = A' \cap B'$

Idempotent laws: $A \cap A = A \,; A \cup A = A$

We prove, by way of example, the first distributive law $A \cap (B \cup C) = (A \cap B) \cup (A \cap C)$. From the definitions, this statement is equivalent to each of the following statements in turn.

$x \in (A \cap (B \cup C)) \leftrightarrow x \in ((A \cap B) \cup (A \cap C))$

$(x \in A) \,\&\, (x \in (B \cup C)) \leftrightarrow (x \in (A \cap B)) \mid (x \in (A \cap C))$

$((x \in A) \,\&\, ((x \in B) \mid (x \in C))) \leftrightarrow (((x \in A) \,\&\, (x \in B)) \mid ((x \in A)) \,\&\, (x \in C)))$

The last statement is seen, however, to be an instance of the tautology $(P \,\&\, (Q \mid R)) \leftrightarrow ((P \,\&\, Q) \mid (P \,\&\, R))$ and is, therefore, true.

Each of the above statements asserts the equivalence of two sets that can be represented by certain subregions of Fig. 3.9. For example, the left-hand side $A \cap (B \cup C)$ of the first distributive law is the shaded region of Fig. 3.9. The reader can verify that the same region represents the right-hand side $(A \cap B) \cup (A \cap C)$, making plausible the equivalence of these two expressions. Every statement in the list can be illustrated in the same manner by use of such "Venn diagrams."

The relation $A \subseteq B$ is equivalent to the equation $A \cap B = A$ or, alternatively, equivalent to the equation $A \cup B = B$. Again, these equivalences follow quickly from the basic definitions by the use of elementary logic.

We have, with these definitions, introduced an *algebra* of sets. What, however, is its relation to the Boolean algebra of statements that we discussed earlier? We shall see that it is, in different guise, the same algebraic system that is used in the calculus of statements or propositions. In other words, this basic study of sets provides another model of Boolean algebra.

Every true statement of the algebra of sets that is formed from the symbols for sets $A, B, C, \ldots$, the symbols for set operations $\cup, \cap, '$, and those for set relations $\supseteq, =$ can be translated into a true statement in the propositional calculus (and conversely) by (1) letting the symbols $A, B, C, \ldots$ represent statements rather than sets, (2) replacing the "$\cup$" by "OR" or "$\mid$," replacing the "$\cap$" by "AND" or "$\&$," replacing "A'" by "$\neg A$," for any A, and (3) replacing "$A \supseteq B$" by "B implies A," or by "$B \to A$" (or "$A \leftarrow B$"), replacing "$A = B$" by "$A \leftrightarrow B$" or leaving it as written.

For example, the first property of complementation becomes, on translation, DeMorgan's law: $\neg(A \,\&\, B) = (\neg A \mid \neg B)$.

Some of the theorems of the algebra of sets involve the null set and the universe. These include the following, in which A is an arbitrary set.

$$\Phi \subseteq A \subseteq U$$
$$\Phi \cap A = \Phi \text{ and } U \cap A = A$$
$$\Phi \cup A = A \text{ and } U \cup A = U$$
$$A \cap A' = \Phi \text{ and } A \cup A' = U$$

(Note the proof of $\Phi \subseteq A$. To show this, we must prove that if $x \in \Phi$ then $x \in A$. But, by the definition of Φ, $x \in \Phi$ is a *false* statement for all x in U. From what we have noted earlier, a false hypothesis implies any conclusion. In particular, it implies in this case that $x \in A$ and, therefore, that $\Phi \subseteq A$.)

Each of these statements similarly corresponds to a true statement in the propositional calculus if, (4) we let U correspond to any statement t that is true, or equal to 1, for all possible truth values of the Boolean variables that appear in it (i.e., t is a tautology, such as "$A \mid \neg A$") and, (5) let Φ correspond to a statement f that is identically false or equal to 0 (the negation of a tautology such as "$\neg (A \mid \neg A)$").

In the propositional calculus a simple algorithm was available to us, namely that of calculating truth tables, to verify whether any given wff was a tautology, or theorem, of the system. The analog of this method, implied by the above, is also applicable in the algebra of sets. We note first that the intersection, union, and complement, when applied to the null and universal sets, satisfy laws that correspond to the truth tables for the AND, OR and NOT of the algebra of statements. Here Φ corresponds to 0, and U to 1. Thus we have, corresponding to the truth table for the AND,

$$\Phi \cap \Phi = \Phi, \quad \Phi \cap U = \Phi$$
$$U \cap \Phi = \Phi, \quad U \cap U = U$$

with similar relations for unions (corresponding to the OR) and complements (corresponding to the negation).

To verify, then, if a statement in the algebra of sets is true for all possible assignments of specific sets to the set variables that appear within it, it suffices to check the truth of the statement for all possible assignments of Φ, U to these set variables. Statements expressing set inclusion can always, from what we have seen, be replaced by equations. Thus, to verify that the statement $A \subseteq (A \cup B)$ is true we first write this relation as the equation $A \cap (A \cup B) = A$. We then check that:

$$\Phi \cap (\Phi \cup \Phi) = \Phi, \quad \Phi \cap (\Phi \cup U) = \Phi$$
$$U \cap (U \cup \Phi) = U, \quad U \cap (U \cup U) = U.$$

Each of these statements can be verified by recalling the properties of intersection and union as they apply to the null set and the universal set. $A \subseteq (A \cup B)$ is thus seen to be true when the variables take on all possible assignments of the null set and the universal set.

We leave to the exercises the proof of the assertion that this procedure suffices to verify the validity of any statement of this kind about sets when the variables are replaced by any sets whatsoever.

3.4   MISCELLANEOUS SPECIAL NOTATION AND ITS USES

We summarize in this section and illustrate the use of some notation that is particularly useful in discussing sets. We have already made use in preceding sections of some of this notation without emphasizing it.

Two special symbols are known as *quantifiers*. These are the *existential* quantifier "∃," which is an abbreviation for "there exists," and the *universal* quantifier "∀," which is an abbreviation for "for all."

Thus "∃$x(x + 3 = 5)$" represents the statement: "there exists an x such that $x + 3 = 5$," which happens to be a true statement. Some implied universe is always understood as the domain in which lies the object whose existence is asserted. In the given example, this universe could be taken to be the natural numbers. Relative to our discussion in Chapter 1, "there exists" does not necessarily mean "we can find."

The statement ∃$x(x^2 - 4x + 5 = 0)$ is false if the allowed universe is the set of real numbers, but it is true if it is the set of complex numbers.

∀$x[(x + 1)(x - 1) = x^2 - 1]$ is the true statement that "for all x, $(x + 1)(x - 1) = x^2 - 1$." The statement ∀$x[(x^2 - 3x + 5) > x]$ is a true statement if the universe is understood to be the totality of *real* numbers.

We can form rather complex statements by using both symbols in the same expression. For example, the assertion

$$\forall n \neg \exists\, x, y, z(x^{n+2} + y^{n+2} = z^{n+2}),$$

where the universe is the set of natural numbers, is the statement of "Fermat's last theorem" that there are no nontrivial integral solutions to the equation $x^m + y^m = z^m$ for any exponent m greater than two. No one knows at this writing if this statement is true or false.

Using our earlier terminology, a *predicate* becomes a statement when it is prefixed with quantifiers relating to all the variables that appear in the predicate. For example, the predicate, or relation defined on the natural numbers, $x \geq y + 2$ becomes the false statement ∃y ∀$x(x \geq y + 2)$ when prefixed by the indicated quantifiers.

A set may be defined explicitly by listing its members, such as in:

$$S = \{1, 2, 3, 4, 5, 6, 7\} \text{ or } T = \{\text{ALPHA, BETA, GAMMA}\}.$$

We may also describe a set by specifying the conditions required for membership in the set, as in writing $V = \{x \mid x > 10\}$ to denote the set of integers x (if the universe is understood to be the natural numbers) such that x is greater than 10.

The graph of the function $y = x^2 + 3$ can be written

$$W = \{(x, y) \mid y = x^2 + 3\}.$$

The set of prime numbers P can be written:

$$P = \{n \mid \neg \exists\, m, p[(m > 1) \,\&\, (p > 1) \,\&\, (n = mp)]\}$$

or equivalently:

$$P = \{n \mid \forall m, p[(n = mp) \rightarrow ((m = 1) \mid (p = 1))]\}$$

with, of course, innumerable other ways of expressing the same set.

The set K of all words in the English language beginning with Q, if the universe is understood to be all English words and WORD denotes an arbitrary English word, is

$$K = \{\text{WORD} \mid \text{HEAD(WORD)} = Q\}.$$

Given a set A, we can form many other sets from its members, by taking them in all possible combinations. The *power set P* of a set A is defined to be the set of all sets S which are subsets of A. We can write this definition as $P = \{S \mid S \subseteq A\}$. Thus, the power set of the set $A = \{1, 2, 3\}$ is $P = \{\Phi, \{1\}, \{2\}, \{3\}, \{1, 2\}, \{1, 3\}, \{2, 3\}, \{1, 2, 3\}\}$. Note that the null set, being included in every other set, is always a member of a power set.

We have already seen the possibility of defining some sets by describing set membership in recursive terms as, for example, the use of the BNF in writing

$$<T> :: = 1 \mid 0 \mid <T> <T>$$
$$<S> :: = 1 \mid 0 \mid 1 <T>$$

to indicate the set S of all binary number representations, omitting superfluous leading zeros.

3.5 THE PRODUCT OF SETS

If M, N are two given sets their product is defined to be the set $L = M \times N$ whose elements are all possible ordered pairs of elements of M and N. That is,

$$L = \{(x, y) \mid (x \in M) \& (y \in N)\}.$$

This is often called the cartesian product of the two sets after Descartes, the seventeenth century French mathematician and philosopher, whose writings included the basic notions of analytic geometry. No diagrams appeared in his work, but he did advance the key idea of identifying the points in the plane by pairs of real numbers. Let X, Y denote respectively the horizontal and vertical axes of a coordinate plane, each calibrated, using current elementary school terminology, as a "number line." The plane is then the product of X and Y, the totality of points in the plane being identified with all possible pairs $\{(x, y)\}$ of real numbers.

Such set multiplication is not commutative, but it is associative. Three-dimensional space is the product $X \times Y \times Z$ where Z is a third axis perpendicular to X, Y.

3.6 THE ROLE OF SET THEORY IN MATHEMATICS
AND IN COMPUTING

One of the great achievements, or perhaps insights, provided by modern mathematics is the realization that all of mathematics can be developed in systematic fashion by starting with literally nothing—namely with the null set Φ—and by studying the properties of new objects, introduced in hierarchical fashion: sets of earlier defined sets, sets of "sets of sets," and so forth. For example, at the beginning of this development the number 1 can be identified with the set $S\ (=\{\Phi\})$, whose sole member is the null set (S, which has a member, is not the same as the null set, which has no members); 2 can be then identified by the set which has both S and Φ as its members $\{\Phi,\{\Phi\}\}$, and so forth. After defining the natural numbers, all mathematical constructs can eventually be described in these terms.

We saw at least one example of the set theoretical approach when we identified a function by its graph, which is a *set* of pairs of elements, one from its domain and the other being the corresponding value in the range of the function.

We go no further in following up on and justifying this provocative assertion concerning the development of mathematics from set theory. For a satisfactory exposition of these ideas would take us far afield of the mathematics directly relevant to computing. In any event, it is reasonable to expect that the notions of set theory, with its accompanying terminology and defined operations, playing such a powerful role in explaining the development of mathematics, should be very useful in computing as well.

In considering the sets that are of consequence in computing we can take a much more restricted approach than appears to be necessary in mathematics, for the sets we may manipulate in computing processes do not include *arbitrary* infinite sets. The elements of the sets we deal with in computing are the natural numbers (strings of bits, or, more generally, strings of symbols), and n-tuples (ordered sets or arrays) of natural numbers or of strings of symbols. But, with our interests restricted to the "constructive," we are not concerned with such things as the arbitrary real numbers or arbitrary point sets of mathematical analysis.

Some programming languages have built-in facilities to perform operations on sets. One of the most widely used interactive languages, APL, has a number of operations available to manipulate n-tuples of numbers. More generally, the programming language whose design most strongly reflects the influence of set theory is SETL, developed at New York University's Courant Institute. This language has the built-in capability to handle as operands sets made up of integers, Boolean elements, bit strings, character strings, labels, and blanks. Set operations such as unions, intersections, forming the power set, checking the inclusion or the equality of two sets, finding the number of elements in a set, defining sets by membership properties, and so forth, are all available to the programmer [6, 8, 9]. For an example of SETL programming showing the use of several set operations, see Fig. 3.10.

A set of articles, authors and keywords are to be referenced by AND, OR specifications on keywords or authors. Input records are stored as relations which are sets of tuples containing keywords, articles, and authors. We first show the setting up of these sets.

```
KEYSET = {<keyword,<article,authors>>}
AUTHORSET = {<author,<article,authors>>}
        define setup (KEYSET,AUTHORSET);
          read (ART,AUTHS,KEYS);.
            (while ART ¬ = Ω)
            (∀x∈ KEYS)
            KEYSET = KEYSET ∪ <x,<ART,AUTHS>>;
            end ∀x;
            (∀x∈ AUTHS)
            AUTHORSET = AUTHORSET ∪ <x,<ART,AUTHS>>;
            end ∀x;
            read (ART, AUTHS,KEYS);
          end while ART;
          return;
        end setup;
```

Now that this input data has been stored as sets we can read in requests to look up articles based on keywords and authors.

Assuming that a request lists a set of keys (SETKYS) that can be either authors or keywords, we can ask for articles (1) written jointly by the authors mentioned in the request (ANDA – ∩ authors), (2) written collectively by the authors mentioned in the request (ORA – ∪ authors), (3) containing all of the keywords mentioned in the request (ANDK – ∩ keywords), (4) containing any of the keywords mentioned in the request (ORK – ∪ keywords).

```
definef lookup (AUTHORSET,KEYSET,REQ,SETKYS);
  collect = φ;
  switch = {<'ANDA',L1>,<'ORA',L2>,<'ANDK',L3>,<'ORK',L4>};
go to switch (REQ);

L1: x ∋ SETKYS;
    collect = AUTHORSET[x]; SETKYS = SETKYS−{x};
    (∀x ∈ SETKYS)
    collect = collect ∩ AUTHORSET[x];
    end ∀x;
    return collect;

L2: (∀x ∈ SETKYS)
    collect = collect ∪ AUTHORSET[x];
    end ∀x;
    return collect;

L3: x ∋ SETKYS
    collect = KEYSET[x];
    SETKYS = SETKYS−{x};
    (∀x∈ SETKYS)
    collect = collect ∩ KEYSET[x];
    end ∀x;
    return collect;

L4: (∀x ∈ SETKYS)
    collect = collect ∪ KEYSET[x];
    end ∀x;
    return collect;
end lookup;
```

Fig. 3.10 An example of SETL programming (courtesy of S. Stolfo).

Most applications programmers, especially those in commercial data-processing organizations, quickly learn that the processing of files and data bases is an extremely important area of modern computer usage. In these applications we deal with collections of related information organized in a variety of ways. There is an ongoing enormous effort devoted to the study of the efficient organization of such information and to efficient methods for retrieving and updating information. In these applications we deal with sets of items, and much of what goes on in the manipulation of such collections of data can be couched in terms of sets. We often distinguish between a *file,* which is a collection of related information, and a *data set,* which is the physical embodiment of a file (e.g., a region of disk memory, a magnetic tape, a deck of cards, etc.).

There are many places where set-related notions are relevant and, by way of illustration, we mention several in passing.

If a file consists of a sequence of pairs of items, $F = \{(x_1, y_1),$ $(x_2, y_2), \ldots, (x_n y_n)\}$ with some ordering $x_1 \leq x_2 \leq \ldots \leq x_n$, we often refer to the *inverted* file as the collection $\{(y_i', x_i')\}$ written with an ordering $y_1' \leq y_2' \leq \ldots \leq y_n'$.

In general there need not be a unique x_i for a given y_i (the inverse of the original graph is a relation, not necessarily a function). The inverted file is usually written with items $(y_i, x_i^{(1)}, x_i^{(2)}, \ldots, x_i^{(p)})$, where each $x_i^{(j)}$ appears in a pair $(x_i^{(j)}, y_i)$ of the given file, or graph.

S	S#	SNAME	STATUS	CITY
	S1	Smith	20	London
	S2	Jones	10	Paris
	S3	Blake	30	Paris
	S4	Clark	20	London
	S5	Adams	30	Athens

P	P#	PNAME	COLOR	WEIGHT
	P1	Nut	Red	12
	P2	Bolt	Green	17
	P3	Screw	Blue	17
	P4	Screw	Red	14
	P5	Cam	Blue	12
	P6	Cog	Red	19

SP	S#	P#	QTY
	S1	P1	3
	S1	P2	2
	S1	P3	4
	S1	P4	2
	S1	P5	1
	S1	P6	1
	S2	P1	3
	S2	P2	4
	S3	P3	4
	S3	P5	2
	S4	P2	2
	S4	P4	3
	S4	P5	4
	S5	P5	5

Fig. 3.11 A suppliers-and-parts data model in relational form, from [3].

A concordance, or alphabetical index of the principal words in a book or in the works of an author, can be viewed as a subset of an inverted file.

A promising approach to data base organization that is being actively pursued is that of *relational data bases* [3]. A set of tabulated data can be viewed as the graph of a relation on a number of variables. Different relationships of importance in the application can be represented by different relations or tables (see Fig. 3.11). In this approach to the design of data base systems several combining operations on relations are defined. These have great utility, and set notation is used in specifying the retrieval of wanted information. For example, with reference to Fig. 3.11 the notation

$$\{SP \cdot P\# \mid SP \cdot S\# = 'S2'\}$$

is a shorthand representation of the request "retrieve the set of P# values from the SP relation which are such that the corresponding S# value is S2" [3].

3.7 THE THEORY OF TRANSFINITE NUMBERS

In this section we consider some aspects of the mathematical study of the infinite and look briefly at a theory that extends the notion of "number" to infinite sets. It may seem strange to include such exotic notions in a discussion of the mathematics that underlies programming, but we shall see that some of the consequences of these ideas anticipate some fundamental results of the theory of computability, and they provide insight to such fundamental questions as: do programs exist to compute all functions?

In 1895 the German-Danish mathematician Georg Cantor startled the mathematical world with a treatment of the infinite that to many seemed bizarre and based more on metaphysical notions than on rigorous mathematical arguments. There is even today no universal agreement that all of Cantor's fundamental arguments are sound, the principal objections being closely related to the caution expressed in the constructivist's approach to mathematics, as mentioned in the appendix to Chapter 1.

What Cantor did in essence was to extend the concept of number so that it becomes meaningful to associate numbers with infinite collections, as well as with finite collections, and, in fact, to introduce an infinite hierarchy of such infinite numbers.

Let us say that two, for the moment finite, classes or collections of things are *similar* if there exists a pairing, in one-to-one fashion, of the elements of one collection with the elements of the other. For example, the dwarfs in the story of Snow White can be so matched with the names of the days of the week; these two collections then comprise two similar classes. For finite collections an effective matching process exists to compare two collections and determine if they have the same number of objects or if one is greater than the other. We then say that two sets have the same *cardinal* number if they are similar (the cardinal number is different from the *ordinal* number, which connotes a position within some ordering, e.g., five vs. fifth). A given number can be considered to be that property of similarity that is shared by some particular set and all other sets that are similar to it. Similarity, being reflexive, symmetric, and transitive, is an equivalence relationship. Thus "five" is the cardinal number for all sets that are similar to the fingers on the normal human hand. Bertrand Russell succinctly gave this definition of number as "the class of all similar classes."

Now there is nothing in this definition of number to prevent us from applying it equally well to collections that are not finite. We then associate the idea of "number" with infinite sets as well as with finite ones.

Consider the set of all the natural numbers $N = \{1, 2, 3, \ldots\}$. Cantor calls the number of the elements in this set (and in every set similar to it) "aleph-null," using the first letter aleph ($\aleph$) of the Hebrew alphabet and writes it as $\aleph_0$ (in anticipation of a sequence of such transfinite numbers requiring higher subscripts for identification). Any set that is similar to the set of natural numbers, and thus has cardinal number $\aleph_0$, may also be called "enumerable," or "denumerable," or "countable." The elements of any such set can be matched with the natural numbers: there is a "first" element, a "second" element, a "third," and so forth. All the elements of an enumerable set can be ticked off or counted so that a positive integer is eventually attached to every element of the set.

This extension of our definition of number to infinite sets leads now to some surprising results. For example, we easily show that the even positive numbers alone comprise a set that is enumerable, or that has the same cardinal number, $\aleph_0$, as does the set of *all* of the natural numbers. The similarity of these two sets is indicated by the following pairing of elements, which associates to every even positive number a natural number, and conversely.

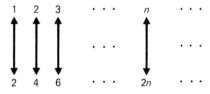

In the sense then of there existing a one-to-one correspondence between these two sets, we see that there are "as many" even numbers as there are natural numbers, or that the two sets have the same cardinal number. Similarly, we can show that the set of all the integers—positive, negative, and zero—is also enumerable. Again, to show this we must indicate how to "peel off" the numbers of this set, identify a first member, a second, a third, and so forth, so that any given member of the set is eventually counted. This is readily done. We can, for example, let every integer correspond to a natural number in accordance with the following scheme. Let 0 correspond to 1, let every positive integer m correspond to $2m$. Let every negative integer $-n$ correspond to $2n + 1$.

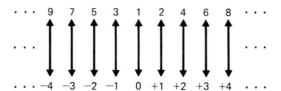

Note that this correspondence scheme is the same as if we represent every positive or negative integer in binary notation using the last bit to represent the sign, 0 if positive, 1 if negative. Zero is represented as 01, the encoding of -0; the string 00 corresponds to no integer.

Extending the number system to include the rational numbers still yields a collection that is denumerable. This can be seen from the diagram below, which shows a procedure for counting the positive rational numbers one by one, thus establishing a one-to-one correspondence between them and the natural numbers.

We write all positive rational numbers of the form p/q in reduced terms, so that p, q have no common divisors. Let the ith row of the tableau in Fig. 3.12 contain all rational numbers with numerator i.

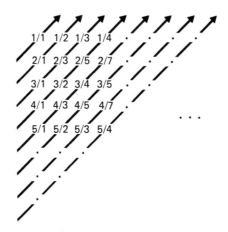

Figure 3.12

By sweeping through this two-dimensional infinite array in the directions indicated by the arrows and moving from left to right, we see that a correspondence can be established with the natural numbers, as implied by the diagram in Fig. 3.13.

We leave it to the reader to extend the argument here given and show denumerability in the two cases (1) where 0 is included with the positive rationals, and (2) where the negative rational numbers are also included.

This argument can be applied more generally to show that any countable set of countable sets is countable. For the elements of such a collection can be written as a square array, as in the above, and we can use the same method for enumerating them as has been applied in this instance.

One may suspect from what we have seen so far that all infinite aggregates are denumerable, and the followers of some mathematical philosophies would hold that this is the only sensible view to take. Consider, however, the following argument, which leads to the conclusion that the class of all nonnegative real numbers that are less than or equal to one is *not* countably infinite.

Write all numbers x that lie between zero and one ($0 \leq x \leq 1$) as infinite decimals. In those ambiguous situations where a number has two such representations, such as $2/5 = 0.4000\ldots = 0.3999\ldots$, we shall agree to use that representation which terminates in an infinite sequence of 9's. Assume now that this set of numbers is denumerably infinite and, therefore, that a list can be written which includes all of them. Suppose, for example, that our assumed enumeration scheme leads to:

We shall now construct a number α which is in the interval from 0 to 1 but which *cannot possibly be* in our assumed list. This construction contradicts the hypothesis that the assumed list includes *all* such numbers, and yet it is a consequence of this hypothesis. By the argument of reductio ad absurdum, the hypothesis must then be false, for it implies its own contradiction.

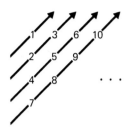

Figure 3.13

We shall write the infinite decimal representation of this new number α by choosing as its first digit one that is different from the first digit of the first number in the above listing, as its second digit one that is different from the second digit of the second number, and so forth. In its k th position we choose a digit different from the kth digit of the kth number in the list. Thus, the number α differs in every position from, in the case of our sample list, the number $0.07646\ldots$, which is read off the diagonal of the indicated array. Let us further agree not to use a zero in each position of the number being constructed. This still leaves us with at least eight possible choices, so this is not a severe restriction. We thereby avoid constructing a number that terminates in an infinite string of zeros and which might then merely be another representation of a number that appears somewhere in the list.

There thus exists a number α which certainly lies between 0 and 1 and yet cannot appear in our assumed list of all such numbers, since it *differs in at least one position* from every number in that list.

We thus conclude that the set of all numbers in the continuum from 0 to 1 is *not* denumerable. The infinitude of points on the real axis is a collection of higher cardinality (or higher "power" in Cantor's terminology) than the natural numbers. The transfinite number for this set is different from $\aleph_0$ and is in fact one of an infinite sequence of such transfinite numbers that emanate from Cantor's theory. (Constructivists, mentioned in the appendix to Chapter 1, would not accept the foregoing argument as a demonstration of the existence of nondenumerable sets of numbers. The procedure for obtaining α would be meaningful within this mathematical philosophy only if it were *effective* in obtaining the successive digits of the decimal representation of α. The conclusion following from the argument advanced here would be not that such a number as α exists, but rather that there is no effective way of generating the infinite number of decimal representations of all numbers between 0 and 1.)

Not only is the set of real numbers of higher cardinal number than the set of natural numbers, but the real numbers comprise in some sense a vastly bigger set. For our argument can be slightly modified to show that *any* interval, no matter how small in length, of the real numbers has a higher cardinal number than the natural numbers.

3.8 IMPLICATIONS OF THE THEORY OF TRANSFINITE NUMBERS TO COMPUTING

The denumerability of the natural numbers implies immediately the denumerability of all finite strings made up of symbols from some finite alphabet. Suppose, for example, that we employ a 256-character alphabet, of which the blank is one character. Then, any finite string of symbols, or word, formed from this alphabet can be considered to be a base 256 representation of one of the natural numbers. This gives an immediate one-to-one correspondence between all such strings and the natural numbers, and, therefore, these strings form a denumerable class. This implies that the class of all possible books written in the English language, the class of all possible programs that can be written in any given programming language, the class of all descriptions of numbers, as in the discussion in Chapter 1 of Berry's paradox, the class of all possible human thoughts (*if* we assume that any thought can be expressed as a string of English words—which assumption is, perhaps, doubtful) are all denumerable classes. To be practical, there is, of course, some upper bound imposed by the real world on the size of each of these classes, and they are, in fact, finite rather than infinite. But, even if we ignore the restraints of a finite world and finite man, these classes are no more than denumerably infinite.

On the other hand, the class of all possible total functions defined with domain equal to the natural numbers and range contained within the natural numbers is nondenumerably infinite. There are several ways of proving this, but one rather immediate proof can be given by following the "diagonalization" argument that we used to show the nondenumerability of the real numbers in the interval from 0 to 1.

Assume that all such functions comprise a denumerable class. We then can list them in tabular form, identifying each function by the string of its values at arguments $1, 2, 3, \ldots$. Suppose, for example, this gives us the form in Fig. 3.14.

Now, paralleling what was done in the case of the real numbers, we form a new function on the natural numbers by writing a string that differs in every position from the corresponding element of the above array such as

$$f: \quad 2, \quad 7, \quad 38, \quad 100, \quad \cdot \quad \cdot \quad \cdot$$

f is certainly not the same as any of the f_i $(i = 1, 2, 3, \ldots)$, since it must differ at one or more arguments from every f_i. Therefore, no such list of all total functions exists; they comprise a nondenumerable class.

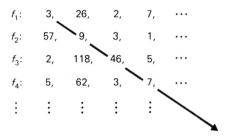

f_1:	3,	26,	2,	7,	⋯
f_2:	57,	9,	3,	1,	⋯
f_3:	2,	118,	46,	5,	⋯
f_4:	5,	62,	3,	7,	⋯

Figure 3.14

On the other hand, the set of possible programs that can be written to compute functions is, from our earlier remarks, a denumerable class. Therefore, there exist functions on the natural numbers that cannot be computed by any program.

This corresponds to a property of the real numbers to which we have alluded. There are only a denumerably infinite number of ways of describing individual real numbers, using any finite vocabulary. For example, "the ratio of the circumference of a circle to its diameter," "the square root of the biggest, in absolute value, of the roots of the equation

$$(x * * 3) - 17 * (x * * 2) + 35 * x - 15{,}735 = 0,"$$

"the limit as $n \to \infty$ of $(1 + 1/n) * * n$," are examples of such descriptions. We have seen, however, that there are (accepting the argument given) a non-denumerably infinite number of such real numbers. Therefore, the great majority, in some special sense, of these real numbers can individually never be identified, named, or described in any manner whatsoever.

This property of the real numbers is reminiscent of the claim by the philosopher Ludwig Wittgenstein that there are facts that cannot be enunciated or expressed. They can only be "known" in a sense by their effects. As he writes in his *Tractatus Logico-Philosophicus,* "There are indeed things that cannot be put into words. They make themselves manifest," and again, "What we cannot speak about, we must pass over in silence." However, in mathematics, we certainly do not remain silent about the totality of real numbers.

EXERCISES

3.1 Draw a circuit, employing switches to represent Boolean variables, that realizes the Boolean expression $X \mid (Y \& Z)$. Write the truth table for this expression.

3.2 Given the following switching circuit where switches (not shown in detail) represent the indicated Boolean variables:

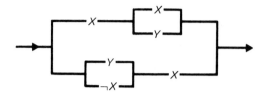

    a. give a Boolean expression that represents the circuit.

    b. write a truth table for the result of (a) and give the disjunctive normal form for the corresponding Boolean expression.

3.3 Let A, B, C be three bits. Write a table that defines for each of the 8 possible combinations of A, B, C that bit D which when added (arithmetically) to the algebraic sum of A, B, C gives an *even* sum (D is called an "even parity bit"). Write a Boolean expression for D in terms of A, B, C using the disjunctive normal form. Draw a logical circuit (using AND and OR gates and inverters) with inputs A, B, C that will give D as output.

3.4 Let A, B, C be three bits. Write the table that shows for each combination of A, B, C the corresponding value of the "majority bit" m where m is 0 or 1, according to which value occurs more frequently among A, B, C. Draw a logical circuit with inputs A, B, C that will give m as output.

3.5 Design a "black box" with three inputs and a single output, employing logical gates and inverters, that gives an output signal when at least one and at most two inputs carry signals (or are equal to 1).

3.6 If the universe is taken to be the first 1,000 positive integers and $\{P(i) \mid i = 1, 2, \ldots, M\}$ is an array of M positive integers ($\leq 1,000$) stored in memory, write a PL/I subroutine (or use any other suitable programming language) for finding the set P', the complement of the set P (denote P' by Q in the program).

3.7 Let $\{P(i) \mid i = 1, 2, \ldots, M\}$ and $\{Q(i) \mid i = 1, 2, \ldots, N\}$ be two arrays of integers stored in memory with $M, N \leq 1,000$. Write a PL/1 subroutine (or use any other suitable programming language) for finding the sets R, defined as $P \cup Q$, and S, defined as $P \cap Q$.

3.8 If $N(A)$ denotes the number of elements in the set A, we can write: $N(A \cup B) = N(A) + N(B) - N(A \cap B)$. Justify this equation. Applying this identity twice we calculate:

$$
\begin{aligned}
N(A \cup B \cup C) &= N(A) + N(B \cup C) - N((A \cap B) \cup (A \cap C)) \\
&= N(A) + N(B) + N(C) - N(B \cap C) - N(A \cap B) \\
&\quad - N(A \cap C) + N(A \cap B \cap C).
\end{aligned}
$$

In a survey it is reported that of 1,000 programmers, 650 habitually flowchart their programs, 788 are skilled COBOL programmers, 675 are men, 278 of the women are skilled COBOL programmers, 440 programmers both habitually flowchart and are skilled in COBOL, 210 women habitually flowchart, and 166 women are both skilled in COBOL and habitually flowchart. Would you accept these data as being accurately reported?

3.9 The set theory formula $(A \cup B)' = A' \cap B'$ is the analog of what statement of the propositional calculus? Prove, by truth tables, this theorem of Boolean logic to which the set formula corresponds. Generalize this formula to give the complement of the union of n sets.

3.10 Let A be the range of the function $f(x) = x^2 + 3$, B the domain of the function $g(x) = x - 25$ where the universe is the set of nonnegative integers $\{0, 1, 2, ...\}$. List the elements of the set $A \cap B'$.

3.11 Illustrate the following set equality by using Venn diagrams and shading the region corresponding to each side of the equation:

$$A \cup (B' \cap C) = (A \cup B') \cap (A \cup C).$$

3.12 Let $A - B$ be the set of those elements that are in set A but not in set B. Express $A - B$ in terms of the set operations $\cup$, $\cap$, $'$ and show by Venn diagrams that

$$(A - B) \cup C = (C \cup A) \cap (C \cup B').$$

3.13 Given any set S formed from the sets A, B, C by the set operations $\cup$, $\cap$, $'$, explain the analog of the disjunctive normal form for S in terms of the Venn diagram. Take as an example

$$S = (A \cup B)' \cap C.$$

3.14 With the same given conditions as in exercise 3.13, express S in the *conjunctive normal form*, i.e., as the intersection of sets which are individually unions of selected sets and of the complements of selected sets. (Hint: Express S' using the disjunctive normal form, then take the complement to obtain an expression for S, using the result of Exercise 3.9.) Cf. Exercise 2.30.

3.15 Given any set theory equation of the form $S_1 = S_2$, where S_1, S_2 are set expressions formed from A, B, C by using $\cup, \cap, '$, show that this is a true equation for arbitrary A, B, C if it is true for any assignment of Φ, U to A, B, C. (Hint: Assuming the hypothesis, show that if any point x is in S_1, it must be in S_2 and conversely, by using the disjunctive normal forms of S_1, S_2, as in Exercise 3.13.)

3.16 Write down the set P, defined as the set of all subsets (the power set) of $\{1, 2, 3\}$. If the set P is taken as the universe, what is the complement of the set B: $\{\{1, 2\}, \{2, 3\}\}$?

3.17 If the universe is the set of natural numbers and $S = \{x \mid x^2 > 5x\}$, $T = \{y \mid \neg(y^2 - 2y = 0)\}$ what is $T' \cup S$?

3.18 If the universe is the set of natural numbers, what is the set Q defined by
   a. $Q = \{n \mid \neg \exists m(2m = n)\}$?
   b. $Q = \{m \mid \forall z[(z \neq 5) \rightarrow ((\exists k(m = z \cdot k)) \rightarrow (z = 1))]\}$?

3.19 Prove that the power set of a given set S has greater cardinal number than S. (Hint: Use the method of reductio ad absurdum. Assume that the elements of the set of all subsets *can* be put into one-to-one correspondence with the elements of S. Then construct a subset of S to which there cannot possibly correspond any element of S.).

3.20 Write a program in any suitable language that will generate *all* pairs of natural numbers (make the substantial and unrealistic simplifying assumption of ignoring the limited word size of any real computer). This result also implies the denumerability of the set of all pairs of natural numbers.

3.21 Show that the points of any two line segments of different length can be put into one-to-one correspondence (i.e., the segments have the same cardinality). Show, also, that any line segment has as many points as an infinite line.

3.22 Following the discussion of the denumerability of the rational numbers we can, in accordance with the following suggested scheme, establish an effective one-to-one correspondence between all *pairs* of nonnegative integers and *single* nonnegative integers.

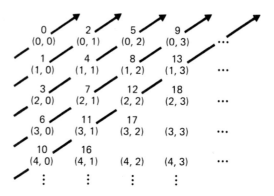

Figure 3.15

Let the pair (x, y) correspond in this fashion to the number z. Write algebraic expressions that give z as a function of x, y and conversely that give x, y as functions of z.

APPENDIX
THE RUDIMENTS OF GRAPH THEORY

Graph theory is a part of combinatorial mathematics, that branch of mathematics that concerns the study of finite sets and problems of enumeration, arrangement, or design. The theory is not, strictly speaking, usually considered to be a part of the foundations of mathematics. Yet a case can be made for so classifying it. In any event, the basic ideas of graph theory are of great importance in the computer sciences, especially in formal linguistics and automata theory. One quickly infers this from the number of illustrations, in works in these areas, that consist of sets of nodes connected in various ways. For these reasons, we include this material as an appendix.

As with all of the mathematics we cite, there is a very extensive literature devoted to this subject. However, it is the basic ideas that are important to the computer scientist, the representation as graphs of a number of structures that appear in computing. We briefly describe the fundamental definitions and vocabulary and give some examples of the representation of graphs and of algorithms related to them.

3.9   SOME FUNDAMENTAL NOTIONS OF GRAPH THEORY

We have repeatedly emphasized that all items represented in a digital computer are strings of binary digits and, therefore, are representations of the natural numbers. This is not, however, very restrictive in applications, and many different kinds of "data structures" are mapped into the natural numbers and thus represented in the computer. One frequently occurring structure in computer science is the class of *graphs*. We are here using this somewhat overworked term with still another meaning.

Graph theory concerns the study of structures that can be drawn in the plane consisting of points, or nodes, and of path segments, not necessarily straight lines, that connect some of these nodes (there may be more than one path segment joining two nodes, and we may have a path segment extending from a node back to itself). We shall consider only finite graphs, i.e., graphs with a finite number of nodes and a finite number of path segments.

Examples.

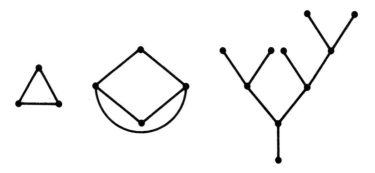

We shall in this section introduce some of the fundamental definitions and notation of graph theory. We shall not go into the extensive body of results that are included in numerous treatises on this subject. For example, see [1, 2, 4, 5, 7].

If all the path segments are oriented, or directed (like one-way streets), the graph is called a directed graph or, more briefly, a *digraph.*

Examples.

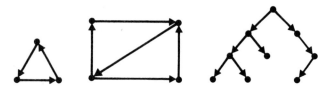

In a digraph each node has an "indegree" (number of incoming path segments) and an "outdegree" (number of outgoing path segments). In computing, most applications of graphs involve digraphs.

Path segments may have numeric "weights" associated with them.

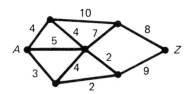

Problem.   Find the "shortest" (least sum of weights) path from A to Z.

The weight associated with a path segment from a node P to a node Q may indicate the distance from a physical point P to a point Q, but in general it can have a meaning and a measure that are unrelated to this distance. If, for example, P and Q denote work stations in some assembly line procedure, the associated weight might indicate the time, or the cost, for a component being manufactured to reach station Q after arriving at P.

Graphs describe the connectivity of the nodes. They do not have properties stemming from the measures of the segments and angles that might appear in a particular drawing of them. Thus, the four graphs in Fig. 3.16 are equivalent. Each indicates that the four given nodes are connected to each other in the same manner. (Such graphs are said to be *isomorphic.*

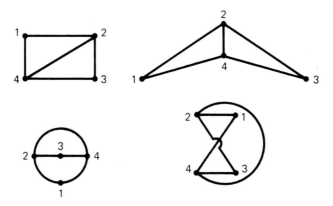

Figure 3.16

Two graphs G, G' are isomorphic if there is a one-to-one onto mapping of the nodes of G to the nodes of G' such that there is a path segment connecting nodes u, v in G if and only if there is a path segment connecting the images u', v' of these nodes in G'. If G, G' are digraphs, the corresponding path segments in G' must be oriented in the same way as those in G.)

A graph is *connected* if every two distinct nodes are joined by a chain of path segments, or simply by a *path;* otherwise, it is said to be disconnected.

The following graph is *not* connected. That is, it includes 5 nodes with connectivity as shown. There is, for example, no path from node 1 to node 4.

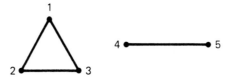

A digraph is *strongly connected* if every node can be reached from every other node by a directed path, i.e., a path whose every segment is traced according to its given orientation.

A directed *tree* (Fig. 3.17) is a connected digraph in which every node, except one, has indegree 1. The exceptional or, as it is often called, the "distinguished" node is called the *root* and has indegree 0. Nodes with zero outdegree are called terminal nodes or *leaves.* In an unweighted tree the

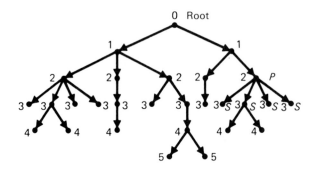

Figure 3.17

length of the (unique) path from the root to any node is taken to be the number of segments in the path and is called the *level* of the node. Usually trees are drawn with the root at the top. An undirected tree is simply a directed tree without the path segment orientations indicated. However, a tree always has an implied orientation given by tracing a path from the root to each of its nodes.

A directed path in a digraph that leads from a node back to that same node is called a *cycle*. A directed tree has no cycles and is an example of an *acyclic* graph. A cycle is *simple* if all its nodes are distinct (i.e., no node appears twice, except for the starting node). If a simple cycle contains all the nodes of a digraph it is called *Hamiltonian* (Fig. 3.18). A path is said to be simple if it does not contain any cycles; it is Hamiltonian if it contains all the nodes of the digraph. We also speak of cycles and Hamiltonian paths in undirected graphs where these terms have the obvious meanings.

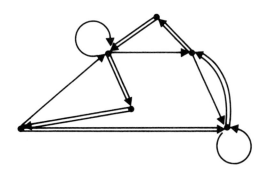

Figure 3.18

The "traveling salesman" problem of determining the shortest path that passes through each of a given set of cities is that of determining a Hamiltonian path of minimum length. (The digraph in this case is weighted, each path segment having its length as its weight.)

The problem of the "knight's tour" in chess consists of moving the knight starting from any given square so that in 64 moves it visits every square on the board and returns to the starting square. In the language of graphs, it is the problem of finding a Hamiltonian cycle in the graph whose nodes are the 64 squares of the board and whose path segments join every pair of squares that are at a knight's move from each other.

A *subtree* of a given tree is the tree obtained by taking any node of the tree as a root and including all path segments and nodes that can be reached by traveling down from that node. If we "prune" a subtree from a given tree, the remaining structure is still a tree.

Family trees are often used in genealogy to describe the lineage of individuals. A tree that shows some of the ancestors of a given individual is a graph that satisfies the conditions for being a tree (assuming no marriages of cousins), the given individual being at the root of the tree. The representation of the descendants of an individual is also a tree if only one parent of each individual in the lineage is shown. If two parents appear for any individual, the representation is a digraph but not a tree.

By analogy with family trees we speak of the relationship between the members of certain pairs of nodes as that between a parent, or father, node and a child, or son, node. (It is difficult to root out all evidence of sexism in the literature.) Thus, in Fig. 3.17 node *P* is the father of four sons labeled *S*.

A tree is a natural generalization of an ordered list. In a list, every element has as its predecessor the element immediately to its left. If we generalize the notion of ordering so that every element in the list is considered a successor of some preceding element, not necessarily the one immediately to its left, we are led to the notion of a tree.

For example, consider the following list in which each element is to be considered a successor of the element written in parentheses next to it.

$$R, A(R), B(R), C(A), D(B), E(B), F(C), G(E).$$

The tree corresponding to this list with its special ordering is:

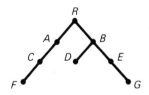

3.10   MISCELLANEOUS EXAMPLES OF
GRAPHICAL STRUCTURES IN COMPUTING

1. The tree structure of expressions (Fig. 3.19): Any binary operation can be represented as a tree:

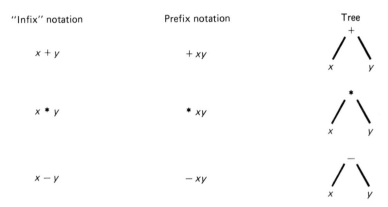

| "Infix" notation | Prefix notation | Tree |

Figure 3.19

By replicating this scheme, a tree can be written down for any complex expression built up by binary operations. Thus, the tree for $((a * b) + c) * (d - (e * f))$ is

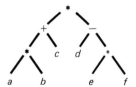

The operands appear at the leaves of such trees, and the level numbers of the operation nodes imply the order in which these operations should be executed in computing the expression. Operations with higher level numbers should be executed before those with lower level numbers. However, the computations corresponding to disjoint subtrees can proceed simultaneously. Thus, in the given example, the multiplication (level 2) in $a * b$ must be executed before the addition (level 1) of $(a * b) + c$. However, the operations in the subtree corresponding to $(d - (e * f))$ can be performed in parallel with those in the subtree for $((a * b) + c)$.

2. A graph can be used to represent the flow, or sequencing of control, of a program. Nodes can correspond to program statements or to blocks (consecutively executed strings) of statements. If i, j denote two nodes, a directed segment $i \rightarrow j$ is taken to mean that control can pass from node i to node j.
Example of a fragment of a program and its flow:

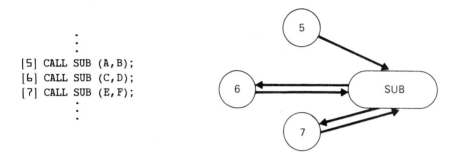

```
      .
      .
      .
[5] CALL SUB (A,B);
[6] CALL SUB (C,D);
[7] CALL SUB (E,F);
      .
      .
      .
```

A program flowchart is a graph with considerable additional information contained at the nodes.

3. The tree representation of the block structure of a program: Nodes may represent the blocks of which a program is constructed. A path segment from node A to node B means that B is a subblock of A (A block as in ALGOL can only be entered from its parent block.)

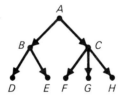

4. The tree representation of structures, or hierarchical collections of data, such as in PL/I: The following example of a declaration represents a simplified payroll file. The entire file is called the EMP_MASTER file. It includes payroll information on each employee. Each record includes (i) information on employee identification (IDENT) consisting of two fields, EMP_NO and NAME, (ii) a field for SALARY, and (iii) information on deductions (DEDNS) consisting of three fields, INSUR, LOAN, and SAVE. The tree

describing the hierarchical organization of data is also shown. The data items appear only at the leaves of the tree.

Example. `DECLARE 1 EMP_MASTER,`
` 2 IDENT,`
`  3 EMP_NO,`
`  3 NAME,`
` 2 SALARY,`
` 2 DEDNS,`
`  3 INSUR,`
`  3 LOAN,`
`  3 SAVE;`

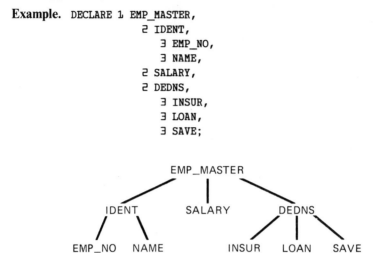

Note that the indented format of this PL/I declaration statement describes the tree structure of this data in an alternate way.

5. In Chapter 9 we make extensive use of trees for the representation of the derivation of sentences in languages. These ideas are based on Chomsky's very important work in linguistics. We elaborate this later but include at this point, without full explanation, a sample tree showing the grammatical derivation of a particular English sentence.

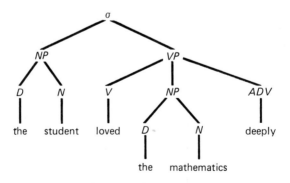

Figure 3.20

In this example of a tree (Fig. 3.20), the symbols have the following meanings:

σ: sentence

NP: noun phrase   N: noun

VP: verb phrase   V: verb

D: determiner   ADV: adverb

3.11 THE ENCODING OF GRAPHS IN THE COMPUTER

It is easy to represent a graph by a list of symbols that can then be represented in memory. We can, for example, represent a digraph by listing each path segment extending from node *a* to node *b* as the ordered pair (*a, b*).

Thus, such a representation of the following graph *G* is indicated:

G: (2, 1), (1, 4), (4, 3), (2, 3), (4, 2)

Trees can be represented more compactly. We can, for example, use a prefix or postfix notation corresponding to the prefix or postfix representation for algebraic expressions and their trees, as we have implied in the preceding discussion of the tree structure of expressions.

Consider the tree in Fig. 3.21 where the level number of each node is written in parentheses next to it.

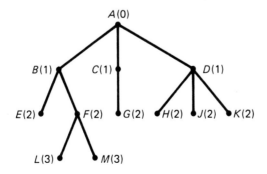

Figure 3.21

A postfix string for this tree is:

ELMFBGCHJKDA

That is, the string $\alpha_1 \alpha_2 \ldots \alpha_n x$ represents the tree:

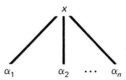

and the notation is extended in obvious recursive fashion to arbitrary trees. (The node x above corresponds to an operation symbol in expressions. The postfix notation applies even if the operation is not binary, but we must then be able to determine the number of operands for a given operation.)

A digraph can also be represented by an "adjacency matrix." A *matrix* in mathematics is a rectangular array of elements, often written as in the following array A of 3 rows and 4 columns.

$$A: \quad \begin{pmatrix} a_{11} & a_{12} & a_{13} & a_{14} \\ a_{21} & a_{22} & a_{23} & a_{24} \\ a_{31} & a_{32} & a_{33} & a_{34} \end{pmatrix}$$

Each element a_{ij} $(i = 1, 2, 3; j = 1, 2, 3, 4)$ in the matrix has in this example two subscripts, the first indicating the row i and the second the column j that contain that element. The matrix A is said to be a 3×4 matrix, indicating the numbers of rows and of columns in that order. These numbers define the "dimensions" of the matrix.

An adjacency matrix is a square matrix in which each row (and column) corresponds to one of the nodes of the graph. We take $a_{ij} = 1$ if there is a path segment directed from node i to node j, and $a_{ij} = 0$ if there is none.

Thus, the adjacency matrix for the graph G above is

$$\begin{pmatrix} 0 & 0 & 0 & 1 \\ 1 & 0 & 1 & 0 \\ 0 & 0 & 0 & 0 \\ 0 & 1 & 1 & 0 \end{pmatrix}$$

If the path segments have weights, we can write down an adjacency matrix that contains these weights as entries, not just 0 and 1. If there is more than one path segment from a node i to a node j, we might wish to indicate the number of such segments in the (i, j) position of the matrix.

In algebra, the addition or subtraction of two matrices of the same dimensions is defined in the following way. If A, with elements $\{a_{ij}\}$, is an $l \times m$ matrix and B, with elements $\{b_{ij}\}$, has the same dimensions, then the matrix $C = A \pm B$ is defined to be that $l \times m$ matrix whose elements $\{c_{ij}\}$ are given by $c_{ij} = a_{ij} \pm b_{ij}$.

As an example we have

$$\begin{pmatrix} 1 & 0 & -2 \\ 3 & 2 & 2 \\ 0 & -1 & 3 \end{pmatrix} + \begin{pmatrix} 2 & 1 & 0 \\ 4 & -3 & 2 \\ 1 & 0 & 4 \end{pmatrix} = \begin{pmatrix} 3 & 1 & -2 \\ 7 & -1 & 4 \\ 1 & -1 & 7 \end{pmatrix}$$

Multiplication of matrices is defined as follows. Let A with elements $\{a_{ij}\}$ be an $l \times m$ matrix and B with elements $\{b_{ij}\}$ be an $m \times n$ matrix. That is, A has the same number of columns as B has rows. The product $C = A \times B$ is then defined to be an $l \times n$ matrix whose elements $\{c_{ij}\}$ are given by the following equation:

$$c_{ij} = a_{i1}b_{1j} + a_{i2}b_{2j} + \ldots + a_{im}b_{mj},$$

or, as it is usually written,

$$c_{ij} = \sum_{k=1}^{m} a_{ik}b_{kj}.$$

Thus, as an example, we can compute the following product of two square matrices of order 3:

$$\begin{pmatrix} 1 & 0 & -2 \\ 3 & 2 & 2 \\ 0 & -1 & 3 \end{pmatrix} \begin{pmatrix} 2 & 1 & 0 \\ 4 & -3 & 2 \\ 1 & 0 & 4 \end{pmatrix} = \begin{pmatrix} 0 & 1 & -8 \\ 16 & -3 & 12 \\ -1 & 3 & 10 \end{pmatrix}$$

Similar matrix operations are useful in dealing with adjacency matrices. Suppose that A is the $n \times n$ adjacency matrix corresponding to a graph H with n nodes. We define the product $A \cdot A = A^2$ to be that matrix which is obtained by following a multiplication rule similar to the one used in algebra but in which *Boolean* addition (the OR) and *Boolean* multiplication (the AND) are used in place of ordinary addition and multiplication. We write then

$$(A^2)_{ij} = \alpha_{ij} = (a_{i1} \& a_{1j}) \mid (a_{i2} \& a_{2j}) \mid \ldots \mid (a_{in} \& a_{nj}).$$

What meaning can be attached to this element α_{ij} in the i,j position of the square of the adjacency matrix? Note that $\alpha_{ij} = 1$ if any one of the products $(a_{ik} \& a_{kj})$ $(k = 1, 2, \ldots, n)$ is equal to 1. That is, $\alpha_{ij} = 1$ if there is any *two-segment* path joining node i to node j, and $\alpha_{ij} = 0$ otherwise.

To illustrate the computation, let G also represent the adjacency matrix for the graph G above. We then have:

$$G^2 = \begin{pmatrix} 0 & 0 & 0 & 1 \\ 1 & 0 & 1 & 0 \\ 0 & 0 & 0 & 0 \\ 0 & 1 & 1 & 0 \end{pmatrix} \overset{\text{Boolean}}{\times} \begin{pmatrix} 0 & 0 & 0 & 1 \\ 1 & 0 & 1 & 0 \\ 0 & 0 & 0 & 0 \\ 0 & 1 & 1 & 0 \end{pmatrix} = \begin{pmatrix} 0 & 1 & 1 & 0 \\ 0 & 0 & 0 & 1 \\ 0 & 0 & 0 & 0 \\ 1 & 0 & 1 & 0 \end{pmatrix}$$

This shows that, for example, there is a two-segment path from node 2 to node 4 but none from node 2 to node 3.

The Boolean analog of the algebraic sum $A + A^2$ is the matrix $A \mid A^2$ defined to be that matrix whose element in the i, j position is $a_{ij} \mid \alpha_{ij}$. If, then, we form the matrix $G \mid G^2$, its elements will indicate whether in graph G node i can be joined to node j by a path of length 1 *or* of length 2. That is

$$(G \mid G^2)_{ij} = G_{ij} \mid (G^2)_{ij}.$$

In our example

$$G \mid G^2 = \begin{pmatrix} 0 & 0 & 0 & 1 \\ 1 & 0 & 1 & 0 \\ 0 & 0 & 0 & 0 \\ 0 & 1 & 1 & 0 \end{pmatrix} \text{ OR } \begin{pmatrix} 0 & 1 & 1 & 0 \\ 0 & 0 & 0 & 1 \\ 0 & 0 & 0 & 0 \\ 1 & 0 & 1 & 0 \end{pmatrix} = \begin{pmatrix} 0 & 1 & 1 & 1 \\ 1 & 0 & 1 & 1 \\ 0 & 0 & 0 & 0 \\ 1 & 1 & 1 & 0 \end{pmatrix}$$

We see that a one- or two-segment path connects any ordered pair of the nodes 1,2,4.

If there are n nodes, then the matrix $A \mid A^2 \mid A^3 \mid \dots \mid A^n$ is the *path matrix*. The element in the (i, j) position is 1 if there is a path *of any length* connecting node i to node j and it is 0 otherwise. (It is sufficient to include paths up to length n because a longer path passing through n nodes must contain a cycle that can be removed, leading to a shorter path.)

If ordinary addition and multiplication are used in forming the powers of the adjacency matrix, the elements of these matrix powers denote the *number* of paths of given length (corresponding to the power) that join node i to node j.

3.12 EXAMPLE OF AN ALGORITHMIC SOLUTION TO A GRAPH-RELATED PROBLEM—THE MINIMAL-PATH PROBLEM

We return to a problem we have already illustrated—that of finding the shortest path between two nodes in a weighted digraph.

Consider the problem of finding the shortest path from node 1 to node 8 in the digraph in Fig. 3.22:

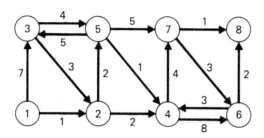

Figure 3.22

We shall solve the problem by following an iterative procedure. The object at each stage of this procedure will be to find additional nodes for which we know the minimal path from node 1. When node 8 appears as one of these additional nodes, we shall have the solution to the problem.

At step 1 we include node 1, for we know the minimal path from node 1 to node 1. It has length 0. Thus, the initial set of nodes for which we know the solution to the minimal path problem is $M_1 = \{1\}$.

We shall continue to generate increasing sets of nodes $M_1, M_2, M_3, \ldots$. At each stage we shall, as follows, add nodes for which we know the solution to finding the shortest path from node 1. After determining all the nodes in set M_k (M_1 offers no problem), we examine all new nodes that are within one path segment of any node in M_k. For each of these new nodes compute the length of a path from node 1 as follows. Suppose the new node N is one path segment from a node P in M_k. Add the length of this path segment to the known minimal distance from node 1 to P. Do this for all possible new nodes. Choose as new members of the set M_{k+1}, where $M_{k+1} \supset M_k$, those nodes that are at the minimal distance, computed in this manner, from node 1. That is, the minimum is to be taken with respect to all of the new nodes that are being considered.

The sets $M_1, M_2, \ldots$ are strictly increasing in the number of their elements. Since there are only a finite number of nodes in the digraph, every node must eventually appear in one of the M's, and we shall then know the solution for that node.

Continuing beyond step 1 we obtain the following sets of nodes for the given problem. We also indicate the minimal path length d_k from node 1 to each of the *new* nodes in the set M_k (that is, to each node of M_k that is not in M_{k-1}).

$$M_1 = \{1\}, \qquad d_1 = 0 \qquad M_4 = \{1, 2, 3, 4, 5, 7\}, \qquad d_4 = 7$$
$$M_2 = \{1, 2\}, \qquad d_2 = 1 \qquad M_5 = \{1, 2, 3, 4, 5, 7, 8\}, \quad d_5 = 8$$
$$M_3 = \{1, 2, 4, 5\}, \quad d_3 = 3$$

The solution to the given problem of finding the shortest path length from node 1 to node 8 is seen to be $d_5 = 8$.

We leave it to the reader to complete the argument that the stated procedure does what we claim and that it always succeeds in determining the shortest path length between a given node and every other node in the digraph.

APPENDIX EXERCISES

A.1 Are the two graphs drawn in (a) isomorphic? in (b)?

a)   b)

A.2 Draw all trees containing seven nodes, showing only trees that are *not* isomorphic.

A.3 Draw a digraph with nodes identified by the numbers 1, 2, 3, 4, 5, 6, 10, 12, 15, 18, 30 so that there is a directed path from node i to node j if and only if i is a divisor of j. Avoid superfluous path segments.

A.4 Draw a directed (from the root) tree of eight nodes where each node is identified by one of the following strings: AN, ANT, ANTIC, CANT, CANTÉR, CANTALOUPE, FRANTIC, MAN, and a directed path from node i to node j exists if and only if j contains i as a substring.

A.5 Draw a digraph whose eight nodes are identified by the subsets of $\{a, b, c\}$ and in which a directed path from node i to node j exists if and only if i is a subset of j. Avoid superfluous path segments.

A.6 Let x, y be three-bit binary words. Consider the relation R defined by: xRy if and only if x, y differ in precisely one position and the sum of the bits in y exceeds the sum of the bits in x. Represent R by a digraph in which each node corresponds to a three-bit number and a directed path segment extends from node x to node y if and only if xRy.

A.7 Show that in any digraph (i) the sum of the indegrees at all nodes, (ii) the sum of the outdegrees at all nodes, and (iii) the number of path segments are all equal.

A.8 Show that if there is a directed path in a given digraph from a node u to a node v, then there is a *simple* directed path from u to v.

A.9 Given the "weighted" adjacency matrix M:

$$\begin{pmatrix} 5 & 2 & 0 & 0 \\ 0 & 0 & 3 & 4 \\ 0 & 0 & 0 & 8 \\ 0 & 4 & 1 & 0 \end{pmatrix}$$

Draw a weighted digraph G of four nodes corresponding to M. Is G connected? Is it strongly connected?

A.10 Given the following digraph G:

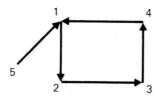

Is G connected? Is it strongly connected? Write down the adjacency matrix A for G. Find, using A, that matrix which indicates for each pair of nodes i, j the number of directed paths from i to j that include precisely two path segments. Find the path matrix for G.

A.11 Let the M nodes of a digraph G be $N1, N2, \ldots, NM$. Suppose that the graph is specified by being given the set of path segments $\{(NI, NJ)\}$ where (NI, NJ) denotes a path segment directed from node NI to node NJ (there may be, as we have noted, more than one path segment from NI to NJ).

     a. Write a program in any suitable language to give as output the indegree of every node.

     b. Write a program to form the adjacency matrix of G and to compute the path matrix of G.

A.12 Write a program in any suitable language to find the shortest path between two nodes of a given weighted digraph G. Assume that the input data consists of the weighted adjacency matrix A of G; that is, $A(I, J)$ is the length of the directed path segment joining node I to node J. However, if $A(I, J) = 0$, this is taken to mean that there is no directed path segment from I to J. Use the method outlined in the text.

REFERENCES

1. Berge, C., *The Theory of Graphs and Its Applications.* Translated by Alison Doig. London: Methuen, 1962.

2. Bellman, R., K. L. Cooke, and J. A. Lockett, *Algorithms, Graphs, and Computers.* New York: Academic Press, 1970.

3. Date, C. J., *An Introduction to Database Systems*. Reading, Massachusetts: Addison-Wesley, 1975.

4. Harary, F., *Graph Theory*. Reading, Massachusetts: Addison-Wesley, 1969.

5. Harris, B., ed. *Graph Theory and its Applications*. New York: Academic Press, 1970.

6. Kennedy, K., and J. Schwartz, "An Introduction to the Set Theoretical Language SETL." *Comp. and Math. with Appl.*, **1** (1975).

7. Ore, O., *Theory of Graphs*. Providence, Rhode Island: Amer. Math. Soc. Colloq. Publ., **38**, 1962.

8. Schwartz, J. T., *Set Theory as a Language for Program Specification and Programming*. New York: Courant Institute of Mathematical Sciences, Lecture Notes.

9. Schwartz, J. T., *An Interim Report on the SETL Project, Installment 1: Generalities*. New York: Courant Institute of Mathematical Sciences, Lecture Notes, February 1973.

4
Recursive Functions

In this chapter we shall follow one of several possible approaches toward making precise the notion of an effectively computable function. We describe the class of partial recursive functions, a class which may, it is believed, be identified with the vaguely defined class of the (partial) effectively computable functions (cf. Church's thesis, below). We shall, in Chapter 5, where we consider the theory of Turing machines, take still another approach to making sharp the intuitive notion of effective computability. Historically, the formulation of the class of partial recursive functions occurred at about the same time (circa 1936) as the establishment of the theory of Turing machines. These theories, concerned with a mathematical development of the class of computable functions before there were any electronic computers, provided an intellectual orientation that many believe was very helpful in preparing for and motivating the advent of the modern computer.

The operations of composition, recursion, and iteration play key roles in these mathematical formulations, and this suggests their importance in programming. These schemes for defining functions are described here in programming, or in flowchart, terms.

The theory of recursive functions and sets is a very fertile field of mathematics (cf. [9]) and would be so even if no high speed computers existed. We introduce a few of the basic ideas and definitions but leave untouched most of the vast mathematical theory. We define the class of primitive recursive functions, a very important subset of the partial recursive functions. Almost all functions computed in practice are in this class.

At the end of the chapter we give a short description of the basic building blocks used in composing flowcharts for the application of the technique of structured programming. Our purpose is not to give an exposition of structured programming, but to show that the small number of basic operations used in this disciplined approach to programming provide complete generality. These operations are sufficient to enable the execution of any computable procedure whatsoever. The proof depends on showing that with these building blocks we are able to compute an arbitrary partial recursive function.

4.1   INTRODUCTION

In considering the underlying mathematics of programming, we are concerned with functions whose domains and ranges are subsets of the natural numbers. (It will be more convenient for us to assume in this chapter that the "natural numbers" include zero. That is, we are now using the term as being equivalent to the "nonnegative integers.") That we are able to dispense with negative numbers and with nonintegral numbers comes as no surprise to anyone with the briefest acquaintance with computers. For, as we have emphasized earlier when considering number representation in the computer, every signed number that is represented within the machine—floating or fixed point—can always be thought of as an integer (the integer corresponding to the string of bits that is used to represent the number in, say, a binary machine). We shall usually assume domains and ranges to be subsets of the natural numbers, but we shall also have occasion to introduce functions defined for more than a single argument, that is, functions whose arguments are r-tuples ($r \geq 1$) of the natural numbers and which assume values that are s-tuples ($s \geq 1$) of the natural numbers. Any such function can always be regarded as a set of functions that take on values that are natural numbers (the s functions that give respectively the components of the s-tuples in the range of f).

In *all* uses of a computer, as we have emphasized, no matter how far removed from mathematics a commercial application may seem, we are computing the values of a function. For, in any data-processing operation, the input can always be read off as a string of bits (a natural number) or as an n-tuple of such strings, and the output can similarly be interpreted. All steps intermediate between input and output then comprise the computation of this function.

4.2   "RECURSIVE" DEFINITIONS

In defining the class of recursive functions, we make use of a technique that appears frequently in mathematics in the definition of certain classes of objects. These classes are defined "recursively" or in terms of themselves. The technique is an example of the genetic methods referred to in Chapter 2 and it consists of the following: we assert first that certain "primitive" objects are in the class being defined. We then describe one or more ways of producing new objects in the class when given some objects already known to be in the class. All members of the class being defined are then taken to be precisely those, and only those, objects that can be obtained by starting with the primitive objects and repeatedly introducing new objects, making use of the stated rules for obtaining these new objects. We have already seen one example of such a technique in the use of recursion in the definition of a function. In this case, the method enables us to compute the value of $f(n)$ once we have obtained the value of $f(n-1)$. (The "objects" being defined are the elements $(n, f(n))$ of the graph of $f(n)$.)

For example, consider the class P of numbers defined in the following way.

Primitive object: 1 is a member of P.

Generating rule: If x is a member of P and y is a member of P (not necessarily distinct from x) then $x + y$ is a member of P.

Very little thought shows that the class P consists of all the positive integers.

In formal logical systems the same procedure is used in defining a class of well-formed formulas (wff's) starting with certain primitive formulas and rules which describe how to formulate new wff's from given wff's. We have seen the technique illustrated in the case of Boolean algebra.

We may, for example, define the class of well-formed parenthetical expressions (PE's) formed from two symbols a, b by writing:

Primitive parenthetical expressions: a and b are well-formed parenthetical expressions.

Generating rules: (1) If E_1, E_2 (not necessarily distinct) are well-formed parenthetical expressions, then (E_1E_2) is a well-formed parenthetical expression. (2) If E_1 is a well-formed parenthetical expression, then (E_1) is a well-formed parenthetical expression.

This scheme admits the following expressions as well-formed. We generate these expressions by several applications of the given rules. The expression on the right-hand side of an arrow is obtained from expressions on the left of the arrow by applying the named rule.

Expression		Generation			
		Rule 1		Rule 1	
$((ab)b)$	a, b	$\rightarrow$	(ab)	$\rightarrow$	$((ab)b)$
		Rule 1		Rule 1	
	a, b	$\rightarrow$	(ab)	$\rightarrow$	$(b(ab))$
$(((b(ab))))$		Rule 2		Rule 2	
		$\rightarrow$	$((b(ab)))$	$\rightarrow$	$(((b(ab))))$

The elegant notational scheme, the Backus-Naur form, which was introduced in Chapter 2, is often used in describing the syntax of programming languages where recursive definitions of symbolic expressions are applied (see Chapter 9). Its use is illustrated in the following application to the last example:

$$<PE> :: = a \mid b \mid (<PE>) \mid (<PE><PE>)$$

This means that the class of well-formed parenthetical expressions, *PE*, can be formed by including *a* or *b* or any *PE* surrounded by parentheses or any juxtaposition of *PE*'s surrounded by parentheses.

PEANUTS   **By Charles M. Schulz**

We now make use of these methods to define several classes of functions. The first step is to define the primitive objects, or basic functions, of these classes of functions.

4.3 THE BASIC RECURSIVE FUNCTIONS

The following three functions are those with which we begin the generation of the classes of the primitive recursive functions and of the partial recursive functions. As might be expected, these three basic functions are, in some sense, the simplest functions that we can consider. We follow the development and notation as in Davis [3].

1. The successor function, $S(x) = x + 1$. For given argument x, the image of x is its successor $x + 1$.

2. The zero function, $N(x) = 0$. For any given argument x, this function is identically zero.

3. The generalized identity functions defined for all i, n, with $0 < i \leq n$, $U_i^{(n)}(x_1, \dots, x_n) = x_i$. For a given n-tuple of arguments, this function is the ith component of the n-tuple.

These functions are the building blocks with which we start in generating the very rich classes we now define. It is seen that they are indeed primitive functions.

Generating Rules

Composition.   Suppose we know that a function $f(y_1, \dots, y_m)$ is in the class being generated. We can apply the composition rule to yield a new function by replacing each of the arguments y_i $(i = 1, 2, \dots, m)$ by any function that has been shown to be within the class.

Thus, in formal terms, if we are given the functions

$$\begin{cases} f(y_1, \dots, y_m) \\ g_1(x_1, \dots, x_n) \\ g_2(x_1, \dots, x_n) \\ \quad \vdots \\ g_m(x_1, \dots, x_n) \end{cases}$$

as members of the class being generated, then the function

$$h(x_1, \dots, x_n) = f(g_1(x_1, \dots, x_n), \dots, g_m(x_1, \dots, x_n))$$

is obtained from these given functions by the operation of composition (cf. Fig. 4.1).

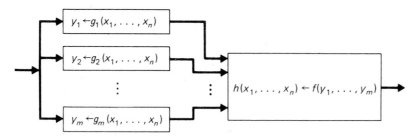

Fig. 4.1   The operation of composition-computation of $h(x_1, \dots, x_n)$.

For example, the function $F(x) = 1$ is obtained by substituting $N(x)$ for x in $S(x)$ as follows:

$$F(x) = S(N(x)) = N(x) + 1 = 1.$$

The function $G(x) = 2$ can then be obtained by

$$G(x) = S(F(x)) = F(x) + 1 = 2.$$

The function $\varphi(x_1, x_2) = 0$ is obtained by the following composition scheme:

$$\varphi(x_1, x_2) = N(U_1^{(2)}(x_1, x_2)) = N(x_1) = 0.$$

The function $f(x, y) = x + 2$, which is not the same as the function $\varphi(x) = x + 2$, is derived as follows:

$$f(x, y) = S(S(U_1^{(2)}(x, y))) = x + 2.$$

Using composition alone, a rather restricted class of functions can be generated from the three basic functions. Note that the SUBROUTINE operation and the MACRO facilities of a number of programming languages provide obvious facilities to use composition within a program.

Primitive Recursion. The rule or operation of primitive recursion is a schema (Fig. 4.2) that defines a new function in terms of two given functions. We show first how this schema defines a function of a single argument. Call the function to be defined $r(x)$. The operation of primitive recursion includes an assignment of some specified value to $r(0)$. It then also includes a procedure to determine $r(k + 1)$, once we have obtained $r(k)$. We write the following equations, where k is a constant and $g(x, y)$ is assumed to be a total function already known to be within the class.

$$\begin{cases} r(0) = k \\ r(x + 1) = g(x, r(x)) \text{ for } x > 0 \end{cases}$$

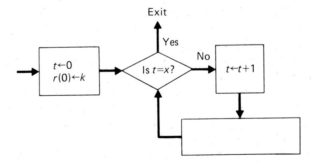

Fig. 4.2   The operation of primitive recursion—computation of $r(x)$.

Thus, starting with $r(0)$, we are able to iterate the second equation to obtain r at any argument.

More generally, we can define a function, $r(x_1, \ldots, x_n)$, of a number of arguments by applying this idea to some one of the arguments. Thus the following equations define $r(x_1, x_2, \ldots, x_n)$ by (1) giving its value for $x_1 = 0$ and arbitrary values of the other arguments, and (2) defining r with first argument $x_1 + 1$ in terms of the value of r with first argument x_1.

$$\begin{cases} r(0, x_2, \ldots, x_n) = f(x_2, \ldots, x_n) \\ r(x_1 + 1, x_2, \ldots, x_n) = g(x_1, r(x_1, x_2, \ldots, x_n), x_2, \ldots, x_n) \end{cases}$$

The function $r(x_1, \ldots, x_n)$ has been defined in terms of the functions $f(x_2, \ldots, x_n), g(x_1, y, x_2, \ldots, x_n)$.

4.4 POSSIBLE PROGRAMMING LANGUAGE FEATURES TO ENABLE THE USE OF FUNCTION-GENERATING OPERATIONS

The operations of composition and of primitive recursion are examples of transformations of functions into functions, as we have discussed this in Chapter 2. They are mappings of a higher order than ordinary functions that map numbers into numbers. In both composition and primitive recursion the input for each operation consists of *functions*, and the output is a *function*. As we have pointed out, most programming languages have facilities to define ordinary functions, i.e., to define procedures whose arguments are variables that are assigned specific numeric values at execution time. After the procedure is defined, a program statement provides these input arguments in a call statement such as, typically

$$Z = \text{FUNCTION}(X1, X2);$$

The output value of the function is assigned to the variable Z when this statement is executed.

However, we need some additional language capability, provided by only a few langauges such as ALGOL 68, in order to be able to cope with the definition of the operations of composition or of primitive recursion. Here, we might want to be able to write, as part of a procedure *definition*, statements like:

$$H(X1, X2) = \text{COMPOS}(F(Y1, Y2, Y3), G1(X1, X2), G2(X1, X2), G3(X1, X2));$$

or

$$R(X) = \text{PRIMREC}\ (K, G(X, Y));$$

These refer respectively to special cases of the operations of composition and of primitive recursion. We have used the upper case equivalents of the identifiers that appeared in our original definitions of these operations.

After defining the functions $H(X1, X2), R(X)$, we should, as before, be able to call them in statements such as:

$$Z = H(X1, X2); \text{ or}$$

$$Z = R(X);$$

The procedures COMPOS and PRIMREC that appear in these procedure definitions use *functions* as their arguments and give as a result a *function*, not a number. In calling COMPOS and PRIMREC the input arguments are other *procedures*, not variables. This is another example of the kind of situation that justifies the extended capability for procedure definitions of ALGOL 68.

We shall make use later of such programming language facilities to describe the generation of functions in the class of partial recursive functions.

4.5 THE CLASS OF PRIMITIVE RECURSIVE FUNCTIONS

Primitive recursion is a powerful operation that can be used to obtain a surprisingly extensive class of functions when used with composition and the basic functions of Section 4.3. We illustrate its application in the following list of some of the functions obtained through the use of primitive recursion and composition (Davis [3]).

1. $\Sigma(x, y) = x + y$

$$\begin{cases} \Sigma(0, y) = y \\ \Sigma(x + 1, y) = S(\Sigma(x, y)) \end{cases}$$

2. $\Pi(x, y) = x \cdot y$

$$\begin{cases} \Pi(0, y) = 0 \\ \Pi(x + 1, y) = \Pi(x, y) + y = \Sigma(\Pi(x, y), U_2^{(2)}(x, y)) \end{cases}$$

3. $P(x) = (x - 1) \quad \text{for } x \geq 1$
   $\qquad\quad = 0 \qquad\qquad \text{for } x = 0$

$$\begin{cases} P(0) = 0 \\ P(x + 1) = x = U_1^{(1)}(x) \end{cases}$$

4.
$$D(x, y) = \begin{cases} x - y & \text{for } x \geq y \\ 0 & \text{for } x < y \end{cases}$$

This last function is the same as the ordinary difference $x - y$ when the result is a natural number. However, negative numbers are excluded from its range and it is defined as 0 when the ordinary difference is negative. It is obtained as follows by primitive recursion and composition from the preceding functions in our list.

$$\begin{cases} D(x,0) = x = U_1^{(1)}(x) \\ D(x, y + 1) = P(D(x, y)) \end{cases}$$

$D(x, y)$ is often written as $x \overset{.}{-} y$.

5. $E(x, y) = x^y$
$$\begin{cases} E(x,0) = 1 \\ E(x, y + 1) = E(x, y) \cdot x = E(x, y) \cdot U_1^{(2)}(x, y) = \Pi \left(E(x, y), U_1^{(2)}(x, y) \right) \end{cases}$$

6. $F(x) = x!$
$$\begin{cases} F(0) = 1 \\ F(x + 1) = (x + 1) \cdot F(x) = S(x) \cdot F(x) = \Pi \left(S(x), F(x) \right) \end{cases}$$

7. $A(x, y) = |x - y| = D(x, y) + D(y, x)$
$$= \Sigma \left(D(x, y), D(U_2^{(2)}(x, y), U_1^{(2)}(x, y)) \right)$$

The list can be extended considerably, and the class of functions so generated is called the *primitive recursive functions*.

DEFINITION: *The class of primitive recursive functions consists of those functions that can be obtained by repeated applications of composition and primitive recursion starting with (1) the successor function, $S(x) = x + 1$, (2) the zero function, $N(x) = 0$, (3) the generalized identity functions, $U_i^{(n)}(x_1, \dots, x_n) = x_i$.*

All of these functions are easily shown to be total since the three basic functions are total and every single application of either composition or primitive recursion applied to total functions can only yield a total function.

First used by Gödel in 1931, this class of functions was called by him the recursive functions. This latter term now has a different, more general meaning, which will be described in the sequel.

The question arises as to whether the class of primitive recursive functions can be equated with the effectively computable (total) functions. It can not be so identified, but it is far from easy to construct a computable function that is not primitive recursive. Almost all of the functions computed on computers (from an earlier remark this can be construed to refer as well to all data-processing operations) are primitive recursive. However, we shall see below a rather bizarre example, Ackermann's function, of a function that is effectively computable but is not primitive recursive. The computation of this function has often been done on machines as a programming tour de force, but it is an interesting question as to whether Ackermann's function is the *only* effectively computable, but not primitive recursive, function that has ever been programmed on digital computers.

4.6   ACKERMANN'S FUNCTION

As extensive as is the class of primitive recursive functions, it does not include the function defined by the following equations:

$$\begin{cases} f(0, n) = n + 1 & (1) \\ f(m, 0) = f(m - 1, 1) & (2) \\ f(m, n) = f(m - 1, f(m, n - 1)) & (3) \end{cases}$$

This is an example of a "doubly-recursive" function and is a special case of a class of functions defined by W. Ackermann [1] and shown by him not to be primitive recursive.

It may not be easy at first glance, especially for the person without much programming experience, to see that equations (1), (2), and (3) provide a proper definition of a computable function $f(m, n)$, a definition that enables one to write a program to compute $f(m, n)$. The reader should compute $f(2, 2)$ if he has not already done this exercise from Chapter 2. The computation will take only a few minutes.

The novice programmer will appreciate the built-in intelligence of a compiler that can cope with this function definition. For example, a PL/I procedure to compute $f(m, n)$ is given below.

```
F: PROCEDURE (M,N) RECURSIVE RETURNS (FIXED);
    DECLARE M,N FIXED;
    IF M = 0 THEN RETURN (N + 1);
    ELSE IF N = 0 THEN RETURN (F(M - 1, 1));
    ELSE RETURN (F(M - 1, F(M, N - 1)));
    END F;
```

We shall see that the given equations (1), (2), (3) define a procedure that generalizes that of primitive recursion. The operation of primitive recursion for the definition of a function can be described with reference to the following diagram.

$$-x\text{------}x\text{------}x\text{------}x\text{------}0\text{---}$$
$$0 \quad\quad 1 \quad\quad 2 \quad \cdots \quad m \quad\quad m+1$$

The operation is applied iteratively on one argument. Given the value of the function at $x = 0$, we can step along the number line computing the

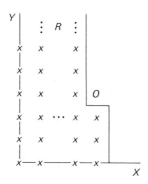

Fig. 4.3 The "doubly recursive" pattern for the computation of Ackermann's function.

value of the function at the next point $x = m + 1$ in terms of the preceding functional value at $x = m$.

Equations (1), (2), (3) enable us to do something similar but in *two* dimensions. With reference to Fig. 4.3, note that we can find, from equation (1), the value of $f(x, y)$ at any point $(0, n)$. Equation (2) gives the value of $f(x, y)$ at $(m, 0)$ if we have previously found the value of $f(x, y)$ at $(m - 1, 1)$. Equation (3) determines $f(x, y)$ at $(m + 1, n)$ if we know the value of $f(x, y)$ at $(m + 1, n - 1)$ and can find $f(x, y)$ at any point on the line $x = m$.

Taking all these details into account we are able to compute the value of $f(x, y)$ at the point labeled O in Fig. 4.3, if we are able to compute the function at any point marked x in region R. From all these remarks, it follows that we can find $f(x, y)$ at every lattice point in the first quadrant of the (X, Y) plane. The description of this *two-dimensional* schema as being *doubly recursive* is justified.

A surprisingly simple flowchart that realizes the procedure we have described is shown in Fig. 4.4. In the course of applying the algorithm to find $f(x, y)$ at the point 0 of Fig. 4.3, we need to obtain the values of $f(x, y)$ at other points in the region R of Fig. 4.3. For example, the first reduction of $f(2, 2)$ involves equation (3), and we need to obtain $f(2, 1)$. Those pairs of coordinates at which the function is needed as the algorithm is elaborated are stored, as they occur in the computation, in a *pushdown store*—a list where the last element recorded is the first one to be read out by the program when the list is accessed (a "LIFO" or "last in first out" list). We call this store the "needed function values stack" (NFVS).

When the NFVS is read, the word at the top will be read and will disappear from the stack, the one below it moving to the top. When a word is

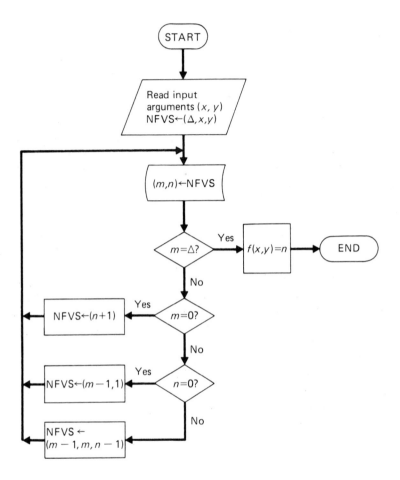

Fig. 4.4 A flowchart for the computation of Ackermann's function.

read we say that we "pop" the stack. The language is, of course, used by analogy to a real stack, such as of cafeteria trays. (See the discussions of "pushdown automata" and of "stack automata" in Chapter 7.)

The pushdown store finds wide application in compiling. For example, it is easily seen that such a device is advantageous in interpreting a string written in the postfix notation defined in Chapter 2. More generally, we shall see examples in Chapter 10 of the use of pushdown stacks in the compiling process.

When we write

$$NFVS \leftarrow (p, q, r),$$

this will mean that the words p, q, r are written, in that order, on the stack. If we start with an empty stack, then, after the execution of this operation, the NFVS will look like

r
q
p

The first word read on a subsequent READ operation will be r. If we execute

$$(a, b, c) \leftarrow \text{NFVS},$$

this shall be taken to mean that r, the first word read, will be stored in c, q in b, p in a, with a similar interpretation for a list of any length.

The procedure described in Fig. 4.4 makes use of a special symbol, or word, Δ that marks the bottom of the stack and is the first word written on an empty stack.

We leave it to the reader to recognize that this procedure realizes the computation of the defining equations for Ackermann's function.

The procedure can be easily programmed on any general purpose computer, given enough storage. (It will be easier, however, if we assume some bound, like one machine word, on the size of the arguments and on all intermediate computed quantities.) It thus appears that this function is effectively computable, and we can compute its value for any given pair of arguments.

However, it is a most remarkable function, and perhaps we should examine more closely our use of the phrase "we can compute." To find, say, $f(2, 2)$ is a trivial computation and $f(3, 3)$, $(= 61)$, can be computed in a tiny fraction of a second on any modern computer.

But $f(4, 4)$ is another story. No one knows with certainty at this time if the universe is finite or infinite. However, current theories with some reasonable evidence to support them (Relativity and the "Big Bang" theories) seem to imply that the universe is finite. It is enormous, however, and we are fairly certain of the existence of many billions of galaxies, most of them containing many billions of stars. The total mass of this finite (if it is) cosmos has been estimated to include something like 10^{80} elemental particles.

If every one of these particles were used in some way to represent one digit in the decimal representation of $f(4, 4)$, not only would they not be sufficient, but *we would not even be able to represent that number which is the number of digits in f(4, 4)* (i.e., $[\log_{10} f(4,4)]$). What meaning then is there in the statement that "we can compute" this function?

It is not very difficult to show that $f(4,4)$ is the same as

$$2 \qquad -3$$

This is an enormous number, larger than the decimal number 1 followed by $10^{19,199}$ zeros. It may seem strange, looking at Fig. 4.4, that $f(x,y)$ can be so large for such small arguments. For, only one box involves any increasing arithmetic operation and that is simply the addition of 1.

We shall omit the proof here that this function, although computable, is not primitive recursive. The argument depends upon the fact that $f(x, x)$ grows more rapidly than any given primitive recursive function. The reader will have an opportunity to prove it as one of the exercises.

4.7 THE CLASS OF PARTIAL RECURSIVE FUNCTIONS

The class of primitive recursive functions can be extended by introducing an additional generating rule.

Minimalization. The operation of minimalization introduces for each given total function $f(y, x_1, x_2, \ldots, x_n)$ a new function $h(x_1, x_2, \ldots, x_n)$ whose value for given $(x_1, x_2, \ldots, x_n)$ is the least y such that $f(y, x_1, x_2, \ldots, x_n) = 0$. We write $h(x_1, x_2, \ldots, x_n) = \min y[f(y, x_1, x_2, \ldots, x_n) = 0]$. Fig. 4.5 shows the schema for a function f that involves a single x.

Example. Let $z = [x/2]$ denote the largest integer that does not exceed $x/2$ (sometimes called the "floor" of $x/2$ and written as $\lfloor x/2 \rfloor$; the "ceiling" of $x/2$, written as $\lceil x/2 \rceil$, is the smallest integer not exceeded by $x/2$). We shall define $z = [x/2]$ by minimalization.

We have

$$z = [x/2] = \min y\,(2(y+1) > x).$$

This is not yet recognizable as an application of minimalization since the expression in parentheses is not of the form $f(y, x) = 0$. We continue:

$$= \min y\,(2y + 2 \ge x + 1)$$
$$= \min y\,(2y + 1 \ge x)$$
$$= \min y\,(x \dot{-} 2y \dot{-} 1 \dot{=} 0).$$

This last expression is clearly recognizable as an application of minimalization (we have used the fact that $a \geq b$ is equivalent to $b \doteq a = 0$).

The function $h(x_1, x_2, \ldots, x_n)$ is not necessarily a total function since there may not be any value of y for which $f(y, x_1, x_2, \ldots, x_n)$ is equal to zero. A programmed search for such a y will never terminate.

Thus, if

$$h(x) = \min y(\mid y^2 - x \mid = 0),$$

$h(x)$ is defined only for arguments x which are perfect squares.

The operation of minimalization, then, may lead to a *partial*, and not total, function when it is applied to a total function.

Comparing Fig. 4.5 with Fig. 4.2, we note that in the case of primitive recursion we are assured of exiting from the loop after some prescribed number of times, known when we enter the loop. However, in the operation of minimalization there is no way of knowing in general at its entry point whether the loop will terminate or how many times it will be executed.

If we extend the class of primitive recursive functions by allowing the operation of minimalization (clearly a computable or programmable operation), we generate a larger class of functions called the *partial recursive functions*. This class includes functions that are not primitive recursive, not only because the new functions obtained may not be total, but it also includes total functions that are not primitive recursive.

Now that, through minimalization, we have introduced functions that are not necessarily defined for all arguments, we must reconsider the meaning of the operation of composition because the functions $f(y_1, \ldots, y_m)$, $g_1(x_1, \ldots, x_n), \ldots, g_m(x_1, \ldots, x_n)$ to which it is applied may not be total. We shall say that the function $h(x_1, \ldots, x_n)$, obtained by replacing each y_i in f by $g_i(x_1, \ldots, x_n)$, is defined at a point $x = (x_1, \ldots, x_n)$ if and only if (1) all the g_i are defined at x and (2) f is defined at $(y_1, \ldots, y_m)$.

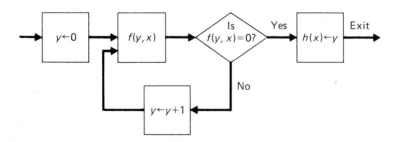

Fig. 4.5   The operation of minimalization—computation of $h(x)$ from $f(y, x)$.

DEFINITION: *The class of partial recursive functions consists of those functions that can be obtained by repeated applications of composition, primitive recursion, and minimalization, starting with* (1) *the successor function,* $S(x) = x + 1$, (2) *the zero function,* $N(x) = 0$, (3) *the generalized identity functions,* $U_i^{(n)}(x_1, \ldots, x_n) = x_i$.

It can be shown (Davis [3]) that the operation of primitive recursion can be dispensed with in defining the class of partial recursive functions *if* we extend the list of assumed basic functions to include (4) $\Sigma(x, y) = x + y$, (5) $D(x, y) = x \doteq y$, (6) $\Pi(x, y) = x \cdot y$. That is, the class of partial recursive functions consists of those functions that can be obtained by repeated applications of composition and minimalization starting with these six given basic functions.

The *recursive* functions (sometimes called the *general recursive* functions) are those total functions which are included in the class of partial recursive functions. Ackermann's function is an example of a recursive function that is not primitive recursive. In programming computers we must try to avoid entering arguments that are outside the domain of a programmed partial recursive function; we do not want infinite loops or endless procedures.

The class of partial recursive functions is very broad and, it is believed, can be identified with the heuristically and vaguely defined class (cf. Chapter 1) of the partial effectively computable functions. Since there is no precise definition of effective computability, the equivalence of the notions of *(partial) recursiveness* and *(partial) effective computability* cannot be proven. It is, rather, an act of faith substantiated by the fact that no one has been able to describe a function that is generally admitted to be effectively computable but which is not recursive. The formal assertion of this equivalence, when stated for total functions, is known as

Church's Thesis: The class of effectively computable functions can be identified with the class of recursive functions.

That any recursive function is effectively computable can be proven by showing that any function obtained by composition, primitive recursion, and minimalization starting with the basic functions is *programmable*. We leave to the reader the problem of recognizing, from the flowcharts for these operations, that if programs are available to compute functions f, g, etc., then we can construct a program to compute any function formed from them by composition, primitive recursion, or minimalization. The programming is trivial *if* we introduce the simplifying assumption that all arguments and intermediate computed quantities are limited to one machine word (or at least some fixed number of words).

If we accept the equivalence of the notion of effective computability and of recursiveness, then in order to prove that a particular function is recursive it will suffice to show that there is some effective procedure—or some program—that will compute it.

4.8   REMARKS ON THE IMPLICATIONS OF THESE FUNDAMENTAL OPERATIONS TO THE FACILITIES THAT MUST BE PROVIDED IN ANY GENERAL PURPOSE COMPUTING DEVICE OR LANGUAGE

We have seen that, accepting the result that the class of recursive functions can be equated with the class of effectively computable functions, the operations of composition, of primitive recursion, and of minimalization play key roles, and any device that purports to provide a general computing capability must be capable of implementing these operations. The operation of *composition* can be interpreted as the providing of a *subroutine* capability—the ability in any computation to replace an argument by the result of another computation.

The operation of minimalization (or that of iteration, cf. below) involves essentially the ability to program a *loop* with a test to determine exit conditions. It uses the DO WHILE operation of structured progamming, which we describe in a later section. The primitive recursion operation is, as has been noted, not quite as powerful as that of minimalization. It also involves the execution of a loop, but in a situation where the number of passes through the loop *have been predetermined,* as opposed to the use of an arbitrary test at each stage to determine if a terminating condition has been attained.

4.9   A PROGRAMMING LANGUAGE PRECL BASED UPON THE GENERATION OF THE PARTIAL RECURSIVE FUNCTIONS

We have mentioned the use of certain extended programming language features to facilitate the description of the generation of functions by the operations of composition and of primitive recursion. We shall elaborate upon these somewhat and shall describe a simple language with facilities for the definition of function procedures, but only procedures that are restricted to the use of composition, of primitive recursion, or of minimalization. These facilities enable the definition of *any* partial recursive function, and Church's thesis implies that this means the definition of any effectively computable function.

We define a rudimental "language" PRECL (Partial RECursive Language) for the description of the partial recursive functions. This language will provide little more than a formalized upper-case restatement of the definitions of functions by composition, primitive recursion, and minimalization. The correspondence between these formal statements and what we have written earlier will be obvious.

Assume that there are three system built-in functions. These are:

$$N(X) = 0;$$
$$S(X) = X + 1;$$
$$U\_I\_N\_(X1, X2, \ldots, XN) = XI; (I, N = 1, 2, 3, \ldots, I \le N).$$

The arguments in these and all other PRECL defined functions are assumed to be natural numbers of any length when these functions are called in assignment statements such as $Z = F(X)$;

The third of the built-in functions, $(U_i^{(n)}(x_1, x_2, \ldots, x_n))$, represents an infinite number of functions corresponding to the possible numeric values assigned to I, N.

PRECL contains procedure definition facilities to allow the definition of functions by composition, primitive recursion, and minimalization. To define a function by composition we write:

DEF H(X1, X2, ..., XN) = COMPOS(F(Y1, Y2, ..., YM),
      G1(X1, X2, ..., XN), G2(X1, X2, ..., XN), ..., GM(X1, X2, ..., XN));

This is the PRECL equivalent of

$$h(x_1, x_2, \ldots, x_n) = f(g_1(x_1, x_2, \ldots, x_n), \ldots, g_m(x_1, x_2, \ldots, x_n)).$$

There are similar PRECL definitions for functions by using primitive recursion or by using minimalization. To define a function by primitive recursion on the first argument we write:

DEF R(X1, X2, ..., XN)
            = PRIMREC(F(X2, X3, ..., XN), G(X1, Y, X2, ..., XN));

Relating this statement to our earlier notation, this statement defines the function $r(x_1, x_2, \ldots, x_n)$ in accordance with the equations

$$\begin{cases} r(0, x_2, \ldots, x_n) = f(x_2, \ldots, x_n) \\ r(x_1 + 1, x_2, \ldots, x_n) = g(x_1, r(x_1, \ldots, x_n), x_2, \ldots, x_n). \end{cases}$$

Similarly, we write

DEF H(X1, X2, ..., XN) = MINIM(F(Y, X1, ..., XN));

to denote $h(x_1, x_2, \ldots, x_n) = \min y(f(y, x_1, \ldots, x_n) = 0)$.

We shall also assume the implicit use of composition, as in most programming languages, in assignment statements where any variable can be replaced by a function defined earlier in a program. That is, we assume we can write such statements as $Z = \text{FUNCT}(F1(X, Y), F2(X, Y, F3(X, Y)))$; with the understanding that when such a statement is executed X, Y will have been assigned numeric values and $F1, F2, F3$ will all have been defined earlier.

Any function can be defined by a PRECL program that shows its derivation as a sequence of function procedure definitions. After definition, the function can appear in an assignment statement. We can illustrate this by writing the complete program for the computation of the function $A(x, w) = |x - w|$. (Here $D(X1, X2)$ denotes the function $x_2 \div x_1$.)

```
/ * PROGRAM TO COMPUTE A(X, W) = | X - W | * /
DEF P(X) = PRIMREC(0, U_1_1(X));
DEF D(X1, X2) = PRIMREC(U_1_1(X2), P(Y));
DEF SIGMA(X1, X2) = PRIMREC(U_1_1_(X2), S(Y));
DEF A(X, W) = SIGMA(D(X, W), D(W, X));
GET X, W; PRINT A(X, W);
END;
```

We are not advocating this language for serious consideration as a competitor for COBOL or PL/I but wish merely to emphasize the constructive aspects of the definition of the partial recursive functions.

4.10 REMARKS ON VOCABULARY—"RECURSIVE," "ITERATIVE"

We have noted that the word "recursive" is used with several different, but related, meanings. Because of the importance of these concepts and the frequent usage of the word, we summarize these different interpretations, giving them in order of increasing precision of meaning.

1. A "recursive" definition of anything is a definition of that thing given in terms of itself. We have noted the use of the BNF notation in the recursive definition of a class of symbolic expressions. In this usage new elements of the class being generated are defined in terms of elements known to be in the class. We have also seen the definition of a recursive procedure as a procedure that can call itself.

We have given an example of a recursive subroutine in Chapter 2. As an additional example of a recursive procedure we indicate the following recursive definition of a function in LISP (LISt Processing language). This language includes a wealth of facilities to manipulate lists of expressions, where these expressions may themselves be such lists. It provides very flexible means for recursive definitions.

The example defines a function LENGTH on the domain of lists. If L is a list, $\text{LENGTH}(L)$ will denote the number of expressions in L. Thus, if L is the list (A CB (B D C) D), the successive expressions of L are A, CB, (B D C), D, and LENGTH(L) = 4. The lambda notation of Chapter 2 is used in LISP to identify functions. If L is a list, the built-in LISP function CDR(L), which maps lists into lists, denotes the sublist obtained by deleting the first element or expression of L. Thus, if L = (A B C D),

$$\text{CDR}(L) = \text{CDR}((A \ B \ C \ D)) = (B \ C \ D).$$

The LISP arithmetic function ADD1 (X), defined for numeric arguments X, gives as result the value of X increased by 1.

DEFINE (((LENGTH (LAMBDA (L)
               (COND ((NULL L) 0) (T (ADD1 (LENGTH (CDR L)))))))))

    The function LENGTH (L) is here defined for a given argument L by scanning the pairs (__) following COND (condition) from left to right. The first element of each pair is a condition, the second element defines the value of LENGTH (L) if that condition is satisfied. Thus, looking at the first pair ((NULL L) 0), if the condition (NULL L) is true (i.e., if the list L is null or empty), then the value of LENGTH (L) is taken to be 0. In the second pair (T (ADD1 (LENGTH (CDR L)))) the condition given is the identically true condition T. This means that the function LENGTH (L), if L is not null, is defined to be LENGTH (CDR L) increased by 1, i.e., one more than the length of the list after deleting the first element of the list. Thus, LENGTH is defined in terms of itself. The definition is recursive. (We have

LENGTH (A B C D) = 1 + LENGTH (B C D) = 2 + LENGTH (C D)
                  = 3 + LENGTH (D) = 4 + LENGTH (NIL) = 4.

"NIL" denotes the null string.)

2. A function definition is often said to be "recursive" with the specific meaning of its being defined by a direct application of primitive recursion. More generally, the word may apply to any definition of a function where the functional value at an argument x can be found from known functional values at (usually) smaller arguments.

Example. The "Fibonacci numbers" are defined by the equations:

$$\begin{cases} F_0 = 0, F_1 = 1 \\ F_{n+1} = F_n + F_{n-1} \end{cases}$$

These equations define the sequence 0, 1, 1, 2, 3, 5, 8, 13, ...

3. A function is recursive if it is a total function in the class of partial recursive functions. From Church's thesis, this is equivalent to saying that it is computable.

Iteration. An "iterative" procedure is one that is repeatedly applied, and iteration is very close in meaning to that of primitive recursion.

For example, if we are given a number N, it can be shown that the following iterative procedure will determine $\sqrt{N}$ to any desired accuracy.

Choose $x_0 (> 0)$ as a first approximation to $\sqrt{N}$, then compute successively:

$$x_1 = \frac{1}{2}\left(x_0 + \frac{N}{x_0}\right)$$

$$x_2 = \frac{1}{2}\left(x_1 + \frac{N}{x_1}\right)$$

$$\vdots$$

$$x_{i+1} = \frac{1}{2}\left(x_i + \frac{N}{x_i}\right)$$

$$\vdots$$

It is not difficult to show that the successive approximations, or "iterates," x_i approach $\sqrt{N}$ ever more closely, and in fact that the number of correct decimal places in x_i approximately doubles at each step.

For example, if $N = 2$ and $x_0 = 1$, we have:

$$x_1 = \frac{1}{2}\left(1 + \frac{2}{1}\right) = 1.5$$

$$x_2 = \frac{1}{2}\left(1.5 + \frac{2}{1.5}\right) = 1.416666667$$

$$x_3 = \frac{1}{2}\left(x_2 + \frac{2}{x_2}\right) = 1.414215686$$

$$x_4 = \frac{1}{2}\left(x_3 + \frac{2}{x_3}\right) = 1.414213562,$$

which is correct to 9 decimal places.

At each stage of this procedure we compute the function

$$f(x) = \frac{1}{2}(x + \frac{N}{x})$$

where $x_{i+1} = f(x_i)$.

We can designate the successive iterates, starting with x_1, as:

$$f(x_0), f(f(x_0)), f(f(f(x_0))), \ldots$$

These expressions are often written as:

$$f(x_0), f^2(x_0), f^3(x_0), \ldots$$

To avoid possible confusion with the powers of $f(x)$, we usually write the latter as $(f(x))^2, (f(x))^3, \ldots$

The definition of the operation of primitive recursion, applied to a function of a single argument x, includes the equation $r(x + 1) = g(x, r(x))$. If no x appears explicitly in $g(x, y)$ (i.e., outside of $r(x)$, as, for example, in $r(x + 1) = r(x) + 2$), the equation has the form $r(x + 1) = G(r(x))$. In this case the function $r(x)$ is defined in terms of the successive iterates of G; $r(1) = G(r(0)), r(2) = G^2(r(0)), \ldots, r(k) = G^k(r, 0), \ldots$.

Iteration may be used as an alternative to minimalization in defining the class of partial recursive functions. This will be described in a later section.

4.11 PRIMITIVE RECURSION AND MATHEMATICAL INDUCTION

The method of mathematical induction for proving theorems is closely related to the operation of primitive recursion. Induction is often used to prove a theorem $T(n)$ that is stated in terms of a parameter n, where n is an arbitrary natural number (e.g., "The sum of the first n positive integers is $n(n + 1)/2$"). The method, which most people have learned in secondary school or introductory college algebra courses, consists of proving a stated theorem to be true for $n = 0$ (or perhaps $n = 1$) and then showing that *if* the theorem is true for $n = k$ (i.e., assume $T(k)$ to be a true statement), then the theorem must be true for $n = k + 1$. That is, (i) $T(0)$ is true, and (ii) $T(k)$ implies $T(k + 1)$. The two parts imply that $T(n)$ is true for all integers n (≥ 0 if we use 0 in the first part, ≥ 1 if we start with 1). We recall the use of the method in the following.

Example. Prove that the sum $S(n)$ of the first n squares is $S(n) = n(n + 1)(2n + 1)/6$.

i. For $n = 1$, $S(1) = 1$, and the theorem is seen to be true for this initial value of n.

ii. Assume that $S(k) = k(k + 1)(2k + 1)/6$. We must prove that $S(k + 1)$ is given by the value of $n(n + 1)(2n + 1)/6$ at $n = k + 1$.
We have

$$S(k + 1) = \sum_{i=1}^{k+1} i^2 = \sum_{i=1}^{k} i^2 + (k + 1)^2$$

$$= S(k) + (k + 1)^2 = k(k + 1)(2k + 1)/6 + (k + 1)^2$$
$$= (2k^3 + 9k^2 + 13k + 6)/6 = (k + 1)(k + 2)(2k + 3)/6,$$

and the proof by induction is complete.

Example. If $f(m, n)$ is the Ackermann function, prove that $f(1, n) = n + 2$.

i. For $n = 0$, $f(1, 0) = f(0, 1) = 2$ and, thus, the given statement is true for $n = 0$.

ii. Assume that $f(1, k) = k + 2$. We must show that

$$f(1, k + 1) = (k + 1) + 2 = k + 3.$$

We have $f(1, k + 1) = f(0, f(1, k)) = f(0, k + 2) = k + 3$. The stated result is then shown to be true.

Using the result that $f(1, n) = n + 2$, we leave it to the reader to show by induction that $f(2, n) = 2n + 3$.

It can be similarly shown that:

$$f(3, n) = 2^{n+3} - 3$$

$$f(4, n) = \left. 2^{2^{\cdot^{\cdot^{2}}}} \right\}_{n+3} - 3$$

(Note that the first two results can be written to conform with this pattern if we write:

$$f(1, n) = 2(n + 3) - 3$$
$$f(0, n) = 2 + (n + 3) - 3.)$$

The operation of primitive recursion provides the definition of a computable function $f(x)$ when we are given its value at $x = 0$ and have a means of computing $f(x)$ at $k + 1$ if we know the value of $f(x)$ at k. Mathematical induction provides the proof of a theorem involving n when we can prove the theorem to be true at $n = 0$ and can prove that the theorem is true at $n = k + 1$ if it is true at $n = k$.

4.12   THE USE OF ITERATION AS AN ALTERNATIVE TO MINIMALIZATION[1]

A variant of the operation of minimalization that can serve equally well in the definition of the class of partial recursive functions is that of iteration as this has been used by Eilenberg and Elgot [7].

Iteration. Let $f(x), g(x)$ be two partial functions known to have distinct domains (that is, they are never both defined for the same arguments). We form a new function $h(x)$ as follows.

Given an argument x (here, x may represent an n-tuple $(x_1, x_2, \dots, x_n)$), either f or g or neither is defined at x.

---

[1] This section can be omitted on a first reading of this material. It covers a topic not normally included in an elementary treatment of this subject area and probably demands a higher level of mathematical sophistication than most of the topics we discuss. We include it because it will facilitate a proof in Section 5.10.

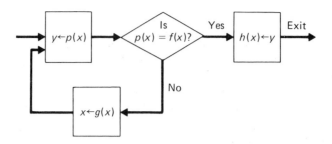

Fig. 4.6   The Eilenberg—Elgot variant of iteration.

Let $f \cup g = p$ denote the function which for a given argument x is equal to $f(x)$ if $f(x)$ is defined, or is equal to $g(x)$ if $g(x)$ is defined. Otherwise, p is undefined at x. We are assured that the definition is unambiguous since f, g have distinct domains. It can be shown, but it is not immediate, that $p(x)$ is partial recursive if $f(x)$, $g(x)$ are partial recursive.

We then define $h(x)$ as follows:

1. If $p(x)$ is defined at x, then if $p(x) = f(x)$ go to (2), else if $p(x) = g(x)$ then go to (3); if $p(x)$ is not defined at x then neither is $h(x)$.

2. $h(x) = f(x)$.

3. Replace x by $g(x)$ and return to (1).

The function $h(x)$ can also be written as $h = f \cup fg \cup fg^2 \cup \ldots \equiv fg^*$. ($g^k$ denotes the function $\overbrace{g(g(\ldots(g(x))\ldots))}^{k \ \ g\text{'s}}$. As noted earlier, it is called the kth iterate of $g(x)$.) $h(x)$ is said to be obtained by iteration from $f(x)$, $g(x)$.

Consider the problem of programming the computation of $p(x)$ with $f(x)$, $g(x)$ being partially computable and not total. If $p(x)$ is defined we must avoid an endless computation of either $f(x)$ or $g(x)$. We can accomplish this by proceeding as follows. Assume that we have procedures available to compute $f(x)$ and $g(x)$. Let these be conducted in parallel, that is, take one or several steps in the computation of $f(x)$, then do the same for $g(x)$ and continue to alternate back and forth between the two procedures for $f(x)$ and $g(x)$ until one or the other terminates. If either procedure terminates, yielding a value of $f(x)$ or of $g(x)$, continue the computation of $h(x)$ with step (2) or with step (3). We are assured that it is not possible for both procedures (for $f(x)$ and for $g(x)$) to terminate for the same argument since the ambiguous situations where both $f(x)$ and $g(x)$ are defined cannot occur.

If a function is obtainable by the operation of minimalization, it is obtainable through the use of iteration. This is quickly seen from the following.

Suppose that $h(x) = \min y[f(y, x) = 0]$ where $f(y, x)$ is a total function of x, y.

Let the function $\varphi(x, y)$ be defined as follows:

$$\varphi(x, y) = \begin{cases} y \text{ if } f(y, x) = 0 \\ \\ \text{undefined if } f(y, x) \neq 0 \end{cases}$$

Let $g(x, y)$ be defined as:

$$g(x, y) = \begin{cases} (x, y + 1) \text{ if } f(y, x) \neq 0 \\ \\ \text{undefined if } f(y, x) = 0 \end{cases}$$

(The range of $g(x, y)$ consists of a set of ordered pairs.)

Thus, $\varphi(x, y)$ and $g(x, y)$ have distinct (complementary) domains. We leave it to the reader to verify that we can then write

$$h(x) = (\varphi \cup \varphi g \cup \varphi g^2 \cup \ldots)(x, 0) = (\varphi g^*)(x, 0).$$

The flowchart of Fig. 4.7 shows the computation of $\varphi g^*(x, 0)$ or, equivalently, of $h(x)$.

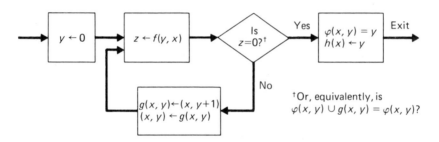

Fig. 4.7   Minimalization viewed as an example of iteration (of the function g).

We can similarly prove the converse, that a function defined by iteration can also be defined by minimalization, but a complete proof will require extensive details (see [7]).

4.13   ON SETS: PRIMITIVE RECURSIVE, RECURSIVE, RECURSIVELY ENUMERABLE

A set is a collection, finite or infinite, of natural numbers or of n-tuples of the natural numbers. We are thus, as noted in Chapter 3, using the word with a more restricted meaning than it has in many parts of mathematics.

Associated with every set, as previously noted, is its characteristic function, that function which for a given argument assumes the value 0 if that argument is in the set, and 1 if it is not. A characteristic function is, then, necessarily total. If the characteristic function is primitive recursive or recursive, we say that the set is, respectively, primitive recursive or recursive.

A larger class of sets is that of the *recursively enumerable* sets. These sets have a generative structure in the sense that each recursively enumerable set is the set of outputs of some computable function.

DEFINITION: *A set is recursively enumerable if it is empty or is the range of some recursive function.*

Note the difference between a recursive set and a recursively enumerable set. Since the characteristic function is recursive or computable when the set is recursive, we are able, given a number, to determine by computing its characteristic function whether or not that argument is in the set. When it is recursively enumerable we may not be able to make such a determination.

In other words, if a set is recursive we can program a computer so that, given an arbitrary argument, the programmed machine will arrive at some conclusion as to whether or not the given argument is in the set. It may be necessary to wait a very long time to make this determination, but we are assured that if we wait long enough a response will be forthcoming as to whether or not the given argument is a member of the prescribed recursive set.

The set of prime numbers is, for example, recursive, for we can easily describe a procedure that will determine if a given argument is prime or not. We can, in a very straightforward manner, divide the given number by $2, 3, 4, \ldots$ trying all numbers up to its square root (that we need not try *all* divisions, but can restrict our inquiry to prime divisors is an obvious saving in efficiency—but we are interested only in the feasibility of the determination procedure). If our search yields no divisors of the given number, that number is, of course, prime.

In the case of a recursively enumerable set we can program a machine to compute successively the members of the set $\{f(0), f(1), f(2), \ldots\}$, and, eventually, every element of the set will appear in its output. However, given an arbitrary number, we cannot, as in the case of a recursive set, be certain of being able to make a determination of whether or not that number is in the set. We may wait a very long time and, perhaps, have our question answered affirmatively by seeing it appear as an output of the computation. However, if the argument is *not* in the set, this negative answer never appears. No matter how long we wait we are never able to abandon our search with assurance that the sought-for argument will not appear in subsequent calculations of the function. In other words, there is a *partial* determination procedure available to answer our question. If the answer is YES, we eventually learn this, but if the answer is NO we can never realize it.

A recursive set is necessarily recursively enumerable. To see this, note that if we have a computational procedure to determine if a given argument is in a particular recursive set, we can modify the procedure so that instead of stopping and giving the answer YES when the argument is in the set, it gives as final result the input argument itself. Also, in those instances where the argument is not in the given set, the procedure is modified to give as output some particular element of the set, and by our assumption there is at least one. The range, then, of the function computed by this procedure is the given recursive set and, therefore, this set is recursively enumerable.

It is not at all easy to give an example of a set that is known to be recursively enumerable but is not recursive. We shall see an example of such a set in Chapter 6 (on the theory of Turing machines). We can perhaps, however, make plausible the fact that being a recursive set is a more demanding condition than being recursively enumerable.

Consider the following function. Let $\psi(x)$ be the smallest number of prime numbers into which x can be partitioned (i.e., the smallest number of prime numbers whose sum is x). The range of this function, since it is obviously programmable, is by definition a recursively enumerable set. Call it S. A famous problem in elementary mathematics, namely Goldbach's conjecture, concerns the question of whether every even number can be expressed as the sum of two primes. It was first posed in 1742, but no one has yet succeeded in solving it completely. Thus, if this conjecture is true, $\psi(2x)$ is equal to 2 for all x (> 1), and S consists of only the number 2.

The range S of $\psi(2x)$ is, by definition, a recursively enumerable set since ψ is a recursive function. The proof that ψ is recursive involves a fair amount of detail if we attempt to show this by generating it using composition and minimalization starting with the three basic recursive functions. However, if we accept Church's thesis, we can argue that since $\psi(2x)$ is obviously a programmable function, then it is recursive.

The range of $\psi(2x)$ is then recursively enumerable, but is it a recursive set? In order to show this, we would have to prove that there is a recursive function which can be used to determine whether or not a given argument is in the range. We do not know how to define such a function. It has been proven by great effort that every even number can be partitioned into not more than 68 prime numbers and, therefore, that no number greater than 68 is in S. However, no one knows at this writing if, for example, 3 is in S and certainly there is no known recursive function that can be used to make this determination for 3 or for any other argument.

The possible—in the sense of conforming to syntactical rules of well-formedness—programs that can be written in any well-defined programming language form a recursively enumerable set. We offer a heuristic argument for this fact. One could program a machine to generate all possible programs with 1 instruction—with 2 instructions— ... and so forth. This set of programs is also recursive; that is, there is a well-defined procedure (effective computation) to determine if a given program is well-formed (see Chapter 9). For, if the program has n instructions, one extravagantly inefficient way of doing this would be to generate all well-formed programs with n instructions and scan this list to determine if the given program is among them.

The set of all theorems in a formal system constitutes a recursively enumerable set (note that here we have a set of character strings, not of numbers). This can be seen by the fact, accepting Church's thesis, that we should be able to describe a mechanical procedure that will churn out all possible theorems. This, under rather general circumstances, can be accomplished by describing a procedure that will go about applying the generating rules, or rules of derivation, starting with the axioms, in all possible ways.

Every reader has studied elementary Euclidean plane geometry and, as noted earlier, has, therefore, seen a prototype of a formal system. However, a good deal of further "formalization" would have to be done before this subject, as it is usually described, would lend itself to such a mechanical theorem-proving procedure. A clearer example for our purpose would be the axiomatic formulation of the propositional calculus, as we have described this in Chapter 2. This schema included four axioms and two rules (substitution and modus ponens) for generating new theorems. It is feasible to write a program that defines a procedure to go about applying these rules to the axioms in all possible ways, generating eventually all possible theorems.

We shall only in the most sketchy way try to make this result credible and generally applicable to formal systems. Thus,

$$A_1, A_3, A_4, G_1(A_1, A_3), G_2(A_3, A_4, G_1(A_1, A_3))$$

might describe the generation of a theorem starting with given axioms A_1, A_3, A_4, and applying certain generating rules G_1, G_2 which take respectively two arguments and three arguments. It will take a lot of work to implement a general procedure of this kind—including substitutions of new arguments for the variables that may appear in the generation scheme—but it can be done.

It is easy to show that any *finite* set of numbers is recursive. All we have to do to program a machine to recognize whether or not a given number is in the set is to store within the machine the numbers in the given set and compare a given argument with each of these stored numbers.

4.14   ON STRUCTURED PROGRAMMING

We shall touch briefly on the mathematical ideas that underlie the technique of structured programming, a discipline for writing programs that has been recently advocated, principally by Dijkstra (cf. [2, 4, 5, 6, 8]), in order to facilitate program development and to minimize programming errors. One key point is the argument [4] that the unbridled use of GO TO's or TRANSFER's in programming leads often to a program with an excessively complex and tortured logical flow, and this makes errors likely and debugging difficult. We have, however, seen that a rather elegant scheme is available to describe the generation of all (accepting Church's thesis) computable functions. That is, we can describe the computation of every such function by starting with a very small number of primitive functions and by cascading, in proper sequence, the repeated application of a very few fundamental operations—composition and minimalization, or composition and iteration. We have also seen that composition and primitive recursion suffice for almost all computable functions that occur in practice.

In looking at the flowchart for the generation of a function such as in Fig. 4.8(a), we do not see an intricate, tortured flow of the kind that might appear in a program that made use of different kinds of atomic steps, especially GO TO operations (Fig. 4.8(b)). Note, in fact, that there are *fewer* processing blocks in Fig. 4.8(b), but Fig. 4.8(a) seems less complicated. In particular, with no GO TO's, the flow is straightforward; the intermediate functions needed in the process are developed using one or the other of the basic operations. Finally, the output function is realized after the necessary preliminary functions have been generated. All of this seems to lend credence to the fact that we can avoid unduly contrived situations in planning program development. We shall not, however, use the schema for the generation of the recursive functions.

It is the idea of repeatedly applying a few simple operations that is exploited in the method of structured programming. This technique is, perhaps, best described as a method for composing, by successive refinements, flowcharts that make use of a very small number of basic building blocks. Flowcharts appear in computing in many ways, often with unclearly specified conventions. In particular, when a directed line joins two parts of a flowchart it may, on occasion, denote a sequencing of events, or a moving of data, or both. We shall assume in the following that a directed line joining two parts of a flowchart indicates not necessarily a moving of data but rather specifies an ordering in time of the sequence of steps involved in the execution of the process. Thus, a self-contained segment of a flowchart will have just one input line and one output line. We shall allow lines to merge, but not split (except through decision boxes).

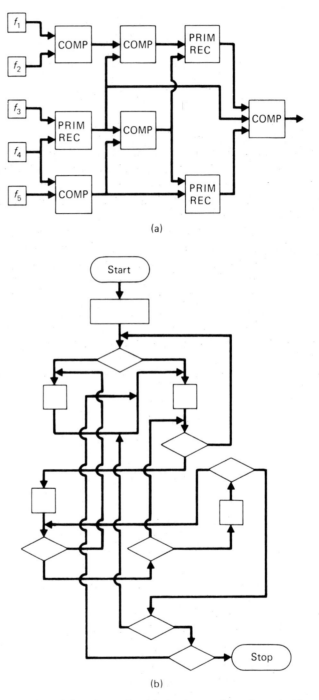

(a)

(b)

Fig. 4.8 Examples of flowcharts for (a) the generation of a primitive recursive function, (b) a procedure with unrestricted use of transfer instructions.

Three basic building blocks are used in composing structured flow-charts. These are:

1. the sequencing of two processes:

2. the conditional test or the "if then else":

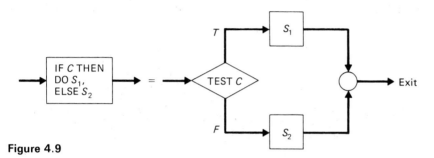

Figure 4.9

3. the "do while":

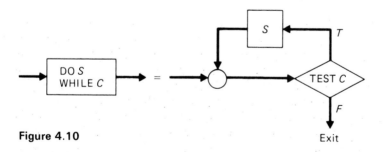

Figure 4.10

Since each of the three building blocks or elements has one input line and one exit line, we can describe in recursive terms the generation of complex flowchart structures from these elements. Every block that denotes a process (the rectangular blocks in the preceding) can be replaced in turn by one of the building blocks, or more generally by a flowchart with one input and one output. (We leave it to the reader to describe this class of flowcharts by an extended BNF that applies to flowcharts in a manner analogous to the application of the BNF notation to sequences of symbols.) The primitive processes in this development can be taken to be the three basic functions $N(x) = 0$, $S(x) = x + 1$, $U_i^{(n)}(x_1, x_2, \ldots, x_n) \doteq x_i$, and the primitive condition can be taken as $x = y$.

The adequacy of the three building blocks to express any computing process whatsoever is demonstrated if we show how to perform the fundamental operations of recursive function theory using them.

Composition (Fig. 4.1) is a direct example of the "sequence" operation and it is so described in Fig. 4.11. Minimalization (Fig. 4.5) is easily described in terms of the "do while" operation as we see in Fig. 4.12.

Fig. 4.11   Composition in terms of the "sequence" operation

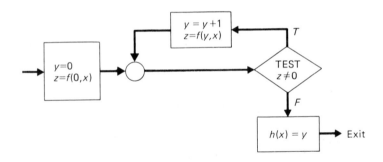

Fig. 4.12   Minimalization using the "do while."

Primitive recursion (Fig. 4.13) and iteration can similarly be easily expressed in terms of the basic building blocks.

We have defined both minimalization and primitive recursion in terms of the "do while." However, pursuant to our earlier remarks, note the difference in its use in these two cases. In primitive recursion an ordinary do loop can be used in program execution. We know at the entry to the loop that it is to be executed x times. In the case of minimalization nothing is known in general, at the entry to the loop, of the number of times the loop will be executed. In the "do while" search for a zero of $f(y, x)$ we are not even

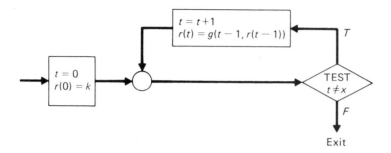

Fig. 4.13 Primitive recursion (defining a function, $r(x)$, of a single argument) using the "do while."

assured in the general case that the search will eventually terminate (the function being computed may not be total).

Thus, there is no question of the universal applicability of these building blocks. The technique of structured programming is then applied by first describing an algorithm and using processing blocks in the flowchart with rather sweeping functional specifications that indicate what the program is to accomplish. Then, by successive refinements the processing blocks are replaced by nested equivalent flowcharts of greater and greater detail until the implementation of the program becomes routine.

EXERCISES

4.1 Show that the following functions of nonnegative integers are primitive recursive:

a. $f(x) = 3x^2 + 5x \doteq 2$

b. $g(n) = 10^n$

c. $\begin{cases} F(n) = 1^3 + 2^3 + 3^3 + \ldots + n^3 \text{ for } n \geq 1 \\ F(0) = 0 \end{cases}$

4.2 If x, y are nonnegative integers and x is divided by y ($\neq 0$), we get a quotient $Q(x, y)$ and a remainder $R(x, y)$, where $R(x, y) < y$, satisfying the equation

$$\frac{x}{y} = Q(x, y) + \frac{R(x, y)}{y}.$$

Show that both $Q(x, y)$ and $R(x, y)$ are recursive functions. (Show that each can be obtained by composition and/or minimalization from functions already shown to be primitive recursive.)

4.3 Assume that a PL/I (or other suitable programming language) subroutine FUNCT(X, Y) exists. Write a segment of code that defines a new function subroutine, $H(X)$, defined by:

$$H(X) = \min \; Y \; (\text{FUNCT} \; (X, \; Y) = 0).$$

4.4 Show that the functions $p = \max(x, y)$, $q = \min(x, y)$ are primitive recursive.

4.5 Let $f(x)$ be defined by:

$$f(x) = \begin{cases} x^2 \text{ if } x \text{ is even} \\ x + 1 \text{ if } x \text{ is odd} \end{cases}$$

Show that $f(x)$ is primitive recursive.

4.6 Show that if $g(x_1, x_2)$ is primitive recursive and if $f(x_1, x_2) = g(x_2, x_1)$ then $f(x_1, x_2)$ is also primitive recursive.

4.7 a. Show that the function $y = [\sqrt{x}]$ (the greatest integer contained in $\sqrt{x}$) is primitive recursive.

  b. Show that $y = [x/3]$ is primitive recursive.

4.8 Describe the class of functions that is generated by starting with the three basic functions: $S(x)$, $N(x)$, $U_i^{(n)} (x_1, x_2, \ldots, x_n)$ and using repeatedly only the operation of composition in all possible ways.

4.9 If $f_0, f_1, f_2, \ldots$ is an enumeration of all singularly (one argument) primitive recursive functions, prove that the binary function $f_x(y)$ of the arguments x, y is *not* primitive recursive.

4.10 Let $f(x)$ be defined by the equations:

$$\begin{cases} f(0) = 1 \\ f(1) = 3 \\ f(x + 2) = (x + 2) \cdot f(x) \text{ for } x > 1 \end{cases}$$

Show that $f(x)$ is recursive.

4.11 If $f(m, n)$ denotes the Ackermann function, compute $f(2, 2)$ by following the flowchart of Fig. 4.4.

4.12 We have proved by induction that $f(1, n) = n + 2$ where $f(m, n)$ is the Ackermann function. Show, similarly, that:

  a. $f(2, n) = 2n + 3$

  b. $f(3, n) = 2^{n+3} - 3$

  c. $f(4, n) = \underbrace{2^{2^{\cdot^{\cdot^{2}}}}}_{n+3} - 3$

4.13 If $f(m, n)$ is the Ackermann function, show that the function $f(x, x)$ is not primitive recursive.

Outline of proof: Let $\varphi(x_1, x_2, \ldots, x_n)$ be an arbitrary primitive recursive function. Show first:

A: There is some number M, depending only on φ, such that

$$\varphi(x_1, x_2, \ldots, x_n) < f(M, \max(x_1, x_2, \ldots, x_n)) \text{ for all } x_1, x_2, \ldots, x_n.$$

Prove A by showing: (1) it is true for the three basic primitive recursive functions $S(x)$, $N(x)$, $U_i^{(n)}(x_1, x_2, \ldots, x_n)$, (2) $f(m, n)$ is increasing in each argument, (3) if a set of functions satisfy property A, then any function formed from them by composition or primitive recursion satisfies A.

Thus, if $\varphi(x)$ is an arbitrary primitive recursive function of a single argument there is some number M such that $\varphi(x) < f(M, x)$ for all x. If $f(x, x)$ is primitive recursive, we can let $\varphi(x)$ be $f(x, x)$ in this inequality. Letting $x = M$, we have a contradiction, and therefore $f(x, x)$ is not primitive recursive.

4.14 Show that if $f(x)$ is a recursive function satisfying $f(n) < f(n + 1)$, then the range of $f(x)$ is a recursive set.

4.15 Assume a stored program computer with only one arithmetic register, an accumulator, and only the following three machine operations:

TR + A: Transfer to location A if the contents of the accumulator are positive.
ADD A: Add the contents of location A to the contents of the accumulator.
STO A: Store the contents of the accumulator, without clearing it, in location A.

Suppose that there is an unlimited store in the machine (or at least that it is as big as we need for any given application), and that the word size is also as big as may be needed. Assume, also, that any needed constants like $0, +1, -1$ are stored permanently in certain fixed locations.

Show that, accepting Church's thesis, this very limited instruction repertoire is adequate to perform any computation whatsoever. A function of N arguments is computed by setting up its arguments in, say, locations $1, 2, 3, \ldots, N$ and putting the result in location $N + 1$. It suffices to prove that the three basic functions can be computed on this machine, and that functions obtained by composition, primitive recursion, minimalization from machine computable functions are, themselves, machine computable.

4.16 Write a program in any suitable language that will generate and emit as output all the prime numbers. Assume that the word size of the machine is unlimited. This result, then, implies that the prime numbers form a recursively enumerable set.

4.17 Write a program in any suitable language that will generate and emit as output all possible pairs of the natural numbers. Assume that the word size is unlimited.

4.18 Write a program in any suitable language that will generate and emit as output all possible programs for the machine of Exercise 4.15, i.e., all possible programs formed from the operations TR +, ADD, STO. Again assume an unlimited word size.

4.19 Show that the operation of iteration (as described by Fig. 4.6) can be obtained from the "sequence," "if then else," and "do while" operations of structured programming.

4.20 Show that the "sequence," "if then else," and "do while" operations of structured programming are describable in terms of the operations of composition, primitive recursion, and minimalization.

4.21 Describe, as implied possible in the text, the class of flowcharts formed from the basic building blocks of structured programming using an extended BNF applicable to flowcharts.

4.22 Show that the iterative algorithm for the computation of $\sqrt{N}$ approximately doubles, with each iterate, the number of correct decimal places in the approximation to $\sqrt{N}$.

REFERENCES

1. Ackermann, W., "On Hilbert's Construction of the Real Numbers," 1928. Translated by Stefan Bauer-Mengelberg in *From Frege to Gödel*. Edited by Jean van Heijenoort. Cambridge: Harvard University Press, 1967.

2. Dahl, O. J., E. W. Dijkstra, and C. A. R. Hoare, *Structured Programming*. New York: Academic Press, 1972.

3. Davis, M., *Computability and Unsolvability*. New York: McGraw-Hill, 1958.

4. Dijkstra, E. W., "GO TO Statement Considered Harmful." *Comm. Assn. Comp. Mach.* **11**, 3 (March 1968).

5. Dijkstra, E. W., "Structured Programming," in *Software Engineering Techniques*. Ed. J. N. Burton and B. Randell. NATO Science Committee, 1969; pp. 88–94.

6. Dijkstra, E. W., *Notes on Structured Programming*. Technological University Eindhoven, The Netherlands, Department of Mathematics, April 1970.

7. Eilenberg, S., and C. C. Elgot, *Recursiveness*. New York: Academic Press, 1970.

8. Linger, R. C., H. D. Mills, and B. I. Witt, *Structured Programming*. Reading, Massachusetts: Addison-Wesley, 1979.

9. Rogers, H. Jr., *Theory of Recursive Functions and Effective Computability*. New York: McGraw-Hill, 1967.

5
Turing Machines and Computability

The English mathematician Alan M. Turing proposed in 1936 that a certain class of ideal machines, now called Turing machines, be considered as computing devices. Although these machines are of the utmost simplicity, it appears that any effectively computable function, no matter how complex it may be, can be computed by a machine in this class if that machine can use as much time and auxiliary storage as may be needed; this statement is known as Turing's thesis. In particular, we can define a certain machine in the class that can simulate any other machine in the class and thus, we believe, compute any effectively computable function. This machine, called the universal Turing machine, is the theoretical prototype of real general purpose computers.

This model of the computing process predated by several years the first large general purpose programmable computing machines, and it has had a profound impact on many areas of computer science. In fact, the fundamental idea of using a programming language that differs from the machine language of the computer which interprets that programming language appears, in essence, in Turing's work. The importance of his ideas may be judged in part by the fact that the annual award of the Association for Computing Machinery for outstanding contributions to computer science is named after Turing.

We see in this chapter that the class of functions that can be defined by Turing machines is the same as the class of partial recursive functions defined in the last chapter. Therefore, the two approaches are equally satisfactory in making precise the notion of an effectively computable function.

However, Turing's approach, with its machine orientation, provides a better model for real computers than the more abstract mathematical framework of recursive function theory.

5.1 MOTIVATIONS UNDERLYING TURING MACHINES

In our discussion of the theory of recursive functions we took a very formal approach in giving a precise meaning to the vague notion of an effectively computable function. There does not seem to be much of heuristic value in the schema we used to define the general recursive functions, and there appears little that might have been motivated by our intuitive impressions of effective procedures. We shall now take another quite different approach toward defining sharply the class of effectively computable functions. This approach will involve the employment of certain highly simplified and idealized machines whose capabilities will be used to give meaning to the notion of effective computability. That is, we shall deal with processes that are machine-like and that therefore bear some resemblance to our use of real computers. However, the device that we shall employ, the Turing machine, will be, in a sense, stripped down to its essentials. It will, it is true, be a computer of sorts but one vastly less efficient and, in compensation, less complex than a modern computer. Any manufacturer who would market such a machine would fail in short order. In order to appreciate the motivation underlying the prescription of this device it is worth reviewing briefly the notions brought out by Turing in his fundamental paper of 1936, "On Computable Numbers With an Application to the Entscheidungsproblem" [5], where he formulates the device that today we call a Turing machine. We shall see that he was guided in part by certain rudimentary impressions of human mental processes.

Turing considered the process of computation as performed by a human and by stripping away the superfluous and extraneous by, in a sense, distilling the situation to its core, he arrived at the fundamental characteristics of these machines. Consider, using the analogy of Rogers [4], a man seated in a room and performing some prescribed computation, defined for given input data, using pencil and paper. Let us suppose that the room has a window in it to permit input information to be given to him on sheets of paper and to allow him to transmit his results in similar form. Assume that he has available to him an unlimited supply of scratch paper to use in the course of his calculations or, better—for the room would be rather crowded with this supposition—that additional paper will be brought to him whenever he needs it. If he accumulates such prodigious intermediate results during the course of the computation that they cannot be accommodated in the room, we shall store these partial results for him outside the room and furnish them to him when he needs them. Suppose that our human computer has been instructed beforehand about the procedure he is to execute when we provide him with input data. He, however, knows no mathematics beyond the most elementary arithmetic operations and knows no shortcuts or deviations from the prescriptions given him.

Let us analyze this situation and try to break it down into atomic steps. We first have the problem of providing input data to our human computer in camera. Consider the sheets of paper we pass through the window to him and that he uses in the course of his calculations. It is helpful, and in no way restrictive, in making our conceptions precise if we assume that he uses paper divided into squares, like graph paper, and that he always writes any character in one of the squares. Does this paper have to be two-dimensional or can we replace it by a one-dimensional equivalent? That is, can we assume a strip or tape divided into squares instead of the two-dimensional arrays of squares on the sheets? The feasibility of doing this is, perhaps, suggested by the fact that we can form an image on a TV screen by scanning the picture over horizontal, or other, lines. If our human computer has sufficient memory, he can then dispense with the two-dimensional format. To avoid requiring him to remember too much, let us permit him to jot down on scratch paper anything he needs to remember. He can then always refer back to this written record when demands on his memory become excessive.

Next, consider the kinds of operations he might perform in the course of the calculations, keeping in mind that he has memorized the procedure that he has been taught to apply. We shall, of course, allow him to write down a statement of this procedure if it is excessively long. Suppose, for example, that he must multiply two multi-digit numbers. In the course of doing this he must perform, say, the partial product 8×7. He reads the 8, he reads the 7 and knows that he must write down a 6, shift one digit position, add the carry of 5, and so forth. To use language that generalizes and at the same time somewhat simplifies this further, we might say that when he is in a certain mental *state*, namely, knowing that he is at a particular point in the multiplication process, he reads an 8 and a 7 and enters another mental *state*, that which dictates his writing a 6 and remembering a carry of 5. On occasion he may erase a character he has written and replace it by another. He may go back and forth on the paper and make reference to, or change, earlier obtained results. If he needs more paper, additional blank paper will be provided him.

These are the things he does—replaces symbols by symbols (including erasing since the blank is considered to be one of the possible symbols), moves to other parts of the paper and at different times invokes some one of a fixed number of small "subroutines." We consider this last operation to be that of entering some mental state. Some fixed number of symbols will always suffice for all purposes and, for any particular algorithmic process, some finite number of states of mind will be adequate. Turing gave an interesting, but perhaps not completely convincing, argument against an infinitude of such mental states. He wrote that "if we admitted an infinity of states of mind, some of them will be arbitrarily close and will be confused." He offered a similar reason for not allowing an infinite alphabet of symbols–that some of them would be blurred if there were too many of them.

Turing then constructs a machine that will do the work of our human computer by enabling it to perform the atomic steps implied by the above considerations. It is interesting to note that at about the same time (1936), and independently of Turing, the American mathematician Emil Post, also seeking to give a formal explication of effectiveness based on an understanding of what takes place in the human brain, arrived at a similar formulation of a machine ("Finite Combinatory Processes, Formulation I" [3]). Post's very brief description, however, is more suggestive than substantive and omits most of the details necessary to a complete description of the

230   A. M. Turing   [Nov. 12,

ON COMPUTABLE NUMBERS, WITH AN APPLICATION TO
THE ENTSCHEIDUNGSPROBLEM

By A. M. Turing.

[Received 28 May, 1936.—Read 12 November, 1936.]

The "computable" numbers may be described briefly as the real numbers whose expressions as a decimal are calculable by finite means. Although the subject of this paper is ostensibly the computable *numbers*, it is almost equally easy to define and investigate computable functions of an integral variable or a real or computable variable, computable predicates, and so forth. The fundamental problems involved are, however, the same in each case, and I have chosen the computable for explicit treatment as involving the least cumbrous technique. I hope shortly to give an account of the relations of the computable numbers, functions and so forth to one another. This will include a development of the theory of functions of a real variable expressed in terms of computable numbers. According to my definition, a number is computable if its decimal can be written down by a machine.

In § § 9, 10 I give some arguments with the intention of showing that the computable numbers include all numbers which could naturally be regarded as computable. In particular, I show that certain large classes of numbers are computable. They include, for instance, the real parts of all algebraic numbers, the real parts of the zeros of the Bessel functions, the numbers π, e, etc. The computable numbers do not, however, include all definable numbers, and an example is given of a definable number which is not computable.

Although the class of computable numbers is so great, and in many ways similar to the class of real numbers, it is nevertheless enumerable. In § 8 I examine certain arguments which would seem to prove the contrary. By the correct application of one of these arguments, conclusions are reached which are superficially similar to those of Gödel†. These results

† Gödel, "Über formal unentscheidbare Sätze der Principia Mathematica und verwandter Systeme, I", *Monatshefte Math. Phys.*, 38 (1931), 173–198.

Fig. 5.1   Allan Turing and the first page of his fundamental paper of 1936.

behavior of the machine. Nevertheless, there are those who believe that the machine we discuss should be called a *Post-Turing* machine in recognition of Post's fundamental contributions. This is yet another of the innumerable examples in the sciences of several individuals arriving at about the same time and independently of each other at the same key idea leading to the solution of a significant theoretical problem.

5.2 ORGANIZATION OF A TURING MACHINE

We now describe the salient characteristics of a Turing machine. These will differ slightly from Turing's original specifications, conforming more closely to modern expositions of the theory.

1. The machine includes a potentially infinite, in both directions, linear tape divided into boxes and read by a read head that scans one box at a time. At any given time the tape is finite, but there is no automatic recognition of the physical ends of the tape. It is potentially infinite in the sense that we assume that a blank square will be appended to the tape whenever needed, when the tape would, otherwise, be pulled through the read head. This corresponds to our assumption that an unlimited supply of paper was available to our human computer.

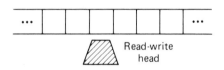

Fig. 5.2   Turing machine tape.

2. Symbols written on the tape are drawn from a *finite* alphabet: $S_0, S_1, S_2, \ldots, S_p$. Usually, S_0 is taken to be the blank B, and S_1 to be the unit 1. One of the basic theorems of the theory states that an alphabet with only *two* characters, B and 1, will suffice in designing a machine to compute any function. This theorem attests to the universality of binary machines; they are just as powerful as decimal machines. (N.B. In a binary machine the 0 bit is the same as the blank B.)

3. The control or processing unit of the machine (thinking of the tape as a peripheral attachment) can assume one of a *finite* number of distinct internal

states or configurations: $q_1, q_2, q_3, \ldots, q_m$. As in the case of the alphabet, it can be shown that we can always design a machine to do what we want that employs only two states, but at the expense of an expanded alphabet. The internal state of a machine completely determines how the machine responds to a symbol being read on the tape.

The "program" for a given machine is assumed to be built in and consists of a set of instructions in the form of *quintuples* which are defined below. A clock is an integral part of the machine, and at each time step the machine executes that one of its quintuples which may apply to the state of the machine and the symbol being read. A particular Turing machine is, then, to be thought of as being comparable to a real computer with a stored program in its memory. Each machine defines one particular mathematical function on input data provided on its tape, rather than being able to compute an arbitrary function. We shall, however, later introduce a *universal* Turing machine which can receive as part of its input data a description of any other Turing machine and then, by simulating the behavior of that machine, compute the same function as the machine it is simulating would do.

Each quintuple $(q_i S_j S_k R q_l, q_i S_j S_k L q_l,$ or $q_i S_j S_k N q_l)$ defines the action of the machine when it is in a particular state reading a particular character. Its format is interpreted as follows:

q_i	S_j	S_k	$R, L,$ or N	q_l
The machine in this state,	reading this symbol on the tape,	will replace it by this symbol,	move to the square on the right (R), or left (L), or not at all (N),	then enter this state.

Here q_l may be the same as q_i and S_k the same as S_j. The behavior of the machine, beginning from some starting position on a given tape, is completely determined by its initial state and by the set of quintuples which are built in. Normally, we shall assume that the initial state of a Turing machine is q_1. With this understanding the machine *is*, in a sense, its set of quintuples, for these specify unequivocally its behavior. It is generally recognized in computing practice that software can be converted into hardware, and conversely. The interchangeability of the two is made striking in Turing's formulation, but there are those who believe that it would have been better if Turing had looked at a set of quintuples as a *program* rather than as a definition of a *machine*.

5.3 THE USE OF TURING MACHINES TO COMPUTE FUNCTIONS

The result of a machine's computation is obtained from the information on its tape if and when the machine stops. That the machine may not stop at all is easily seen. Suppose the two quintuples

$$q_1\, S_2\, S_2\, R\, q_3 \text{ and } q_3\, B\, B\, L\, q_1$$

both appear in the machine, and the read head is positioned as shown on the tape in Fig. 5.3 while the machine is in state q_1.

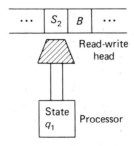

Figure 5.3

It is easily recognized that in this situation the machine will seesaw interminably between the two squares shown.

We have two choices in determining how the machine will stop. We can either introduce a special STOP, or quiescent, state q_ω which has no successor states under any conditions (i.e., no quintuple begins with q_ω), or we can say that the machine will stop when it is in state q_i scanning symbol S_j if it contains no quintuple beginning $q_i S_j$. We shall adopt the former convention. A little thought will show that the difference between the two conventions is insubstantial. We can always, with slight modifications, go from a machine that does not have a special stop state to a machine that employs one, as implied by one of the exercises.

There is one important restriction in writing down the quintuples of a machine to perform some task. We cannot include two quintuples which are contradictory in that they instruct the machine to do two different things under the same conditions. This would occur if we were to allow two different quintuples with the same two starting symbols $q_i S_j$. If, for example, the two quintuples

$$q_2\, S_3\, S_2\, R\, q_3 \text{ and } q_2\, S_3\, B\, L\, q_1$$

both appear in the machine, the situation will be ambiguous when the machine is in state q_2 scanning S_3 on its tape. If we allowed the machine to follow, in random fashion, one or the other of the two quintuples, it would not have the deterministic behavior that we expect of an effective procedure.

With these assumptions, then, a given Turing machine, i.e., a given set of quintuples, will act to transform in some manner a particular starting tape made up of characters drawn from its alphabet. Starting in the specified initial state, it defines a particular function on tapes with designated starting squares, mapping initial tapes into final tapes and final read head positions. The map or function is defined for a given starting tape and starting position if the machine eventually stops after starting on the tape. If it never stops because it enters an endless loop in moving over some finite segment of the tape, or because it extends without limit the tape, the map or function for that machine is undefined for that starting tape and starting position.

Consider, for example, the machine consisting of the two quintuples,

$$\{q_1 \ 1 \ 1 \ R \ q_1, \ q_1 \ B \ 1 \ R \ q_2\},$$

and employing as alphabet the two characters $\{B, 1\}$. Assume that the machine starts in state q_1 and that q_2 is the STOP state.

It is clear that this machine will, when it starts on some particular 1 in a tape made up of blanks and 1's, move to the right to find the first blank. It will then change this blank to a 1, move one square to the right and stop.

On the other hand, the machine that uses the same alphabet and consists of

$$\{q_1 \ 1 \ 1 \ R \ q_2, \ q_2 \ B \ B \ L \ q_1, \ q_2 \ 1 \ 1 \ L \ q_1\}$$

will, when it starts on a 1, go immediately into an endless loop moving back and forth between its starting square and the one to the right.

5.4 THE INSTANTANEOUS DESCRIPTION OF A TURING MACHINE

Consider the problem of interrupting the operation of a Turing machine when it is about to begin the execution of some particular quintuple and recording that information needed to resume the computation at some later time—that is, all the information that completely determines the subsequent course of the machine's actions. The analogous problem for real computers has been frequently studied in setting up backup and recovery procedures. These are of special importance when there is concern about the possible failure of a computer system during a very lengthy data processing task, or in situations where it is necessary to anticipate system interrupts to allow execution of a high priority job. In the case of Turing machines, the problem has a simple solution. All we need record at the given instant are (1) the internal state of the machine, (2) the list of symbols that are written on the tape, and (3) the identity of the tape square currently being scanned by the read head.

We can encode all of this information in a string of symbols as follows. Suppose the machine is in state q_3, that the information on the tape is $S_2 S_1 S_2 S_0 S_2 S_3 S_1$, and that the read head is positioned over the third square from the left. We represent all of this information by writing

$$S_2 S_1 q_3 S_2 S_0 S_2 S_3 S_1$$

The position of q_3, just before the symbol that is about to be read, indicates the location of the read head. Such a string of tape symbols together with one state symbol constitutes an "instantaneous description" of a Turing machine. If we omit the state symbol, the resulting string is the *tape description* alone.

If a machine eventually stops after starting in some initial instantaneous description, ID_i, we can consider the terminal instantaneous description, ID_t, to be the "result" of the computation. The machine effects a transformation, or mapping, from instantaneous descriptions into instantaneous descriptions: $ID_i \rightarrow ID_t$. In fact, every single quintuple determines a partial function on instantaneous descriptions. For example, the quintuple $q_2 S_2 S_3 R q_1$ causes the instantaneous description $S_3 S_4 S_0 q_2 S_2 S_1 S_1$ on a particular machine to be succeeded by $S_3 S_4 S_0 S_3 q_1 S_1 S_1$. A computation on a Turing machine proceeds as an eventually terminating sequence of instantaneous descriptions, as determined by its quintuples. If the machine does not eventually stop, no computation is defined.

A machine "snapshot," as this term is used on real machines, is analogous to the instantaneous description of a Turing machine. A snapshot includes all information of interest to the programmer in determining, at a designated point during a computation, what transformations the program has accomplished at that point in its execution. It includes much of the information that would be needed to resume the computation at that point.

5.5   REPRESENTATION OF INPUT AND OUTPUT DATA

In order, now, to use a Turing machine to compute a mathematical function, we must indicate how the input data will be encoded on the starting tape or is mapped into the initial instantaneous description, and also how the output will be represented on the final tape or how the terminal instantaneous

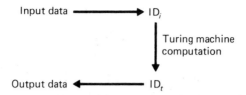

Fig. 5.4   The encoding of input data and the decoding of the output.

description is mapped into the output data (Fig. 5.4). For these purposes we adopt the following conventions for the representation of input and output data.

1. We shall use the most primitive of all notational schemes to represent numbers—the unary system which employs only one symbol, 1, and represents numbers as strings of 1's.

   An input argument, m, will be represented on the input tape as a string of $m + 1$ 1's. Letting $\overline{m}$ be the machine tape representation of m, we have

$$\overline{5} = 111111$$
$$\overline{0} = 1$$

If we were to use m 1's instead of $m + 1$ 1's to represent the number m, then 0 would have to be represented by the blank B in a binary Turing machine. This would prevent our using B as a spacer, which is an essential element in any data representation scheme.

   An n-tuple of input arguments will be represented on the input tape as the n-tuple of the representations of the individual arguments, separated by intervening blanks. That is,

$$\overline{(m_1, m_2, \ldots, m_n)} = \overline{m}_1 B \overline{m}_2 B \ldots B \overline{m}_n$$

   Usually, but not always, we shall assume that a machine starts in state q_1 with the read head over the leftmost 1. The initial instantaneous description, then, of a machine with the n-tuple $(m_1, m_2, \ldots, m_n)$ on its starting tape is:

$$\bigstar\, q_1 \overline{m}_1 B \overline{m}_2 B \ldots B \overline{m}_n\, \bigstar$$

where the asterisks are special end-of-tape marks (cf. below).

2. We shall assume an equivalent representation scheme for the output data. Some authors [1] take the result of a computation to be the number of 1's appearing on, and possibly scattered over, the tape when a machine stops, but the reasons for deviating from the input format are not compelling. The

advantage of taking the number of 1's on the final tape as the result is that, then, *every* Turing machine defines some partial function on n given arguments. It can be shown, however (see the exercises), that any machine employing the more relaxed output representation can be replaced by one that gives its results in the same format as is used for the input data.

By using the same formats for both input and output we admit the possibility of the result of a computation being an n-tuple of numbers. We further assume that the final read head position is over the leftmost 1 on the tape.

In fact, one might be made a little uneasy if the result of a calculation is taken to be simply the number of 1's on the final tape, where the 1's are scattered, and no end-of-tape marks are used. For, the external observer who tallies these 1's is then tacitly recognizing the ends of the tape, a function that the machine cannot perform (see the remarks under Section 5.7, 1. "Searching for a symbol on the tape").

5.6　ADDITIONAL CONVENTIONS

Our schemes for the representation of input and output data now enable us to consider the problem of defining Turing machines to compute various mathematical functions. Before doing this, however, we shall impose additional conventions on the Turing machines that we shall design (by listing their quintuples) to perform various functions. These conventions, as well as those already given, are essentially the same as, but deviate slightly from, those that Davis [1] stipulates for what he calls "regular" Turing machines. The principal purpose of imposing these conventions is to facilitate composing or "tying" machines together. Suppose that a particular machine Y is available to perform some desired transformation on the data appearing on a machine tape or, equivalently, on instantaneous descriptions. It may be very convenient in designing another machine Z if it is possible to take advantage of the existence of Y. That is, by entering some state, say q_α, in the course of its computation, Z will start simulating Y. The computation on Z can then continue from the point at which Y would have stopped. In other words, we might want to make use of Y as a "subroutine."

3. With this goal in mind it will be helpful for us to employ special end-of-tape marks to signal the two squares at the two ends of the tape. We shall use the asterisk ✶ for this purpose. As was pointed out earlier, however, nothing prevents our moving beyond these end-of-tape marks because of the assumption that a blank square will always be appended to the tape when it would otherwise be pulled through the read head. If, therefore, we wish to

extend the tape, we can execute small "routines" such as

$$q_i \ast B R q_l, \ q_l B \ast L q_i$$

or

$$q_i \ast B L q_l, \ q_l B \ast R q_i$$

which erase the end-of-tape marks and move them to the right or to the left.

4. We shall often assume, as indicated above, that the start state of a machine is q_1. Note, however, that a renumbering of the states of a machine will certainly have no effect on its operation. In particular, if all state indices of a given Turing machine Z are increased by the same amount, so that q_1 becomes q_α, then the machine with renamed states, starting in state q_α, will have the same behavior as Z. In general, we shall assume that all the state indices i of a regular Turing machine lie in the interval $\alpha \le i \le \omega$ where q_α is the START state and q_ω is the STOP state. As indicated, q_ω has no successor state under any conditions, for no quintuple of Z begins with q_ω.

We shall require further that when Z stops in state q_ω the read head will be situated over the leftmost 1 on the tape. Thus, the configuration of the tape and the read head when the machine stops conforms to the standard starting configuration, and the machine is in a sense "ready" to start a new computation.

5. If a machine does not stop after starting on some input tape, the partial function determined by the machine will be undefined for the input argument(s) represented on the tape.

We shall say that a Turing machine that satisfies conventions 1–5 is a *regular* Turing machine.

If a function is partial recursive, it can be computed on some (regular) Turing machine. With the stated conventions, every regular Turing machine defines, for every m, a partial function of m arguments. If the result given by an arbitary Turing machine is taken simply to be the number of 1's on its output tape, it can be replaced, as we have indicated, by a regular Turing machine that computes the same function. It turns out that the class of functions defined by all Turing machines is precisely the class of partial recursive functions. We shall not give the proof of this fact in complete detail but shall give it in a manner sufficient to demonstrate the plausibility of the result.

A demonstration of the fact that every partial recursive function is computable by some (regular) Turing machine might proceed along the following lines:

1. Show that each of the three basic recursive functions, $S(x) = x + 1$, $N(x) = 0$, $U_i^{(n)}(x_1, x_2, \ldots, x_n) = x_i$, can be computed by some regular Turing machine.

2. Show that if we form new functions from Turing machine computable functions by using any one of the operations of composition, primitive recursion and minimalization, the new functions so formed will be Turing machine computable.

Since every partial recursive function is obtainable from the basic recursive functions by some finite number of applications of the operations of composition, primitive recursion, and minimalization, it will follow from 1 and 2 that every such function is Turing machine computable.

The proofs of 1 and 2 are exercises in programming, and the techniques that must be employed are recognizable to any programmer versed in (real) machine language programming. In every case we must construct a machine to do the required job, and this construction, or writing of the quintuples, is an act of programming. Unless otherwise stated, it will be assumed in the sequel that the machines we use are binary, i.e., they use the alphabet $\{B, 1\}$ except for the end-of-tape mark $\ast$. (As previously noted, however, even this special symbol can be dispensed with at the expense of adding more quintuples.)

The act of designing a Turing machine by specifying its built-in program of quintuples is, perhaps, the ultimate in machine language programming and bears a close resemblance to microprogramming. With no complex or extended operations available, everything takes place in a binary Turing machine at the bit level—that is, all functions must be computed by taking steps that involve one bit at a time. It is true that our procedures lack any parallelism or other efficiency—there being no built-in composite operations, not even the fundamental arithmetic operations. There is, however, one aspect of generality that is obtained as a compensation for the extremely simplistic approach to machine processing that we take. That is, our procedures will work on operands of completely arbitrary length. The handling of multiprecision arithmetic operations on a modern computer is not a trivial task and some practical bound exists on the lengths of operands and results, even if unlimited secondary storage is assumed. But the Turing machines we shall define will handle operands of any length whatsoever. Our procedures will never assume any upper bound on the lengths of the strings of bits that represent in unary notation the arguments, intermediate computed quantities, or results in a calculation.

Let us take the first step in the proof, that of showing that the successor function, $S(x) = x + 1$, is Turing machine computable.

Assuming the initial state to be q_1, we must design a machine that will transform the initial instantaneous description corresponding to the argument m

$$\bigstar \, q_1 \, \overline{m} \, \bigstar$$

into the terminal instantaneous description

$$\bigstar \, q_\omega \, \overline{m+1} \, \bigstar$$

where q_ω tentatively denotes the STOP state. To achieve this we need only add 1 to the string of 1's representing m.

Consider the following two-state machine, S, with q_2 as its STOP state.

$$\{q_1 \, 1 \, 1 \, L \, q_1, \; q_1 \bigstar 1 \, L \, q_1, \; q_1 \, B \bigstar R \, q_2\}$$

It is quickly seen that this machine accomplishes the desired task. It begins by moving to the square on the left of the initial read head position and it changes the $\bigstar$ to a 1. It moves another square to the left where a new blank square is appended, changes this blank to an $\bigstar$, goes to the right and stops in state q_2.

Thus, S computes, when given a single argument x on its input tape, the successor function $S(x) = x + 1$.

The programming of $N(x) = 0$ is just as easy. This time we must transform an initial instantaneous description

$$\bigstar \, q_1 \, \overline{m} \, \bigstar$$

into

$$\bigstar \, q_\omega \, \overline{0} \, \bigstar$$

Define the machine N as follows:

$$\left\{ \begin{array}{ll} q_1 \, 1 \, B \, R \, q_1 & q_2 \bigstar \bigstar R \, q_3 \\ q_1 \bigstar B \, L \, q_2 & q_3 \, B \, 1 \, R \, q_4 \\ q_2 \, B \, B \, L \, q_2 & q_4 \, B \bigstar L \, q_5 \end{array} \right\}$$

Given an arbitrary input argument, N will erase all symbols to the right of the left $\bigstar$. It then skips back over the intervening blanks to the left $\bigstar$, goes to the right one square and writes a 1. It moves another square to the right, writes an $\bigstar$, moves to the left and stops in state q_5. The result then for all arguments is a single 1, the machine representation of 0.

The third of our basic recursive functions, the identity function, $U_i^{(n)}(x_1, x_2, \ldots, x_n) = x_i$, involves two arbitrary constants, i, n. For each different assignment of these two parameters we have a different machine, a machine which, when given an n-tuple of numbers on its input tape, will give as output the ith component of that n-tuple. A machine to compute

$U_2^{(3)} (x_1, x_2, x_3) = x_2$ is given below. The necessary modifications to obtain a machine for other values of i, n are obvious.

$$\left\{ \begin{array}{lll} q_1\,1\,1\,L\,q_2 & q_3\,1\,1\,R\,q_3 & q_5\,B\,B\,L\,q_5 \\ q_2 \star B\,R\,q_2 & q_3\,B\,B\,R\,q_4 & q_5\,1\,1\,R\,q_6 \\ q_2\,1\,B\,R\,q_2 & q_4\,1\,B\,R\,q_4 & q_6\,B \star L\,q_7 \\ q_2\,B\,B\,R\,q_3 & q_4 \star B\,L\,q_5 & q_7\,1\,1\,L\,q_7 \\ \underline{\quad\quad} & \underline{\quad\quad} & q_7\,B \star R\,q_8 \end{array} \right\}$$

We leave to the reader the verification of the behavior of this machine in its computation of $U_2^{(3)} (x_1, x_2, x_3)$.

5.7 SOME ELEMENTARY DATA-HANDLING OPERATIONS

Rather simple machines have sufficed to compute the three basic functions. We now further illustrate the art of Turing machine programming by writing some "routines" to accomplish a few simple data-handling tasks that are needed in subsequent sections. These will not be complete and regular machines but will simply be parts of machines designed to accomplish certain intermediate operations.

1. *Searching for a symbol on the tape.* With the assumption that all pertinent information on the tape lies between two programmed end-of-tape marks, $\star$, on the left and right ends, it is a trivial matter to search the tape for the occurrence of a given symbol. Note that the problem is not solvable if there are no end-of-tape marks, for a search in either direction will be interminable when the symbol does not appear on the tape.

Assume that we seek the leftmost occurrence of the symbol $\#$, starting from some arbitrary initial square. We move to the left until we reach the left $\star$. We then reverse direction and scan each symbol as we move to the right. If $\#$ is not encountered before the right $\star$, it does not appear on the tape.

In the following list of quintuples, a dash, –, should be taken to be any symbol of the machine's alphabet except $\star$ and $\#$. The suggested machine fragment begins in state q_1 and terminates in state q_3. If the search for $\#$ is successful, the terminal read head position is over the leftmost occurrence of $\#$. If the search is unsuccessful, the read head will be over the right end-of-tape mark. In both cases, the machine finishes in state q_3.

$$\left\{ \begin{array}{ll} q_1\,-\,-\,L\,q_1 & q_2\,-\,-\,R\,q_2 \\ q_1\,\#\,\#\,L\,q_1 & q_2\,\#\,\#\,N\,q_3 \\ q_1 \star \star R\,q_2 & q_2 \star \star N\,q_3 \end{array} \right\}$$

2. *Copying data.* Consider the problem of copying a segment of the tape that lies between two symbols P, Q onto a segment of the tape that begins

with the symbol M at its left end, where M does not lie between P and Q. Assume that the segment to be copied is a string formed from the symbols 0, 1 and that we begin with the read head over the left boundary symbol P in state q_1. We shall use two intermediate symbols α, β to mark the positions of 0, 1 respectively while they are being copied. The machine finishes in state q_9 with its read head positioned to the right of the data just copied.

Move data

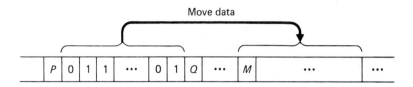

P	0	1	1	$\cdots$	0	1	Q	$\cdots$	M	$\cdots$	$\cdots$

$q_1\,P\,P\,R\,q_2$

$q_2\,0\,\alpha\,R\,q_3$ α is used to mark a 0 that is to be copied;

$q_3\,-\,-\,R\,q_3$ skip to right over all symbols except M;

$q_3\,M\,0\,R\,q_4$ replace M by the 0 being copied;

$q_4\,-\,M\,L\,q_5$ rewrite M on the next square to the right;

$q_5\,-\,-\,L\,q_5$ skip to left over all symbols except α;

$q_5\,\alpha\,0\,R\,q_2$ restore α to 0 and look at next symbol;

$q_2\,1\,\beta\,R\,q_6$ β is used to mark a 1 that is to be copied;

$q_6\,-\,-\,R\,q_6$ skip to right over all symbols except M;

$q_6\,M\,1\,R\,q_7$ replace M by the 1 being copied;

$q_7\,-\,M\,L\,q_8$ rewrite M on the next square to the right;

$q_8\,-\,-\,L\,q_8$ skip to left over all symbols except β;

$q_8\,\beta\,1\,R\,q_2$ restore β to 1 and look at next symbol;

$q_2\,Q\,Q\,R\,q_9$ Q signals end of data; move to right and stop in state q_9.

With the facility to copy data, it is easy to see that we can simulate a peripheral store on a machine. We can use the tape to the right, say, of the right ∗ for this purpose. It is helpful to use a special symbol, such as the M in the preceding discussion, to mark the right end of this peripheral store. This symbol will indicate the starting location for the next data entry to be stored.

3. *Packing data.* Suppose, next, that there are a number of 1's scattered over the tape between the two asterisks. We shall pack these 1's so that they are consecutively written starting at the left ∗. We begin with the read head over this mark and the machine in state q_1. The machine finishes with the data packed and the read head over the right ∗ bounding the packed 1's. All other symbols are erased.

$q_1 * * R q_2$
$q_2 - - R q_2$　　　skip to the right over all symbols except 1, α;
$q_2 \, 1 \, \alpha \, L q_3$　　　when a 1 is encountered, change it to α;
$q_3 - - L q_3$　　　skip to the left over all symbols except 1, $*$;
$q_3 * * R q_4$　　　when either $*$ or 1 is encountered, move to the
$q_3 \, 1 \, 1 \, R q_4$　　　right and prepare to write 1;
$q_4 - 1 R q_2$　　　write a 1 after the $*$ or last written 1;
$q_2 \, \alpha \, B \, R q_2$　　　erase the α used to mark the last 1 copied and
　　　　　　　continue search;

$q_2 * B L q_5$　　　if $*$ is encountered the search for 1's is over; erase the
　　　　　　　$*$ and
$q_5 - B L q_5$　　　skip back over intervening squares, erasing them, until
　　　　　　　we reach either $*$ or 1;
$q_5 * * R q_6$　　　if we reach the $*$ while in state q_5 there are no 1's;
$q_5 \, 1 \, 1 \, R q_6$　　　go to the last written 1;
$q_6 \, B * L q_7$　　　write $*$ to its right;
$q_7 \, 1 \, 1 \, R q_8$　　　and stop in state q_8 over the $*$.

5.8　SOME MORE COMPLEX MACHINE OPERATIONS

We sketch briefly the design of various machines that perform procedures that attest in part to the fact that a Turing machine can be designed to compute any effectively calculable function.

1. On designing one machine to do the work of k given machines: suppose we are given k regular Turing machines $Z_1, Z_2, \ldots, Z_k$ where the ith machine Z_i computes the function

$$f_i : (m_1, m_2, \ldots, m_n) \to r_i .$$

Let us design a machine Z which, given the input $(m_1, m_2, \ldots, m_n)$, will compute the string of results $(r_1, r_2, \ldots, r_k)$ of all k machines.

$$F : (m_1, m_2, \ldots, m_n) \to (r_1, r_2, \ldots, r_k).$$

This can be done in a number of ways and the programming is quite straightforward.

One approach might include, in part, changing and adding to the quin-tuples of each Z_i to yield a machine Z_i' that performs as Z_i does, but, by always shifting over k squares when Z_i shifts one square, uses every kth square of the tape starting with the one under the read head, in the same way that Z_i uses the consecutive squares of the tape. If, for example, we are given three machines Z_1, Z_2, Z_3, the modified machines Z'_1, Z'_2, Z'_3 would use respectively the squares labeled A, B, C in the following diagram.

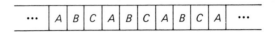

The quintuples for the composite machine Z are then written to accomplish the following tasks:

a. Given the tape representation of the input data $(m_1, m_2, \ldots, m_n)$, rewrite it so that every 1 in an argument and every B spacer is replicated k times.

b. Execute Z'_1 then move to the beginning of the input data for Z'_2. Enter the starting state for Z'_2 (assume the state indices of Z'_2 to be chosen so that they do not conflict with those of Z'_1), execute Z'_2 and successively all Z'_1 $(i = 2, 3, \ldots, k)$. The individual results will appear in every kth square in accordance with our scheme for tape usage.

c. "Collect" the individual results which are written in our staggered notation and form the tape representation of the k-tuple of results. Position the read head over the leftmost 1 when stopping.

2. On simulating a machine that employs k (> 1) tapes using a machine with only one tape: suppose we were to generalize the notion of a Turing machine so that it employed more than one tape. Replace the quintuples by sextuples $q_i\, S_j\, S_k\, M q_l\, t$ (where $M = R$, or L, or N, and $t = 1, 2, \ldots, k$). We take the last symbol t to indicate that control is transferred to a read head that scans the tth tape. This means, then, that at the next time step the machine will be in state q_l reading the symbol under the read head that scans the tth tape. Would such an increased facility give us a more powerful machine, one that is capable of computing a function that cannot be computed on any Turing machine limited to one tape?

It is easy to see that the answer is negative. We need only show that a machine with k tapes can be simulated on a machine with one tape. We omit the details, noting only that the same device for the tape representation of information as was used in the preceding example can be employed here, together with a special mark to indicate the position of the read head on each of the k simulated tapes. Each sextuple, then, is a kind of macro instruction that can be replaced by a set of quintuples to accomplish the desired function on the machine with one tape that simulates the k-tape machine.

The operations of composition, primitive recursion, and minimalization applied to Turing machine computable functions yield Turing machine computable functions. We shall not carry through all the programming details needed to give a complete and explicit proof of this result but we sketch the constructions of the Turing machines that perform the desired tasks, based on the flowcharts of Figs. 4.1, 4.2, and 4.5. Our "proofs" will simply consist of showing that each operation defined in a flowchart box can be accomplished by some Turing machine and that we can, using the techniques we have illustrated, form "composite" machines that realize the complete procedure including the handling of control functions and the flow.

Consider the operation of composition. The problem is as follows: we are given for each function $g_i(x_1, \ldots, x_n)$, $i = 1, 2, \ldots, m$, a Turing machine Z_i that computes it. We are also given a Turing machine Y that computes the function $f(y_1, \ldots, y_m)$. We must construct a Turing machine that computes the function $h(x_1, x_2, \ldots, x_n) = f(g_1(x_1, x_2, \ldots, x_n), \ldots, g_m(x_1, x_2, \ldots, x_n))$. The biggest part of the construction is realized by our stated result on the design of one machine that does the work of k (> 1) given machines. This result implies that we can define a single machine Z that computes the m-tuple of results $g_1(x_1, \ldots, x_n)$, $g_2(x_1, \ldots, x_n), \ldots, g_m(x_1, \ldots, x_n)$. It only remains to "compose" this machine Z with a machine that behaves as Y does. We call this latter machine Y'. It computes the same function that Y does, but its states must be renumbered, as implied in the preceding, so that it begins in the stop state of Z.

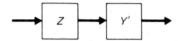

Primitive recursion is handled in a similar manner. Consider the case where we define a function $r(x)$ of a single argument (Fig. 4.2). We are given that $r(0) = k$, and we are given a machine Y that computes $g(x, y)$. We seek a machine Z that will compute $r(x)$ defined by the equations

$$\begin{cases} r(0) = k, \\ r(x + 1) = g(x, r(x)) \quad \text{for } x \geq 0. \end{cases}$$

Again, it is a straightforward construction to obtain Turing machines that effect the transformation of each of the boxes of the flowchart in Fig. 4.2. The decision box is realized by comparing two arguments t, x (cf. the exercises) and entering one state if they agree, another if they do not. We leave the details to the reader as well as the handling of the more general statement of primitive recursion where it is used to define a function $r(x_1, x_2, \ldots, x_n)$ of n arguments.

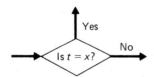

No new problems appear in considering minimalization. The transformation or decision indicated in each box of the flowchart in Fig. 4.5 can be accomplished by a Turing machine, and these machines can be composed, using the techniques we have described, to form one machine Z, where Z computes the function

$$h(x) = \min y[f(y, x) = 0].$$

Again, the generalization to

$$h(x_1, x_2, \ldots, x_n) = \min y[f(y, x_1, x_2, \ldots, x_n) = 0]$$

is straightforward.

It then follows from our earlier remarks that any function in the class of partial recursive functions is computable by some Turing machine. It remains to show that any Turing machine computable function is a partial recursive function. This result will complete the demonstration of the fact that the two classes, the partial recursive functions and the partial Turing machine computable functions, are equivalent. Toward this goal we must first describe everything that takes place on a Turing machine—its writing of tape symbols, moving the tape, changing states, and so forth—in terms of the natural numbers and of arithmetic operations.

5.9   THE ARITHMETIZATION OF TURING MACHINES

We referred briefly in Chapter 2 to the technique of arithmetization which is a useful tool in mathematical logic. Recall that it consists essentially of simulating a system in computational terms—of mapping, in invertible fashion, all the objects of the system into the natural numbers and all the operations and relations on these objects into arithmetic functions and relations. To apply it to the study of Turing machines we must describe all of the salient elements of Turing machines: states, quintuples, tape symbols and descriptions, instantaneous descriptions, and related notions in terms of the natural numbers. Parts of our problem can be handled in a very straightforward manner, for those things that can be represented as finite sequences of symbols drawn from a finite alphabet are immediately representable as natural numbers. If, for example, we have an alphabet of 15 symbols then, as we have seen, any word formed with the symbols of this alphabet can be considered an integer written in a base 15 notation. It follows that all of the things we have listed are integers in some extended base notation. For example, any single quintuple can be written, ignoring subscripted notation, as a string made up of symbols from the list $0, 1, 2, \ldots, 9, Q, S, R, N, L$ (such as $Q2S17S3RQ11$ for the quintuple $q_2 S_{17} S_3 R q_{11}$) and is, thus, some base 15 number.

In mapping a *sequence* of strings of symbols in invertible fashion into a single string of symbols we must be able to recover each individual string of the sequence from the single string. This is, of course, immediate if we can recognize the beginning and end of each individual string for it is then trivial to "parse" the concatenation of all the individual strings. If we have a *set* of strings where the ordering is immaterial, such as in the listing of quintuples comprising a Turing machine, we can choose an arbitrary ordering or sequence and map this into the integers.

The number into which we map, by some appropriate scheme, the set of quintuples of a machine is called the "description number" (as used by Turing), or the "index number" or, for a particular method of representation described below, the "Gödel number" of the machine. For example, if we consider the two-state, three-symbol machine that we have defined to compute $S(x) = x + 1$, its description number, using the simple encoding scheme we have described, might be taken as the base 15 number:

$$Q1S1S1LQ1Q1S2S1LQ1Q1S0S2RQ2$$

This string can be parsed in obvious fashion to recover the individual quintuples from the description number since each quintuple is of fixed length. The $\ast$ is identified as S_2. A description number obtained for a machine by this method is, of course, not unique since each different ordering of the quintuples leads to a different description number.

The mathematical logician Kurt Gödel has used an encoding scheme [2], that bears his name, to encode as natural numbers both finite sequences of symbols and sequences of sequences of symbols. His method has certain technical advantages. The numbering scheme is applied in the following way. The alphabet of symbols that may appear in strings are encoded as natural numbers. Let us suppose that the ith symbol S_i is represented by the number k_i. Then the number corresponding to the string of length p,

$$S_{i_1} S_{i_2} \ldots S_{i_p},$$

is taken to be the following product formed from the first p prime numbers. (We denote the ith prime number by $Pr(i)$, so that $Pr(1) = 2$, $Pr(2) = 3$, $Pr(3) = 5$, etc.)

$$\cdot\ 2^{k_{i_1}} 3^{k_{i_2}} 5^{k_{i_3}} \ldots (Pr(p))^{k_{i_p}}$$

That is, the numbers k_i appear as exponents of the successive prime numbers. Thus, if we encode A as 1, B as 2, C as 3, then the "Gödel number" for the string BAC is

$$2^2 3^1 5^3 = 1{,}500.$$

If, conversely, we are given the Gödel number of a string, we can recapture the symbolic string that it represents by factoring it into a product of primes and reading off the exponents of these prime factors, in order of increasing magnitude of the primes (a basic result of elementary number theory is that this factorization can be done in one and only one way).

A refinement of this encoding scheme permits the representation of sequences of sequences. If we are given the finite sequence $S_1, S_2, \ldots, S_p$ where each S_i is a *sequence* of symbols, then we can associate a Gödel number with each S_i (call it $gn(S_i)$) by the above scheme. We can then form the product

$$2^{gn(S_1)} \, 3^{gn(S_2)} \ldots (Pr(p))^{gn(S_p)}$$

to represent the sequence of sequences. A necessary property of this encoding, in order for it to be of use in applying the technique of arithmetization, is that it be invertible. We must, therefore, be able to distinguish between the Gödel number of a sequence of *symbols* and the Gödel number of a sequence of *sequences*. One immediate way of accomplishing this is not to use the number 2 as any of the numbers k_i used to represent the symbols of the alphabet. We leave it to the reader to recognize why this will result in an easily recognizable distinction between the Gödel numbers of the two kinds of sequences.

With the use of such numbering schemes (sometimes the term "Gödel number" is used indiscriminately in the literature with the meaning of "description number"), we can represent not only strings, such as instantaneous descriptions, in the form of natural numbers, but we can represent sequences of instantaneous descriptions as well. Again, to the computer programmer the feasibility, at least, of the above mappings contains no surprises. As we have remarked several times, all data that appear in a machine, no matter how varied its format, can always be read out as the natural numbers whose binary representations are the strings of bits that represent these data items in the machine. This includes not only object data but programs as well.

5.10 "PROOF" THAT IF A FUNCTION IS TURING MACHINE COMPUTABLE THEN IT IS PARTIAL RECURSIVE[1]

We shall, following our usual practice, provide only the skeleton of a proof of this result, omitting most of the technical details. We must show that if we have a Turing machine computation represented schematically as in Fig. 5.4,

---

[1] This section, based upon Section 4.12, is more demanding, mathematically, of the reader and can be omitted in a first exposure to this material.

then there is a partial recursive function f that effects the same transformation of input into output.

We sketch out a proof along the following lines. We shall first make plausible that a single quintuple defines a function that is partial recursive on the numbers representing instantaneous descriptions. Assuming this to be true, we next consider a Turing machine Z of n (> 1) quintuples. Each of these quintuples defines a function on instantaneous descriptions that is partial recursive, *and* these functions have disjoint domains since no two quintuples can, by definition, apply to the same instantaneous description. Let those quintuples that cause the machine to enter a STOP state be designated by $P_1, P_2, \ldots, P_m$. We suppose that each P_i defines, by hypothesis, a partial recursive function f_i on instantaneous descriptions.

Let the other quintuples of the machine, those that do not take it into a STOP state, be designated by $M_1, M_2, \ldots, M_p$, and let each such quintuple M_i similarly define a partial recursive function g_i on instantaneous descriptions.

Using the notation of Chapter 4, we assume the result that if f, g are two partial recursive functions with disjoint domains, then the function $f \cup g$ is a partial recursive function. Let, then,

$$f_1 \cup f_2 \cup \ldots \cup f_m = f,$$
$$g_1 \cup g_2 \cup \ldots \cup g_p = g.$$

We then leave it to the reader to see that the function fg^* defined in Chapter 4 as

$$fg^* = f \cup fg \cup fg^2 \cup \ldots$$

is the function defined by the machine Z. If we accept the fact that fg^* is partial recursive when f and g are, the result follows immediately.

Returning to our initial hypothesis, we consider the effect of a single quintuple and ask if this can be described as a partial recursive function on instantaneous descriptions. We shall only consider one example of a quintuple and shall omit all the technical details necessary to a proper consideration of all three types of quintuples. Let us suppose that the quintuple M is

$$q_2\, S_2\, S_3\, R\, q_3$$

and consider the function $M : \mathrm{ID} \to \mathrm{ID}$ that this quintuple defines on instantaneous descriptions. Let us use the first scheme we indicated for representing instantaneous descriptions as base 15 numbers. Consider then the base 15 description number

$$N_1 = S3\,S4\,Q2\,S2\,S3\,S1.$$

It is mapped by M into N_2, $M: N_1 \rightarrow N_2$, where N_2 is the base 15 number

$$N_2 = S3\,S4\,S3\,Q3\,S3\,S1.$$

We leave it to the reader to see that the arithmetic function defined by M, $N_2 = m(N_1)$, is given by the following equations, using the notation of Chapter 4. Recall that $[P/Q]$ denotes the greatest integer in the quotient P/Q and $R(X, Y)$ is the remainder when X is divided by Y.

$$d = \min k[R(\mid ([N_1/15^k] - Q2S2) \mid, 15^4) = 0]$$
$$N_2 = m(N_1) = 15^{d+4}[N_1/15^{d+4}] + 15^d (S3Q3) + R(N_1, 15^d)$$

From its definition, d is the number of symbols following an occurrence of the four-digit base 15 number $Q2S2$ in the description number N_1. If N_1 does not include these four consecutive symbols, i.e., the quintuple M is not applicable to it, then d and the function m, which depends upon d, are not defined on N_1.

From the results of Chapter 4 and the associated exercises, it is quickly seen that m is a partial recursive function. We further assume that, in similar manner, the functions defined by arbitrary quintuples can be shown to be partial recursive.

This completes our fragmented proof of this theorem. The method of proof is primarily of interest to us in our survey because of the use of the technique of arithmetization, of casting everything relevant to the behavior of Turing machines within the domain of the natural numbers.

In Chapter 4 we described Church's thesis, a statement which equates the class of effectively computable functions with the class of recursive functions. Now that we have, in a fashion, demonstrated that the class of partial recursive functions is identical to the class of Turing machine computable functions, it follows that if Church's thesis be true, the notion of Turing machine computability can be used in similar fashion to make precise the idea of effective computability. The statement of the equivalence in this form is generally known as

> *Turing's Thesis:* The class of effectively computable functions can be identified with the class of Turing machine computable functions.

Perhaps Turing's thesis is more satisfying than Church's thesis in giving precise meaning to the vague notion of effective computability because of the underlying motivations of Turing as we have described them. If we had first stated Turing's thesis as our fundamental tenet, then Church's thesis would have been a consequence of it.

5.11 SOME IMPLICATIONS TO THE "REAL" WORLD OF COMPUTING

We shall see in the next chapter some consequences of the theory of Turing machines which are of a negative character in that they assert certain fundamental limitations to the powers that we can hope to incorporate within a computing device or program. It turns out that certain functions, or decision-making procedures, simply cannot be programmed no matter how clever we are.

We note, however, at this point some positive inferences that can be drawn from the theory of Turing machines. First, accepting Turing's thesis, we see that any digital computer that has adequate command structure to simulate an arbitrary Turing machine can, if given adequate peripheral storage and ignoring limitations of time, compute any function or do any data-processing task whatsoever. It takes very little to be able to simulate a

Fig. 5.5   Emil Post and his paper on finite combinatory processes.

Turing machine, and any real computer has the capacity to do this if it has some very modest amount of internal storage (with, of course, the very necessary assumption of an unlimited supply of peripheral storage being available). We leave the further consideration of this matter to the exercises.

Thus, ignoring the fundamental and very practical questions of efficiency, ease of programming, and so forth, all computers are of equal power in the sense any function that can be computed on any one of them can be computed on any other. Further, very modest facilities of high speed storage and of instruction repertoire will suffice to give a computer this ability to simulate an arbitrary Turing machine and, therefore, to perform any calculation at all. This last statement is far from obvious. For example, the handling of multiprecision arithmetic is not at all a trivial task on a real

Fig. 5.6 Pictured above are four people who played key roles in the construction of the IAS (Institute for Advanced Study) computer. From left to right they are: Julian Bigelow, chief engineer; Herman H. Goldstine; Robert Oppenheimer, Director of the Institute; and John von Neumann. The early work of Drs. Goldstine and von Neumann on the planning and coding of problems for a stored program machine had a profound effect on the development of the modern digital computer.

computer, but the stated result implies that with rather limited facilities (except for the unbounded peripheral store) arithmetic with arbitrarily large operands can be handled on a quite small machine.

We turn next to some implications to the study of programming languages. Sometimes in 1954, IBM's Applied Science Department sought some outside confirmation of the worthwhileness of its modest investment in developing a compiler for the then newly proposed FORTRAN programming language, the language that was to become the first widely used problem-oriented programming language and whose name, in fact, has become almost a household word. A presentation of the language was given to IBM's most distinguished consultant, the great mathematician John von Neumann, in order to elicit his opinion of its merit. He seemed, to the author, to be somewhat bored by the proceedings and, yes, he did at the end acquiesce in a recommendation that the project be pursued but, on theoretical grounds, seemed to dismiss the whole development as but an application of the idea of Turing's "shortcode." Later, in his monograph on "The Computer and the Brain" [6], he elaborated somewhat on this imputed contribution of Turing. He described this, in essence, as a code that enabled one to use a machine as though it were another machine with a more convenient and a richer repertoire of commands than its own basic command set. That is, one machine can simulate another with a more advantageous code structure.

The author has not succeeded in finding any reference to the term "shortcode" in Turing's work, but it has been suggested (by Stefan Bauer-Mengelberg) that von Neumann may have been making reference to Turing's use in his 1936 paper, cited earlier, of "abbreviated tables." Turing had used tables at one point in this paper to specify the behavior of a given machine, giving in different format the same information that is contained in the description number of a machine or, equivalently, in the machine's set of quintuples (see Fig. 6.1). Each row of a table corresponded to a different state of the machine and each column to a different symbol of the alphabet. The entry then in the ith row and jth column of the table indicated the machine's actions to be taken when in state q_i it scans symbol S_j (i.e., the symbol to be written, the nature of the movement of the tape, the state to be entered.)

Turing then described in this tabular form certain machines to perform frequently needed tasks, similar to those we have used in the preceding discussion. By using these machines as (we might call them today) macro operations, he could design other machines in a much more economic fashion. These other machines, by entering certain special states, could, when desired, "invoke" along lines we have described the actions of the earlier defined machines.

It is apparently this intimation of a fundamental notion of programing languages that von Neumann related to one of the early models of modern programming languages.

EXERCISES

5.1 Show that a quintuple, $q_i\ S_j\ S_k\ N\ q_l$, can always be replaced by a set of quintuples, each of which involves tape movement.

5.2 Define a (regular) Turing machine that computes the function $f(N) = 4$.

5.3 Define a (regular) Turing machine that computes the function $g(N) = 2N$.

5.4 Define a (regular) Turing machine that computes the function

$$\begin{cases} f(0) = 3 \\ f(N) = 2 \text{ if } N > 0 \end{cases}$$

5.5 Define a (regular) Turing machine that computes the function

$$\begin{cases} f(N) = 2 \text{ if } N \text{ is even} \\ f(N) = 3 \text{ if } N \text{ is odd} \end{cases}$$

5.6 Define a (regular) Turing machine that computes, for given argument N, the remainder when N is divided by 3.

5.7 Define a (regular) Turing machine that computes the function $z = \max(x, y)$.

5.8 Define a Turing machine that, starting on a standard input tape of $n + 1$ 1's, will transform the input into a string of $n + 1$ fields where each field is 1001. Assume the alphabet of the machine is $\{B, 0, 1, \star\}$, where B is the blank and $\star$ is the end-of-tape mark.

5.9 Give an example of a well-defined function that can *not* be computed on any real computer (with necessarily finite storage), but which can be computed on some Turing machine.

5.10 Suppose we introduce a representation scheme for negative integers, as well as the natural numbers, on a Turing machine tape. Let $\eta 1^{m+1}$, where 1^{m+1} denotes a string of $m + 1$ 1's, be the tape representation of $-m$ where $m > 0$. Define a Turing machine that computes $x - y$ where x, y are arbitrary integers (positive, negative, or zero).

5.11 Define a Turing machine that, given as input two bit strings X, Y of equal length N and separated by a blank B ($\star\ XBY\ \star$), will yield as output a bit string Z of the same length where each bit Z_i ($i = 1, 2, \ldots, N$) is given by $Z_i = X_i \mid Y_i$ in terms of the corresponding bits of X, Y.

5.12 In Turing's original 1936 paper, he assumed machine tapes that could be extended in only one direction. That is, his tapes had a special beginning tape mark but could only be extended at the other end. Show that a machine employing the convention of two-ended extendible tapes can always be replaced by one with his more restricted convention.

5.13 Suppose we change the output convention so that the result given by an arbitrary Turing machine is taken to be the number of 1's on its final tape, where these 1's may not be consecutively written. Show that such a machine can be replaced by a regular Turing machine that computes the same function.

5.14 We adopted a convention of using special STOP states. Show that a convention whereby a machine stops when it is in state q_i scanning S_j on its tape and no quintuple begins $q_i\, S_j$ – – – could equally well have been adopted.

5.15 Design a Turing machine fragment that will compare two nonoverlapping fields G_1, G_2 on the tape. Assume that both fields are made up of 0's and 1's, that the symbol A marks the left and right squares flanking G_1, and the symbol B is similarly used to bound G_2 (and these are the only occurrences of A, B on the tape). Let the read head start over the left symbol A with the machine in state q_1. Position the final read head over the left A if the two fields agree and over the left B if they do not.

5.16 Sketch a proof that any Turing machine employing an alphabet with more than two characters can be replaced by one that employs only two, $\{B, 1\}$, and computes the same function of a single argument.

To be specific, suppose that a Turing machine Z uses five symbols $\{B, 1, \alpha, \beta, \gamma\}$, and show that it can be replaced by a machine Z' using only $\{B, 1\}$. (Assume that the end-of-tape mark $\ast$ is in Z's alphabet.)

Skeleton of Proof: (i) Each symbol of the five should be encoded as a field made up of the symbols $B, 1$; (ii) the input tape $\ast\, \bar{n}\, \ast$ must be encoded; (iii) each quintuple of Z must be replaced by a set of quintuples in Z'; (iv) at the end of the simulation of Z by Z', the encoded symbols on the tape of Z' must be properly decoded.

5.17 Show that if Turing machines were designed to operate on two-dimensional "tapes" of squares instead of the one-dimensional tapes used in the definition in the text, they would not be any more powerful, i.e., they would not be able to compute any functions not computable on Turing machines using one-dimensional tapes. (Hint: Sketch out a method for simulating any two-dimensional tape Turing machine on a machine using a one-dimensional tape.)

5.18 A real number x between 0 and 1 is said to be Turing machine computable if a Turing machine exists that computes the successive digits in the infinite decimal representation of x (i.e., assume that the machine does not stop, but continues indefinitely to write the successive digits of x on its tape). Show that there are a denumerably infinite number of such computable numbers. (Turing's original paper was written in terms of such computable numbers rather than computable functions. The two notions are essentially equivalent. Cf. Chapter 6.)

5.19 Sketch out an informal but convincing plan to demonstrate that any stored program computer with which you are familiar can be programmed to simulate any Turing machine Z if it is given as input the set of quintuples defining Z and an arbitrary initial tape on which Z starts. Assume that an unlimited peripheral store (e.g., an infinite supply of magnetic tapes) is available.

5.20 Sketch the design of a Turing machine U that can do what is asked in problem 5.19. That is, U receives as input the set of quintuples defining an arbitrary Turing machine Z together with an arbitrary initial tape segment on which Z might start. U should then produce the same output as Z would produce. U is a "universal" Turing machine (cf. Chapter 6).

5.21 In Chapter 4 we defined a recursively enumerable set to be the set of numbers in the range of some partial recursive function. This is then equivalent to saying that such a set is the set of outputs of some Turing machine. Show that a recursively enumerable set can equally well be defined as the *domain* of some partially computable function.

REFERENCES

1. Davis, M., *Computability and Unsolvability.* New York: McGraw-Hill, 1958.

2. Gödel, K., "Über formal unentscheidbare Sätze der Principia Mathematica und verwandter Systeme I" *Monat. Math. Phys.*, 38 (1931). Translated by Jean van Heijenoort ("On Formally Undecidable Propositions of Principia Mathematica and Related Systems I") in *From Frege to Gödel,* Ed. by Jean van Heijenoort, Cambridge: Harvard University Press, 1967.

3. Post, Emil L. "Finite Combinatory Processes, Formulation I." *Journal of Symbolic Logic* 1 (1936). Reprinted in Martin Davis, ed. *The Undecidable. Basic Papers on Undecidable Propositions, Unsolvable Problems and Computable Functions.* Hewlett, N.Y.: Raven Press, 1965.

4. Rogers, Hartley, Jr. "The Present Theory of Turing Machine Computability." *Journal of the Society for Industrial and Applied Mathematics* **7**, 1 (March 1959).

5. Turing, Alan M. "On Computable Numbers, With an Application to the Entscheidungsproblem." *Proceedings of the London Mathematical Society,* 2nd Series, Vol. 42, pp. 230–265, 1936; Correction, ibid. Vol. 43, pp. 544–546. Reprinted in Martin Davis, ed. *The Undecidable, Basic Papers on Undecidable Propositions, Unsolvable Problems and Computable Functions,* Hewlett, N.Y.: Raven Press, 1965.

6. Von Neumann, John. *The Computer and the Brain.* New Haven: Yale University Press, 1958.

6

The Universal Turing Machine, Some Implications of the Theory of Computability, Variants of Turing Machines

In this chapter we introduce the universal Turing machine, that machine which can simulate any given Turing machine whose quintuples are provided as input data to it. It is this machine that is comparable to the general purpose stored program computer which can compile and execute any given input program.

As powerful as is the universal Turing machine, there are problems that cannot be solved on it and, therefore, in view of Turing's thesis, problems for which no algorithmic solution exists. The prime example of this is the halting problem, the problem of determining whether or not an arbitrary given Turing machine will eventually halt after that machine starts on a given input tape in some arbitrary specified starting condition. This impossibility result has negative implications to the possible design of diagnostic programs. We cannot, in complete generality, analyze an arbitrary given object program and determine whether or not a computer executing that program will eventually stop.

The impossibility of an effective solution to the halting problem enables us to define a function on the integers that is not computable by any algorithm and therefore not computable by any machine. In a discussion of the "busy beaver" problem, we give another and surprisingly simple example of a noncomputable function.

We look at some possible variations of Turing machines. Can we contradict Turing's thesis and increase the powers of these machines by using more than one tape or by, say, using tapes that are not linear, or one dimensional, but tapes of dimension two or more? The answer is no. However, we can improve the efficiency of many procedures by introducing such additional features. We also look briefly at a possible violation of a fundamental characteristic of effective processes. We allow Turing machines to be nondeterministic. Again, after a suitable definition of what it might mean to execute a procedure on such a machine, we find that these machines cannot do anything that an ordinary deterministic Turing machine cannot do.

We consider still other variants of Turing machines that are closer to the stored program computer—Wang machines and the "register machines" of Shepherdson and Sturgis. These all provide alternative models of the computing process and all can be shown to be identical in computing power to the class of Turing machines, i.e., a Turing machine computable function can be computed on these other devices, and conversely. Another model is provided by the "cellular automata" of von Neumann that were introduced by him primarily to study the possibility of reproduction by automata.

There are a number of formal systems that emulate Turing machines, and we look at some of these as symbol manipulation systems. The relevant ideas here find particular application to the study of formal languages. The impossibility of solution to the halting problem can be used to show that certain problems expressed as "games" with symbols have no solution. We refer in passing to Minsky's ingenious demonstration, along these lines, that the problem of "Tag," a very simply defined symbol manipulation game, has no effective solution.

Turing, in his original paper [18], discussed computable "numbers" rather than computable "functions." A computable number is an infinite decimal whose successive digits can be computed by some algorithm. These are, of course, the numbers of prime concern to us in computing. To compute the successive digits of a real number is not, however, the only way to specify a real number, and we can also consider the class of "decimally approximable numbers" (cf. the text). There may be such decimally approximable numbers that are not computable in the first sense.

The existence of noncomputable functions implies that "most" real numbers are not computable or even decimally approximable. These indescribable numbers exist (perhaps) in some sense, but to a large extent their decimal representations must remain forever unknown to us.

We close with comments on some results of Gödel on the "incompleteness" of mathematical systems. We can enunciate theorems in any nontrivial mathematical system that are true but cannot be proven within that system.

This seems to imply fundamental limits on our ability to discover all truths within a mathematical system. These results are closely allied to the non-computability results of Turing machine theory, and we speculate briefly on some of their implications.

6.1 THE UNIVERSAL TURING MACHINE

We have seen how Turing machines can be defined to compute any member of a very large class of functions—the partial recursive functions—and we have noted the plausibility of Turing's thesis that any effectively computable function can be computed by some Turing machine. Each Turing machine computes one particular function. These machines, then, are not counter-parts of existing general purpose programmable digital computers for any one of the latter can be programmed to compute an *arbitrary* computable function if adequate peripheral storage is made available. A Turing machine should, rather, be compared to a real computer that has been programmed to compute one particular function.

If we are given the description, or listing of quintuples, of a particular Turing machine we certainly can follow or simulate its behavior without actually building it. In fact we have, throughout the discussion of these machines, been able to talk about them and follow their behavior without working with a physical realization of them. We recognize this procedure itself of describing and simulating the detailed behavior of Turing machines as being effective. Therefore, in consideration of Turing's thesis, we do not find surprising the fact that we can prescribe a Turing machine U which will receive as input the description of, or list of quintuples in, a particular machine M in addition to a copy of an input tape t and will mimic or imitate the behavior of M when M starts on the tape t. In other words, U receives as input (Q_M, t), where Q_M is the list of quintuples of M, and t is an arbitrary input tape. U then simulates the behavior of M when M starts on tape t. The machine U is called a universal Turing machine because of its ability to imitate any given Turing machine. It is analogous to a real computer, operating under a "load and go" programming system, that receives as input an arbitrary program P and accompanying input data D and then compiles and runs P, using input data D. Any real computer can easily be pro-grammed, and this has frequently been done, as a universal Turing machine if it has some very modest internal storage facilities and access to an unlim-ited source of secondary storage.

In his 1936 paper Turing described how to go about defining a universal machine. As indicated earlier, he suggested storing in the form of a table (cf. Fig. 6.1) the information represented by the quintuples of the machine being simulated. The universal machine would then refer to these tables in order to take the necessary actions at each step. This implementation of an "inter-

	0	1
q_1	$1, R, q_2$	q_{STOP}
q_2	$0, R, q_3$	$1, R, q_2$
q_3	$1, L, q_3$	$1, L, q_1$

Fig. 6.1 Description of a Turing machine as a table. The states correspond to the rows, the alphabet symbols to the columns. The entry in the second row and second column corresponds to the quintuple q_2 1 1 $R\,q_2$. How many 1's will this machine print if it starts in state q_1 on a blank tape?

preter" constituted one of the very first systems programming efforts some dozen years before the first real general purpose electronic computers appeared on the scene. We have indicated enough of the possibilities in Turing machine programming to imply that this result can be achieved, and we leave the further detailed planning of such a procedure to the reader (cf. the exercises, Chapter 5).

Perhaps the most direct way to do the simulation on a real stored program computer would be to mimic the steps that are executed on a universal Turing machine. If shortcuts are attempted in programming a stored program computer this may not lead to a completely general simulator. For example, if the stored program machine is to have all the powers of a universal Turing machine, it should be able, in principle, to simulate an arbitrary Turing machine even if the number of states in that machine were so large as to require more than one machine word, or even more than the entire internal memory of the machine, to represent them. If such complete generality is demanded in the simulation process, it seems that the best course of action might be to copy the actions of a Turing machine that is programmed or defined as a universal machine.

We have throughout our discussion of Turing machines considered the set of quintuples of a machine to be the analog of a program in a real computer. In the case of a universal Turing machine, it is the description, or set of quintuples of the machine being simulated, that is represented on the input tape which is the counterpart of the program in a stored program machine.

6.2   THE HALTING PROBLEM

Let us consider the following problem that is associated with every given Turing machine Z and some input tape t. Let Z start computing on tape t. We ask, will Z eventually halt?

We certainly can in many cases solve this problem rather easily. For example, consider the following problem.

Let machine Z consist of the following quintuples:

$$\left\{\begin{array}{lll} q_1\,1\,1\,R\,q_2 & q_3\,B\,B\,L\,q_2 & q_5\,B\,B\,L\,q_4 \\ q_2\,B\,B\,L\,q_1 & q_3\,1\,1\,R\,q_4 & q_5\,1\,1\,L\,q_4 \\ q_2\,1\,1\,R\,q_3 & q_4\,1\,1\,R\,q_5 & q_4\,B\,B\,L\,q_{\text{STOP}} \end{array}\right\}$$

It involves a trivial analysis to see that Z, starting in state q_1 at the first 1 of a single input argument, will stop on any input tape that contains precisely three consecutive 1's and that otherwise it will enter a never-ending loop.

We ask, however, the following more general question. Is there some one effective procedure that will in all cases resolve this question for us? Or, in view of Turing's thesis: can we define a Turing machine which will receive as input the description of an arbitrary Turing machine Z and of any starting tape t and determine whether or not Z will eventually stop after starting in its start state q_1 on tape t? This is the statement of the halting problem.

The answer to this question is NO and we sketch below, in heuristic fashion, an argument leading to this conclusion. This is based on a discussion in Minsky [12]. We use the method of reductio ad absurdum, i.e., we assume that the answer to our question is YES and we then show that this leads to a contradiction.

Suppose we try to answer the question by actually running, or at least simulating, machine Z starting on tape t. Then, if Z does stop we, of course, have the answer YES–but if Z does not stop we can at no point in time be certain of this and be assured of a NO answer.

Assume that a machine to solve the halting problem does, in fact, exist. Call it H. Then H, when given as input the descriptions (Z,t), gives an answer YES (or 1) if machine Z eventually stops after starting on tape t and gives the answer NO (or 0) if Z never stops after starting on t.

Modify H, by adding quintuples, to produce a machine H^* which instead of giving the answer "1" in the instance where Z would stop, enters an endless loop. It is easy for anyone with a little programming experience to see that this can be done, although not all the details are trivial. If H is regular and we are given a listing of the quintuples of H, we can recognize the STOP state of H (the state with highest index) and we can write additional quintuples causing the machine to enter an endless loop, instead of stopping, when the answer 1 is obtained. We must add quintuples that (1) will check to see if the answer is 1 when the machine stops and (2) will then cause an endless loop in this circumstance. Some of the devices of Chapter 5 are useful here, and we leave the details of the programming to the reader.

The machine H^* is not yet in a form suitable to exhibit a contradiction. We further modify it, introducing a small "preprocessing" operation to produce a machine H^{**} that does the following. When H^{**} starts on a tape containing only a description Z of a Turing machine, it will duplicate this description giving (Z, Z) and will then continue its computation as H^* would have done if it had started on the tape (Z, Z).

Consider now the behavior of H^{**}. Given a description of a Turing machine Z, it will go into an endless loop if Z would eventually stop when it starts with its own description Z on its tape, and it eventually stops and gives the answer 0 (NO) if Z would not have stopped after starting with its own description on its tape. Now, since by our assumptions Z can be the description of *any* Turing machine, let it in particular be that of H^{**}. We then have:

> H^{**} will go into an endless loop when it starts with its own description on its tape <u>if</u>–H^{**} will eventually stop when it starts with its own description on its tape and:

> H^{**} will eventually stop (and give the answer 0) when it starts with its own description on its tape <u>if</u>–H^{**} will not stop after starting with its own description on its tape.

The contradiction at which we have arrived implies that our initial assumption that such a machine as H exists is false. Therefore, *there is no effective procedure* to solve the general halting problem.

One immediate consequence of this result is that it is not possible to write a general diagnostic program that is capable of analyzing an arbitrary object program and of determining whether or not that object program will, during execution, enter an endless computation. (For, if this could be done we would be able to solve the halting problem by simulating on a real computer the behavior of the Turing machine Z starting on tape t.) As a theoretical limitation to the sophistication we can hope to build into our diagnostic programs this is, however, not too serious. The theory applies and the limitation exists when we consider computing devices that can simulate a universal Turing machine, that is, devices that are potentially infinite in the sense of having access to an unlimited supply of secondary storage. In practice, however, there is, of course, some limitation to the amount of storage that is available, and our devices are not so much Turing machines as they are examples of finite automata (see Chapter 8). Procedures *do* exist to solve such problems as the halting problem for finite machines. It is easy to show that if a finite machine follows an infinite procedure it must eventually repeat itself and then start cycling—or looping. But, unfortunately, the detection of this involves in general astronomically long procedures that have little practical value.

6.3 DECISION PROBLEMS

Decision problems are problems where we seek an effective or algorithmic procedure to resolve each of a set of questions. The formulation of each question depends upon the assignments of specific numerical values to certain parameters. For example, find an algorithm to answer the question, "Is N a prime number?" A positive solution to a decision problem means that we can program a computer to answer any particular question within the class of possible questions. A demonstration that a decision problem has no solution implies that we can never hope to program a computer, or to build a machine, that will answer all the questions we allow. This does not preclude the possibility of solving the problem for some special cases. What is wanted is an algorithm that will solve every possible problem in the class of problems.

Consider the following question: "Is it possible to find whole numbers x, y that satisfy the equation $3x + 6y = 151$?"

We leave it to the reader to see that the answer to this question is NO. This problem is, however, *not* an example of a decision problem—there being no parameters in the statement of the question awaiting assignment before the question becomes meaningful.

The following, however, is an example of a decision problem: "For given natural numbers a, b, c is it possible to find integers x, y that satisfy the equation $ax + by = c$?"

The enunciation of an algorithm using the numbers a, b, c that will lead to an answer to this question would be an affirmative solution to the decision problem for this class of questions (i.e., for each assignment to a, b, c there is a different question). A positive solution to this decision problem would consist of an algorithm that for given a, b, c will lead to a YES or NO answer to the question. It is not difficult to show that this particular decision problem is solvable and that a necessary and sufficient condition for a solution to exist is that the greatest common divisor of a, b divide c. The Euclidean algorithm, described in Chapter 1, can thus be used to obtain such a decision-making algorithm for this problem.

A decision problem is *undecidable* if we can demonstrate that no algorithm exists to resolve all the questions raised by the problem. The halting problem is then an example of such an undecidable problem.

6.4 VARIATIONS OF THE HALTING PROBLEM

A large number of problems related to programming diagnostics, when stated in their most general terms, can be shown to be undecidable on the basis of the undecidability of the halting problem. Following is a list of decision problems, each of which is undecidable. The proof of undecidability in each case proceeds in the following vein.

Assume that the given problem is decidable. We then show that if this is the case we can describe an effective decision procedure for the halting problem. We conclude, therefore, that the given problem is undecidable.

1. Given an arbitrary Turing machine Z, an initial tape t, and symbol s, decide if Z will ever print the symbol s on its tape during the course of a computation starting with the tape t (the printing problem).

2. Given an arbitrary Turing machine Z, find a binary machine Z' with the smallest number of quintuples that computes the same function as Z.

3. Given arbitrary Turing machines Z, Z', determine if Z and Z' are equivalent in the sense of computing the same function.

4. Given an arbitrary Turing machine Z, find a machine Z' that computes the same function as Z and does this in least time (the smallest number of steps) for each argument.

5. Given an arbitrary Turing machine Z, find the smallest number in the domain of the function defined by Z.

All general optimizing problems involving the search for least time, shortest program, least storage requirements, etc., are undecidable problems. We illustrate the reduction to the halting problem and the use of the method of reductio ad absurdum by showing that the printing problem mentioned in (1) is undecidable.

Assume that (1) is decidable. We show how, under this hypothesis, we can resolve the halting problem. We shall describe an algorithm that will, given the description Z of a Turing machine and of a tape t determine whether or not Z eventually stops after starting on t. Define a new machine Z' which behaves like Z *but* instead of stopping when Z does, Z' enters a new state and prints on its tape a symbol σ, that is not in the alphabet used by machine Z, before stopping. We can use the techniques we have seen earlier to accomplish this. We add new quintuples to Z so that, at those points where Z stops, the revised machine Z' will go on to print σ before stopping. Now we ask if Z' ever prints the symbol σ, using the fact that (1) is decidable. If the answer is YES, this means that Z would have stopped; if the answer is NO, then Z would have engaged in an endless computation. In other words, we have solved the general halting problem on the assumption that (1) is decidable. Therefore, (1) is not decidable.

If (3) were decidable then so would (2) be decidable. For we can, for $k = 1,2,3,\ldots$, effectively generate all sets of k quintuples for a binary machine using not more than $2k$ states (this number is an extravagant bound on the number of different states that might be used in a machine of k quintuples). For each such set of quintuples we can determine, because of our hypothesis, (i) if this set defines a Turing machine Z', and (ii) if Z' is equivalent to the given machine Z. This procedure is clearly effective and must culminate in the discovery of a binary machine that is equivalent to Z and involves the smallest possible number of quintuples.

Now (2) is not decidable. Again, using the method of reductio ad absurdum, we show that if (2) were decidable then so would the halting problem be decidable. Given the description Z of a Turing machine and of a tape t we describe a procedure to be executed by a machine Z' that will resolve the halting problem for machine Z and input tape t.

Design Z' so that, when it receives an input argument k, it writes tape t and then simulates the behavior of Z, starting on input tape t, through k steps. If Z would have stopped in k or fewer steps, then Z' is programmed to give zero as its result. If Z would *not* have stopped within k steps, then Z' writes the value of k itself as its final result. Z' computes a total function.

If, then, Z' gives the same result for all input arguments as does the function $f(x) = x$, this means that Z never stops after starting on tape t. The determination of whether or not Z' computes the function $f(x) = x$ will resolve the halting problem for machine Z starting on tape t. Now, if (2) were decidable, we would be able to determine whether or not Z' computes the function $f(x) = x$. For, the minimal quintuple Turing machine that computes $f(x) = x$ (the identity function $U_1^{(1)}(x) = x$) has only two states (prove this). By examining the minimal machine that is equivalent to Z' we could decide this matter. Hence, (2) is not decidable.

(In the above we could have designed a machine Z' that would take the descriptions of Z and input tape t as input values in addition to the number of steps k. Our argument could easily be extended to apply to such a machine.)

We leave it to the reader to devise similar arguments to show that (4), (5) are also undecidable.

All these results imply similar conclusions for real digital computers. It is not possible, given any general purpose (in the sense that it has adequate facilities to simulate the universal Turing machine) computer, to write general diagnostic programs for this machine that are capable of analyzing arbitrary programs and of answering such questions as: (1) Will a given program lead, when executed, to an endless computation? (2) Will a given program during execution write the number 2 in location 1000? (3) Will a given word in the machine be executed as an instruction or used as a data item? (4) Will a given tape unit be used in the course of the calculation? (5) Do two given programs lead to the same result for all possible arguments? (6) What is the shortest program equivalent to a given one? (7) Will a particular instruction ever be executed? and so forth.

The proofs we have given for similar results in the theory of Turing machines apply, mutatis mutandis, to these situations. We repeat below the proof of (1) in the language of a stored program computer.

Assume that a diagnostic program D were available that could receive as input (P, I) where P is an arbitrary program and I is arbitrary input data, and make a determination of whether or not P when executed using data I will eventually stop. Modify D to produce a program $D**$ which

1. given input data I will produce a copy of it, setting up (I, I) in proper format for use by D,

2. by adding appropriate transfer instructions to D will cause an endless computation when D would otherwise halt after giving the answer YES, but $D**$ will function as D does when the answer is NO.

As before, then, if we give the input data $D**$ to $D**$ we have

1. If $D**$ stops after starting with input data $D**$, then $D**$ does not stop after starting with input data $D**$.

2. If $D**$ does not stop after starting with input data $D**$, then $D**$ does stop after starting with input data $D**$.

Our hypothesis then must be false, and no such diagnostic program exists.

6.5   A NONCOMPUTABLE FUNCTION

Having demonstrated the impossibility of an effective solution to the halting problem, we can now easily give an example of a function that most will agree to be well-defined but which is not computable. It is not computable in the sense that no algorithm to compute it can be formulated—no program written in any language—no machine plugboard wiring scheme set up—no formulation in terms of recursive functions—no symbol manipulation scheme—to yield its values for all arguments. These assertions are based on our acceptance of Turing's thesis which identifies the notions of effective computability and of Turing machine computability, for what we show is that no Turing machine exists to compute the function we shall describe.

We consider the following function $\phi(x)$

$$\phi(x) = \begin{cases} 0 \text{ if } x \text{ is not the Gödel number of a Turing machine} \\ 1 \text{ if } x \text{ is the Gödel number of a Turing machine } X, \text{ and } X \\ \text{eventually stops after starting with } x \text{ on its tape} \\ 2 \text{ if } x \text{ is the Gödel number of a Turing machine } X, \text{ and } X \\ \text{never stops after starting with } x \text{ on its tape.} \end{cases}$$

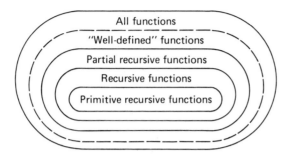

Fig. 6.2 The relative inclusion properties of various classes of functions.

$\phi(x)$ is not computable. If it were, the Turing machine that computes it would provide a general solution to the halting problem, and we have seen that this problem does not have any general solution.

We thus have seen evidence for the relative inclusion properties of the classes of functions indicated in Fig. 6.2.

The dotted-line boundary of the class of well-defined functions is used to indicate the fuzzy character of that which may be intended by "well-defined." Not everyone will agree that our example of a noncomputable function meets criteria for being well-defined that should properly apply. A mathematical constructivist would certainly not accept the application of such a condition as "X never stops after starting with x on its tape" in determining that $\phi(x) = 2$. The usual finitistic demand of constructivity would not allow the use of such a decision that is based upon a nonverifiable behavior.

As mentioned earlier, just about all of the functions that are computed in practice are primitive recursive functions. We rarely are concerned with partial functions, except in cases of programming errors, or with functions that are recursive, but not primitive recursive. As we have noted, all data-processing operations as well can be viewed mathematically as the computation of functions and these then are essentially all primitive recursive.

6.6 A RECURSIVELY ENUMERABLE SET THAT IS NOT RECURSIVE

Consider the set $S = \{x \mid \phi(x) = 0 \text{ OR } \phi(x) = 1\}$. This is the set of all numbers x that are either not Gödel numbers of Turing machines or that are the Gödel numbers of machines which eventually stop after starting with their own Gödel number on their input tape. This set of numbers is recursively enumerable, for we can define a procedure as follows, using the universal Turing machine, to search for all numbers x that satisfy either the condition $\phi(x) = 0$ or $\phi(x) = 1$.

We can, for example, execute the following procedure.

1. Given an arbitrary input number u, find a pair of natural numbers (x, y) uniquely determined by u. Use a method for obtaining the pair corresponding to a given u that will give *all* possible pairs (x, y) as u assumes all values (cf. Exercise 4.17).

2. Check if x satisfies the conditions for being the Gödel number of some Turing machine. If x is not such a number, let x be the output number.

3. If x is the Gödel number of some Turing machine X, then simulate X, using the universal Turing machine, through y steps. If the simulated machine X stops after precisely y steps, let x be the output of this computation. If the simulated machine X does not stop after the yth step, give as output the Gödel number of any Turing machine that defines a total function (i.e., one that eventually stops for any input argument).

The outputs of the machine that executes this procedure will be precisely the set of elements in S. Thus S is a recursively enumerable set.

Now, we shall show that the set $S' = \{x \mid \phi(x) = 2\}$, the complement of S, *cannot* be recursively enumerable. For we shall see that if S' were recursively enumerable we would be able to define a procedure that would determine for any given number x whether $\phi(x) = 0, 1,$ or 2; that is, we would be able to compute the noncomputable function $\phi(x)$, a contradiction.

Suppose, then, that S' is recursively enumerable, as well as S. We can then define the following procedure to compute $\phi(x)$. This procedure is similar to that which we considered in the computation of $p(x) = f(x) \cup g(x)$ included in the discussion of iteration in Section 4.12. We execute a procedure that seesaws back and forth between two given procedures, one of which is unending. If we know that in all cases one of the two given procedures must terminate, then the seesaw procedure must terminate for any argument.

For given input argument x,

1. take one step of the procedure used to generate the elements of S, searching for x, then

2. take one step of the procedure that generates the elements of S', searching for x, then return to (1).

Since x is either in S or in S' this procedure must terminate at either (1) or (2). In either case we shall know the value of $\phi(x)$ when the procedure ends.

Our argument shows in general that if any set T and its complement T' are both recursively enumerable, then T must be recursive.

The set S is thus recursively enumerable, but it is not recursive; the condition for being recursive is more demanding than that for being recursively enumerable. We have also exhibited a set S' that is not even recursively enumerable.

6.7 TURING MACHINES ARE EFFECTIVELY ENUMERABLE

We can define an algorithm that will generate or list all possible Turing machines. This is true for machines with arbitrary alphabets, but it suffices, from what we have said about the universality of binary machines, to consider only such machines. The result is obtained in a very straightforward manner.

A Turing machine is defined by listing all its quintuples. Given n states, $q_1, q_2, \ldots, q_n$, of a machine, there are $12n^2$ possible quintuples that one can write (this is seen by counting the number of ways in which $q_i \, S_j \, S_k \, M q_l$ can be formed where there are n possible q's, 2 possible S's and 3 possible M's—$R, L,$ or N). Any n-state machine is a subset of these quintuples and there are 2^{12n^2} possible subsets to consider. This number is then an upper bound on the number of n-state Turing machines. Some of these sets of quintuples must be rejected as the definition of a machine because of the incompatibility of the quintuples (no two can begin with the same $q_i \, S_j$). We can implement a procedure (cf. the exercises) that will assign successively the values $2, 3, 4, \ldots$ to n and for each assigned value will generate all possible sets of quintuples, giving as output those sets that provide definitions of Turing machines. Every possible Turing machine on a binary alphabet will be obtained, and the descriptions of these machines therefore form a recursively enumerable set.

Each of these machines defines a partially computable function. (Distinct machines do not necessarily define distinct functions.) Although these machines are effectively enumerable, we shall see in the discussion of computable numbers (Section 6.17) that a subset of them, those machines that define total functions, cannot be effectively enumerated.

6.8 THE BUSY-BEAVER PROBLEM

Consider the following problem suggested and analyzed by T. Rado [10, 15]. Suppose that Z_n is a binary (alphabet $B, 1$) Turing machine of n states $q_1, q_2, \ldots, q_n$. Let such a machine start in state q_1 on a blank tape. Either it eventually stops or it does not. If it does stop, count the number of 1's on the tape after it has stopped. The problem is to find the maximum number of 1's, call it $\Sigma(n)$, that can be produced as output by any n-state machine if and when it halts. Perhaps the name of the problem was suggested by the image of the machine busily piling up 1's as a beaver might accumulate sticks.

(Fig. 6.1 shows a 3-state machine that will print 6 1's on a blank tape. Can you do better with three states?)

It is easy to see that such a maximum must exist, or that $\Sigma(n)$ is defined for every $n > 1$. There are only a finite number of n-state Turing machines on a binary alphabet to consider. Only a finite number of these will eventually halt after starting on a blank tape and one (or more) of this finite set of machines will print the greatest number of 1's.

Can we effectively find $\Sigma(n)$? Or, in other words, can we provide an algorithm that will determine the maximum output for a given arbitrary value of n? The determination of the maximum of a finite set of numbers is a trivial problem when all numbers in the set are given. However, this is not quite what we have here. There are only a finite set of n-state machines that eventually halt, but these machines are not completely known to us.

For some particular and small n we may well be able to determine those machines that halt. For example, if $n = 3$ and one of these states, q_3, is designated as the stop state, the only machines that can be defined are trivial. A very small analysis leads to the conclusion that the two quintuple machine

$$\begin{cases} q_1\,B\,1\,R\,q_2 \\ q_2\,B\,1\,R\,q_3 \end{cases}$$

is a 3-state machine that writes the maximum number of 1's, and we have $\Sigma(3) = 2$.

But, can we define an effective procedure that provides the answer for general n? It turns out that no such algorithm is possible.

Let us look at a closely related problem which is somewhat easier to analyze and which provides a very simple example of a noncomputable function. The example is due to C. Dunham [6]. Suppose that a Turing machine of n states starts in state q_1, not on a blank tape, but on one that has the number n on it. As before, consider the maximum number of 1's that such a machine can give as output when it stops. Let $\phi(n)$ designate this function of n. It follows, from the same argument we have given for $\Sigma(n)$, that $\phi(n)$ is the maximum of some finite set of numbers and is, therefore, well defined for any n. We show that $\phi(n)$ is not computable by any Turing machine.

Suppose that $\phi(n)$ were computable. Then the function $1 + \phi(n)$, or $S(\phi(n))$, would also be computable. Let Z be a Turing machine that computes the total function $1 + \phi(n)$ and suppose that it is a machine of m states. (Assume that Z's output value is represented simply by the number of 1's on its tape when it stops.)

But $\phi(m)$, by definition, is greater than or equal to the output (number of 1's) of any m-state machine that starts with m on its tape. Therefore, we have

$$\phi(m) \geq 1 + \phi(m),$$

which is impossible. Hence, no machine such as Z exists, and the function $\phi(n)$ is not computable by any Turing machine. By Turing's thesis, it is not computable by any algorithm.

We shall leave a similar but somewhat more complicated analysis for the function $\Sigma(n)$ to the exercises. This function, too, is a noncomputable function. It can also be shown that $\Sigma(n)$ grows more rapidly than any computable function.

6.9   VARIATIONS OF THE TURING MACHINE. MACHINES WITH MORE THAN ONE TAPE OR WITH HIGHER DIMENSION TAPES

A number of modifications of Turing machines have been studied. In no case, because of Turing's thesis, do these modified characteristics enable the computation of functions that cannot be computed on a Turing machine that conforms to our definition, but they do on occasion make it possible to perform certain operations more efficiently. Some of these modified machines play important roles in complexity theory and in formal linguistics (cf. Chapters 10, 11).

In the last chapter we saw that we could simulate on an ordinary one-tape Turing machine any k-tape Turing machine, one that might employ sextuples instead of quintuples, using the 6th symbol to specify one of k (> 1) tapes that is to be read next. Having more tapes does not, therefore, increase the power of the machine, but it does facilitate some processes. For example, it is convenient for a universal Turing machine to employ two tapes, one to contain the quintuples of the machine it is simulating and the other tape to contain the input data and "work space" for the computation.

Similarly, if we extend the concept of the tape to include multidimensional physical arrays (e.g., a tape as a matrix of symbols), it is a straightforward but tedious task to simulate the actions of such a machine on a machine that uses a normal linear tape. We omit the details.

6.10   NONDETERMINISTIC TURING MACHINES

We have imposed the requirement on the set of quintuples defining a Turing machine that only one quintuple can begin with a given pair of a state symbol q_i and alphabet symbol S_j. This is necessary to avoid the ambiguous situation where two quintuples might dictate that the machine take two different actions under the same conditions, i.e., for the same given instantaneous description. If we remove this restriction, with the understanding that the machine can execute, by chance, one of a number of equally applicable quintuples beginning with the same first two symbols, the behavior of the machine will no longer be deterministic, and we leave the domain of the effective and of machine-like processes. We can, however, still consider the possibility of a terminating sequence of instantaneous descriptions that *may* result from the machine's selection of certain quintuples at points where it has a choice of more than one.

Consider the following set of quintuples

$$\left\{ \begin{array}{lll} q_1\,1\,1\,L\,q_1 & q_3\,1\,B\,R\,q_3 & q_3\,*\,*\,R\,q_4 \\ q_1\,1\,B\,R\,q_3 & q_3\,*\,B\,L\,q_4 & q_4\,B\,1\,R\,q_5 \\ q_1\,*\,1\,L\,q_1 & q_3\,B\,B\,L\,q_3 & q_5\,B\,*\,L\,q_6 \\ q_1\,B\,*\,R\,q_2 & \rule{1.5cm}{0.4pt} & \rule{1.5cm}{0.4pt} \end{array} \right\}$$

This "machine," having two quintuples beginning $q_1\,1\,\ldots$, is nondeterministic. For given input argument x, it will compute either $S(x) = x + 1$ or $N(x) = 0$, according to which of the two quintuples it elects to execute when in state q_1 reading the first 1 of the input argument.

It is reasonable to ask if nondeterminism makes it possible to compute functions that cannot be computed on an ordinary (deterministic) Turing machine. In a superficial sense the answer is yes, because it is trivially possible to define a nondeterministic Turing machine (cf. the exercises) that, following a random procedure, will give as a possible result for given input argument any number whatsoever. Therefore, we might say that any function at all is "computable" in that some actions the machine might take for given input will lead to the correct functional value as output.

This would be a useless concept, however, for we would have no way of knowing most of the time if the result the machine gives is the correct functional value or not. Therefore, we shall, in general, make use of nondeterministic machines in a rather restricted way. We shall use them not for the computation of arbitrary functions, but to make binary decisions, to accept or reject a given input string, i.e., to give a result of 1 or 0. We shall say that if *some* path the machine *might* follow after starting on a given input string leads to an accept decision, say a 1, the result will be taken to be 1. If the machine, no matter what choices of quintuples it makes, never gives the answer 1 (either because it does not halt, or because it gives only the answer 0), we shall say that the input string is rejected or the result is 0. (If the machine never halts when the result is 0, it defines a partially computable function. We know the result when it is 1, otherwise we do not.)

Such a nondeterministic machine can be replaced by a deterministic machine that gives the same result as the nondeterministic machine would give with a suitable set of choices of quintuples in the ambiguous situations. We sketch this result in cursory manner and describe a procedure that is inefficient but is deterministic. We assume a machine that either eventually stops and gives the correct result or that may go on indefinitely.

A computation on a deterministic machine is a sequence or chain of instantaneous descriptions (ID's). Graphically, it is a stark tree devoid of forked branches, a tree where each node represents an ID, with only one branch coming out of that node (outdegree 1) directed to the successor ID. A "computation" on a nondeterministic Turing machine Y is a particular path through a tree of ID's, as in Fig. 6.3, where some of the nodes may have outdegree greater than 1. A fork with several branches corresponds to the situation where there is more than one quintuple beginning with the same $q_i S_j$.

The basic idea in the construction of the equivalent deterministic Turing machine is to trace out systematically all possible paths of a given length k on Y, searching for a path that leads to a stop state. If this search for a terminating path is unsuccessful, we can increase k and extend all paths to this greater length, continuing the search for a stop state. If any terminating path exists, we shall eventually find it, otherwise the search is unending. For any given path length there are only a finite number of paths that need be considered since the number of ambiguous quintuples is finite, i.e., there is a bound on the number of outgoing branches at any fork of the tree.

We describe in more detail a possible construction for the simple case where there are two different quintuples corresponding to a given $q_i S_j$.

Initial ID

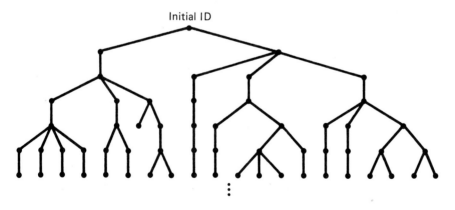

Fig. 6.3 Possible computational paths in a nondeterministic Turing machine. Every node is an ID and all possible sequences of ID's have been traced up to six steps. Only one path has led to a stop state before the completion of six steps.

Generate all possible strings of length p that are made up of two digits 1, 2–corresponding to the two possible quintuples. Let each such string, e.g., 11212..., prescribe, as follows, the selection of one of the two quintuples when the ambiguous situation is encountered during the course of a computation. The first time a fork is reached in a computation, execute the first quintuple, the second time the first quintuple, the third time the second quintuple, and so forth. The string defines the sequential decisions to be made.

Continue a computation until either the machine halts or k steps have been executed. If any decision string of length p is exhausted before k steps have been executed, extend these strings and continue the procedure.

The procedure can be generalized to handle any number of ambiguous quintuples and must eventually find a terminating path of ID's if one exists.

In this discussion we have been concerned only with the question of whether or not *some* computational path exists that leads to a certain terminal state. However, we also have occasion in the study of automata to consider "probabilistic," or "stochastic," machines. These are machines that also display a form of nondeterministic behavior, but where more information is available and relevant to the behavior of the machine. As in the above, several different steps may be taken at certain points in a machine procedure, *but* we possess additional information about the likelihood of occurrence of each of these events (cf. exercises Chapter 7). In these situations we are able, using this given information on the probabilities of occurrence of certain machine responses, to consider not merely the *possibility* of a particular course of machine actions but also the *probability* of such occurrence. There is, thus, a difference in meaning between the words "nondeterministic" and "probabilistic" in referring to the behavior of a machine.

A number of other simple models for the computing process have been suggested. The goal in some cases has been to study machines that are closer to real digital computers in possessing stored programming capabilities. The hope has been that the theory emanating from the study of such devices might then have more import with respect to the use of real computers.

6.11 WANG MACHINES

Hao Wang [20] has proposed a machine, as a base for the study of computability, that employs a stored program, but does not exploit the self-modifying capability of real machines. His "B machine" uses a tape which, as in Turing machines, is divided into squares and can be indefinitely extended. The machine also has an expandable storage for the accommodation of an arbitrarily large stored program. The machine can perform four kinds of operations. In each case we indicate the quintuples of a Turing machine that will perform analogous operations:

(1) $\rightarrow$: shift the tape to read the square one position to the right.

$$\{q_\alpha \, B \, B \, R \, q_{\alpha+1}, q_\alpha \, \bigstar \, \bigstar \, R \, q_{\alpha+1}\}$$

(2) $\leftarrow$: shift the tape to read the square one position to the left.

$$\{q_\beta \, B \, B \, L \, q_{\beta+1}, q_\beta \, \bigstar \, \bigstar \, L \, q_{\beta+1}\}$$

(3) $\bigstar$: mark the square of the tape under scan.

$$\{q_\gamma \, B \, \bigstar \, N \, q_{\gamma+1}, q_\gamma \, \bigstar \, \bigstar \, N \, q_{\gamma+1}\}$$

(4) C_n : jump (transfer) to the instruction at location n if the square being scanned is marked.

$$\{q_\delta \, B \, B \, N \, q_{\delta+1}, q_\delta \, \bigstar \, \bigstar \, N \, q_n\}$$

Each square on the tape contains either the mark $\bigstar$ or a blank B (the alphabet consists of two characters). The machine has no separate halt instruction but stops when there is no instruction telling it what to do next. By convention, every program has as its two last statements $N - 1. \rightarrow ., N. \leftarrow .$ where the location of the instruction precedes the operation symbol. Instructions are executed sequentially except when the flow is affected by the execution of a jump instruction. Note that it is not possible to erase the mark $\bigstar$; there is no instruction to erase.

If we designate the location and operation symbol of each instruction as the pair $<\alpha, \beta>$, then a program to find and stop at the nearest blank to the right of a square initially under scan would be:

$$<1, \bigstar >, <2, \rightarrow >, <3, 2>, <4, \rightarrow >, <5, \leftarrow >$$

($<3, 2>$ is the instruction at location 3: "jump to location 2 if the square being scanned is marked.")

Somewhat different conventions are used for the tape representation of data—necessitated by the fact that there is no erasing. Alternate squares, consisting of P-squares, or principal squares, and A-squares, or auxiliary squares, are used to represent information. A string of n marked P-squares with unmarked A-squares between them is used to represent the number n.

It can be shown that the three basic primitive recursive functions are computable by B-machines and that the operations of composition, primitive recursion and minimalization applied to B-computable functions lead to B-computable functions. Thus, B-machines can be used to compute any partial recursive function. The converse statement, that any function computed by a B-machine is partial recursive is even more straightforward and follows from our ability to simulate a Wang machine using a Turing machine. We leave to the reader the recognition of the feasibility of doing this.

Another machine that is not quite stripped down to its essentials but one that is easier to use is also defined by Wang. This is his "W machine," and it includes the operation of erasing. It has five operations: $\rightarrow, \leftarrow, \ast, C_x, E$. The auxiliary tape squares are not needed for a W machine. It has been shown (Shepherdson and Sturgis [16], C. Y. Lee [9]) that the jump instruction ("jump if marked to __") can equally well be replaced by a "jump if blank to __" instruction. This question had been raised by Wang in his paper but left unanswered.

6.12   REGISTER MACHINES OF SHEPHERDSON–STURGIS

J. C. Shepherdson and H. E. Sturgis have introduced another model for a universal computing device [16]. Their machines, like the Wang machines, have separate stores for instructions although they also do not exploit this by modifying their own instructions. Again, there is the goal of further bridging the gap between theoretical and real computers, and this has been achieved in several ways. As noted earlier, Turing machines are rather awkward devices to use. They can only scan one digit or bit at a time, they have only one read head and one tape, all of which limitations cause difficulties and lead to ponderous computational procedures. The Shepherdson–Sturgis machines avoid some difficulties by using, as their fundamental components, registers assumed to have the capacity to hold natural numbers (including zero) of any size. Instructions are normally executed sequentially but may carry identifiers, or labels, needed in the execution of a jump instruction. Several different versions of these machines are given, but the basic operations can be stated as in the following.

The operations given below differ slightly from those given by Shepherdson–Sturgis. This variation is due to S. Eilenberg.

$P(n)[E]$:   Add 1 to the number in register n and jump to the instruction at E.

$D(n)[E_1, E_2]$:   Subtract 1 from register n if it is not empty and jump to the instruction at E_1. If register n contains 0, jump to the instruction labeled E_2.

The machine stops if no instruction with the specified label for the successor instruction appears in the program. It is assumed that an unlimited number of registers is available, but the execution of each program involves only a finite number of these registers, the others remaining empty during the computation.

A program to move the contents of register m into register n is:

[1]: $D(n)[1, 2]$
[2]: $D(m)[3, -]$
[3]: $P(n)[2]$

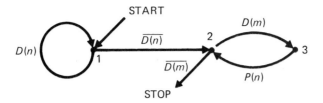

Figure 6.4

We are able to represent such programs conveniently in graphical form. Each node represents one instruction location in the program. One or two exit lines from each node indicate the succession of instructions. Thus, the above program can be depicted as in Fig. 6.4.

The two paths from node 1 correspond to the two possibilities: $D(n)$ when we are able to decrement register n, and $\overline{D(n)}$ when we cannot decrement this register because it is empty.

If it is necessary to avoid erasing register m when copying into register n, we can copy m into a third register at the same time it is copied into n, and m can then be restored from this third register at the completion of the copying into n.

Addition of the contents of two registers is shown in Fig. 6.5. This program erases register 1, 2 in the addition process. By using additional registers we can, as indicated above, avoid this situation if it is desired.

Again, these few remarkably simple machine functions are sufficient to compute any partial recursive function and, therefore, in view of Church's thesis, to compute any effectively computable function.

To compute a function $f(x_1, x_2, \ldots, x_n)$, the input values of the arguments are assumed to appear initially in registers $1, \ldots, n$. A special register y will be reserved to contain the result. If the machine does not stop, then f is not defined for the given arguments; if it does stop, the result $f(x_1, \ldots, x_n)$

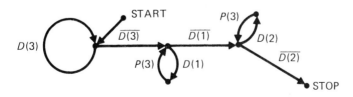

Fig. 6.5 Example of a program that will add the contents of registers 1, 2 and put the result in register 3 after having erased it.

appears in register y. We further assume that our machines will always preserve the input arguments in the input registers.

The proof, which is straightforward, consists of (1) writing programs for the basic partial recursive functions and (2) showing that if programs are available to compute certain given input functions, then we can write programs for new functions obtained from these by composition, primitive recursion, and minimalization. Any skilled programmer should be able to carry through the details of the proofs.

6.13   CELLULAR AUTOMATA

The basic ideas for these machines are due to J. von Neumann [19], who introduced them, probably not because of interest in them per se, but rather as vehicles to study the feasibility of designing automata to reproduce themselves. Other names for cellular automata are "tessellation structures" and "iterative circuit computers" [7, 17].

Consider a two-dimensional lattice of squares extending indefinitely in all directions (Fig. 6.6).

Let us suppose that each square, such as A, is a finite machine that can assume any one of N states: $\sigma_1, \sigma_2, \ldots, \sigma_N$. All squares are identical in their structure, but at any given time they may, of course, be in different states. As with most of the machines we consider, a clock regulates their behavior (these are examples of synchronous machines and of finite automata, cf. Chapters 7, 8). At each time step, every machine A assumes a state which is determined by the states of its four neighboring squares B, C, D, E (with each of which it shares one side) and of itself at the preceding time step. One of the possible states is a "quiescent" one and if a given square and its four

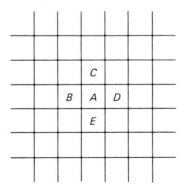

Figure 6.6

neighbors are in this quiescent state at time t then the given square remains in this same state at time $t + 1$ (some of its neighbors, of course, possibly influenced by nonquiescent squares, may at time $t + 1$ no longer be in a quiescent state). If all squares in the array arrive at the quiescent state at the same instant, no further changes of state are possible.

At the beginning of the operation of such a cellular automaton, all squares, except for some finite number, are assumed to be quiescent. The

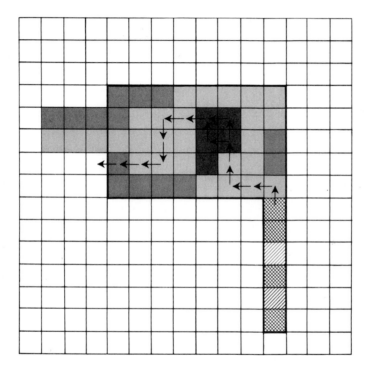

Fig. 6.7 Von Neumann Machine is theoretically capable of reproducing itself. This is a highly simplified diagram of its conceptual units. The darkest squares are the "nerve cells" of the "brain." The next lightest squares are "muscle cells." The next lightest are transmission cells. The crosshatched squares are the "tail" which bears the instructions of the machine. The double hatching represents an "on" signal; the single hatching, an "off" signal. The empty squares are units of the environment which the machine manipulates. The arrows indicate that instructions are coming from the tail, on the basis of which the brain instructs a muscle cell to act on its surroundings. The machine has sent out a "feeler" to the left. Reprinted with permission from John G. Kemeny, "Man Viewed as a Machine," *Scientific American,* April 1955.

"input" information is represented by the configurations of these nonquiescent starting states of the automaton. The termination of operation occurs when the total configuration of states of the squares ceases to change (or some authors [3, 4, 8] have found it more convenient to consider the operation ended when some predesignated square enters a particular distinguished state). A "computation" then can be defined if we encode the input data so that input values are translated into particular patterns of state configurations and, similarly, decode in some fashion a terminal configuration to give output values.

Von Neumann described (his work was elaborated posthumously by A. W. Burks [19, 3]) a universal cellular automaton that is capable of computing, as described above, any partially computable function and which also has self-reproductive capabilities. Reproduction is meant in the sense that certain initial configurations of cell states result in copies of these configurations appearing in areas of the machines that were entirely quiescent at time $t = 0$.

We have described two-dimensional cellular automata, but the extension to cellular automata of any dimension is straightforward. In particular, a one-dimensional cellular automaton is a machine that is very close to being a Turing machine, and we leave the details of the demonstration of this fact to the exercises.

6.14 A TURING MACHINE AS A SYMBOL MANIPULATION SYSTEM

We have noted that the arithmetization of Turing machines enables us to describe and study their behavior within a formal system and with no further recourse to their "machine" characteristics. We have implicitly done this in an even more simple way by following the behavior of a Turing machine as a sequence of instantaneous descriptions, which are symbolic strings, and we shall now describe this approach in a more systematic manner.

Every quintuple determines a transformation on instantaneous descriptions. We shall formally describe these transformations as schemes for rewriting symbolic strings. The quintuples will be interpreted as rewriting rules that result in the replacement of several symbols in an instantaneous description by other symbols.

Let u, v represent arbitrary finite strings of the symbols in a given machine's alphabet, including as a possibility the empty or "null" string, and let x denote an arbitrary symbol of the alphabet. We have then the following interpretations as rewriting rules of the three kinds of quintuples.

$$q_i S_j S_k N q_l : u q_i S_j v \to u q_l S_k v$$

This means that the result of executing the given quintuple is to transform a given ID $uq_i S_j v$ into the ID $uq_l S_k v$.

We similarly describe the effects of the other two kinds of quintuples.

$$q_i S_j S_k Rq_l: \begin{cases} uq_i S_j xv \to uS_k q_l xv \\ \\ uq_i S_j \to uS_k q_l B \end{cases}$$

The second part of this rule conforms to the machine's behavior when there is no symbol on the tape following S_j, the symbol under the read head. In this case, a blank square is appended to the tape. Similarly, we have

$$q_i S_j S_k Lq_l: \begin{cases} uxq_i S_j v \to uq_l xS_j v \\ \\ q_i S_j v \to q_l BS_j v \end{cases}$$

A Turing machine, then, being a set of quintuples, defines a set of rewriting rules. Starting with any given ID of a deterministic Turing machine, only one rewriting rule can possibly be applied to that ID since no two quintuples begin with the same q and S. A computation is, as previously noted, a sequence of instantaneous descriptions,

$$(ID)_1 \to (ID)_2 \to \ldots \to (ID)_n$$

where each $(ID)_k \to (ID)_{k+1}$, $k = 1, 2, \ldots, n - 1$, in the chain is the result of the application of one of the quintuples in the machine. $(ID)_n$ includes the stop state and so has no successor.

If an ID, such as $(ID)_n$ in this case, results from a chain of applications of any number of quintuples or rewriting rules, starting with, say, $(ID)_1$, we may write

$$(ID)_1 \to * (ID)_n$$

to indicate this fact. (The arrow without the star indicates the application of one rewriting rule.)

We could very well have started the discussion of Turing machines from this point of view of using rewriting rules and instantaneous descriptions without ever mentioning the physical characteristics of these machines or the heuristic considerations that led to their formulation. This would, however, have been a rather sterile beginning and done little to support our belief that such machines can execute arbitrary effective calculations.

The idea of using rewriting rules in symbol manipulation systems will be applied extensively in the discussion in Chapter 9 of formal languages. Sets of such rules will comprise what will be called a "phrase structure grammar" within that context.

6.15   THE USE OF "NORMAL" REWRITING RULES AND SOME SPECIAL SYMBOL MANIPULATION SYSTEMS

It is possible to accomplish the transformation on ID's that results from the execution of quintuples by using rewriting rules that are somewhat different in interpretation from those we used in the last section. We shall now use rules that transform certain prefixes of finite strings into suffixes.

Let g, h be finite strings of symbols. A rule, written as $g \to h$, is *not* taken now to mean that we replace g by h in place. Rather, an application of this rule transforms the string gu, where u is an arbitrary finite string, into the string uh, i.e., $gu \to uh$.

Rules of this kind are called *normal* rewriting rules or *normal* productions. We shall show by illustration that we can use such rules to accomplish the transformations of the last section.

We change the convention for writing an ID so that it always begins with a state symbol. Assume that the information to the left of the read head (up to the end-of-tape mark) is cut off and attached to the right end of the string of the tape data. Use one end-of-tape mark or asterisk instead of the two marks that would be next to each other as a result of the first step. Thus, the

ID $\boxed{\ast\ S_2 S_1 S_2 \mid q_3 S_4 S_1 \ast}$ becomes $q_3 S_4 S_1 \ast S_2 S_1 S_2$. Let us call an ID written

with this new convention a "normal" ID.

Now, considering ID's written in this manner, it is possible to accomplish all the necessary transformations corresponding to quintuples by using normal rewriting rules. These rules will involve repeatedly peeling off a prefix of two symbols from the front end of a string and appending a suffix, determined by that prefix, to the right end of the string.

Consider first a quintuple of the type $q_i S_j S_k N q_l$ which we have seen to determine the transformation $u q_i S_j v \to u q_l S_k v$. This is accomplished by the set of normal rewriting rules:

$$q_i S_j \to q_l S_k$$
$$\sigma\tau \to \sigma\tau \qquad \text{(where } \sigma \text{ is any symbol except a}$$
$$q \text{ and } \tau \text{ is any symbol at all)}$$

For example, the quintuple $q_2 S_1 S_2 N q_3$ transforms the ID $\ast S_1 S_3 q_2 S_1 S_0 \ast$ into the ID $\ast S_1 S_3 q_3 S_2 S_0 \ast$. The equivalent transformation is accomplished by writing the normal rules

$$q_2 S_1 \to q_3 S_2$$
$$\sigma\tau \to \sigma\tau$$

We write the succession of strings obtained by applying these rules:

$$q_2 S_1 S_0 \star S_1 S_3 \rightarrow S_0 \star S_1 S_3 q_3 S_2 \rightarrow S_1 S_3 q_3 S_2 S_0 \star \rightarrow q_3 S_2 S_0 \star S_1 S_3$$

If there had been an odd number of symbols in the string, the device would still work, but we would have to "circulate" through the string two times, e.g., $q_2 S_1 S_2 N q_3$ transforms $\star S_1 S_3 q_2 S_1 S_0 S_2 \star$ into $\star S_1 S_3 q_3 S_2 S_0 S_2 \star$. The normal rules would effect the following transformations:

$$q_2 S_1 S_0 S_2 \star S_1 S_3 \rightarrow S_0 S_2 \star S_1 S_3 q_3 S_2 \rightarrow \star S_1 S_3 q_3 S_2 S_0 S_2 \rightarrow S_3 q_3 S_2 S_0 S_2 \star S_1$$
$$\rightarrow S_2 S_0 S_2 \star S_1 S_3 q_3 \rightarrow S_2 \star S_1 S_3 q_3 S_2 S_0 \rightarrow S_1 S_3 q_3 S_2 S_0 S_2 \star \rightarrow q_3 S_2 S_0 S_2 \star S_1 S_3$$

The other two kinds of quintuples can be handled in like manner. Consider $q_i S_j S_k R q_l$. For example, $q_2 S_1 S_2 R q_3$ transforms $\star S_1 S_3 q_2 S_1 S_0 S_2 \star$ into $\star S_1 S_3 S_2 q_3 S_0 S_2 \star$.

We first try the normal rules

$$q_2 S_1 \rightarrow S_2 q_3$$
$$\sigma \tau \rightarrow \sigma \tau$$

We then have:

$$q_2 S_1 S_0 S_2 \star S_1 S_3 \rightarrow S_0 S_2 \star S_1 S_3 S_2 q_3 \rightarrow \star S_1 S_3 S_2 q_3 S_0 S_2 \rightarrow S_3 S_2 q_3 S_0 S_2 \star S_1$$
$$\rightarrow q_3 S_0 S_2 \star S_1 S_3 S_2,$$

which is correct.

However, while these rules work for this type of quintuple if there are an odd number of symbols in the string, they do not work if there are an even number; the cycling will go on indefinitely, e.g.,

$$q_2 S_1 S_0 \star S_1 S_3 \rightarrow S_0 \star S_1 S_3 S_2 q_3 \rightarrow S_1 S_3 S_2 q_3 S_0 \star \rightarrow S_2 q_3 S_0 \star S_1 S_3$$
$$\rightarrow S_0 \star S_1 S_3 S_2 q_3 \rightarrow \ldots$$

There are a number of devices we might use to get around this difficulty. Let us use the following rules where we introduce the special symbol η.

$$q_2 S_1 \rightarrow S_2 q_3' \qquad S_2 q_3' \rightarrow \eta S_2 q_3$$
$$\sigma \tau \rightarrow \sigma \tau \qquad \eta \tau \rightarrow \tau$$

(σ is any symbol except a q or η; τ is any symbol at all, and $\sigma \tau \neq S_2 q_3'$)

Now, if there are an even number of symbols, $S_2 q_3'$ will move to the head of the string and then the parity of the string will be changed by appending the three symbols $\eta S_2 q_3$. Later the η will be erased.

Thus we have

$$q_2 S_1 S_0 \star S_1 S_3 \rightarrow S_0 \star S_1 S_3 S_2 q_3' \rightarrow S_1 S_3 S_2 q_3' S_0 \star \rightarrow S_2 q_3' S_0 \star S_1 S_3$$
$$\rightarrow S_0 \star S_1 S_3 \eta S_2 q_3 \rightarrow S_1 S_3 \eta S_2 q_3 S_0 \star \rightarrow \eta S_2 q_3 S_0 \star S_1 S_3 \rightarrow q_3 S_0 \star S_1 S_3 S_2$$

We leave it to the reader to verify that these rules will also yield the correct result if there are an odd number of symbols in the string.

In case there are no tape symbols to the right of the scanned square, the execution of the quintuple $q_i S_j S_k R q_l$ must result in a blank square (S_0) being appended to the right end of the tape. We can accomplish this in our example by adding the rule

$$q_3 * \rightarrow q_3 S_0 *$$

Again, the reader can verify that the initial normal ID $q_2 S_1 * S_2 S_1$ will be correctly transformed into the ID $q_3 S_0 * S_2 S_1 S_2$ as a result of all these rewriting rules.

The third type of quintuple $q_i S_j S_k L q_l$ is handled in analogous fashion and we omit the details.

Summarizing what we have done, it appears that any Turing machine computation can be accomplished by a restricted type of string manipulation. Starting with a string representation of an initial ID, we repeatedly peel off prefixes of fixed length 2 and append a transformed version of each prefix as a suffix to the string. The transformations continue until a stop state symbol appears at the head of the string.

6.16 THE PROBLEM OF "TAG"

We look next at a still further restricted type of string transformation, similar to the one discussed in the preceding use of normal rules, but where the transformation at each step depends only on the first symbol of the prefix.

E. L. Post, in 1921 [14], considered such string manipulations of which the following is an example.

Starting with some finite string of 0's and 1's:

1. if the first digit is 0, delete the first two digits and append 1 to the string.

2. if the first digit is 1, delete the first two digits and append 010 to the string.

Repeat the procedure, continuing to apply the appropriate rule at each step as long as there are at least two digits left in the string.

If, for example, we start with the string 01000 we have:

$$01000 \rightarrow 0001 \rightarrow 011 \rightarrow 11 \rightarrow 010 \rightarrow 01 \rightarrow 1$$

and we can go no further.

If we start with the string 110100, we have

$$110100 \rightarrow 0100010 \rightarrow 000101 \rightarrow 01011 \rightarrow 0111 \rightarrow 111 \rightarrow 1010$$
$$\rightarrow 10010 \rightarrow 010010 \rightarrow 00101 \rightarrow 1010 \rightarrow \ldots$$

With the second occurrence of 1010 we see that this sequence of transformations will continue indefinitely.

The problem of Tag for a given set of rules and a given starting string is
to determine if the string will eventually be exhausted or if the transformations will continue indefinitely. The name "Tag," suggested by B. P. Gill,
comes, of course, from the childhood game and the vision of the right end of
the string "chasing" the front end.

The problem that we have given as an example is not difficult to analyze.
However, some others of this type are quite intractable. For example, Post
considered the following tag problem with "deletion number" 3 and rules:

1. if the first digit is 0, delete the first three digits and append 00 to the
string.

2. if the first digit is 1, delete the first three digits and append 1101 to the
string.

We may succeed in analyzing the behavior of Tag for a particular given
input string, but we ask the more general question. Is there some effective
procedure that will determine for an arbitrary starting string whether or not
the transformations will continue indefinitely? We do not know if there is
such an effective procedure that will resolve the problem just stated.

More generally, Minsky [11] has shown that there is no effective procedure that will take as input the rewriting rules of an arbitrary Tag system
together with some arbitrary given starting string and arrive at a determination of whether or not the game of Tag will end for that starting string.

Minsky proved this result by showing that if the Tag problem could be
solved, then we would have a solution to the halting problem. In the last
section we saw that a Turing machine computation can be performed using a
rewriting system that is very similar to a Tag system, but where the rewriting
rules depend upon the *two* symbols of each prefix, not just the *first* symbol as
in a Tag system. Minsky's result is based upon his demonstration, using some
ingenious coding schemes, that a Turing machine computation can be expressed as a rewriting system in which each normal rule depends only upon
the first symbol of the prefix, i.e., a computation can be expressed as a Tag
system. The problem, then, of whether or not an arbitrary game of Tag ends
can be equated to the halting problem for an arbitrary Turing machine.

Since Tag systems provide still another model of the computing process,
any machine that can apply an arbitrary Tag process can serve as a universal
Turing machine. Very simple universal Turing machines have been designed
by Minsky to handle the general Tag system. At this time it appears that his
machine with a 4 symbol alphabet and 7 internal states is the "smallest"
universal machine that is known. It is the smallest such machine in the sense

that the product of the number of symbols in its alphabet and the number of its states is less than that of any other known machine that can cope with a general Tag system. (See Section 11.5, "Complexity of Machines.")

Minsky has also shown that such machines can do without some of the properties of a normal Turing machine if we allow the use of more than one tape. A remarkably frugal universal machine that he has described employs a single tape with two read heads and without the ability to read or write on the tape but only to sense the end of the tape.

6.17 COMPUTABLE NUMBERS

In his fundamental paper [18], Turing considered computable *numbers* rather than computable *functions*. The computable numbers are those real numbers such as

$$\sqrt{2} = 1.414213562\ldots$$

whose infinite decimal (or in any radix) expansions can be computed by some effective process. In this case, the machine does not halt but continues indefinitely, emitting as output the successive digits of the infinite expansion of the number being computed. (Assume a separate output tape.)

On the face of it, the problems of computing numbers and of computing functions appear to be different, but they are in essence the same. The (total) computable functions correspond in one-to-one fashion to the computable numbers. If a machine computes, say, some binary real number between 0 and 1, it can be modified to compute the function corresponding to that number, and conversely. We leave to the exercises the details of an effective correspondence between the total functions on the natural numbers and the real numbers. This correspondence justifies the last statement.

Without loss of generality we can consider only the real numbers between 0 and 1. We have seen that there are a nondenumerably infinite collection of such numbers. However, the *computable* real numbers form only a denumerably infinite class by virtue of the fact that there cannot be more computable numbers than there are Turing machines, and we have seen that all Turing machines can be enumerated. "Most" real numbers are not computable since the real numbers comprise an infinitude of higher order. This is said in the sense that the computable numbers can be matched in one-to-one fashion with the members of a subset of the real numbers, but not conversely.

Although there is a one-to-one correspondence between the computable numbers and the integers, i.e., the computable numbers can be enumerated, this correspondence is not effective. There is no algorithm to compute the integer to which each computable number corresponds (and conversely). We can prove this result by using a "diagonalization" argument similar to that we used in showing that the real numbers were nondenumerable.

Suppose that there *were* an effective correspondence between the computable numbers and the integers. With no loss of generality (cf. the exercises) we can restrict the computable numbers to those lying between 0 and 1.

$$1 \leftrightarrow \alpha^{(1)} = .\alpha_1^{(1)}\alpha_2^{(1)}\alpha_3^{(1)} \ldots$$
$$2 \leftrightarrow \alpha^{(2)} = .\alpha_1^{(2)}\alpha_2^{(2)}\alpha_3^{(2)} \ldots$$
$$3 \leftrightarrow \alpha^{(3)} = .\alpha_1^{(3)}\alpha_2^{(3)}\alpha_3^{(3)} \ldots$$
$$\vdots$$

The set $\{\alpha^{(i)} \mid i = 1, 2, \ldots\}$ is assumed to include all computable numbers between 0 and 1.

If the correspondence is effective, this means that if we are given an integer, we can compute the (quintuples of the) Turing machine that computes the corresponding real number, and conversely. We can then compute that real number to any number of decimal places.

Such a correspondence is, however, impossible for we now describe a computable real number β that cannot possibly be in the supposed list of all computable numbers. Compute each digit β_i $(i = 1, 2, \ldots)$ in the decimal expansion of β by the equations

$$\beta_i = \alpha_i^{(i)} - 1 \text{ if } \alpha_i^{(i)} > 1$$
$$= 2 \qquad \text{if } \alpha_i^{(i)} = 0 \text{ or if } \alpha_i^{(i)} = 1$$

This construction assures that β differs in at least one position from every number $\alpha^{(i)}$ in the list. Further, we avoid the ambiguous representations of the finite decimals (e.g., $0.43000\ldots = 0.42999\ldots$). The procedure is clearly effective and leads to a number β that is computable but cannot be in the list, since it differs in at least one position from every number in the list. Our hypothesis that such an all-inclusive list exists must be wrong and, therefore, the computable real numbers are denumerable but cannot be effectively enumerated.

The computable numbers are tempting as a basis for constructive mathematics, but they have, however, from a constructive point of view, some properties that seem to limit their applicability. For example, the sum of two computable numbers is a computable number (cf. the exercises). We might say that the computable numbers are "closed" under addition, which is an essential property of a collection of objects known as a *field* in mathematics. It seems reasonable to expect then that we can *construct* the sum of two computable numbers. But, as pointed out by J. Myhill [13], this is not necessarily the case. We may be able to compute two numbers α, β, without being able to find even the first digit of $\alpha + \beta$.

For example, let $\alpha = 0.666\ldots$ be defined as follows. The ith digit α_i of α is set equal to 6 if the ith decimal place in the infinite expansion of π *is not* the first occurrence of the beginning of a string of 10 consecutive 5's and let $\alpha_i = 7$ if the ith decimal in π *is* the first occurrence of the beginning of such a string.

Let $\beta = 0.333\ldots$ be defined in similar fashion. Define $\beta_i = 3$ if the ith digit in the infinite expansion of π is not the first occurrence of the beginning of a string of 10 consecutive 7's in π and $\beta_i = 2$ otherwise.

Now no one knows if 10 consecutive 5's or if 10 consecutive 7's occur in π. Such strings have not appeared among the several thousand decimal places to which π has been computed, but we have no theory at this time that implies that they will or will not appear somewhere in the infinite decimal expansion of π.

We have the following possibilities:

$\alpha + \beta = 1$ if there are no strings of 10 consecutive 5's or of 10 consecutive 7's in π.

$\alpha + \beta > 1$ if a string of 10 consecutive 5's appear before a string of 10 consecutive 7's.

$\alpha + \beta < 1$ if a string of 10 consecutive 7's appear before a string of 10 consecutive 5's.

Although we can compute α and β to any desired number of places, we do not know how to go about computing even the first digit of $\alpha + \beta$.

For reasons related to these matters, E. Bishop, in his book on *Constructive Analysis* (cf. Chapter 1), has used not the computable numbers but, rather, the *decimally approximable* numbers as the foundation of constructive analysis. A real number ρ is called decimally approximable if, given any positive rational number ε, no matter how small, we can find a number d with a finite number of decimal places such that $|\rho - d| < \varepsilon$.

With respect to our example, both α and β are decimally approximable. Their sum $\alpha + \beta$ is also decimally approximable although we do not know how to compute its decimal representation. Apparently we can verify constructively that such a number is decimally approximable although we cannot do the same for the property of being computable.

6.18   INTIMATIONS OF GÖDEL'S RESULTS

Following the treatment in Arbib [1, 2], we give a partly heuristic, partly formal discussion of some of the results and consequences of Gödel's investigations in mathematical logic on the incompleteness of formal systems. These results have been stated by von Neumann to be the most significant mathematical discovery of the first half of the twentieth century.

Recall that we briefly introduced the notion of a formal system in Chapter 2 and described in Chapter 4 the generation of all the theorems of a formal system as the generation of a recursively enumerable set. What Gödel showed, among other things, was that any formal system that is "rich" enough to enable us to describe within the system the basic operations and relations of arithmetic is "incomplete" in the sense that *there exist true statements or theorems within the system that cannot be obtained from the axioms and rules of inference of the system.* Thus, in all nontrivial systems ("nontrivial" meaning that at least elementary arithmetic is describable within the system) of mathematics, there are truths which cannot be discovered by working entirely within the system.

We shall attempt to make this result plausible and we give the skeleton of a proof along the following lines.

Let us consider a particular mathematical system S. Our assumption that the system is adequate to discuss within it the relations and operations of elementary arithmetic implies, in particular, that we are able to talk about Turing machines and their operations in terms using the arithmetization techniques of Chapter 5. For example, we have seen how to represent the instantaneous descriptions of Turing machines as natural numbers and how to describe the transition of these descriptions as the results of functions determined by the quintuples which define the machine. The quintuples in turn can also be represented by natural numbers.

Within the system S we shall be able to write out some proofs for particular Turing machines leading to conclusions that these machines do or do not eventually stop after starting with a description (Gödel number) of themselves on their input tape.

For example, consider the proof that the binary Turing machine, whose stop state is q_2, consisting only of the quintuples

$$Q: \{q_1 \, 1 \, B \, R \, q_1, \; q_1 \, B \, B \, N \, q_2, \; q_1 \, * \, * \, N \, q_2\}$$

will always stop eventually when it starts on an input tape that contains its own description. Such a proof might consist of statements indicating that *any* instantaneous description to which Q can be applied can contain only a finite number of 1's and, therefore, is eventually transformed into an instantaneous description which is terminal.

Since all our proofs are given within the framework of the formal system S, it is possible, as noted in Section 4.13, to write a program (or design a Turing machine) that will go about putting together in all possible ways sequences of applications of the rules of inference to the axioms and to theorems proven from them. That is, as indicated earlier, the theorems of our system form a recursively enumerable set.

Now, some of the theorems emitted by the machine executing this procedure will be of the form:

"N is the Gödel number of a Turing machine that never stops when it starts with N on its tape."

We next modify our procedure as follows. We revise our program so that it receives as input a number M and then goes about searching for a theorem "M is the Gödel number of a Turing machine that never stops when it starts with M on its tape." If it eventually generates such a theorem, then our new procedure stops, indicating a successful conclusion to its search. Let P be the Gödel number of a Turing machine designed to execute this procedure. We show the following properties of P.

1. P is the Gödel number of a Turing machine that never stops when it starts with P on its tape.

2. Statement (1) is *not* one of those theorems discovered by procedure P.

We prove (1) by assuming that it is *not* true and then showing that this assumption implies that it *is* true. Then, it must be true by the method of reductio ad absurdum. The proof follows.

If (1) is not true, this means that P eventually stops when it starts with P on its tape—or that the procedure succeeds in finding a theorem of the form "P is the Gödel number of a Turing machine that never stops when it starts with P on its tape." But this is the statement of (1). Thus, if (1) is not true, then it is true, and we have shown (1) to be true.

On the other hand, (1), which we now know to be true, asserts that procedure P never stops when it starts with P on its tape. Therefore, (2) is true.

We have, then, discovered a theorem, namely (1), that is *not* among those theorems that the procedure M can generate, or, equivalently, that P can verify. Our system S is then incomplete in that any procedure, utilizing all the axioms and rules of the system which generates all theorems obtainable from them, *cannot yield* a certain theorem that we have shown by other arguments to be true.

6.19   DISCUSSION OF THE INCOMPLETENESS RESULTS AND SOME POSSIBLE IMPLICATIONS TO THE QUESTION OF WHETHER OR NOT MAN IS A MACHINE

Some authors have interpreted these incompleteness results to imply that the human brain is not a machine. For, the argument goes, Man, possessing Gödel's results on incompleteness, is able to enunciate, as we have done in the preceding Section, a theorem that is true but is not provable within any formal system. Any machine, as discussed in Chapter 2, can be described in terms of a formal system. Hence, Man can display a theorem not provable by any machine.

As has been noted, however (Davis [5]), the argument is faulty. For we can certainly program the use of Gödel's incompleteness theorem within a machine just as it is used by Man. Any computer so endowed could equally well state a theorem not provable within any formal system, or by any machine program, *if it is given that program* (or the Gödel number of the Turing machine that performs this computation).

However, the incompleteness result does seem to imply that *if* the human brain is a machine (and its operations are describable as a formal system), then the brain can never discover the description of its own workings. For, if it could do this, then Gödel's result indicates that the brain could prove a theorem which is beyond its proving capability. However, these arguments seem to shed no light on the question of whether or not the brain is a machine. In all of this discussion we have left undefined the word "machine."

EXERCISES

6.1 Show that *if* a Turing machine existed that could solve the halting problem, it would be possible to define a Turing machine that could decide the truth or falsity of Fermat's last theorem (THEOREM: There do not exist any positive integers satisfying the equation $x^n + y^n = z^n$ for $n > 2$). Show the result by actual construction of a machine, not by resorting to the fact that a false hypothesis implies any statement at all.

6.2 Show that there is no effective procedure to determine if two arbitrary given Turing machines both eventually halt for the same input arguments.

6.3 Show that there is no effective procedure to determine the smallest element in the domain of an arbitrary partially computable function.

6.4 Show that there is no effective procedure to determine for an arbitrary given Turing machine a machine which computes the same function and employs the smallest possible number of steps for every argument.

6.5 Show that there is no effective procedure to determine if an arbitrary given Turing machine computes a function that is identically equal to 2 for every argument.

6.6 Show that if the halting problem could be solved for an initial blank tape, then it could be solved for an arbitrary initial tape.

6.7 Write a program in any language that executes a decision procedure to determine for given input values of a, b, c if there exist natural numbers x, y that satisfy the equation $ax + by = c$.

6.8 Show that no diagnostic program exists that will determine for an arbitrary given machine language program (for any stored program computer) whether a given memory location will be used, during the execution of that program, as the location of an instruction or as the location of a data word. (This result explains in part the difficulty of constructing a translator that is completely general to translate programs written in one machine language into programs written in another machine language.)

6.9 Write a program in any language that will generate for given input n all n-state Turing machines. This will show that the class of Turing machines can be effectively enumerated (i.e., they comprise a recursively enumerable set).

6.10 Construct a possible solution to the busy beaver problem for machines of 7 states. That is, define a binary Turing machine of 7 states that will eventually halt and will write the largest possible number of 1's on an initially blank tape.

6.11 Show that the function $\Sigma(n)$ (the maximum number of 1's that can be printed on a blank tape by any binary n-state machine) is not a computable function.

Hint: Suppose that function $\Sigma(x)$ *were* computable. Let, then, the machine $M_{\Sigma(x)}$ that computes $\Sigma(x)$ have k states. Modify $M_{\Sigma(x)}$ to obtain a machine $M_{\Sigma(\Sigma(x))}$ that computes $\Sigma(\Sigma(x))$. Suppose that $M_{\Sigma(\Sigma(x))}$ has k' states. Next, define a machine for given x, $/\!/^x$, that transforms a blank tape into the representation of x and then continues its computation, functioning as $M_{\Sigma(\Sigma(x))}$ does, i.e., $/\!/^x: B \to \bar{x} \to \Sigma(\Sigma(x))$. This can be done with $x + 1 + k'$ states. From the definition of $\Sigma(x)$, we then have $\Sigma(x + 1 + k') \geq \Sigma(\Sigma(x))$. But, this is impossible for *all* x since $\Sigma(x) > x + 1 + k'$ for sufficiently large x, and $\Sigma(x)$ is an increasing function of x.

6.12 Define a Turing machine, and mode of operation, that makes use of three tapes—an input tape that can only be read, a working tape that can be used for reading or writing in a manner similar to tape usage on a conventional machine, and an output tape that can only be written. Show that such a machine can be simulated by a conventional one-tape machine.

6.13 Define a nondeterministic Turing machine that will give as a possible result, for any input argument x, any number whatsoever.

6.14 Design Wang B-machines that will compute the three basic primitive recursive functions $S(x) = x + 1$, $N(x) = 0$, $U_i^{(n)}(x_1, \ldots, x_n) = x_i$. Follow the conventions indicated in the text.

6.15 Design a register machine that will compute the product function $\Pi(x, y) = xy$. Assume that x is in register 1, y in register 2. Put the result in register 3. Make use of as many registers as you need.

6.16 Following the discussion in the text give a precise definition of a one-dimensional cellular automaton and of a computation on such a machine. Show that such a machine can be simulated by a Turing machine and, conversely, that any Turing machine can be simulated by a one-dimensional cellular automaton.

6.17 Show that any quintuple of the form $q_i S_j S_k L q_l$ can be simulated by the use of normal rewriting rules.

6.18 Write a program in any language that will generate all possible pairs of the natural numbers. This will imply that the set of all number pairs is a recursively enumerable set. (Assume that machine word lengths are unlimited.)

6.19 Show that any Turing machine that makes use of four states q_1, q_2, q_3, q_4 can be replaced by a machine that makes use of only two states, at the expense of an expanded alphabet. The methods used can be applied to "reduce" any n-state machine to a 2-state machine. (In designing the 2-state machine, do not "waste" a state by using a special stop state. Assume, rather, the convention of Exercise 5.14 to determine when the machine stops.)

6.20 Show that the class of real numbers has the same cardinal number as (i.e., can be put into one-to-one correspondence with) the class of total functions defined on the natural numbers. Consider only the real numbers in the interval $0 \leq x < 1$, then generalize to all real numbers.

6.21 Show that the class of *all* (binary) computable numbers has the same cardinal number as the class of (binary) computable numbers lying inside the interval from 0 to 1.

6.22 Show that any real number whose binary representation is computable has a computable decimal representation, and conversely.

6.23 Let α, β be two computable numbers ($0 \leq \alpha, \beta < 1$) whose infinite binary representations are defined as the outputs of two given Turing machines Z_α, Z_β. Prove that $\alpha + \beta$ is computable although we are not necessarily able to define the Turing machine that computes it.

REFERENCES

1. Arbib, M. A., *Brains, Machines and Mathematics.* New York: McGraw-Hill, 1964.
2. Arbib, M. A., *Theories of Abstract Automata.* Englewood Cliffs, N.J.: Prentice-Hall, Inc., 1969.
3. Burks, A. W., ed., *Essays on Cellular Automata.* Urbana, Ill.: University of Illinois Press, 1970.
4. Codd, E. F., *Cellular Automata.* (Assn. Comp. Mach., Monogr. Ser.) New York: Academic Press, 1968.
5. Davis, M., ed., *The Undecidable. Basic Papers. Undecidable Propositions, Unsolvable Problems, and Computable Functions.* New York: Raven Press, 1965.
6. Dunham, C., "A Candidate for the Simplest Uncomputable Function." *Comm. Assn. Comp. Mach.,* **8,** 4 (April 1965).
7. Holland, J. H., "Iterative Circuit Computers: Characterization and Resume of Advantages and Disadvantages." *Proceedings of the Symposium on Microelectronics and Large Systems.* Washington, D.C.: Spartan Press, Inc., 1965.

8. Holland, J. H., "Universal Spaces: A Basis for Studies of Adaptation," in E. R. Caianiello, ed., *Automata Theory*. New York: Academic Press, Inc., 1966.

9. Lee, C. Y., "Categorizing Automata by W-Machine Programs." *J. Assn. Comp. Mach.*, **8,** (1961).

10. Lin, S. and T. Rado, "Computer Studies of Turing Machine Problems." *J. Assn. Comp. Mach.*, **12,** 2 (April 1965).

11. Minsky, M. L., "Recursive Unsolvability of Post's Problem of 'Tag' and Other Topics in the Theory of Turing Machines." *Ann. Math.* **74** (1961).

12. Minsky, M. L., *COMPUTATION: Finite and Infinite Machines*. Englewood Cliffs, N.J.: Prentice-Hall, Inc., 1967.

13. Myhill, J. "What Is a Real Number?", *Amer. Math. Mon.* **79** (1972).

14. Post, E. L., "Absolutely Unsolvable Problems and Relatively Undecidable Propositions—Account of an Anticipation," 1941. In [5].

15. Rado, T., "On Non-Computable Functions." *Bell System Tech. J.* **41,** 3 (May 1962).

16. Shepherdson, J. C., and H. E. Sturgis, "Computability of Recursive Functions." *J. Assn. Comp. Mach.*, **10** (1963).

17. Thatcher, J. W., "Universality in the von Neumann Cellular Model." *Univ. Michigan Tech. Rep.*, 1965.

18. Turing, A. M., "On Computable Numbers with an Application to the Entscheidungsproblem." *Proc. London Math. Soc.*, 2nd Ser. **42,** 1936, pp. 230–265; Correction, ibid., **43,** pp. 544–546. Reprinted in [5].

19. Von Neumann, J., *Theory of Self-Reproducing Automata*. Ed. by A. W. Burks. Urbana, Ill.: University of Illinois Press, 1966.

20. Wang, H., "A Variant to Turing's Theory of Computing Machines." *J. Assn. Comp. Mach.*, **4** (1957).

7
General Remarks
About Automata

Automata are constructions of mathematics more than of engineering. They are of interest insofar as the kinds of symbol manipulation schemes that they can execute. We have seen a prime example of an automaton in the Turing machine. The universal Turing machine can execute an arbitrary effective procedure (Turing's thesis). There are, however, many limited procedures of significance that can be accomplished with devices that are restricted in some way by comparison to the universal Turing machine—especially in lacking the ability to provide as much peripheral storage (tape) as the machine may need in the course of a computation. Any real computer is, of course, restricted in this way with some practical bound on time and on its storage capacity, and is thus, in a practical sense, not an example of a universal Turing machine.

The notions of state and of state transition are, as seen in Turing machines, fundamental to any discussion of automata.

A hierarchy of automata can be described. The simplest kind, sometimes called a "mechanism," has no tape, or "external environment." It simply follows a succession of states. A Turing machine that can only move in one direction over its input tape is an example of a "finite automaton." Other modifications may restrict in various ways the freedom of access of the machine to its peripheral store; examples of this are pushdown store automata, i.e., machines with a "last in—first out" memory stack, and stack automata. In this chapter we briefly introduce a variety of different automata without considering the functions they can perform. Chapters 8 and 10 go further into the uses of some of these devices.

These machines are also called "logical automata." Their states and state transition rules can be realized by assemblages of fundamental logical components. We have noted this in part in the discussion of Chapter 3 on the applications of Boolean algebra. We look again at the logical gates that can be used to implement arbitrary Boolean functions, and we consider a variant of these gates, the McCulloch-Pitts neurons that arose from a consideration of the characteristics of the neurons in an animal nervous system. We also look at some single (or universal) logical elements that can be used as the building blocks for the circuitry of any logical automaton.

Feedback is essential to the design of more powerful automata. We are using the term here to refer to circuits where signals can be "fed back" to earlier components that have already appeared in the circuit flow through the automaton. This is a special case of a universal characteristic of self-regulating systems of all kinds. Feedback is reminiscent of the use of recursion in the definition of functions.

There are times when we want to follow random, not deterministic, processes in a computer, and we look briefly at ways—"Monte Carlo" methods—for doing this in a deterministic machine.

The power of computing devices can be extended by attaching an "oracle" to them, a device that can answer questions beyond the capacity of any computer not so equipped. The idea is reminiscent of those computer applications that call for human judgmental input in some man-machine interactive usage.

We close this chapter with a look at the provocative question raised by Turing in his paper, "Can a Machine Think?"

7.1   WHAT IS AN AUTOMATON?

Webster defines an automaton as "a machine or control mechanism designed to follow automatically a predetermined sequence of operations or respond to encoded instructions." In automata theory we study such devices, but it never becomes necessary actually to build them, for the automata we study are idealized machines whose behavior can be completely explained in terms of some formal descriptive system where we manipulate symbols instead of hardware. We have seen this idea amply illustrated in the case of Turing machines. However, of course, we often hope to learn, in our study of these devices, information that will be of help to us in designing real computing devices. The *machine* concept underlying automata is, nevertheless, not at all superfluous for it may provide a compelling picture of the effectiveness (where such is the case) of the procedures defined by an automaton's behavior, and it may allow more simple and elegant descriptions of the

Fig. 7.1 The three fundamental phases of any information processing.

processes being executed than would the symbolic treatment alone. Thus we often use the word "machine" interchangeably with "automaton."

As with real computing devices there are always three functions to consider in discussing automata: (1) input, (2) processing, (3) output (Fig. 7.1). These may take a variety of forms, and input or output may be, in some cases, limited to being part of an internal configuration or even may apparently be lacking, but they are always represented in some way. As with the real devices that provide much of the underlying motivation for the study of this subject, automata are devices that transform information into information.

A Turing machine is an example of such a device. Let us recall its salient characteristics. First, it assumes at any time one of a finite number of internal *states,* where we think of the tape as being external to the control part of the machine. It has a built-in clock and at regular time steps it reads its tape, which is its sole "environment." The information on each tape square consists of a symbol which is one of a finite set of such possible symbols. Its internal state determines how, in response to its reading of a tape symbol, it changes or leaves unaltered its internal state and changes or leaves unaltered the tape symbol it has read. It can move to the right or to the left on the tape, or it may not move at all, and it is assumed that the machine has an inexhaustible supply of blank tape available to it.

Not only is the Turing machine a prototype of a mathematical automaton, but the universal Turing machine is in some respects (i.e., as implied by Turing's thesis) the most powerful possible automaton. A number of interesting lesser devices can be obtained by restricting in various ways the behavior of the universal Turing machine.

Automata theory has come to have a number of different "flavors" and orientations. This, perhaps, is in part responsible for the difficulties librarians have in classifying new books on the subject, for these seem to appear at random in categories reserved for mathematical logic, abstract algebra, electrical machines and switching theory, linguistics, etc. Some parts of the subject matter are close to engineering, with great attention given to the physical realization, from basic building blocks, of machines with specified characteristics. At the other end of the spectrum, the subject matter lends itself to the application of abstract algebraic theory and, when so described, seems to deviate widely from the "real" world of computing—with possible applications hoped for at some future time.

7.2 THE NOTIONS OF "STATE" AND OF A "MECHANISM"

The "state" of an automaton at any instant completely determines its behavior in response to its environment and to time. Everything relevant to this behavior is summed up in the notion of its state. Every automaton follows certain rules that specify its behavior for every possible state of the automaton.

As we have noted in discussing Turing machines, the "state" at any moment of a computer program being executed could be interpreted, like the "instantaneous description" of a Turing machine, to be the complete set of information that would have to be recorded if the program were interrupted at that instant, with the expectation of continuing the procedure from that point at some later time. The "state" determines the future course of the program's execution.

The simplest kind of automaton that can be conceived is one with a finite number of states that responds not at all to its environment but is influenced only by time as measured by a built-in clock. Such a device has at times been called a "mechanism," as in Murray [3]. A mechanism is, as perhaps might be expected, not a particularly interesting device with its "autistic" ignoring of any external environment and with no input or output. Its behavior is completely determined by the rules governing the transition of its states. If, for example, a mechanism has three states, which we can designate A, B, C, and the succession of states is $A \to B$, $B \to C$, $C \to A$, we might indicate this by the directed graph (shown in Fig. 7.2), where each node identifies one of the states and the directed path segments indicate the possible state transitions.

This, for example, describes the behavior of a traffic light that cycles through

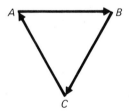

Fig. 7.2 State transition diagram for a particular mechanism of three states.

Green, Yellow, and Red, the "state" for this mechanism being its color, the only thing of consequence in describing its behavior.

We might also describe the transition of states in a mechanism by writing a square array, or matrix, with one row and one column corresponding to each state and the entry in each position of the array being 1 or 0 according to whether or not the successor of the state corresponding to the row is the state corresponding to the column. The matrix is, of course, the same as the connectivity matrix for the digraph (see Appendix to Chapter 3) that represents the mechanism.

Thus, the matrix conveying the same state transition information as the above graph is its connectivity matrix

$$\begin{array}{c} \\ A \\ B \\ C \end{array} \begin{array}{ccc} A & B & C \\ \begin{bmatrix} 0 & 1 & 0 \\ 0 & 0 & 1 \\ 1 & 0 & 0 \end{bmatrix} \end{array}$$

It is immediate to see that a mechanism must always cycle or enter a loop. For, in writing down the sequence of states assumed by the mechanism, starting with any given state, $S_{i_1} \rightarrow S_{i_2} \rightarrow S_{i_3} \rightarrow S_{i_4} \rightarrow \ldots$, we must eventually encounter a repetition of a state, there being only a finite number of different states. When a repetition occurs, the behavior of the mechanism repeats itself starting at that point. Included in this, of course, is the possibility of the repetition cycle or loop being of length one if a state appears which is its own successor. Such a self-succeeding state is sometimes called a "quiescent" state, for once the mechanism has entered it no further changes of state can occur.

A state transition diagram may have a more complicated appearance, such as in Fig. 7.3. This shows the state transitions for a particular mechanism of 31 states. If this mechanism starts in any one of its 31 states, it must eventually enter one of two possible cycles. One cycle contains five states and the other contains three states. That part of a state transition diagram that leads into a node of a cycle is a directed tree. There may be more than one branch leading into each node of the tree, but only one branch can be directed out from each node because each state of the mechanism has a single, unique, successor state. Every tree has a root which is a node that is part of a cycle. A mechanism is completely described graphically by a collection of such trees and cycles. Murray calls such a graph an "iterative structure" [3]. Even a mechanism acts as a device to transform information. It carries any given internal state, its "input," into some particular cycle (which may be a single quiescent state), its "output."

One way of generalizing the notion of a mechanism is to consider devices where the successor state of a given state is not uniquely determined

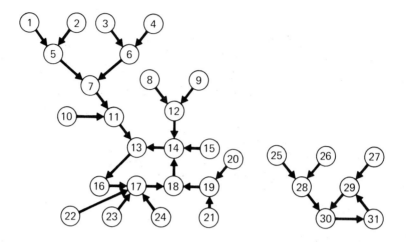

Fig. 7.3 State transition diagram for a particular mechanism of 31 states.

but, rather, where several successor states may occur. Further, we can suppose that a particular probability of occurrence is associated with each successor state when a state transition occurs. The transition diagram in this case may not include trees, for more than one outward directed segment may lead from each node.

We have used the idea of state in discussing Turing machines. Although a Turing machine has only a finite number of internal states, it is *not* a mechanism, for with its use of the tape that constitutes its environment, it has external input and output. If the tape is considered part of the machine, then the analog of "state" is the machine's "configuration" or "instantaneous description," which, as we have seen, includes a description of the tape's contents as well as of the location of the read head. In this case, the number of possible configurations is infinite and again the machine cannot be thought of as a mechanism.

Returning to questions related to those briefly discussed in Chapter 1, it seems plausible that the universe is not a mechanism. If it were, it would eventually loop. As we have already noted, it seems unlikely that it satisfies the condition of being synchronous (cf. discussion of "Clock" in Section 7.3), of a finite number of states, and deterministic.

7.3 A CLASSIFICATION OF AUTOMATA

There are, in essence, five salient characteristics that are of significance in describing the automata that are of interest to us. We describe these, following a classification given by Alonzo Church.

1. Causality: deterministic or nondeterministic. In discussing the transition of states in an automaton, we have indicated that, as in a Turing machine, the successor state to a given state may be uniquely determined by that state and the symbol being read. However, we can also consider the possibility of the sequencing of states being nondeterministic with any one of several successor states possibly appearing after a state transition. We may, in some instances, have information of the probability of occurrence of each of the possible successor states. We always want real computing devices to be deterministic in this sense. (If we want a random behavior in the course of a calculation, we can achieve it by Monte Carlo techniques, cf. below.) The occurrence of machine errors may, of course, introduce undesired nondeterminism. A nondeterministic automaton is not quite the same as a "probabilistic" automaton. In the latter case we assume that information is available concerning prescribed probabilities governing possible state transitions where there may be more than one successor state. In the case of a nondeterministic automaton no such information is available, the state transitions occurring purely at random.

2. Size: fixed, growing, or infinite. Since, in studying automata, we are motivated by a desire to achieve a better understanding of real devices and their use by finite man, we rarely consider properties of infinite automata. We do, however, study devices that can increase in size, with no restriction on ultimate size during use, and a Turing machine is an example of this. Recall that in discussing the operation of a Turing machine we assumed that we would never run out of tape—that a blank square of tape would be appended when, otherwise, the read head would be positioned beyond the end of the tape. We could also have considered the tape to be infinite, but this would have been wasteful for, at any given time, only a finite portion of the tape can contain nonblank information. Thus, if the tape is considered part of it, a Turing machine is an example of a *growing* automaton. As we have noted earlier, this is a departure from reality, for there is always some practical bound on the size of the auxiliary storage that can be assumed to be available in using a real device. However, in most cases such a restriction seems to lessen our ability to obtain interesting theoretical results.

3. Input/Output: discrete or continuous. The tape input and output for a Turing machine consists of sequences of symbols drawn from a finite alphabet. Almost all automata studied have similar restrictions on the nature of their input and output. We assume that the discrete symbols of the alphabet used by a given automaton are recognizable by the machine with no possibility of error. Often in practice, we are concerned with the use of computers where analog, continuous signals serve as input or output, as in process control or laboratory automation applications. In these cases, electrical input or output signals may be measured in several ways, such as voltages or as

current intensities. In all such applications, however, signals in this form have to be transformed through converters (analog to digital or digital to analog) in order to make use of digital computers in the process.

4. Clock: synchronous or nonsynchronous. In most cases, we imagine a sequence of discrete events occurring within an automaton rather than that the automaton is a continuously varying machine. It is convenient to think, then, of a clock governing the actions of the automaton. At each new time step, the automaton changes its state and/or the scanning of its environment in a way determined by its design and past history. We may think of these time steps as being equally spaced, but this is only a convenience to avoid an apparently useless generalization. Further, as in our consideration of the size of an automaton, we never have occasion to assume an infinite past in considering the history of an automaton. An infinite past can be rejected as a consequence of our rejecting infinite size. For, if an infinite past were necessary, it would seem that the memory required for it would physically have to be of infinite size. Time, then, can be measured by discrete instants as $t = 0, 1, 2, \ldots$ As with growing automata, we assume that no bound exists on the length of a time sequence in following an automaton's behavior.

5. States: finite or infinite. Just as we rejected infinite size and infinite histories of automata, so do we have little reason to deal with infinite state automata. As pointed out earlier, if we think of the environment of an automaton as being part of that automaton, then we do in most cases have to think of a potentially infinite number of states. The configuration, or instantaneous description, of a Turing machine would be in this situation a more apt notion than its state. This is an arbitrary choice, however, and invariably in automata theory we restrict the notion of state to be that of the *internal* state, where the environment with which the automaton interacts is external to it, and we are always concerned with devices that have a finite number of such internal states. In fact, if we insist on a finite size, but nevertheless infinite state device, then we would have to worry about Turing's objection to such devices. The machine would not be able to differentiate between every pair of states if their number were infinite, and there would be a "blurring" of states.

Thus, Turing machines are examples of automata that are growing, deterministic, discrete, synchronous and, if we distinguish between internal states and configurations, of a finite number of states. The other models of universal computing devices briefly mentioned in Chapter 6, Wang machines, Shepherdson-Sturgis machines, and cellular automata are similarly describable as devices with these characteristics if we properly identify the internal states, input and output, in each case.

Fixed size, deterministic, discrete, synchronous, finite state machines are called simply "finite automata" and they comprise another category of machines that play a very significant role in automata theory. They are discussed in Chapter 8.

7.4 FUNCTIONS PERFORMED BY AUTOMATA

In essence, three functions are performed by different kinds of automata— they *recognize* or *accept, generate,* and *compute.* However, the recognition and generating functions can both be interpreted as special cases of the compute function.

1. Recognizing (or accepting): We may, for example, consider such tasks accomplished by automata as (a) determining whether a given finite sequence of letters drawn from the English alphabet contains the substring *ABBA,* (b) recognizing the prime numbers, (c) recognizing if a given expression in a program is well-formed according to the rules governing the formation of such expressions within the programming language being used. In all of these cases, we want to give as input to the automaton the string of symbols, or the number, to be tested and we want to receive as output the decision that the input item is or is not a member of the class of objects that the automaton accepts. Note that we usually want a clear decision on rejection as well as on acceptance—a firm YES or NO, and not an equivocal answer.

2. Generating: We have considered the notion of a recursively enumerable set of numbers. Such a set can be generated and is the list of numbers emitted as the successive outputs of some Turing machine obtained from inputs $0, 1, 2, \ldots$. In general, we may use automata designed to generate sequences of numbers or to generate strings of symbolic expressions. It is meaningful, for example, to study an automaton or its equivalent formal system that generates all the well-formed strings in some formal language (cf. Chapter 9).

3. Computing: The universal Turing machine and its equivalent models are, as implied by Turing's thesis, capable of carrying out any effective calculation. The functions of recognizing and generating are special cases of this. For example, the YES or NO decision of an automaton acceptor can be interpreted as "0" or "1," and the process is then obviously the calculation of a function. In many cases, however, we consider devices that are restricted in some way and that do not have the complete power of the universal Turing machine.

7.5   THE RANGE OF AUTOMATA

A mechanism is the simplest possible form of an automaton. The universal Turing machine is, on the other hand, the most powerful possible automaton that executes effective procedures. In view of Turing's thesis, it can perform any computation at all that one can hope to do by some effective device. If we restrict in various ways the facilities of such a machine (especially by limiting the ability to extend its tape indefinitely), we are led to other kinds of automata having limited powers. These restricted machines are used in automata theory to define functions or procedures that are proper subsets of the computable functions or of general effective procedures. We shall also, by studying these restricted machines, gain insight, especially in the study of computational complexity and of formal lingusitics (including programming languages), into the kinds of machine facilities needed to accomplish various tasks of importance in these studies.

In the case of a mechanism, where there is no tape or any information to be gleaned from the mechanism's environment, the behavior can be specified simply by stating the rules governing the succession of states, i.e., by naming for each given state q_i its successor state q_j.

If a Turing machine is prevented from moving back over its input tape, it becomes an example of a finite automaton. At this point we only briefly introduce this very important class of automata; Chapter 8 will be devoted to a more detailed discussion of them. There are principally two kinds of finite automata, those that can only read their input tape and those that can write on it. The first is used to recognize or accept tapes. Such a machine starts reading its input tape in a prescribed starting state and "accepts" this tape if it finishes its reading in one of a set of acceptance states. These machines are generally assumed to read their tapes in one direction only. We shall in fact see in Chapter 8 that providing such an automaton with the ability to read its tape backwards as well as forwards does not enhance its powers.

The second kind of finite automaton can write on its input tape and can thus transform an input sequence of symbols into an output sequence; it is therefore called a sequential machine.

It is perhaps instructive to compare the ways of prescribing the behavior of the four kinds of automata we have mentioned.

Mechanism.   Behavior can be specified by writing expressions of the form $q_i q_j$ indicating that state q_i is succeeded by state q_j.

Finite automaton recognizer.   Behavior can be specified by writing expressions of the form $q_i S_j q_l$ indicating that when the machine is in state q_i scanning the tape symbol S_j it enters state q_l and moves to the right on the tape. The end of the tape can be sensed.

Finite automaton sequential machine.   Behavior can be specified by writing expressions of the form $q_i S_j S_k q_l$ indicating that when the machine is in state q_i *scanning the tape symbol* S_j it enters state q_l, writes S_k on the square being scanned and moves to the right on the tape. As before, the end of the tape can be sensed. (In a "Moore" machine the output symbol S_k is determined uniquely by q_l. In a "Mealy" machine, the output symbol is determined by the *transition* from state q_i to q_l, and, therefore, different outputs can occur for the same successor state q_l. See Chapter 8.)

Turing machine.   Behavior can be specified by writing expressions of the form $q_i S_j S_k M q_l$, as we have already described at some length. When the machine is in state q_i, scanning the tape symbol S_j, it replaces S_j by S_k, enters state q_l and moves to the right (R), or to the left (L), or not at all (N), according to the value of M.

In all of these cases, when the automata are understood to be deterministic, no two controlling expressions can begin with the same symbol(s) (the same q_i in the case of mechanisms or the same $q_i S_j$ in the other three types of machines). In all cases a standard starting state is assumed.

7.6   MACHINES WITH PUSHDOWN STORES AND MACHINES WITH STACKS

Still other kinds of machines intermediate between finite automata and the universal Turing machine are of special importance, both in complexity studies and as recognition devices for the well-formed sentences of certain classes of formal languages (cf. Chapters 9 and 10).

These machines are obtained by restricting in certain ways the behavior of Turing machines. Before looking at some of the details of these restrictions, it is suggestive to revise slightly the physical model of the Turing machine that we have given earlier. We assume a machine that has *two* tapes and *two* read heads—one tape for input only, the other a work tape (Fig. 7.4). As before, the control section of the machine can assume only a finite number of internal states. The input tape, once mounted, can be read only, the work tape is used in the same way as before, it is extendable and can be read or written on.

In order to specify the behavior of such a device we must, of course, modify the quintuples of the ordinary Turing machine to allow the use of either tape. This can be done in several ways. We can distinguish between two kinds of internal states for the Control. In any state of one kind the machine scans and responds to the symbol under the read head on the input tape, in the other kind of state it scans and responds to the symbol under the

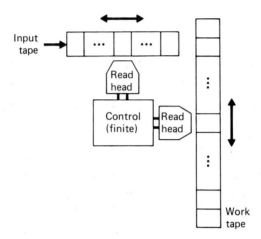

Fig. 7.4   A Turing machine with a separate input tape.

read head on the work tape. The details of the construction are of little significance, and it is easy to see that such a machine, equipped with a separate input tape, can be designed to be equivalent to any ordinary Turing machine. We leave it to the reader to see that, by using methods we have already discussed, an ordinary one-tape Turing machine can always be defined to simulate a machine with a separate input tape. Conversely, any Turing machine with a separate input tape can always begin by copying its input on its work tape and then proceed like an ordinary one-tape Turing machine. It will be desirable in Chapter 11 to consider a further refinement in the organization of a Turing machine. We shall at times assume that a separate (write-only) output tape is included, as well as a separate (read-only) input tape.

We now restrict the nature of the work tape to obtain a pushdown automaton and then a stack automaton.

A pushdown automaton (PDA) can read its input tape in only one direction, and it uses a work tape that can be likened to a stack of cafeteria trays (Fig. 7.5). At any time, the read head scans only the symbol at one end (the top) of the tape or stack. If this symbol is read, the tape moves (up) so that the next symbol appears under the read head, and the symbol read is "popped" from the top of the stack. If a symbol is written, the tape, or stack, is pushed down, and the new symbol appears at the top of the stack under the read head.

The work tape, or "peripheral store," in this case is often described as a LIFO ("last in-first out") store or as a FILO ("first in-last out") store. We shall see (Chapter 10) that with the use of a PDA it is possible to do some

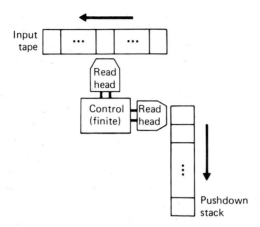

Fig. 7.5 A pushdown automaton. When the stack moves up, entries disappear from the top.

things that cannot be done with any finite automaton. Also, the universal Turing machine can do some things that are beyond the capacity of any' PDA.

A stack automaton (SA) resembles a PDA, but it has the additional ability to read its input tape in both directions. It can also move back and forth over its stack but it can only read, not write, at any point in the interior of the stack. Like a PDA, it can only write a symbol at the top of the stack. An SA can do some things that are beyond the capability of any PDA, but it too is not equivalent to a universal Turing machine.

The preceding discussion implies the following ranking of automata.

```
MECHANISMS < FINITE AUTOMATA < PUSHDOWN AUTOMATA
                < STACK AUTOMATA < UNIVERSAL TURING MACHINE
```

We write $\alpha < \beta$ to denote that the class of machines β can perform any of the processes performed by machines of the class α, but not conversely.

This is not at all a complete listing of automata and their relative powers. A number of special devices have been introduced in connection with the study of a variety of problems in computer science.

7.7 NONDETERMINISM AND MONTE CARLO METHODS IN COMPUTING

In referring to causality in automata, we briefly alluded to the fact that we may wish to introduce random processes into a calculation. We have seen a situation requiring this when we referred in the Appendix of Chapter 1 to the analysis by digital simulation of the behavior of a gas. Recall that the problem was approached by looking at the gas as a collection of a large number of randomly moving particles. By sampling computationally these particles and by following the individual behavior of each particle in the sample, we could average these behaviors over the whole sample and thus estimate physical properties of the total population of particles that comprise the gas. This technique, an example of a *Monte Carlo* procedure, first introduced apparently by S. Ulam in early research on nuclear fusion, finds wide application in the social sciences (where the population might be a human one) as well as in mathematics and the natural sciences. In these situations we usually have statistical information available about the distribution, or probability of occurrence, of the values of the relevant variables. For example, in studying a gas, we may have some statistical information about the possible velocities of the individual particles. Individually, these will vary, but they may do so only in conformance with some known statistical distribution. In other cases we may have no such information, and the variables may occur with entirely random values.

In these instances, how can we pick a random value for a variable as a step in an algorithm? In the case of the particles of a gas, we might, for example, wish to assign a random value to the direction in which a hypothetical particle is moving. How, then, can we turn a deterministic device into a nondeterministic one, or at least simulate a nondeterministic one? How can we toss a coin during a computation?

One way to simulate this last act would be to store a table, or list, with a large number of randomly occurring H's (heads) and T's (tails) where this list of symbols has been obtained through some previously applied procedure. An algorithm requiring such random input could, when it needs it, read the next symbol in the table. There are, however, some surprisingly simple arithmetic techniques for generating sequences of numbers that exhibit the properties of random sequences. This makes it unnecessary in most instances to store a table of random values.

An original suggestion for doing this appears to be due to von Neumann, and we shall describe this as the first of two different techniques for generating random numbers.

We shall show how to generate a sequence of H's and T's that looks like a random sequence. We use the "middle squaring" method suggested by von Neumann.

Start with, say, a four digit number. We use 3569 as an illustration. Square this number getting

12 | 7377 | 61

Use the middle four digits 7377 and repeat the operation getting

$$54 \mid 4201 \mid 29$$

A third application gives

$$17 \mid 6484 \mid 01$$

This is done repeatedly and we obtain the sequence

$$3569 - 7377 - 4201 - 6484 - 0422 - 1780 - 1684 -$$
$$8358 - 8561 - 2907 - \ldots$$

We next translate these four digit numbers into H's and T's by writing an H when a number is between 0 and 4999 and writing a T if the number is between 5000 and 9999. We obtain:

$$\text{H–T–H–T–H–H–H–T–T–H–} \ldots$$

Clearly, the amount of "randomness" in a sequence so generated depends to a great extent on the starting number. If we had begun with the number 0023 we would have generated the sequence 0005 – 0000 – 0000 – ..., not a very "random" sequence.

The question of what exactly constitutes a random sequence of numbers is not easily answered. We can say that a sequence is *not* random if it possesses some order or regularity, but the nature of "order" is vague (we shall attempt to clarify this notion in Chapter 11). We expect, for example, that in a very long sequence of random digits there should be about as many 7's as 4's, that a 5 should appear next to a 2 about as often as it appears next to a 3, that the digits in even positions should be just as random as those in odd positions, and so forth. In practice, a battery of statistical tests are often applied to determine if a given sequence seems to have the properties of randomness.

Any particular algorithm for generating a sequence of numbers, by the very meaning of "algorithm," does not generate a random sequence—since the outputs *are* obtained by a well-defined, deterministic and not random, procedure. In fact, a method such as the one we have described must eventually start repeating its outputs. There are only a limited number of four-digit numbers, and no matter what number we start with, a repetition must eventually occur, after which the sequence "cycles." For these reasons, the sequences generated by such methods are usually called "pseudorandom." However, they still may serve very well the purposes of using random numbers in a calculation. If a "random number generator" produces a very large number of outputs before these start repeating (i.e., the "period" is very long), and the sequence of digits satisfies a number of statistical tests for randomness, the use of these numbers in a computation requiring random inputs will usually be quite satisfactory. There is in fact one additional advantage of these pseudorandom numbers. That is, it is possible to repeat a computation for possible verification. This is in no way possible for truly random numbers, since the repetition of a run will involve *different* random numbers.

The middle squaring technique is in general not as good (re length of period and the results of statistical tests for randomness) as the following method, which is widely employed. We define a procedure recursively in terms of two given constants a, m that have no common divisors. Start with an arbitrary odd number ($<m$), multiply by a and take the remainder after dividing this product by m. Let the resulting number be r_1. To get r_2, multiply r_1 by a and take the remainder after dividing the product ar_1 by m. Continue the procedure, obtaining r_{i+1} from r_i ($i = 2, 3, \ldots$), generating the sequence of pseudorandom numbers $r_1, r_2, r_3, \ldots$.

It is convenient to use here some special notation of number theory that appears frequently in computer-related topics. If the two numbers b, c both give the same remainder when each is divided by the number m, which is equivalent to saying that the difference $b - c$ is a multiple of m, we write:

$$b \equiv c \ (\text{mod } m)$$

This is read as "b is congruent to c modulo m."

Example. $13 \equiv 5 \ (\text{mod } 4)$.

We can now write an equation that defines r_{i+1} in terms of r_i.

$$r_{i+1} \equiv ar_i \ (\text{mod } m), \text{ where } 0 < r_{i+1} < m$$

If $m = 2^k$ is used in this algorithm on a machine whose word size is k binary bits, then r_{i+1}, the remainder after dividing ar_i by m, is simply the right-most word in the product ar_i.

Good results are obtained if a is taken close to the square root of m and congruent to 3 or 5 modulo 8. In this case, the cycle length can be shown to be 2^{k-2}.

For example, if a machine word is 8 bits, we take $m = 2^8 = 64$ and choose $a = $ (say) 13. If we start with the number 15, we obtain

$$r_1 \equiv 13 \times 15 \ (\text{mod } 64) \equiv 3$$
$$r_2 \equiv 13 \times 3 \ (\text{mod } 64) \equiv 39$$
$$r_3 \equiv 13 \times 39 \ (\text{mod } 64) \equiv 59$$
$$r_4 \equiv 13 \times 59 \ (\text{mod } 64) \equiv 63$$
$$r_5 \equiv 13 \times 63 \ (\text{mod } 64) \equiv 51$$

These pseudorandom numbers 3, 39, 59, 63, 51,... are all odd, but they can be converted into random two-digit numbers in the interval from 1 to 32 by adding 1 and dividing by 2.

7.8 THE BUILDING BLOCKS OF AUTOMATA

Much of science is concerned with the attempt to explain the complex as hierarchical structures of the simple. For example, until recently, a rather small number of elemental physical particles were considered adequate to explain the physical and chemical behavior of all matter. A profusion of recently discovered particles seems in part to belie this goal, but many scientists still have an almost religious belief in a fundamental underlying simple (but not obvious) structure of the universe.

Several kinds of elemental devices may be assumed as the units from which automata can be realized and we consider a few of these.

1. Logical elements. In the logical design of real computers we have emphasized that by cascading possibly large numbers of a few functionally simple logical organs, AND and OR gates and inverters (along with additional delay units), we can assemble logical and control circuits to execute the most complex functions.

We assume, when a network of such organs appears, that it forms part of a synchronous machine, with a clock governing its operation. At each time step these organs accomplish their tasks and their output lines carry the output signals at the beginning of the next time step. Synchronization of these signals is then usually required and delay organs may be needed to make sure that the several signals that may be input to an organ arrive at the same time.

As noted in Exercise 2.21, we can get by with either the AND and NOT organs or with the OR and NOT organs alone. In each case, the missing organ can be replaced by a network employing only the other two. For example, the circuit in Fig. 7.6 can be replaced by the circuit in Fig. 7.7, which employs only AND and NOT organs.

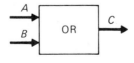

Figure 7.6

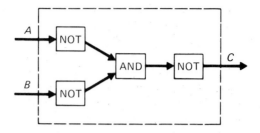

Figure 7.7

The logical equation

$$A \mid B = \neg(\neg A \mathbin{\&} \neg B).$$

provides the specifications for connecting the AND, NOT organs to form the equivalent circuit. Note that there is one significant difference in the use of Fig. 7.7 as opposed to that of Fig. 7.6. If one time step is required for the functioning of every basic organ, then Fig. 7.7 involves a total delay of three time steps while Fig. 7.6 requires only one time step. It might then be necessary to use time delay organs in any circuit where Fig. 7.6 is replaced by Fig. 7.7, in order to assure the synchronization of signals.

We similarly can use only OR and NOT organs by taking advantage of the Boolean equation $A \mathbin{\&} B = \neg(\neg A \mid \neg B)$.

Any Boolean logical expression can then be represented as a network of such basic organs, and this network can be put together in obvious fashion directly from the given expression.

2. McCulloch-Pitts neurons.   Motivated to a large extent by a partial understanding of the mechanism of human nerve cells, McCulloch and Pitts in [2] showed how networks composed of elemental organs that are modeled after the neuron can represent logical functions.

The following salient facts are known about the neuron.

1. All neurons in the brain seem to be identical in structure.

2. There appear to be inhibitory inputs to neurons. When a stimulus appears on one of these inhibitory inputs, the neuron is prevented from firing. (A neuron is said to "fire" when it discharges or emits an electrical signal.)

3. There is associated with every neuron a certain threshold of stimulant activity. Any stimulus below this threshold results in no apparent activity. All stimuli above the threshold seem to have the same triggering effect. The

behavior of the neuron seems to be an "all-or-nothing" event. It either fires or it does not. That is, it seems to have a binary character with no intermediate level output signals playing any role.

4. There appears to be a fantastically complex "wiring" arrangement of the neurons through their axons and dendrites.

5. Although there is no precise "clock" governing a synchronized functioning of all neurons, some aspects of neural behavior conform to a discrete, digital character. After a neuron fires, there is an "absolute refractory period" of about 5 milliseconds during which no excitatory signal can cause the neuron to fire again.

It has often been emphasized that the preceding remarks, which provide some motivation for the specification of McCulloch-Pitts neurons, reflect a quite superficial understanding of the behavior of the nervous system, and it is not in any way claimed that the results obtained from the study of the idealized neurons we describe provide any great insight into the behavior of the brain. In recent years we have learned that the individual neuron is far more complex than it was orginally perceived to be, and its interpretation as a "trigger" appears to be simplistic. We have learned very little about how mental functions, especially with regard to memory and the "higher" thought processes, are effected within the brain and we know little that is helpful to us in designing more sophisticated computing devices. As von Neumann has noted, the ancient Greeks thought that human memory resided in the diaphragm, and we have not made great progress in achieving an improved understanding of this phenomenon since then—even though we know the diaphragm plays no role in it.

A McCulloch-Pitts neuron, then, is an organ with a number of input leads and one output lead.

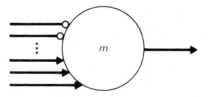

The input leads are of two types: excitatory inputs and inhibitory inputs. The end bulbs of the inhibitory inputs are represented as small circles, and arrow heads designate the excitatory inputs. If at time t the number of stimulated excitatory input leads is greater than or equal to some threshold value shown as *m* in the figure, and none of the inhibitory leads are stimulated, then at time $t + \delta$, where δ is the assumed constant time step, the output lead will be stimulated and it will transmit its signal to other neurons to which it may be connected. In drawing networks of such neurons, there is the constraint that output lines can split, but no merging of lines can occur.

If the number of stimulated excitatory inputs is not at least equal to the threshold number of the neuron, or if any one of the inhibitory inputs carries a signal at time *t*, then the neuron will not fire at time $t + \delta$.

With such organs, we can easily put together assemblages, as shown in Fig. 7.8, to realize the AND, OR, NOT of logic. To achieve the NOT, however, we must assume a constant source of stimuli at every time step. A neuron with threshold 0 can also be used for this function.

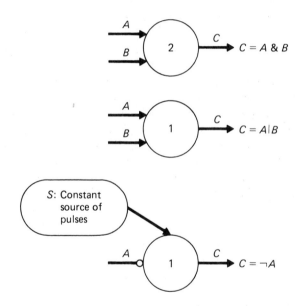

Fig. 7.8 The AND, OR, NOT represented by neurons.

The unit delay element of this type is:

In [5], von Neumann uses a slightly modified version of the McCulloch-Pitts neuron. His neurons fire at time $t + \delta$ if the number of stimulated excitatory inputs *exceeds* the number of stimulated inhibitory inputs by the threshold value, instead of their being prevented from firing by a signal being transmitted to any one of the inhibitory inputs.

Figure 7.9 shows a network of McCulloch-Pitts elements which accomplishes the function of a half-adder. Its output at time $t + 2\delta$ is the right-most bit of the binary sum of the two inputs A, B at time t, i.e., it computes the function $S = (A \ \& \ \neg B) \mid (\neg A \ \& \ B)$.

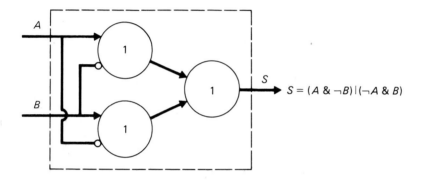

Figure 7.9

In the animal nervous system, certain neurons are specialized and receive stimuli directly from sensory organs such as the eye or ear, while others transmit their output signals directly to effector organs or muscles. These, then, can be considered to fulfill input and output functions and to be analogous to those McCulloch-Pitts neurons that might play this role in an automaton.

7.9 UNIVERSAL LOGICAL ELEMENTS

We have noted that the AND and NOT organs, or the OR and NOT organs, suffice to put together a network corresponding to any logical expression of the propositional calculus. The number of essential organs can be reduced still further for there are several single logical organs which can be used to put together any logical circuit.

The NOR element. The NOR (neither A nor B) function is defined by the following table:

A	B	NOT(A OR B) or NOR (A, B)
0	0	1
0	1	0
1	0	0
1	1	0

NOR(A, B) is true only when A and B are both false. This binary operator is often denoted as $A \uparrow B$, and we can write $A \uparrow B = \neg(A \mid B)$.

It is then a simple matter to express the AND, OR, NOT operations in terms of the NOR for we have:

$\neg A = \neg(A \mid A) = A \uparrow A$

$A \mid B = \neg(A \uparrow B) = (A \uparrow B) \uparrow (A \uparrow B) = {\uparrow}{\uparrow}AB \uparrow AB$, if written in prefix, or Polish, notation

$$A \& B = \neg(\neg A \mid \neg B)$$
$$= (\neg A) \uparrow (\neg B)$$
$$= (A \uparrow A) \uparrow (B \uparrow B)$$
$$= {\uparrow}{\uparrow}AA \uparrow BB \text{ in prefix notation}$$

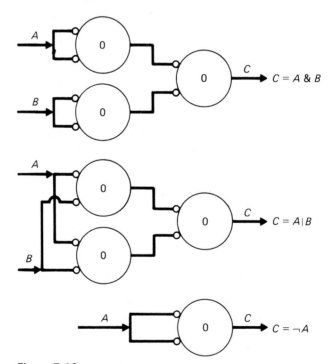

Figure 7.10

The McCulloch-Pitts neuron which realizes the NOR function is:

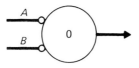

Using this element and following as blueprints the equations for the AND, OR, NOT we have the circuits shown in Fig. 7.10. Any logical circuit can be assembled from elements of this kind.

The NAND element.   Another element that is universal is the NAND ("not and") that is "dual" to the NOR. A NAND B means NOT (A AND B) and is often written with a special symbol, the "Sheffer stroke." (We distinguish between the Sheffer stroke and the OR of PL/I by using a boldface vertical line.) That is,

$$A \mathbin{\mathbf{|}} B = \neg(A \,\&\, B).$$

We similarly can express the AND, OR, NOT in terms of the NAND as follows.

$$\neg A = \neg(A \,\&\, A) = A \mathbin{\mathbf{|}} A$$
$$A \,\&\, B = \neg(\neg(A \,\&\, B)) = \neg(A \mathbin{\mathbf{|}} B)$$
$$= (A \mathbin{\mathbf{|}} B) \mathbin{\mathbf{|}} (A \mathbin{\mathbf{|}} B)$$
$$A \mid B = \neg(\neg A \,\&\, \neg B) = (\neg A) \mathbin{\mathbf{|}} (\neg B)$$
$$= (A \mathbin{\mathbf{|}} A) \mathbin{\mathbf{|}} (B \mathbin{\mathbf{|}} B)$$

Another organ whose possible use has at various times received a good deal of attention is the *majority* organ that has 3 input lines and whose output, as implied by its name, is the state that appears more often in the three input lines. Its output then indicates the majority state of its inputs. Denoting this logical function by $M(A, B, C)$, its truth table is:

A	B	C	$M(A, B, C)$
0	0	0	0
0	0	1	0
0	1	0	0
0	1	1	1
1	0	0	0
1	0	1	1
1	1	0	1
1	1	1	1

The McCulloch-Pitts neuron that computes this function is:

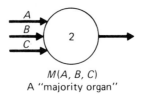

$M(A, B, C)$
A "majority organ"

It is easy to get the AND and OR in terms of this organ *if* we allow constant sources of signals for the 1 and for 0.

$$A \& B = M(A, B, 0)$$
$$A \mid B = M(A, B, 1)$$

NOT A cannot be obtained from the majority organ, but by the "double line trick" that is next described we can dispense with the need for it.

This device, as described by von Neumann, consists of using *two* lines l_1, l_2 to represent each Boolean variable. A "0" is represented by a signal on one line, say l_1, and no signal on l_2. A signal on l_2 with none on l_1 represents a "1." No use is made of the possible configurations where both l_1, l_2 carry signals or where both do not carry signals. This inefficiency of representation might, however, be considered an advantage in error detection. If a signal on a line is "dropped" the resulting configuration (no signal on l_1 or on l_2) could be recognized as being illegitimate, marking the occurrence of an error.

This representation scheme could in fact also be viewed as the simplest possible example of the use of a parity bit for checking. Suppose we were to use, as first described, a single line to represent a 0 or a 1, but we accompany this bit with an *odd* parity bit, i.e., an additional bit chosen to make the total number of bits in any representation an odd number. The resulting configuration is, of course, identical to what we have described as the double line trick.

The NOT is then obtained by simply "crossing" the wires as in the following sketch.

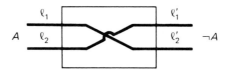

A new majority organ would have to be used, but this can easily be designed using two of the old majority organs (Fig. 7.11).

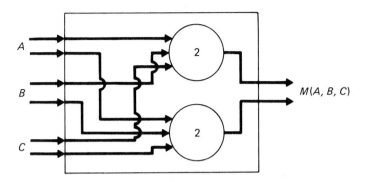

Figure 7.11

This organ then can be used as the sole building block for any logical circuit if each Boolean variable is represented by a pair of line signals.

7.10 FEEDBACK AND MEMORY

The vital role that feedback plays in a great variety of systems was recognized by Norbert Wiener in his book *Cybernetics* [8]. Whether we are considering systems of biological, physical, or sociological (among others) origin, feedback seems to be a pervading phenomenon. As examples, we mention the following:

1. The feedback information that the eye sends back to the brain as the hand reaches for an object; the information is used to guide the hand and to stop its motion when it reaches the desired object.

2. The feedback information that a gyrocompass senses and transmits back to an automatic pilot when an airplane deviates from a prescribed course; the information is used to control the airplane's rudder and return the airplane back to its designated flight path.

3. The feedback information that a governor senses when an engine runs faster or slower than a prescribed setting; the information is used to slow down or speed up the engine.

4. The feedback from the economy in the form of information about the money supply that is used by the Federal Reserve Bank to adjust interest rates and thus influence the economy (even when a clear understanding of cause and effect in this situation seems to be lacking).

5. The feedback from its citizenry that is key to the conduct of a democracy.

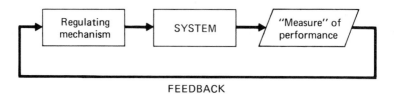

FEEDBACK

Figure 7.12

In all of these cases the behavior of the system is influenced by the ongoing performance of that system. Some *goal* is sought in each case, even though in nonmathematical systems the goal may not be sharply defined. Some regulating mechanism uses the feedback information in such a way as to get "closer" in some sense to the goal (Fig. 7.12).

Learning and memory in animals are involved in biological systems with forms of feedback. The experience of the individual in interacting with its environment is remembered and is used to modify its future behavior.

In the mathematics of computing, the operations of primitive recursion and of minimalization can, with some relaxing of terms, be considered forms of feedback. This is perhaps best seen from the flowcharts for these operations (Figs. 4.2, 4.5).

In the case of primitive recursion, the "goal" is to find $f(x)$ at $x = n$, being given $f(x)$ at $x = 0$ and being given a procedure to find $f(x)$ at successive arguments. A test is made to see if $f(x)$ has been determined at $x = n$; if not, the argument is advanced by 1 and f is recomputed. In the case of minimalization, the "goal" is to find, for given x, the smallest y that gives $f(x, y) = 0$. The goal-seeking procedure here is simply to step along through successive values of y, searching for the smallest y that makes f vanish.

In the logical circuits we have so far looked at, the flow of signals through the circuit was such that there was no backtracking. Once a particular gate or neuron had appeared in the circuit path, there was no way for its output to influence the future behavior of that gate. If we allow signals to be fed back into earlier parts of the circuit, this will be an example of feedback. Without such feedback, these circuits will have rather limited capability and will not be very interesting. They will be able, it is true, to compute any Boolean function of a given set of inputs, but they will not possess "memory," and their usage will be rather limited. If the maximum path as a signal passes from input to output is through a chain of n gates, then the total time of passage is $n\delta$, where δ represents the basic time step and is also assumed to be the time for a signal to pass through any one logical gate. If we assume that fresh signals appear at the input ports of the circuit at each time step, then the machine's output at any time t is governed solely by the input signals received during the preceding n steps, i.e., during the interval from $t - n\delta$ to t.

With the use of feedback circuits, we are able to implement "memory" in automata circuits rather easily. For example, the following neuron has its output fed back to its input. If this neuron ever receives a pulse or a "1" signal it "remembers" the event in that it will, on every succeeding time step, give a 1 as output.

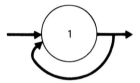

As a further illustration of feedback, we give a somewhat more complicated example from von Neumann's fundamental paper [5]. Figure 7.13 shows a "scalar by two," a circuit that will emit an output pulse for every two input pulses (1's) it receives, no matter what period of time elapses between consecutive 1's. The neurons function according to the von Neumann convention. They will fire at the next time step only if the number of stimulated excitatory inputs exceeds the number of stimulated inhibitory inputs by the threshold figure. We leave it to the reader to see that the machine functions as prescribed.

It is the use of feedback that enables us to design real devices with memory and control functions. These devices have powers that extend beyond the simple ability to compute a Boolean function of n inputs for fixed

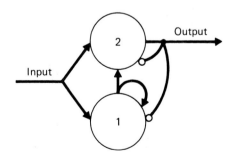

Fig. 7.13   A machine that gives one output pulse for every two input pulses.

n. Using feedback we can design machines that behave as any given finite automaton. That is, we can put together a machine employing a circuit of gates or neurons that will function as the given finite automaton would for any input sequence of characters. We are assuming that each character appears as a pattern of input pulses and that a sequence of *n* characters is represented by the inputs at *n* consecutive time steps.

We can design such a machine that will recognize the same set of finite sequences as any given finite automaton recognizer. We can also design a machine that will transform input sequences into output sequences, defining the same mapping on sequences as any given finite sequential machine.

If such a machine can "grow" with no limit on its size, i.e., universal organs will be "added" to the automaton when it signals a need for such organs, we can design a machine to simulate any Turing machine, including the universal Turing machine.

7.11   ORACLES

One device that has been suggested to augment the powers of the Turing machine and thus enable the computation of functions that are not recursive is to endow a machine with an "oracle" that is capable of answering some questions that are beyond the capability of any Turing machine (Fig. 7.14). Typically what is done is to assume that the oracle can, when interrogated in the course of an otherwise effective procedure, indicate whether or not a given number is in some prescribed set, i.e., the oracle is able to determine the value of the characteristic function of that set for a given argument. If the set is recursive, the oracle adds nothing to the powers of a universal Turing machine[1] for, in this case, we could "program" the computation of the characteristic function. However, if the set is not recursive, then a machine having access to such an oracle can do some things that cannot be done by a universal Turing machine.

Fig. 7.14   A Turing machine equipped with an oracle.

---

1. However, the machine may be able to do some things far more efficiently if the function performed by the oracle is complex.

The situation may well be likened to some computer applications that involve man-machine interaction—situations where the computer interrupts the execution of a procedure at certain points in order to allow a human to make some judgmental decision and then give the computer information to be used in continuing the procedure. Such applications as computer-aided design, or those experiments in artificial intelligence that involve human guidance and the use of heuristic methods at strategic points, are illustrations of this. In these situations it is not easily seen how the role played by the human can be dispensed with by extending or refining the algorithm being executed.

In [1], Davis describes an additional type of quintuple (he actually uses quadruples) for Turing machines equipped with an oracle. Assume that the oracle is able to determine set membership in a particular set S (primarily of interest when S is nonrecursive). The quintuple

$$q_i S_j N q_k q_l$$

is taken to mean that the Turing machine that includes this quintuple will take the following action when it is in state q_i scanning the symbol S_j. It will enter either state q_k or state q_l (i.e., it executes a conditional branch) according to whether or not the "content" of the tape (i.e., the number of 1's on the tape), at the time of execution of this quintuple, is in the set S. The read head position and the scanned symbol S_j are left unaltered.

Let us, for example, design an oracle machine that will, for given n, answer the question of whether or not there are n consecutive 7's in the infinite decimal expansion of π. Let S be the set of numbers n having this property.

We assume a Turing machine Z_0 equipped with an oracle that can recognize membership in the set S. Let Z_0 be defined as follows. (We assume all our prior stated conventions concerning input and output representation in Turing machine calculations.)

$$\left\{\begin{array}{ll} q_1 1 B R q_2 & q_4 1 B R q_4 \\ q_2 1 N q_3 q_4 & q_4 * B L q_8 \\ q_3 1 B R q_3 & q_8 B B L q_8 \\ q_3 * B L q_5 & q_8 * * R q_9 \\ q_5 B B L q_5 & q_9 B 1 R q_{10} \\ q_5 * * R q_6 & q_{10} B 1 R q_{11} \\ q_6 B 1 R q_7 & q_{11} B * L q_{12} \\ q_7 B * L q_{13} & q_{12} 1 1 L q_{13} \end{array}\right\}$$

The quintuple $q_2 1 N q_3 q_4$ indicates that when Z_0 is in state q_2 scanning a 1, it will next enter state q_3 or state q_4 as determined by the content c of the tape. If there are c consecutive 7's in the decimal expansion of π, it will enter state q_3, if not it enters state q_4. When Z_0 starts a calculation with the input representation of the number n, it gives as a result the answer 0 if $n \in S$ and the answer 1 if $n \notin S$. No one at this time knows if an ordinary Turing machine can be designed to compute this particular function, but this oracle-equipped machine does compute it. Of course, the "heart" of the procedure is the decision made by the oracle, the rest of the "computation" being trivial.

7.12   AUTOMATA AND THINKING—THE TURING TEST

A question that has been frequently raised is whether the brain (in particular the human brain) can be explained in terms of automata concepts. A number of analogies, occasionally specious, have been made between the machine and the brain, and at times the hope has been expressed that a better understanding of the brain will lead to more powerful automata and computing devices and, conversely, that an understanding of automata will provide a key to the understanding of the brain. Suggestive of the question being considered, we have noted Boole's "laws of thought," and we have briefly cited some simple analogies between neural behavior and the McCulloch-Pitts neurons that can serve in the construction of logical automata.

The ongoing activities touching on these questions are very widespread. Such loosely defined areas of investigation as cybernetics ("the study of control and communication in the animal and the machine") and artificial intelligence encompass a great number of topics relevant to this matter. The existence of a large number of phenomena and occasional partial explanations for these seem to offer provocative evidence of the feasibility of an automata-like theory that would explain the brain and its functions. We are here thinking of such things as the apparent role that electrical signals of digital form play in the human nervous system; the localized functions of the brain; the presence of an associative memory in humans; the apparent existence of resonating circuits in the brain as one form of memory; instinct as inherited memory; the nature of information obtained through the senses, including visual perception in lower organisms; the genetic code; and so forth. The list is very long, pointing to the possibility of mechanical explanations for mental processes.

However, it would be very wrong to conclude that the case is clear that the brain can be explained as an automaton. The results obtained to date have been fragmented and partial, often suggestive more than substantive, and far from offering any clear theory that can cope with the grand problem of the brain. Early forecasts of rapid progress in artificial intelligence have not materialized, as the great difficulty of the relevant problems has become more clear. Many are gaining new respect for the inherent profundity of the structure of the human brain. The whole matter is not in our view appropriate for further discussion in a treatment of the mathematical basis of computing procedures.

There is, however, one aspect of this question, as it has been discussed by Turing, that relates to programming. In a paper written for popular consumption and reprinted with the title "Can a Machine Think?" [4], Turing considers the feasibility of programming a machine to think. Before answering the question of the paper's title, it would appear necessary to define sharply what it means for a machine to "think." It is very difficult, if not impossible, however, to do this, and Turing cleverly bypasses the need to provide such a definition. Instead, he suggests the following "game," which recalls perhaps the story of "The Lady or the Tiger."

Fig. 7.15   The Turing Test

A closed room contains either a human or a machine. A typewriter outside the room provides the only way of getting information into or out of the room. A person, unaware of what is inside the room, is allowed to ask questions through the typewriter of the "thing" in the room, and he receives answers on the typewriter. After some period of interrogation, he must decide whether a human or a machine is responding to his quesitons. The question of whether a machine thinks is transformed into the question, "Can a machine be programmed to deceive a human interrogator into believing that a human is responding to his questions rather than a machine?"

Turing presents an argument that makes plausible the fact that a machine can be programmed to do fairly well in deceiving a human interrogator.

Suppose the machine is asked to give the product of 34,578,246 by 842,623,129, or to divide 56,785,281 by 12,613,177 to 10 decimal places. It could be programmed to delay somewhat in returning its answer in order to conform to the time that might be required for the average human to do these computations unaided. Also, it should, perhaps, occasionally give a wrong answer in doing arithmetic, since infallibility in this area would be more characteristic of machines than of men.

If the machine were asked to explain the implications of relativity theory to the behavior of pulsars (or whatever), it could throw up its hands with "that's way beyond me" or "I have no knowledge of higher physics." After all, how many humans could give an intelligent response to such a question?

If we ask "Who do you think will win the next World Series?", it could very well come back with "I believe the Yankees have a very good chance." A question concerning the intepretation of a line in some modern poem could evoke the response "It makes no sense to me" or "I have no taste for that stuff."

And so forth. Turing's argument is quite persuasive of the feasibility of coping with all situations. He goes further in fact and makes a concrete estimate of how long he thinks it would take to write a comprehensive set of programs that would enable a machine to perform well at this imitation game. He reasons as follows in arriving at his estimate.

The average human brain has about 10^{10} neurons. Supposedly, however, we use only a fraction of our potential, and the imitation game might be played with a brain of far fewer neurons. Turing assumes that a brain of 10^9 neurons (a "child brain") properly utilized, would suffice to play the game. Then, he takes the crucial step of equating the neuron with a binary bit (in line with our discussion introducing the McCulloch-Pitts neurons). He, therefore, estimates the magnitude of the program required to play the game well at 10^9 bits.

Assuming, then, that a programmer can produce debugged code at a rate of about 1,000 bits per day (i.e., about 125 machine bytes on models of the IBM models 360/370 series—a not unreasonable estimate for machine language coding), he estimates that some 3,000 man-years would be needed to come up with a good comprehensive set of programs. That is, a team of 60 programmers could, perhaps, pull it off in about 50 years.

Some parts of Turing's argument are somewhat dubious, such as the equating of neurons to bits. However, some recent experiments in artificial intelligence make it quite reasonable that Turing's conclusion, that the imitation game can be executed by a machine in a convincing manner, is valid. For example, it has been reported [6, 7] that human subjects interacting with Weizenbaum's psychotherapy program, ELIZA, frequently believe that it is a human who is sympathetically asking questions of them in an interactive dialogue, and not a machine.

There is a related question bearing on this matter that can be approached in a similar manner. This is the question of whether or not a machine can have self-awareness or consciousness. It does not seem feasible to provide any objective definition of "self-awareness" that would lend itself to a decision procedure by anyone communicating with the subject about whom the question is being asked. However, the question can be transformed, analogously to the above, into "Can a machine be programmed to deceive a human interrogator into believing, from the machine's responses, that it has self-awareness?" The question of whether or not a machine can be "alive" can be analyzed in similar manner.

EXERCISES

7.1 Two mechanisms are essentially identical, in the sense of having the same behavior, if one can be derived from the other by simply relabeling its states (i.e., they are isomorphic). How many different, or nonisomorphic, mechanisms of 4 states can be designed?—of 5 states?—of 6 states—of 7 states?

7.2 Let a mechanism be "probabilistic" in the sense that the transition from state i to state j occurs with some known probability a_{ij}, where $0 \leq a_{ij} \leq 1$. The behavior of such a mechanism of n states can then be specified by an nth order matrix A where the element in the ith row and jth column is a_{ij}. From the definition of a_{ij} it follows that for each i, $\sum_{j=1}^{n} a_{ij} = 1$. Show that the probability that state i is succeeded by state j after *two* state transitions is $(A^2)_{ij}$, the element in the i, j position of the algebraic square of matrix A. More generally, show that the element $(A^k)_{ij}$ represents the probability that state i is succeeded by state j after k state transitions.

7.3 Suppose we consider the instantaneous descriptions of a Turing machine with a fixed size, nonextendable, tape to be the machine's internal states. That is, assume that the machine stops when the execution of some quintuple calls for moving beyond the end of the tape. Can such a machine be viewed as a mechanism?

7.4 Show that it is not possible to build a device that will receive an input stream of x pulses and emit an output stream of x^2 pulses—or of 2^x pulses—for all x.

7.5 Show that it is not possible to build a finite machine that will recognize all tapes, made up of strings of 0's and 1's, that contain the same number of 0's as of 1's.

7.6 If the state transition probabilities of a three-state probabilistic automaton are given by the matrix

$$A = \begin{pmatrix} \dfrac{1}{2} & \dfrac{1}{2} & 0 \\[2mm] \dfrac{1}{4} & \dfrac{2}{4} & \dfrac{1}{4} \\[2mm] \dfrac{1}{3} & \dfrac{1}{3} & \dfrac{1}{3} \end{pmatrix}$$

where a_{ij} is the probability that state i is succeeded by state j, then write and execute a program to compute the probabilities b_{ij} that the initial state i will change to state j after a very large number of state transitions.

7.7 Draw two different networks for $(x_1 \overline{x_2} + x_3) \, (x_1 + x_2 \overline{x_3} + x_2)$ using neurons with threshold functions of 1 or 2. (N.B $\overline{x} \equiv \neg x,\ x + y \equiv x \mid y$.)

7.8 Draw a net of neurons that will give an output signal from inputs a, b, c if and only if $a \,\&\, (\overline{b} \mid c) = 1$.

7.9 Design a "scalar by 10" circuit using von Neumann neurons. This is a device that emits one output pulse for every 10 input pulses.

7.10 Draw a circuit using only majority organs that realizes the Boolean function $\neg A \,\&\, (B \mid C)$ (i) using a constant source of pulses, (ii) using the "double line" trick.

7.11 Show that if $x \,\#\, y \,\#\, z$ represents the majority bit $m(x, y, z)$ then $x \,\#\, y \,\#\, z = xy + xz + yz$, and $f(x, y, z) = (x \,\#\, y \,\#\, f(x, \overline{x}, z)) \,\#\, (\overline{x} \,\#\, \overline{y} \,\#\, f(x, \overline{x}, z)) \,\#\, f(x, x, z)$, where f is an arbitrary Boolean function of three variables.

7.12 Write a subroutine in any suitable programming language that will generate a random number each time it is called. Use the recurrence relationship $r_{i+1} \equiv a r_i$ (mod m). Assume that the word length of the machine is 32 binary bits and pick a value for a as suggested in the text.

7.13 Write a Monte Carlo routine to compute the area under the curve $y = f(x)$ and bounded by the lines $x = 0$, $x = 1$. Assume that $0 \leq f(x) \leq 1$ and that a subroutine $F(X)$ can be called to compute $f(x)$. Obtain the area by repeatedly picking a point at random in ("throwing a dart" at) the unit square and counting the percentage of times that the selected point lies under the curve $y = f(x)$ (e.g., if 38% of a large number of randomly selected points lie under the curve, the area is estimated to be 0.38).

7.14 Assume that a Turing machine T is equipped with an oracle that recognizes the elements of a recursive set S. Show that such a machine can be replaced by a machine T' that computes the same function as T and does not use an oracle.

REFERENCES

1. Davis, M., *Computability and Unsolvability.* New York: McGraw-Hill, 1958.

2. McCulloch, W. S. and W. Pitts, "A Logical Calculus of the Ideas Immanent in Nervous Activity." *Bull. Math. Biophys.*, **5** (1943).

3. Murray, F. J., "Mechanisms and Robots." *J. Assn. Comp. Mach.*, **2**, 2 (April 1955).

4. Turing, A. M., "Computing Machinery and Intelligence." *Mind* 59 (n.s. 236). Reprinted as "Can a Machine Think?" in *The World of Mathematics*, Vol. 4. Edited by J. R. Newman. New York: Simon and Schuster, 1954.

5. Von Neumann, J., "Probabilistic Logics and the Synthesis of Reliable Organisms from Unreliable Components." *Automata Studies.* Edited by C. E. Shannon and J. McCarthy. Annals of Mathematics Studies, No. 34. Princeton, N.J.: Princeton University Press, 1956.

6. Weizenbaum, J., *Computer Power and Human Reason.* San Francisco: W. H. Freeman, 1976.

7. Weizenbaum, J., Letter "Computers as 'Therapists'." *Science,* **198,** 4315 (October 28, 1977).

8. Wiener, N., *CYBERNETICS, or Control and Communication in the Animal and the Machine.* New York: John Wiley, 1948.

8
Finite
Automata

Finite size machines with a finite number of possible states comprise a very important class of automata. These machines, together with the associated notion of a "state transition system," find wide application, especially, as we shall see in Chapter 9, to the theory of formal languages (including programming languages). Finite automata are closer to reality than the potentially infinite machines represented by Turing machines, and most problems associated with them are more manageable. There is, for example, an algorithm that will determine the smallest machine, in the sense of having the smallest number of states, that is equivalent to a given machine. The corresponding problem for Turing machines is impossible of general solution.

Finite automata have, however, limited powers. Turing's thesis does not apply to them, and they cannot execute arbitrary effective procedures. It is not even possible for such a machine to multiply two arbitrarily big numbers, although it can add such numbers. Finite automata are primarily used as acceptors, devices that will recognize the members of certain sets of finite strings formed from some alphabet. Each such automaton "defines" a set of such finite strings, or of finite tapes, those strings that cause the machine to enter an acceptance state after reading them. We can define precisely, in genetic or recursive terms, those sets of tapes that are so definable by a finite automaton. These sets are known as the regular sets.

We also look briefly at sequential machines, those finite machines that transform input sequences of symbols into output sequences. Nondeterminism, in the case of finite machines, is a useful concept, and we see that any nondeterministic machine can be replaced by an equivalent deterministic one.

Finite automata were first systematically studied in a mathematically structured way by Rabin and Scott [10].

8.1 WHAT THEY ARE

As mentioned in the preceding chapter, finite automata are fixed size, deterministic, discrete, synchronous, finite state machines. They form perhaps the most widely studied class of automata [4]. Although mechanisms can be considered to be members of this class, only machines that have input—that in a sense communicate with their external environment—are of real interest. All real computers, because there is always some practical bound on the size of auxiliary storage that can be assumed for them, are examples of finite automata rather than of Turing machines. If so viewed, however, the number of states these computers can assume is so prodigious as to allow few of the results of finite automata theory to find fruitful application to them. For example, if a peripheral store of 10^8 bits is assumed for a given machine, the number of states for that computer (recall that we must now think of these states as being the machine's "instantaneous descriptions") is more than $2^{(10^8)}$, a truly vast number.

Except for mechanisms, every finite automaton has an associated input alphabet Σ. It may also have an output alphabet, which may or may not be the same as the input alphabet. Finite automata read finite strings of symbols and may or may not produce strings of symbols as output. We usually assume some standard starting state for a given machine. The machine then reads the first symbol in the string and in response to this symbol it (1) enters another state (which can be the same as the preceding one), (2) may or may not give an output symbol, and (3) moves to read the next symbol in the string. It continues reading the symbols of the string until the string is exhausted, a condition that the machine is able to recognize, and it stops at this time.

We have two kinds of output from these machines. In some cases, the only output is the *state* of the machine after it has read the (finite) input sequence. In other kinds of machines the machine may print a symbol after each input symbol is read, and the output consists of a string of the same length as the input string.

8.2 HOW THEY ARE DESCRIBED

To specify the behavior of a finite automaton we must indicate (1) the state in which it starts, (2) how it changes its state in response to each successive symbol that is read, and (3) how it produces its output.

The symbols of the input alphabet can be taken, as pointed out earlier, to be entire words, or even sentences, if there are only a finite number of these. The actual physical format of the input strings is not important, and this can take such forms as a sequence of symbols on a tape, a deck of cards containing the individual symbols, a time-sequenced array of communication signals received at a terminal, and so forth. The significant thing is that the input, and the words "finite string" connote this, can always be described as an ordered, finite, one-dimensional array (or vector) of data. We frequently refer to these input strings as tapes.

We can usually assume, with no loss of generality, an alphabet consisting only of the symbols 0, 1. As in our earlier discussion of Turing machines, this is not at all a significant restriction. We consider first a machine whose output is determined solely by the terminal state of the machine after it has read the input sequence.

Consider, then, the diagram in Fig. 8.1 of a machine M.

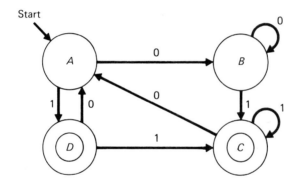

Fig. 8.1   State transition diagram of a finite automaton M.

This figure shows the state transition diagram for a particular finite automaton M with four possible states: A, B, C, D. M has as input alphabet $\{0, 1\}$, i.e., it reads binary strings. The assumed starting state at the beginning of the reading of an input string is shown as A, and the state transitions in response to successive input symbols are shown in obvious fashion by the directed line segments. This automaton is an "acceptor"; it either "accepts" or "rejects" a binary tape after reading it. The acceptance, or "favorable," states are C and D, shown by the double boundary lines for these two states. The automaton accepts a given tape if and only if it is in state C or in state D after having read the tape. It is often convenient (and mathematically desirable) for us to consider the fictitious null tape as a bona fide tape. If the start state happens to be an acceptance state, then the automaton would accept this null tape, which is often denoted as Λ.

Thus, M will accept the tape:

$$11010001$$

for it finishes in state C, an acceptance state, after reading this tape. It will reject the tape:

$$01010100$$

after finishing its reading in state B, an unfavorable state.

Note that tapes of arbitrary length can be read and that this particular automaton accepts an infinite set of tapes. We can, for example, by iterating any number of times the substring 10 in the first part of $101010\cdots1001$ obtain an accepted tape. (This set of tapes can be designated as $\{(10)^n 01 \mid n \geq 0\}$.) In fact, it is easily shown that M accepts any tape terminating with a 1.

The behavior of this automaton can also be described by a *transition matrix*. The matrix corresponding to M is shown in Fig. 8.2.

State	Input symbol 0	1
A	B	D
B	B	C
C	A	C
D	A	C

Fig. 8.2 Transition matrix for the automaton M.

The matrix shows the state transitions of M (if in state A it reads a 1 then it enters state D, etc.) and an additional indication of the start state and of the acceptance states is necessary to specify the machine completely.

A diagram such as Fig. 8.1 is sometimes said to define a "state transition system." Sometimes this term is restricted in usage to systems with a unique favorable state as well as a unique starting state.

8.3 SEQUENTIAL MACHINES

The automaton M has the simplest possible output. It only gives a binary decision—"accept" or "reject," "yes" or "no." We can consider machines that have an additional output capability of writing an output symbol after each

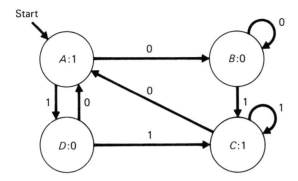

Fig. 8.3 Example of a Moore machine. The machine writes an output symbol for each state entered.

new symbol of the input tape is read [11]. There are two possibilities in specifying the nature of this output. The machine can write an output symbol at each state transition $S_i \rightarrow S_j$, or the machine may be such as to write an output symbol after entering a new state. In the latter case, the output symbol is determined solely by the state it enters after a state transition and is not influenced by the predecessor state.

A *Mealy* machine is one that gives its output when it makes a state transition; a *Moore* machine is one that gives an output that is determined solely by the state entered at each time step.

Figure 8.3 shows a modification M' of machine M, with an output symbol shown for each state entered. M' is a Moore machine. We no longer designate any acceptance states, which were needed to signify the more restricted output of machine M. It is, however, still necessary to specify a starting state.

We assume here an output alphabet $\{0, 1\}$ that is the same as the input alphabet, but this restriction need not apply and a different output alphabet can be used.

If M' reads the tape

$$11010001,$$

it will yield as output another tape or sequence

$$01101001$$

of the same length as the input tape. We assume that the first symbol will be printed after leaving the start state A, i.e., a symbol is printed when each new state, after the first, is entered. The output string is then of the same length as the input string.

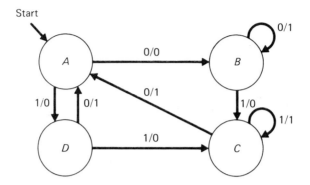

Fig. 8.4 Example of a Mealy machine. The machine writes an output symbol at each state transition.

M' acts to transform sequences into sequences and is an example of a *sequential machine* or, as it is sometimes called, of a *transducer*.

A Mealy machine (Fig. 8.4) is also a sequential machine, but it produces an output symbol that depends on each state transition rather than depending only on the successor state obtained. Figure 8.4 shows such a modification M'' of M.

Again, the output alphabet is assumed to be $\{0, 1\}$ and the start state is A. This time two symbols α/β are associated, not with each state, but with

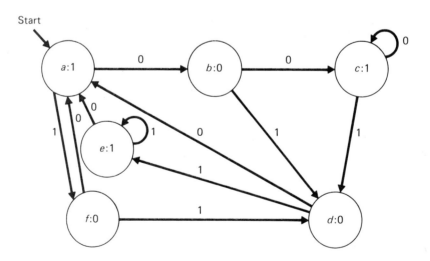

Fig. 8.5 A Moore machine that is equivalent to the Mealy machine M''. It gives the same output string as does M'' for any given input string.

each state transition. The first of these symbols designates the input symbol that causes this particular transition, and the second is the ouput symbol produced when this state transition occurs.

Given the same input sequence as before

$$11010001,$$

M'' will produce as output

$$00101010.$$

It is easy to see that, by introducing new states, any Mealy machine can be replaced by a Moore machine that produces the same output sequences. For example, the machine of Fig. 8.4 can be replaced, by introducing additional states, by the machine of Fig. 8.5.

Similarly, any Moore machine can be replaced by an equivalent Mealy machine. We leave to the reader the required construction.

From a certain theoretical perspective, implied by the use of algebraic structures in studying these matters, the Moore model of a sequential machine is preferable to the Mealy machine.

8.4 FINITE AUTOMATA AS RECOGNITION DEVICES

We have already seen, in our first example M of a finite automaton, how such a machine can be used to define a set of tapes or sequences. That is, a particular set of tapes will be defined by a given machine if that machine accepts those and only those tapes that are in the given set. In this case, we say that the machine *defines,* or *accepts,* or *recognizes* that set of tapes. Consider, for example, the set of all tapes made up of 0's and 1's that have a number of 1's (sometimes, as previously noted, called the "content" of the tape) that is divisible by 3. It is easy to see that this set is defined by the finite automaton whose state transition diagram is shown in Fig. 8.6.

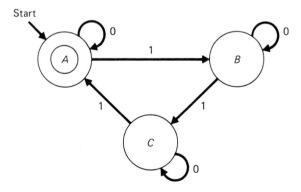

Fig. 8.6 A finite automaton that accepts binary strings containing a number of 1's that is a multiple of 3.

On the other hand, no finite automaton can be designed that will recognize precisely those tapes whose content is a prime number or, as another example, whose content is a perfect square. We shall prove, by the method of reductio ad absurdum, the first of these assertions. Assume that we *can* design a finite automaton P to recognize all sequences of 0's and 1's with a prime number of 1's. Let us suppose that the following tape t is such a sequence:

$$10110011011 \cdots 1$$

Since there are an infinite number of primes, t can be assumed to have a length that exceeds any number we please.

Consider the states of P after reading each symbol in the string t and suppose that the sequence of states assumed by P is as shown in Fig. 8.7.

Since there are only a finite number of states, it is clear that if the automaton reads a very long string of symbols (at least longer than the number of states the automaton can assume), a repetition of some state must appear in listing the successive states assumed. Thus, in Fig. 8.7, the first recurrence of a state is that of C. This is the state of P before and after reading the bracketed segment s. This means that if we insert additional copies of s in the tape immediately after its first occurrence, we must obtain a new tape that is still accepted by P. We can replicate s any number of times, and Fig. 8.8 shows a tape with two additional copies of s inserted after its first occurrence.

The tape of Fig. 8.8 is accepted if the tape of Fig. 8.7 is accepted. Further, the replicated segment s can be repeated indefinitely.

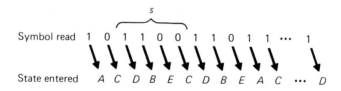

Fig. 8.7 An assumed sequence of successive states of an automaton in reading the binary tape t.

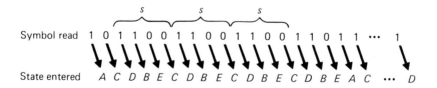

Fig. 8.8 The tape t with two copies of the segment s inserted after its first occurrence.

Let us suppose that the original number of 1's in tape t is m and that there are n 1's in the segment s. The content then of a tape with k additional copies of the segment s inserted is

$$m + k \cdot n.$$

If, now, all of these tapes are accepted by P, as they must be under our assumptions, each of them must have a prime number of 1's. Hence, $m + k \cdot n$ must be a prime number for all values of k. But this cannot be, for if we take $k = m$, we then have:

$$m + k \cdot n = m + m \cdot n = m(1 + n)$$

which is composite, not prime. Hence, our assumption that a finite machine exists that will recognize all binary tapes whose content is prime is false. We leave it to the reader to show by a similar argument that no finite automaton can recognize those tapes whose content is a perfect square. Those sets of tapes that are accepted by some finite automaton are called *regular* sets. We have seen that those binary tapes which have a number of 1's that is a multiple of 3 form a regular set, while those that have a prime number of 1's do not comprise a regular set.

We describe a class of sets in recursive terms and indicate how the class can be generated by repeatedly performing certain fundamental set operations after starting with certain basic sets. When performed on sets of tapes, these operations will yield new sets of tapes. They are:

1. *union*—if S, T are sets of tapes, let R be the set consisting of all tapes that are either in S or in T. Using ordinary set notation, we write $R = S \cup T$.

2. *complex product*—if S, T are sets of tapes, let Q be the set consisting of all tapes obtained by taking any tape of S and appending to it any tape of T. We write $Q = S \times T$.

3. *closure*—if S is a set of tapes, let S^2 denote $S \times S$, let S^3 be $S \times S \times S$, etc. We also write S^0 to denote the null tape, i.e., the tape with no symbols. The closure of S is then defined to be the set P of all tapes which are in S^k for some k. We write $Q = S^* = S^0 \cup S^1 \cup S^2 \cup \dots$

To illustrate these definitions, if
$S = \{ABC, ABAB, CB\}$, $T = \{B, CAB, ABC\}$,
we have:

$$S \cup T = \{ABC, ABAB, CB, B, CAB\}$$
$$S \times T = \{ABCB, ABCCAB, ABCABC, ABABB, ABABCAB,$$
$$ABABABC, CBB, CBCAB, CBABC\}$$
$$S^* = \{\Lambda, ABC, ABAB, CB, ABCABC, ABCABAB, ABCCB,$$
$$ABABABC, ABABABAB, ABABCB, CBABC,$$
$$CBABAB, CBCB, \dots\}$$

It can be shown (Rabin, Scott [10]) that the class of regular sets, those sets that can be recognized by some finite automaton, is made up of finite sets of sequences and of those sets that can be formed from them by repeated applications of the operations of union, complex product, and closure. We shall return later to a proof of this result.

8.5   WHAT FUNCTIONS CAN A TRANSDUCER COMPUTE?

A Turing machine, with its inexhaustible supply of tape, is a growing automaton and not a finite automaton. If, however, we consider a Turing machine that can move in only one direction on its tape, say to the right, then it becomes an example of a finite automaton. The machine is now prevented from writing a string of more than one symbol on the tape and reading all this information at some later time. With this limitation, the machine can "remember" only a finite, fixed amount of information concerning its past, for no matter how long a section of tape it has read, the internal state that it is in after having read this tape is its only means of retaining information about it. This limitation severely restricts the machine's ability to compute.

That a sequential machine can be replaced by a Turing machine that moves its tape in only one direction is perhaps most easily seen by considering a specific machine, like that of Fig. 8.3, and the construction of a Turing machine that will perform the same function. It is a simple matter to see that the following set of quintuples defines such a machine:

$$\left\{ \begin{array}{llll} q_A\,0\,0\,R\,q_B & q_B\,0\,0\,R\,q_B & q_C\,1\,1\,R\,q_C & q_D\,0\,1\,R\,q_A \\ q_A\,1\,0\,R\,q_D & q_B\,1\,1\,R\,q_C & q_C\,0\,1\,R\,q_A & q_D\,1\,1\,R\,q_C \end{array} \right\}$$

We consider next a machine that can add two binary integers. Let us suppose that the input tape, read from right to left, includes first the two low order digits of the two addends, then the next two digits, and so forth. We shall assume that if one addend is shorter than the other, zeros will be used to fill in the high order positions so that there will be matching pairs of digits in all positions. Our machine will read this input tape from right to left and will write as output the binary sum of the two numbers. Since we can only write each successive bit of the output sum after having read a pair of input bits, we shall write the successive bits of the result at every other time step and shall use some spacer symbol, say an asterisk, between these successive bits. The sum may be one bit longer than the addends. We therefore shall presume two zeros at the end of the tape to allow time to write the leading bit of the sum. Thus, to add 110101 and 11011 we shall have as input tape 00101101100111. The desired output is 1 * 0 * 1 * 0 * 0 * 0 * 0 *.

A Mealy machine that will accomplish this addition is shown in Fig. 8.9. Recall that we assume the input tape is read from right to left.

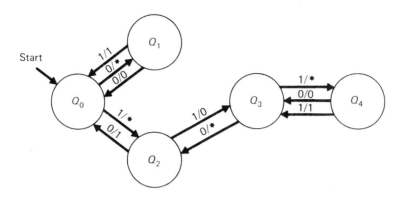

Fig. 8.9 A sequential machine that can add two binary words.

The following conditions hold in each of the machine states:

Q_0: start in this state, or it signifies that the new carry bit from adding a pair of corresponding input bits is 0.

Q_1: first bit of a pair is 0 and the last carry bit is 0.

Q_2: either the first bit of a pair is 1 or the last carry bit is 1, but not both.

Q_3: the new carry bit from adding a pair of bits is 1.

Q_4: the first bit of a pair and the last carry bit are both 1.

Addition along these lines is then clearly feasible. After the machine has read parts of the two addends the number of things that must be "remembered" to continue the process is quite limited, and operands of any length are handled.

The situation is, however, very different when it comes to multiplication. Here, the memory requirements are out of hand and no machine of a fixed number of states (and therefore fixed memory capability) can retain all the information needed in multiplying two binary numbers of arbitrary length. Suppose, for example, that the two operands are each of length $2s$ bits. Let us write them as $p = a \cdot 2^s + b$ and $q = c \cdot 2^s + d$ where a, b, c, d denote the s-bit numbers formed by the leading and trailing halves of each operand.

$$p: \overbrace{\text{x x} \dots \text{x x}}^{a} \overbrace{\text{x} \dots \text{x}}^{b}$$

$$q: \overbrace{\text{x x} \dots \text{x x}}^{c} \overbrace{\text{x} \dots \text{x}}^{d}$$

The product then is

$$pq = ac \cdot 2^{2s} + (ad + bc)2^s + bd.$$

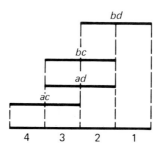

Fig. 8.10 *pq* (four *s*-bit fields)

If the machine has read the last s bits of each operand, i.e., numbers b, d, it may have given as output some part of the full product. However, it can no longer refer to this output because of the restriction that it cannot read information that it has written earlier. Its only way of retaining information about b, d, these first parts of the operands, is by the state it assumes after reading them.

From the equation for pq it is seen that the product is obtained by adding the $2s$-bit partial products, shifted as shown in Fig. 8.10.

We see that the bits of field 3 in pq depend upon b, d as well as a, c. To be more precise, suppose, for example, we consider the multiplica-

tion of $m = 2^{2s} + 2^s$ by itself ($m = \overbrace{100\cdots01}^{s}\overbrace{00\cdots0}^{s}$). The product is $2^{4s} + 2^{3s+1} + 2^{2s}$. That is, it looks like

$$\overbrace{100\cdots01}^{s-2}\overbrace{00\cdots01}^{s}\overbrace{00\cdots0}^{2s}$$

Consider the behavior of a finite machine M that attempts this multiplication along the lines we have described.

Suppose M has read each of the two operands from right to left through the 1 in the $s + 1$st position

$$\cdots\overbrace{100\cdots0}^{s}$$

It presumably has written that part of the product consisting of the $2s$ trailing 0's and the preceding 1.

$$\cdots\overbrace{1000\cdots0}^{2s}$$

But, the machine must now remember after continuing the reading of the 0's of the operands that a 1 is to be written in the $3s + 2_{nd}$ position from the right.

$$\cdots 1\overbrace{00 \cdots 0}^{s}1\overbrace{000 \cdots 0}^{2s}$$
$$\uparrow$$

However, s can be an arbitrarily large number, and M can only be in one of some fixed number of possible states at any time. Therefore, M cannot remember an arbitrarily large number, and it is not possible for it to do multiplication of arbitrarily large operands. In order to cope with this problem, the machine would have to be a growing, or unbounded, automaton, not a finite automaton.

8.6   NONDETERMINISTIC FINITE AUTOMATA

The finite automata we have so far described are deterministic machines. When such an automaton reads an input symbol σ while it is in a given state q, it enters a unique successor state q', determined by q and σ, at the next time step. If we modify this behavior to allow, as in our discussion of nondeterministic Turing machines (Fig. 8.11), more than one possible successor state, the machine will be a nondeterministic finite automaton (NDFA). We also assume that the machine can have more than one starting state.

The NDFA A has two possible start states and it has two possible responses when it is in state q_4 reading a 1. It can either enter state q_1 or state q_2.

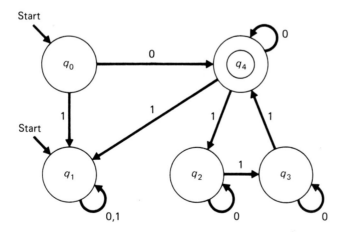

Fig. 8.11 An example of a nondeterministic finite automaton A.

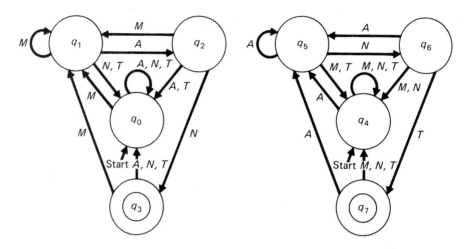

Fig. 8.12 A NDFA, C, that recognizes strings terminating in either MAN or ANT. It has two start states, q_0, q_4 and recognizes one or the other of the two types of strings according to whether it starts in q_0 or in q_4.

We define the recognition of a finite string t by a NDFA to mean that the automaton *can* enter an acceptance state after reading t. That is, *some* selection of successor states during the reading of t will lead to an acceptance state. Thus, our example A will accept any string of 0's and 1's that begins with a 0 and contains $3k$ 1's (where k is some integer, possibly zero). Such strings can also lead to the unfavorable state q_1, but we consider them accepted since there is a feasible path of successive states leading to the acceptance state q_4.

The NDFA is a very useful concept and we are often able to define an accepting automaton more simply than by using a deterministic machine.

Consider the problem of designing a machine that will read strings made up from the letters A, M, N, T and will accept any string that terminates with one or more consecutive occurrences of the word MAN or with one or more occurrences of the word ANT.

A NDFA that will do this is shown in Fig. 8.12. The state graph for this machine C is not connected. The machine is nondeterministic because it can start in either state q_0 or state q_4.

8.7 SOME MISCELLANEOUS NOTATION USEFUL IN DISCUSSING FINITE AUTOMATA

If A denotes an arbitrary finite automaton, let $T(A)$ designate the set of tapes, or finite sequences, accepted by A.

Let q_i, q_j represent two states of the automaton A. Suppose a finite sequence t is such that if A starts in state q_i and reads t, it finishes in state q_j. We may write t: $q_i \rightarrow q_j$. Let "tapes (q_i, q_j)" be the set of all such tapes t. That is, these tapes, when read by A, will cause A to make a sequence of state transitions leading from state q_i to state q_j (i.e., such strings identify directed paths from q_i to q_j in the digraph that represents the state transitions of A).

In the case of the automaton M of Fig. 8.1, we can write 1011: $B \rightarrow C$ or 1011 $\in$ tapes (B, C), i.e., if M starts in state B and reads 1011, it finishes in state C.

Suppose q_0 is the start state of an automaton A and that $\{q_f \mid f \in F\}$ is the set of acceptance states, i.e., F is the set of acceptance state indices. We can then write

$$T(A) = \bigcup_{f \in F} \text{tapes}\,(q_0, q_f)$$

In the case of a NDFA B, tapes (q_i, q_j) represents those strings that *could* lead from state q_i to state q_j for some selection of successor states, where the state transitions are ambiguous.

If we let S denote the set of indices of start states in B, we can write

$$T(B) = \bigcup_{s \in S, f \in F} \text{tapes}(q_s, q_f)$$

If A_1, A_2 are two automata, they are "equivalent," or $A_1 = A_2$, if they accept the same tapes, i.e., if $T(A_1) = T(A_2)$.

If t is some tape, say $\sigma_1 \sigma_2 \cdots \sigma_n$, then t^* denotes that tape written backwards, i.e., $t^* = \sigma_n \sigma_{n-1} \ldots \sigma_1$. If S is a set of tapes, S^* is the set of tapes of S written in reverse order.

If A is an arbitrary finite automaton (possibly a NDFA) let A^* be the automaton obtained by (1) reversing all the arrows of the directed path segments in the state transition diagram of A, and (2) letting the start state(s) of A^* be the acceptance states of A, and letting the acceptance states of A^* be the start state(s) of A. The automaton A^* is not necessarily deterministic if A is deterministic. It is called the "dual" of A. The dual of the automaton M of Fig. 8.1 is shown in Fig. 8.13. This machine M^* is a nondeterministic machine.

From its construction, it is immediate that the dual A^* of an automaton A accepts the tapes accepted by A *if those tapes are written in reverse order*, i.e., we can write

$$T(A^*) = (T(A))^*$$

Note that the dual of an automaton and, generally, that any NDFA need not have a defined response for every state-symbol combination. For example, if M^* is in state B reading a 1, there is no successor state defined. We can, if we

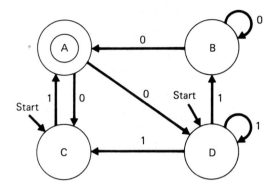

Fig. 8.13   The dual M^* of the finite automaton M.

wish, introduce a fictitious "reject", or nonacceptance, state to which a transition is made in this circumstance. It is not, however, necessary. A tape is accepted by a NDFA only if the tape defines *some* path through the transition diagram leading from a start state to an acceptance state. The existence of incompletely defined paths does not affect the applicability of this definition.

8.8   CONSTRUCTING A DETERMINISTIC FINITE AUTOMATON THAT IS EQUIVALENT TO A GIVEN NDFA

We show that any NDFA can be replaced by a deterministic machine that recognizes precisely the same set of tapes. The construction, which is widely applied, is known as the "subset construction."

We shall first describe it and shall then illustrate its application to a given NDFA.

Given a NDFA B, we construct a new automaton B whose states are identified in its state transition diagram as *subsets* of the states of B.

Let the start state Q_s of B be the *set* of start states of B, i.e.,

$$Q_s = \{q_s \mid s \in S\}$$

where S is the set of start state indices in B. If σ, a letter of B's alphabet, causes, when read, a transition in B from any state q_s to a state q'_s, where there is, perhaps, more than one q'_s,

$$\sigma: q_s \to q'_s \text{ in B,}$$

then let the successor state of Q_s in B when σ is read be Q'_s,

$$\sigma: Q_s \to Q'_s \text{ in } B,$$

where Q'_s is the *set* of states q_s in B that are possible successor states of one of the q_s ($s \in S$) when B reads σ, i.e.,

$$Q'_s = \bigcup_{s \in S} \{q'_s \mid \sigma: q_s \to q'_s \text{ in B}\}$$

The construction continues along these lines. For any given state Q in B, where Q is identified as a subset of the states of B, the successor state Q' in B when the symbol σ is read will be the *set* of states of B that are possible successors of any state in the subset Q when the symbol σ is read, i.e.,

$$\sigma: Q \to Q' \text{ in } B \text{ where}$$
$$Q' = \bigcup_{q_s \in Q} \{q'_s \mid \sigma: q_s \to q'_s \text{ in B}\}$$

The acceptance states of B are taken to be those subset states that include an acceptance state of B as one of the members of the subset.

We illustrate the construction by applying it to the NDFA C of Fig. 8.12. Here, there are two start states q_0, q_4. Therefore, the start state for the

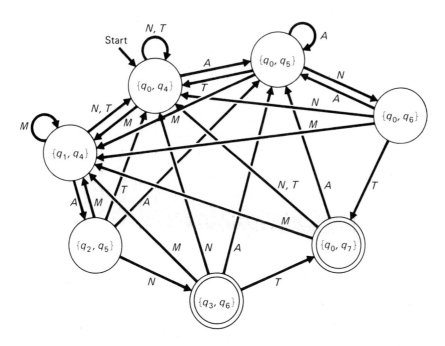

Fig. 8.14 A deterministic automaton C that is equivalent to the NDFA C. The start state is $\{q_0, q_4\}$. The acceptance states are $\{q_3, q_6\}$ and $\{q_0, q_7\}$.

equivalent deterministic finite automaton is the subset $\{q_0, q_4\}$. If, say, an M is read, the successor state will be the subset $\{q_1, q_4\}$. We leave it to the reader to see that repeated constructions of the subset states lead to the deterministic machine C that is equivalent to the NDFA C.

To show that the automaton B, obtained by the subset construction from the NDFA B, accepts precisely the same set of tapes as B ($T(B) = T(\mathrm{B})$), we must prove that any tape accepted by B is accepted by B, and conversely.

Suppose that t is a tape in $T(\mathrm{B})$, $t\colon q_s \rightarrow q_a$ where q_s is a start state of B and q_a is an acceptance state. Let t be the string of characters $t_0 t_1 \cdots t_n$. Consider the chain of successive states assumed by B as it reads t from left to right.

$$q_s \xrightarrow{t_0} q_1 \xrightarrow{t_1} q_2 \xrightarrow{t_2} \cdots \rightarrow q_n \xrightarrow{t_n} q_a$$

Suppose that B, as it reads t, assumes a chain of states

$$Q_s \xrightarrow{t_0} Q_1 \xrightarrow{t_1} Q_2 \xrightarrow{t_2} \cdots \rightarrow Q_n \xrightarrow{t_n} Q_a$$

By the subset construction we have $q_s \in Q_s, q_1 \in Q_1, q_2 \in Q_2, \ldots, q_n \in Q_n$, $q_a \in Q_a$. Since the acceptance states of B are defined to be those subset states that contain an acceptance state of B, it follows that Q_a is an acceptance state of B, and, therefore, t is accepted by B.

Next, we must show the converse, that any tape accepted by B is accepted by B. Let t be a tape that is accepted by B, $t\colon Q_s \rightarrow Q_a$, where Q_s is a start state of B and Q_a is an acceptance state. Again, consider the chain of states assumed by B as it reads t.

$$Q_s \xrightarrow{t_0} Q_1 \xrightarrow{t_1} Q_2 \xrightarrow{t_2} \cdots \rightarrow Q_n \xrightarrow{t_n} Q_a$$

By the subset construction, each state of B that is in the subset Q_a must be a successor state under t_n of some state of B that is included in the subset Q_n. Now Q_a, being an acceptance state of B, contains at least one acceptance state q_a of B, and q_a is then a successor state under t_n of a state q_n of B that is contained in Q_n. That state q_n must similarly be the successor state under t_{n-1} of a state q_{n-1} that is contained in Q_{n-1}. Repeating the argument for each symbol in t we see that the tape t must effect a transition in B from some state q_s in the subset Q_s to the state q_a in Q_a.

But Q_s is, by definition, the set of *all* the start states of B. Therefore, q_s must be a start state of B and t defines a transition in B from a start state q_s to an acceptance state q_a, and $t \, \varepsilon \, T(\mathrm{B})$.

We have thus shown that B and B accept the same set of tapes.

8.9   ANY REGULAR SET CAN BE RECOGNIZED
BY SOME FINITE AUTOMATON

To prove this result we must show that (1) any finite set of tapes is accepted by some finite automaton, and (2) if V, W are two sets of tapes that are accepted by finite automata, say $V = T(A)$, $W = T(B)$, then there exist automata that accept the sets $V \cup W$, $V \times W$ and V^*.

We leave it to one of the exercises for the reader to see that any finite set of tapes

$$V = \{v_1, v_2, \ldots, v_n\},$$

where each v_i is a finite string of symbols from some alphabet, is accepted by some finite automaton.

Similarly (cf. the exercises), it is not difficult to write down the state transition diagrams for automata that recognize $V \times W$ and V^* if we are given the state transition diagrams for the automata A, B that recognize V, W respectively.

With the tool of the NDFA at our disposal, we can also prove the result for $V \cup W$. Our construction of the finite automaton of Fig. 8.14 that is equivalent to the NDFA of Fig. 8.12 illustrates a technique that can be applied to any two automata with distinct state transition graphs. If we are given these diagrams for the automata A, B, where $V = T(A)$, $W = T(B)$, the two disjoint-state graphs can be viewed as a single-state transition system for a NDFA with two start states, and the subset construction yields a finite automaton that recognizes $V \cup W$.

The converse of this theorem is also true. That is, any set that is recognized by some finite automaton is a regular set. It can be proven by induction on the number of states in the automaton, and we omit the details of the proof.

The two results imply that the regular sets are the same as the recognizable sets, those sets that can be recognized by a finite automaton.

8.10   REGULAR EXPRESSIONS, A NOTATION
FOR THE REGULAR SETS

A special notation, closely related to the recursive definition of the class of regular sets that we have given, is often used to describe the regular sets. We have seen that this class of sets is made up of the finite sets of finite sequences on some alphabet and those sets that can be formed from the finite sets by repeated applications of the operations of union, complex product, and closure.

This leads to the following definition of the class of regular expressions. Every regular expression will be a descriptor of some regular set.

Suppose that Σ: $\{\sigma_1, \sigma_2, \ldots, \sigma_n\}$ is some finite alphabet. We define the following class of expressions.

1. Any symbol of Σ is a regular expression.
2. If E, F are regular expressions then so is $(E \vee F)$.
3. If E, F are regular expressions then so is (EF).
4. If E is a regular expression then so is $E*$.

We can restate this definition more compactly using the BNF.

$$\sigma ::= \sigma_1 \mid \sigma_2 \mid \ldots \mid \sigma_n$$
$$E ::= \sigma \mid (EE) \mid (E \vee E) \mid E*$$

The *meaning* of this notation is based on our definition of the class of regular sets.

Any symbol σ ($\sigma \varepsilon \Sigma$) will, of course, denote the set consisting of the single string σ of length 1.

If E, F are respectively the regular expressions for the two sets E, F then:

1. $(E \vee F)$ is the regular expression for the set E $\cup$ F.
2. (EF) is the regular expression for the set E $\times$ F.
3. $E*$ is the regular expression for the set E $*$.

It is easily shown that, from these definitions, $((E \vee F) \vee G)$ and $(E \vee (F \vee G))$ are regular expressions for the same set E $\cup$ F $\cup$ G. Similarly $((EF)G)$ and $(E(FG))$ are regular expressions for the same set E $\times$ F $\times$ G. That is, the parentheses in these expressions conform to an associative law, and we can without confusion write expressions such as $(E \vee F \vee \ldots \vee G)$ or $(EF \cdots G)$.

We give some examples of the use of the notation.

1. $(0 \vee 1) * 1$ denotes the set of all finite binary sequences that terminate in a 1.
2. $0(10) * 1$ denotes the set of sequences $\{01, 0101, 010101, 01010101, \ldots\}$ while $(01) *$ is the union of these sequences and the null string, i.e., $(01) * = (0(10) * 1 \vee \Lambda)$.
3. The machine M of Fig. 8.1 accepts the set of tapes denoted by $(0 \vee 1) * 1$.
4. The NDFA C of Fig. 8.12 accepts the set of tapes denoted by $(A \vee M \vee N \vee T) * (\text{MAN} \vee \text{ANT})$.

8.11   THE MINIMIZATION OF FINITE AUTOMATA

A very practical problem is the following. Let A be a given deterministic finite automaton. Find an automaton with the smallest number of states that is equivalent to A, i.e., accepts precisely the same set of tapes.

We shall describe without proof an elegant procedure for solving this problem. The reader is referred to [1, 3, 7, 9] for a proof that this procedure does what is claimed.

Given the automaton A:

1. Construct the dual A* of A.
2. Apply the subset construction to A* obtaining an equivalent deterministic version B of A*. B recognizes the tapes accepted by A, written backwards.
3. Construct the dual B* of B.
4. Apply the subset construction to B*, obtaining an equivalent deterministic version C of B*. C recognizes the same tapes as A, and C will have the smallest number of states of any finite automaton equivalent to A.

We shall illustrate this construction by finding a smallest automaton that recognizes the same tapes as does the machine *M* of Fig. 8.1 We have already taken the first step of the minimization procedure in defining *M* *, the dual of *M*, in Fig. 8.13.

The subset construction applied to *M* * gives the following deterministic automaton *P*. Note that we have had to introduce a state corresponding to the null set Φ since states *C, D* have no successor in *M* * when 0 is read.

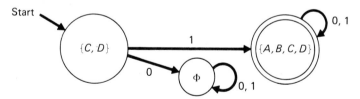

We next execute the third step and construct *P* *, the dual of *P*. We have relabeled the states; their names have no bearing on the behavior of the automaton.

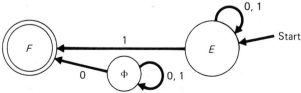

In the last step we apply the subset construction to $P*$. In this case, it has the effect of removing the state corresponding to the null set.

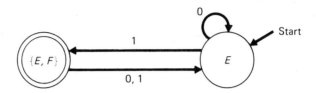

We have obtained a two-state automaton that recognizes the same set of tapes as does the four-state automaton M. We see, perhaps more clearly, that M recognizes any binary sequence that terminates in a 1.

8.12 FINITE AUTOMATA THAT CAN READ THEIR TAPES BACKWARDS

Suppose we revise the description of a finite automaton so that, like a Turing machine, it can move its input tape in either direction. Would this ability of the machine to range back and forth over its input tape extend its powers as a recognition device, i.e., would such a machine then be able to accept a set of tapes that no finite automaton limited to the forward reading of its tape could accept? Perhaps surprisingly, the answer is no. We shall see that a finite automaton that can read its input tape in both directions can always be replaced, as a recognition device, by one that reads its tape in only one direction.

It is this theoretical result that implies in principle the feasibility of such programming constructions as single pass compilers that can produce an object program after passing once through a source program.

We can prove the result as follows. Suppose that B is a machine that can read its tape backwards as well as forwards. Let its behavior be determined by writing "quadruples" of the form $q_i S_j M q_l$, where M is R or L, with the meaning that when B is in state q_i reading the symbol S_j, it goes either to the right or to the left on the tape and enters state q_l. As with normal finite automata, B can sense the end of its tape, and certain of its states are acceptance states.

Suppose that, at some time step, B is reading a symbol on its tape as in the following diagram, that it is in state q_i and must move to the left (i.e., it is executing a quadruple of the form $q_i S_j L q_l$). Let w represent the section of tape that has already been read by B.

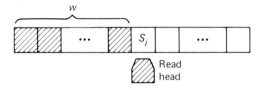

We ask the following question. Can the machine be modified to "re-member" enough about its past reading of w so that, when B is called upon to reenter w from the right, the modified machine (call it C) can determine the state *in which B would next emerge from w on the right.* If the machine C could do this, it would not be necessary for it to move backwards through w and we could replace B with the forward reading automaton C. The "states" of C would include this "remembrance" of tapes read. Clearly, this cannot be done on a finite machine if there is too much to remember. The "instruc-tions" for determining the next state in which B leaves w would have to be of a fixed bound in size, no matter how long the tape segment w is. We shall show that it is possible to do this.

Suppose that we carry, along with the present state q_i of the machine B, a function on states defined in the form of a table. The table indicates for each state in which B might make its next move to the left that state in which B would again arrive (if it does) at the tape symbol currently being scanned. This function is, in general, partial, for the machine conceivably might enter a loop and never emerge from w after reentering it.

State in which B might reenter w from the right	State in which B would next emerge from w on the right
q_0	q_{i_0}
q_1	q_{i_1}
$\vdots$	$\vdots$
q_{n-1}	$q_{i_{n-1}}$

Let us make such a stored table a part of the control of the machine C and consider the "states" of C (call them Q_i) to consist of a state q_i of B accompanied by such a table. Every right-hand entry in the table is one of the states of B, or it is an indication that B would enter an endless loop and never emerge on the right from w after reentering it in the state named in the left-hand column. Since only a finite number of tables can be written, it follows that there are only a finite number of configurations or states Q_i that can be used to define the one-way automaton C that will replace B.

By example, we next show that it is possible to continually update and redefine the table as C moves through w in one direction. The changes of state in C will include this transition of tables. When C starts reading the tape, the associated function, or table, is nowhere defined. If, at any point, B would have moved to the left on its tape, C will be able to determine from its stored table the state in which B would next arrive at the symbol being scanned, making it unnecessary for C actually to read the tape backwards.

It is not difficult to see how to determine the revisions of the table as C moves through the tape. Suppose that at some point the table in C is given in part as follows:

State in which B might reenter w from the right	State in which B would next emerge from w on the right
q_0	q_1
q_1	q_4
q_2	q_2
q_3	q_2
q_4	q_0
$\vdots$	$\vdots$

Let us suppose that B includes, among others, the following quadruples:

$$\left\{ \begin{array}{ll} q_0 1 L q_0 & q_3 1 L q_2 \\ q_1 1 R q_4 & q_4 1 L q_1 \\ q_2 1 R q_3 & \text{———} \end{array} \right\}$$

Suppose that, while reading a particular tape, B arrives at the point where it is in state q_3 scanning a 1, as shown in the following tape segment:

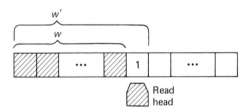

B must now execute $q_3 1 L q_2$. It then reenters w in state q_2. From the table, it will next emerge from w, the section of tape to the left of the current position of the read head, in state q_2. It would then execute $q_2 1 R q_3$ and leave w' $(= w1)$ on the right in state q_3.

We can similarly analyze every possible reentry state in which B might move back into w' from the right, and get a revised table for C to be carried along, listing the next state in which B would emerge from w' after reentering it. We leave it to the reader to check the entries in the following table. The letter p for reentry state q_4 denotes that B will enter an endless loop if it reenters w' in state q_4.

State in which B might reenter w' from the right	State in which B would next emerge from w' on the right
q_0	q_4
q_1	q_4
q_2	q_3
q_3	q_3
q_4	p
$\vdots$	$\vdots$

For any given two-way automaton B we can go through an analysis of this kind. We describe how the pair (q_i, T), where q_i is a state of B and the function T is, as we have specified it, a table of "reentry and emergence" states, is succeeded by the pair (q_i', T') when B reads a symbol σ of its input alphabet. The states of the equivalent one-way automaton C are these pairs (q_i, T), i.e., we can write, in describing the behavior of C,

$$\sigma\colon Q \to Q'.$$

where Q is the pair (q_i, T) and Q' is the pair (q_i', T').

The point is simply that C "remembers" by its state Q at any moment (where Q includes a table T), the effect on B of a backwards move into the segment of tape that has already been read by C.

Thus, we can see that any two-way recognition automaton can be replaced by an equivalent one-way automaton.

8.13   TREE AUTOMATA

We have noted in the appendix to Chapter 3 that a tree structure is a generalization of a finite sequence. Just as an ordinary finite automaton recognizes a particular set of finite sequences, a *tree automaton* recognizes a set of trees with labeled nodes. It thus is a generalization of an ordinary finite automaton. The trees we consider have at each node a symbol drawn from some finite alphabet Σ, and associated with each such symbol x is a non-negative integral valued "weight" $\sigma(x)$. If the symbol x appears at a node of a tree, a number of branches, equal to the symbol's weight $\sigma(x)$, emanate from that node. The symbols at the terminal nodes or leaves have weight 0.

As implied by our earlier definition, Σ^* denotes the set of all finite strings, including the null string, that can be formed from the symbols of Σ.

The strings in Σ^* accepted by an ordinary finite automaton can be thought of as trees if we introduce an additional and terminal symbol # (or we can use the symbol Λ for the null string). If we then give each symbol in Σ a weight of 1 and assign a weight of 0 to #, the trees which can be drawn are in one-to-one correspondence with the strings $\#\Sigma^*$, or with Σ^*. In each tree, # appears at the terminal leaf. Any given finite automaton will accept some subset of these trees.

The tree for the string ABC:

($\# ABC$ is the postfix string representation for this tree.)

There are several schemes for identifying a tree as an ordered string of symbols. We shall, as we have done in the appendix to Chapter 3, use the postfix notation of Brainerd [2]. Recall that we assign the string $\alpha_1 \alpha_2 \cdots \alpha_n x$ to the tree:

The notation is extended in recursive fashion to arbitrary trees.

Example. If $\Sigma = \{+, \times, -, a, b, c\}$ with $\sigma(+) = \sigma(\times) = \sigma(-) = 2, \sigma(a) = \sigma(b) = \sigma(c) = 0$, then any well-formed algebraic expression containing some of the letters a, b, c and using only binary operations $+, \times, -$ is representable by a tree; e.g., $a + ((b - c) \times b)$ is represented by the tree:

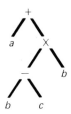

In "postfix" notation, this tree is represented by the string $a\,b\,c\,-\,b\times\,+$.

The behavior of a tree automaton is a generalization of that of an ordinary finite automaton in the sense that its state transition function is defined on n-tuples ($n \geq 1$) of states. We describe the automaton's "reading" of a tree, which may be given in the postfix form as defined above or in graphic form. A state is assigned to each node as follows. (a) The automaton enters a state at each of the terminal nodes, determined by the labels at these nodes. We think of the automaton having an initial state s_0. On reading a symbol α_i of weight 0 (i.e., a symbol at a terminal node) the automaton enters some state s_i. We write α_i: $s_0 \to s_i$. (b) The automaton moves up through the tree. Consider a subtree such as α. After the automaton has assigned states to nodes $\alpha_1, \alpha_2, \ldots, \alpha_n$ and has read x, the n-ary state transition function determines the state to be assigned at the node labeled x.

If the automaton, when it reaches the root, is in one of a designated set S of "favorable" states, the tree is accepted by the automaton. It is readily seen that an ordinary finite automaton cannot necessarily accept the strings which in postfix form identify a family of trees (e.g., $\{\alpha^{n+1} + {}^n \mid n \geq 0\}$ with $\sigma(\alpha) = 0$, $\sigma(+) = 2$, cannot be recognized by any finite automaton, but we can define a tree automaton that will accept trees with these postfix representations).

For applications of tree automata to the study of programming languages, see [5, 6].

EXERCISES

8.1 Design, i.e., draw the state transition diagram of, a finite automaton that reads strings on the alphabet $\{0, 1\}$ and recognizes precisely the strings 101 and 1110.

8.2 Design a finite automaton that reads strings made up of letters in the word CHARIOT and recognizes those strings that contain the word CAT as a substring.

8.3 Design a finite automaton that reads strings on the alphabet $\{0, 1\}$ and recognizes those strings whose content (number of 1's) is divisible by 2 or by 3.

8.4 Is $\{0^n 10^n \mid n \geq 0\}$, where 0^n denotes a string of n 0's, a regular set? Prove your answer.

8.5 Determine if the set of sequences on $\{0, 1\}$ in which the number of 0's is equal to the number of 1's is a regular set.

8.6 Let $V = \{v_1, v_2, \ldots, v_n\}$ be a finite set of tapes where each v_i, $i = 1, 2, \ldots, n$, is a finite string of symbols from some finite alphabet. Show that V is a regular set.

8.7 Design a finite automaton that will recognize the set of strings $\{a^n b a^k \mid (n \geq 1)\,\&\,(k \geq 0)\}$, where a^r denotes a string of r a's.

8.8 Prove that the set of strings on the alphabet $\{0, 1\}$ that contain a number of 1's which is a perfect square is not a regular set. (*Hint:* the difference between consecutive squares increases indefinitely.)

8.9 Given an alphabet Σ and a finite automaton M that recognizes the set of sequences E. Is the set $\Sigma * E$ a regular set?

8.10 Find a regular expression E for the sequences accepted by the finite automaton in Fig. 8.15.

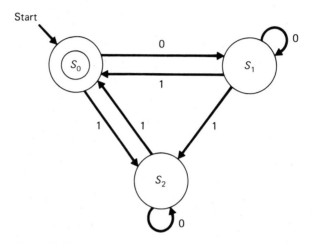

Figure 8.15

8.11 Find a regular expression E for the sequences accepted by the machine in Fig. 8.16.

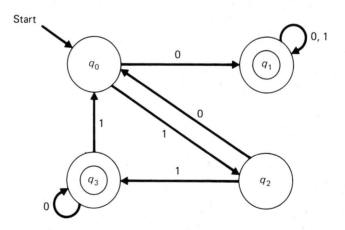

Figure 8.16

8.12 Define two finite automata that recognize the sets of sequences with the following regular expressions:

    a. $(a \vee bcd)$ ✱ bcd b. $(0 \vee 1)$ ✱ 111

8.13 For A a given finite automaton of r states prove that $T(A)$ is infinite if and only if it contains a tape of length n with $r \leq n \leq 2r$.

8.14 If E is a regular set, is its complement $\bar{E}$ necessarily a regular set? Prove that if E, F are regular sets so are the sets $E \cap F$ and $E - F$ (defined as $E \cap \bar{F}$).

8.15 Given the state transition diagrams of two finite automata A, B that recognize respectively the sets V, W show how to obtain state transition diagrams for automata that recognize $V \times W$ and V ✱.

8.16 Given finite automata A, B defined by the state transition diagrams shown in Fig. 8.17, design a deterministic finite automaton that recognizes $T(A) \cup T(B)$.

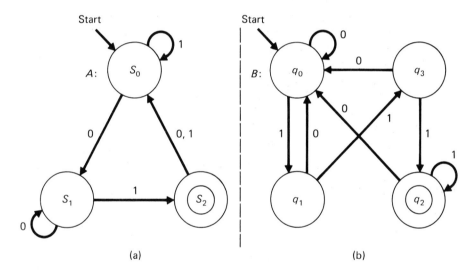

Figure 8.17

8.17 Design a Moore machine that will read sequences made up of the letters A, E, I, O, U and will give as output the same sequences except that in those cases where an I directly follows an E, it will be changed to a U.

8.18 Design a Moore machine that will read sequences of binary bits and write the hexadecimal character $(0, 1, 2, 3, 4, 5, 6, 7, 8, 9, A, B, C, D, E, F)$ for each consecutive field of 4 bits. Write blanks (b) between the hexadecimal characters and write a special symbol ✱ if the last field read is not precisely 4 bits long. Assume a special flag # appears at the end of the binary string.

8.19 Given the state transition diagram in Fig. 8.18 for a finite automaton A:

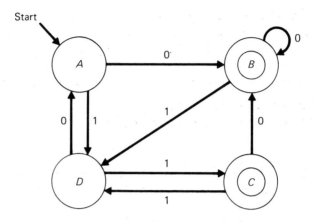

Figure 8.18

a. Draw the state transition diagram for a nondeterministic finite automaton that accepts the tapes $T(A)$ written backwards.

b. Give the state transition diagram for a deterministic finite automaton that accepts these backwards written tapes.

8.20 Find the minimum state deterministic finite automaton that recognizes the same sequences as the machine with the state transition diagram in Fig. 8.19.

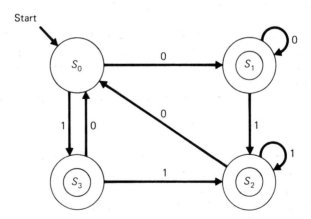

Figure 8.19

8.21 Find the minimum state deterministic finite·automaton that recognizes the same sequences as does the machine with the state transition diagram shown in Fig. 8.20.

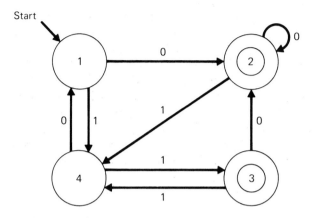

Figure 8.20

8.22 Write a program in any suitable language to execute the state minimization procedure described in the text. The input and output should be descriptions of state transition diagrams.

8.23 Define a tree automaton that will accept all trees with postfix notations $\{\alpha^{n+1} + {}^n \mid n \geq 0\}$, where $\sigma(\alpha) = 0$, $\sigma(+) = 2$.

REFERENCES

1. Beckman, F. S., *Categorical Notions and Duality in Automata Theory.* IBM Research Report RC 2977, July 28, 1970.

2. Brainerd, W. S., "The Minimalization of Tree Automata." *Information and Control,* **13** (1968).

3. Brzozowski, J. A., "Canonical Regular Expressions and Minimal State Graphs for Definite Events." *Proceedings of the Symposium on the Mathematical Theory of Automata.* Polytechnic Institute of Brooklyn, April 1962.

4. Ginsburg, S., *An Introduction to Mathematical Machine Theory.* Reading, Massachusetts: Addison-Wesley, 1962.

5. Gorn, S., "An Axiomatic Approach to Prefix Languages." *Symposium on Symbolic Languages in Data Processing, Rome, 1962. Proceedings of the Symposium Organized and Edited by the International Computation Center, Rome, March 26–31, 1962.* New York: Gordon and Breach, 1962.

6. Gorn, S., "Language Naming Languages in Prefix Form." *International Federation of Information Processing Societies, Working Conference on Formal Languages*. Vienna, 1964. Published in *Formal Language Description Languages for Computer Programming*. Ed. T. B. Steel, Jr. Amsterdam: North-Holland Publishing Company, 1966.

7. Kameda, T., and P. Weiner, *On the Reduction of Non-Deterministic Automata.* Technical Report No. 57, Department of Electrical Engineering Computer Sciences Laboratory, Princeton University, 1968.

8. Kameda, T., "Some New Useful Concepts in Automata Theory." *Proceedings of the Hawaii International Conference on System Sciences,* 1968.

9. Mirkin, B. G., "Dual Automata." *Kibernetika,* No. 1 (1966).

10. Rabin, M. O., and D. Scott, "Finite Automata and Their Decision Problems." *IBM J. Res. Devel.,* **3** (1959).

11. Raney, G. N., "Sequential Functions." *J. Assn. Comp. Mach.,* **5** (1958).

12. Steel, T. B., Jr., ed. *Formal Language Description Languages for Computer Programming.* Amsterdam: North-Holland Publishing Company, 1966.

9
Formal Languages— Introduction

One of the most successful uses of a mathematical approach in coping with important problems of programming is the application of the theories of formal languages and of automata to compiler design and development. In recent years there has developed a very extensive body of literature devoted to these matters, and the subject matter has been so well formalized and organized that much of it is now taught at the undergraduate level. Compiling has gone a long way from Art to Science.

The natural languages are the spoken languages such as English, French, Russian, and so forth. Formal languages on the other hand consist of sets of symbolic strings with some mathematical structure usually imposed. Programming languages are examples of formal languages, the "sentences" of a programming language being the well-formed programs that can be written following the rules (the grammar) of the language.

There is, of course, a great distinction between natural languages and formal languages. However, some ways of specifying grammars are usefully applied to both kinds of languages. In particular, this is true of some very important work of N. Chomsky on the definition of languages by "phrase structure" grammars. These grammars make use of "rewriting rules" to define the well-formed sentences of a language, and these notions have strongly influenced the teaching of grammar in the elementary schools. This approach includes rules for generating the correctly formed sentences of a language rather than providing rules for determining directly if a sentence is well-formed. A sentence is generated by starting with a special symbol and applying a chain of rules that allow designated substrings of symbols to be replaced by other substrings. Each properly formed sentence of the language can then be "derived" in this manner from the starting symbol. These ideas are applicable as well to formal languages and lead to a sweeping classification of such languages.

One very important class of languages is that of the "context-free" languages. In these languages sentences are derived by using restricted rewriting rules which enable the replacement of a single symbol, at each stage of a derivation of a sentence, by a substring of one or more[1] symbols. A language is context free in the sense that each such rule can be applied no matter what other symbols of a string accompany the particular symbol being rewritten.

The rules governing the formation of the well-formed sentences of a language determine the *syntax* of that language while *semantics* concerns the study of the assignment of meaning to sentences. In the case of programming languages the syntax of a language determines when a program is well-formed, i.e., acceptable to a compiler for that language, while the semantics determine for a given program how, when executed, its output is determined from its input.

Given a possible sentence of a language, to *parse* that sentence is to determine if it is well-formed and, if so, to describe its formation by showing its grammatical derivation. A grammar that allows some well-formed sentences to be parsed in more than one way is said to be ambiguous, and usually (but not always) we avoid ambiguous grammars in defining programming languages. Programming languages are defined by grammars that are almost context free. The parse of a program written in some programming language with specified grammar provides information that a compiler can use to construct an equivalent object program.

We look briefly at some techniques for parsing the sentences of context-free languages, giving the reader a taste of the multitude of strategies that can be used for these procedures. It should be emphasized that we only sample the substantial work in this area, and the reader is advised to study some of the recent books on compiler design and on formal languages for more comprehensive treatments of these topics.

9.1   NATURAL LANGUAGES AND FORMAL LANGUAGES

The "natural" languages are the languages spoken by Man. These number well over 1,000, and the richer languages, those with substantial bodies of literature, have undergone centuries of growth and refinement with increas-

---

[1]   Except for the derivation of the null string when it is a sentence in the language. See footnote on p. 310.

ing expressive powers for the description of the world and for ideas of subtlety, depth, and sensitivity. Unlike programming languages, these languages were not formed ab initio by any committee representing prospective users, but their considerable vocabularies and facilities for expression are largely consequences of this evolutionary development. There have been some notable attempts to introduce internationally used semi-artificial languages, such as Esperanto, constructed by one or several people with the laudable goal of reducing the barriers of communication among the peoples of the Earth, but these have never enjoyed any great or continuing success. Relevant to this, it is of interest to note the reportedly furious reaction of the philosopher Ludwig Wittgenstein to such languages. This was based on his profound conviction that languages should grow organically, that they should develop only by natural evolutionary processes and by that extended usage which leads to continual refinements and needed innovations, and that they must not be issued full-blown from the minds of any small number of people. The more widely used programming languages do, of course, go through extended periods of enrichment and revision based on feedback from their users, but, invariably, even the first versions of these languages are completely viable. Voltaire's remark that "no language has been formed by an assembly of logicians" does not apply to programming languages.

It would, perhaps, be a great convenience if we could bypass the need for computer users to learn programming languages and arrange for them to communicate directly with machines, without any restrictions, in their own natural language, supplemented by the language of mathematics. But, of course, this asks for too much from the computer at the present stage of development of artificial intelligence. Natural languages are intended for communication between people and in their entirety are too rich for communication with machines. More important, they are often ambiguous in usage, and the resolution of these ambiguities is not at all easy. We are here thinking not so much of the kind of confusion that results from grappling with ideas that are somewhat vague and elusive, difficult to verbalize and make precise, such as, say, in the writings of some philosophers, but rather with problems incident to the nature of language itself. Suppose, by way of an example somewhat less contrived than Groucho Marx's "I shot an elephant in my pajamas" that we read, out of context, the well-formed sentence "He made her well." It is not possible to tell whether the "he" is a doctor, a sculptor, a shipbuilder, a well-digger or, perhaps, the Creator of Eve.

Such imprecision is, of course, intolerable in defining an algorithm. We leave to the reader the recognition of the problems the computer would face in trying to interpret a seemingly well-formed command such as the following request to retrieve information from a hypothetical, and rather bizarre, personnel file:

LIST THE IDENTIFICATION NUMBERS OF ALL EMPLOYEES
THAT ARE PRIME AND CONTAINED IN THE DISTRICT 3 AND
MANAGEMENT PERSONNEL FILES, THAT RESIDED IN NEW
YORK CITY BEFORE 1970 OR WHO HAVE EXEMPT STATUS,
EXCEPT FOR THOSE WHO EARN MORE THAN $40,000, OR
HAVE AS MANY AS THREE CHILDREN, AND OWN A DOG OR
A CAT, WHO ARE ALSO FLUENT IN FRENCH, AND WHO HAVE
A SPOUSE WHO IS A MEMBER OF A LARGE WOMEN'S ORGA-
NIZATION.

Commas or other punctuation marks are not sufficient to make the
meaning here transparent. We would have to supplement our natural language description with additional specifiers, some of which might play in
part the role of parentheses in algebraic expressions, in order to make such
an ambiguous instruction unequivocal. Or, perhaps, we can conceive of an
interactive dialogue that will enable the computer to elicit the information it
needs to clarify this strange request for information. Natural languages are,
when used in an unrestricted way, clearly not ideally suited for communication with the computer. They contain ambiguities, both in the meanings of
words and in the ways in which sentence structure may be interpreted.

We generalize the notion of language to include not only such structures
as programming languages but, more generally, arbitrary collections of
strings of symbols as well. Assume a finite alphabet, say $\{A_1, A_2, \ldots, A_n\}$. A
formal language, then, is often defined as *any* subset of the denumerably
infinite set of finite strings that can be formed from these symbols. This may
perhaps be criticized as being an unduly broad definition for it follows from
it that such sets of strings as the works of Shakespeare, the set of binary
encoded pictures of the surface of Mars transmitted by Viking I, the set of all
closing prices for a given year on the New York Stock Exchange, and so
forth, are all authentic examples of languages just as well as those natural
and artificial languages whose structures are really of interest to us. Additional structure will, however, always be required in practice. When we study
artificial languages such as the statements of the propositional calculus or,
appropriate to our principal concern, particular programming languages,
formal rules will be additionally given that spell out which of the infinite set
of possible strings are bona fide, well-formed sentences of the language.
Invariably, a finite set of rules for the formation of sentences will be adequate in these cases to generate an infinite set of well-formed sentences. A
formal language is a mathematical structure akin to the formal systems
mentioned in Chapter 2.

Given any particular language, the language we may use to describe that language is called a *metalanguage* (Webster: meta—beyond, transcending, higher) just as "metamathematics" refers to the subject that is concerned with the nature of mathematics—its meaning, methods of proof, and so forth. That we need such an additional language is clear for it seems evident that we cannot describe a given language completely in terms of itself. The situation may, perhaps, be likened to the fact that a person who requires reading glasses for close viewing needs another instrument with which to examine those glasses. When English-speaking people begin the study of French, we might consider the metalanguage used to be English while the language studied, the *object language,* is French. While the metalanguage for the study of the early programming languages was always English (or some other natural language) the formal study of programming languages now frequently involves the use of specially designed metalanguages [4, 5, 6, 7, 8, 9] that are better suited to the task of defining programming languages.

9.2 SYMBOLIC MANIPULATION SYSTEMS—REWRITING RULES

In a superficial sense, all verbal arguments, all mathematical proofs, all chains of logical reasoning that are expressible as sequences of mathematical or verbal statements can be considered to be chains of symbolic strings where each string is obtained from its predecessors by applying hopefully well-defined rules or arguments. In general, these rules may, of course, be quite complex, imprecise, and even perhaps not universally accepted as being valid. We shall, in this section, consider a highly simplified situation where each string of symbols in a deriving chain is obtained from the preceding string by replacing selected symbols in the string by one or more symbols. These substitutions will be defined by a finite number of certain *rewriting rules.* A finite set of these rules will show how a possibly infinite set of strings can be formed. A rewriting rule is also called a *production,* and we shall use the two terms interchangeably in the following.

We begin by defining a very simple formal language. The methods used illustrate general procedures that will be given later. Assume an alphabet consisting of the three symbols $\{\sigma, 0, 1\}$. We describe how to produce certain finite strings of 0, 1 by repeatedly applying rewriting rules, starting with the symbol σ. These rules enable us to replace σ whenever it appears in a string by the sequence of symbols on the right-hand side of any one of the following rewriting rules:

$$\sigma \to 0\,\sigma\,0 \qquad \sigma \to 11$$
$$\sigma \to 1\,\sigma\,1 \qquad \sigma \to 00$$

We can continue to apply successively some of the rewriting rules until we use one of the last two rules and no symbol σ remains in the string. Thus, we can produce the string 1001111001 by starting with σ and choosing at successive steps the appropriate one of the above replacement rules to achieve the following:

$$\sigma \Rightarrow 1\,\sigma\,1 \Rightarrow 10\,\sigma\,01 \Rightarrow 100\,\sigma\,001 \Rightarrow 1001\,\sigma\,1001 \Rightarrow 1001111001$$

It is seen that we can similarly obtain, starting with σ, *any* string of 0's and 1's which is of even length and of which the right-hand half is the mirror image of the left half. These strings comprise the *language* generated by these particular rules. This language has been defined by describing its strings as the outputs resulting from certain well-defined procedures rather than by stating procedures to verify if any given string is or is not a string in that language. Using the vocabulary of Chapter 4, this language has been defined as a particular *recursively enumerable* set of strings but not as a *recursive* set of strings (although, in this case, the set of strings is recursive as well).

These ideas have been notably applied by Chomsky [2, 3] in his invention of "phrase structure grammars" as a first step toward defining the well-formed sentences of natural languages. One key idea here is that while it is very difficult to give rules to determine if a sentence in a natural language is well-formed (that is, to recognize such strings as being elements of a recursive set), it is a much more manageable procedure to define the well-formed sentences as those that can be obtained by applying certain simple rewriting rules. That is, a simple method is used to define these well-formed sentences as the elements of a recursively enumerable set. Before Chomsky's work expositions of grammar were largely based on complex rules for determining if a given sentence is well-formed.

We illustrate these notions in the following example. Take the special symbols of a rewriting system to be:

S, NP, VP, ADV, ART, ADJ, N, V, PREP

(S = sentence, NP = noun phrase, VP = verb phrase, ADV = adverb, ART = article, ADJ = adjective, N = noun, V = verb, PREP = preparation.) Let the terminal vocabulary, those symbols that may appear in the final strings generated, be:

the, of, cow, moon, cheese, green, jumped, is made, over.

Each word or phrase in the terminal vocabulary is being considered here as a single symbol or element of the vocabulary.

Let the following rewriting rules be given:

$$\begin{array}{ll} S \to NP\ VP\ NP & V \to \text{is made} \\ NP \to N & V \to \text{jumped} \\ NP \to ART\ NP & N \to \text{cow} \\ NP \to PREP\ NP & N \to \text{moon} \\ NP \to ADJ\ N & N \to \text{cheese} \\ VP \to V & ART \to \text{the} \\ VP \to V\ ADV & PREP \to \text{of} \\ & ADJ \to \text{green} \\ & ADV \to \text{over} \end{array}$$

The sentence:

the moon is made of green cheese

can then be obtained as follows from the symbol S using the rewriting rules.

$S \Rightarrow NP\ VP\ NP \Rightarrow ART\ NP\ VP\ NP \Rightarrow$ the NP VP NP
$\Rightarrow$ the N VP NP $\Rightarrow$ the moon VP NP $\Rightarrow$ the moon V NP
$\Rightarrow$ the moon is made NP $\Rightarrow$ the moon is made PREP NP
$\Rightarrow$ the moon is made of NP $\Rightarrow$ the moon is made of ADJ N
$\Rightarrow$ the moon is made of green N
$\Rightarrow$ the moon is made of green cheese

We have in this derivation applied only one rewriting rule at each transformation. This is consistent with the assumption that in writing "left $\to$ right" we interpret "$\to$" to mean that the string "right" can be obtained from the string "left" by the application of one rewriting rule.

The derivation of this sentence can also be described as follows in the form of a tree (called a *syntax tree*). This has the advantage of showing at a glance how the sentence of terminals can be derived from the initial symbol. The final sentence is made up of the leaves of the tree (Fig. 9.1), read from left to right.

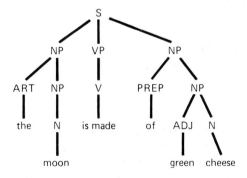

Figure 9.1

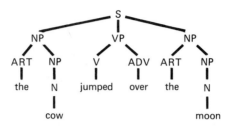

Figure 9.2

Similarly, the sentence

the cow jumped over the moon

can be derived from S by a succession of applications of the rewriting rules. This can be shown by the tree in Fig. 9.2.

In addition to these meaningful sentences, a number of other nonsensical strings can equally well be formed from the use of the rules, such as:

the cow is made of green moon, or
the cheese jumped over the cheese.

The rules, not concerned with the meaning of words, serve in a very limited way to recognize if a generated sentence is sensible but principally are used to guide the formation of strings of words where the various parts of speech follow each other in proper order.

9.3 FORMALIZATION OF THESE SYSTEMS

A widely occurring mathematical structure of algebra that plays a key role in the study of formal languages and of automata is the *free monoid*.

A *monoid* consists of a set S of objects $\{\ell, m, n, \dots\}$ together with a rule (often called a "multiplication" rule even though it has in general nothing to do with arithmetic multiplication) that defines for each ordered pair m, n of objects an object in S. That is, the rule is a binary function $S \times S \to S$ that maps ordered pairs of objects in S into S. We can then consider the "product" mn to be that object in S into which the pair m, n is mapped. This mapping is required to satisfy two conditions:

1. the combining rule is associative, that is, $(\ell m)n = \ell(mn)$

2. there is an element e in S called the unit element, or the identity, which when combined in either order with any element of S leaves it invariant. That is, $em = me = m$.

In elementary mathematics the natural numbers form a monoid if addition is taken to be the rule used in defining the combining of elements, and if 0 is considered the identity element. The two required properties are satisfied, for we have for any natural numbers l, m, n:

$$(l + m) + n = l + (m + n) \text{ and } 0 + m = m + 0 = m.$$

If the ordinary multiplication of integers is taken as the combining rule, the natural numbers again form a monoid if the unit 1 is taken to be the identity element.

Suppose we were to take the domain of objects to be the positive rational numbers and division to be the operation used in the combining rule so that lm has the meaning of $l \div m$. This structure fails to be a monoid on two counts. The associative law is not satisfied since $(l \div m) \div n \neq l \div (m \div n)$, and the only candidate for an identity element, 1, does not satisfy $1 \div l = l$ for arbitrary l.

Given any alphabet, not necessarily finite, $\Sigma = \{\alpha_1, \alpha_2, \dots\}$, a *free monoid* is defined based on that alphabet. Introduce as objects the words or finite strings that can be formed by concatenating or juxtaposing the symbols in Σ.

If, then, we are given two words $u = s_1 s_2 \cdots s_m$, $v = t_1 t_2 \cdots t_n$ where each s_i and t_i is a letter of the alphabet Σ, we can form a new word

$$uv = s_1 s_2 \cdots s_m t_1 t_2 \dots t_n$$

by concatenating u and v.

The associative law is automatically satisfied since the same string results from forming $(uv)w$ as from forming $u(vw)$.

We further provide an identity element by introducing as a well-defined word the null or empty string Λ (often written as ε), a "string" that contains no symbols of the alphabet. This object then satisfies for any word u the condition

$$u \Lambda = u = \Lambda u.$$

The null string may perhaps be considered to be a fictitious object, but it is no more so than the number zero. Consider the probable historical evolution of the number system. The positive integers $1, 2, 3, \dots$ were clearly representable by classes containing $1, 2, 3, \dots$ fingers, pebbles, sticks, or whatever. The number zero is a more sophisticated and abstract notion, less tangible in that not holding up any fingers would surely have seemed to primitive Man to be a not very convincing illustration of such a concept. The printing of the null string similarly creates a problem. When, as in the ALGOL 60 report [7], the null string, called therein the empty string, is defined as

$$<\text{empty}> ::=$$

it is implicit that the empty region on the right of ::= does not include the rest of the universe but is restricted to the line on which it is printed. This situation can be helped by, and is part of the reason for, introducing delimiters to flank every possible string. Examples of such delimiters are BEGIN, END, or our use of asterisks (Chapter 5) in the representation of information on a Turing machine tape. We might then write

$$<\text{empty}> ::= * *$$

to represent the null string. With this convention, however, we would have to use such delimiters as boundary marks for every string that might appear in the system.

This monoid formed from Σ is called a free monoid and is designated as Σ^* (the notation is consistent with the use of the star in regular expressions). If the null string is excluded, the resulting collection, no longer a monoid, is sometimes called the *positive closure* of Σ and designated as Σ^+. Any language L that is based on some vocabulary V is a subset of V^*. It may or may not include the null word Λ.

Given any word u in Σ^*, the powers of u, $\{u^n \mid n = 1, 2, \ldots\}$, are defined in the obvious way by concatenation. Thus u^n is the string formed by writing u n times. $0^n 1^n$ is then the string formed by writing n 0's followed by n 1's. If u is an arbitrary string in Σ^*, $|u|$ denotes the length of, or number of symbols in, u. The length of the null string Λ is taken to be 0. If $u = vw$, we have $|u| = |v| + |w|$. If neither v nor w is equal to Λ then v is called a *head* of u and w is a *tail* of u.

In defining a language L we assume a finite vocabulary $V = \{w_1, w_2, \ldots, w_n\}$. It is the elements or words of this vocabulary that are the symbols of the "alphabet" in the definition of a free monoid, and not the individual letters of which these words are composed. Thus, as in the examples we have cited of Chomsky's use of rewriting rules in studying natural languages, each English word in the vocabulary is one of the "symbols" of the alphabet as well as the nonterminal symbols that appear in the rewriting rules.

In describing the grammars of programming languages, programs, i.e., the well-formed "sentences" of these languages, are strings of atomic elements, some of which will be words composed of more than one character such as IF, THEN, MOVE, $>=$, etc. Often, these elements of programming vocabularies are called *tokens*.

Those elements of the vocabulary V that may appear in a string of L are called *terminals*. Letting T be the set of terminals, the nonterminals are the elements of $V - T$. These may appear in the rewriting rules of a grammar G that defines the (properly formed) sentences of L.

Given a vocabulary V, including a subset of terminals T, a grammar G consists of a finite set of rewriting rules or productions $\{\alpha \to \beta\}$ where α, β are elements of V^* and $\alpha \notin T^*$. (Thus, α cannot be the null string.) Further, one distinguished nonterminal element, say σ, is specified. Given a string $s = u\,\alpha\,v$ in V^*, an application of the rewriting rule $\alpha \to \beta$ allows us to replace α by β yielding the string $t = u\,\beta\,v$. We indicate this by writing

$$u\,\alpha\,w \Rightarrow u\,\beta\,v$$

by one application of the rewriting rule or production $\alpha \to \beta$.

We say that the string s "directly produces" the string t or, inversely, that t "directly reduces" to s.

If we have a chain of such direct productions of strings, called a *derivation,*

$$s_1 \Rightarrow s_2 \Rightarrow s_3 \Rightarrow \ldots \Rightarrow s_n,$$

we write that $s_1 \Rightarrow * s_n$ and say that s_1 "produces" s_n or that s_n can be "derived" from s_1. We shall also say that s produces s and take $s \Rightarrow * s$ to be a bona fide chain, arising from zero applications of a rewriting rule.

Given a vocabulary V with specified terminals T, a distinguished nonterminal symbol σ, which serves as the "starting symbol," and a grammar G, the language $L(G)$ that is defined by G is the set of all strings of terminals that can be produced by σ. That is,

$$L(G) = \{x \mid (x\,\varepsilon\,T^*)\,\&\,(\sigma \Rightarrow * x)\}$$

The strings of terminals produced by σ are the *sentences* of the language L. The intermediate strings $s_2, s_3, \ldots, s_{n-1}$ that are formed in the course of a derivation are called *sentential forms*. These contain nonterminals.

Suppose that a grammar leads to a derivation of the form

$$u \Rightarrow * \cdots u \cdots$$

where u, a nonterminal, appears somewhere in the right side of the derivation in addition to some other unspecified symbols. Then the grammar is said to be *recursive* in u.

The grammar for the fragment of English that we described in the preceding section is recursive in the nonterminal NP since NP $\to$ ART NP is one of its rewriting rules and thus NP $\Rightarrow$ ART NP is a direct derivation. This gives rise to an infinite set of sentences containing the phrases

the moon, the the moon, the the the moon, ...

These examples of possible sentence structure again illustrate some of the limitations of these ideas in defining good English usage. However, we leave it to the reader to define the recursive grammar that would justify to any desired length Gertrude Stein's

a rose is a rose is a rose ....

The Backus-Naur form for linguistic definition that was introduced in Chapter 2 is a slight notational variant on the use of rewriting rules. Recall that, for example, we defined the class K of nonnegative integers written with possible leading zeros by writing

$$<\text{digit}> ::= 0 \mid 1 \mid 2 \mid 3 \mid 4 \mid 5 \mid 6 \mid 7 \mid 8 \mid 9$$
$$<K> ::= <\text{digit}> \mid <K> <\text{digit}>$$

This is equivalent to the set of rewriting rules:

$$<\text{digit}> \to 0$$
$$<\text{digit}> \to 1$$
$$\vdots$$
$$<\text{digit}> \to 9$$
$$<K> \to <\text{digit}>$$
$$<K> \to <K> <\text{digit}>$$

The distinguished initial symbol in this example is $<K>$. BNF conventions imply that all nonterminals are flanked by wedges $<...>$, and the expression $A \to B_1 \mid B_2 \mid ... \mid B_n$ is shorthand for the set of productions $A \to B_1, A \to B_2, ..., A \to B_n$. The symbol "::=" is equivalent to the arrow "→" of our notation.

The class of representations for the nonnegative integers is the language defined by this grammar, or $\{x \mid <K> \Rightarrow * \ x\}$, where x is a string of terminals.

9.4   A CLASSIFICATION OF LANGUAGES

Chomsky [3] has classified grammars and the languages they define into four types according to properties of the rewriting rules or productions of the grammar. This classification is usually known as the *Chomsky hierarchy*. The four classes are not exclusive, each being, with one qualification, included within its predecessor. A language is of a given type if it can be defined by a grammar of that type.

A type 0 grammar has no restrictions on its rewriting rules $\alpha \to \beta$ beyond what we have already stated. This is then the most general class, including all the others. Such a grammar is also called a *phrase structure grammar*. It can be shown that every language defined by a type 0 grammar is a recursively enumerable set of its sentences and, conversely, that every recursively enu-

merable set of strings on some alphabet can be defined by a type 0 grammer
(cf. the exercises). That is, the set of outputs of any Turing machine using an
arbitrary alphabet is a language defined by a type 0 grammar. This follows
from the fact that, if we are given the quintuples of any Turing machine, we
can write down a grammar (cf. the exercises) that defines derivations identical to the sequences of instantaneous descriptions appearing in an arbitrary
computation. An appeal to Church's thesis makes plausible the converse
statement, that if we are given any type 0 grammar we can define a Turing
machine that will give as its outputs the sentences of the language generated
by that grammar.

A type 1 grammar has the restriction on each of its rewriting rules $\alpha \to \beta$
that the length of α does not exceed the length of β, i.e., $|\alpha| \le |\beta|$. Thus,
the successively generated strings of any derivation are nondecreasing in
length. It is easy to show (cf. the exercises) that such a grammar can always
be replaced by, that is, the same language can be defined by, a grammar
whose productions are all of the form $A \alpha B \to A \beta B$ where A, B are arbitrary
strings, $|\alpha| = 1$, and β is any string other than the null string. That is, such a
rewriting rule enables us to replace the nonterminal α by β whenever α is
flanked by, or appears in the "context" of $A \ldots B$. Because of this, the type 1
languages are known as the *context-sensitive* languages. Since any derivation
involves monotonic increasing strings, no context-sensitive language can
include the null string.

A context-sensitive language is a recursive set. We can define an algorithm, exploiting the fact that the sentential forms of derivations never
decrease in length, to determine if a given terminal string S of length l is or is
not a sentence of the language. This can, for example, be done by a brute
force method of generating recursively, applying the productions of the
grammar, all possible strings of length $1, 2, 3, \ldots, l$ and determining if S is
among the last of these.

However, not all recursive sets can be generated by context-sensitive
grammars, and the context-sensitive languages comprise a *proper* subset of
the recursive sets.

A type 2 grammar is one whose productions are of the form $\alpha \to \beta$ where
$|\alpha| = 1$, i.e., α is a single nonterminal, and β is an arbitrary string. We
admit the possibility of β being the null string so we cannot be sure that all
derivations entail a sequence of nondecreasing strings. These languages are
called the *context-free* languages since any rewriting rule applied in a direct
derivation results in the replacement of a nonterminal α by a string β no
matter what the context of α or, that is, no matter what other symbols appear
in the string containing α. It is this class of languages whose study finds the
greatest application to programming languages and is, therefore, of greatest

interest in our survey. Programming languages are in general *not* context free (see Chapter 10), but they come close, in a sense, to being so.

The context-free languages that do not contain the null string form a proper subset of the context-sensitive languages. We shall see that the set of binary sequences $\{0^n 1^n 0^n \mid n \geq 1\}$ is a context-sensitive language that is not context free. Any context-free language that contains the null string is, of course, not context sensitive.

When a context-free language is an infinite set of sentences it is because any grammar defining it must be recursive in some nonterminal u.

The type 3 grammars are restricted to productions of the form $\alpha \rightarrow A\beta$ and $\alpha \rightarrow A$ where α, β are nonterminals and A is a terminal or the null string (such a grammar is sometimes called a "right linear grammar"). Clearly, the languages generated by such grammars are a subset of the context-free languages since the productions of a type 3 grammar satisfy the condition for those of a type 2 grammar. We remark that such a language is a regular set, that is, one defined by a finite automaton. Conversely, every regular set can be defined by a type 3 grammar. These languages form a proper subset of the context-free languages. For example (cf. the exercises), the set of binary strings $\{0^n 1 0^n \mid n \geq 1\}$ is a context-free language that is not a regular set.

The Chomsky hierarchy is far from exhausting the classes of formal languages that are of importance in the study of programming languages, and several more restricted classes will be mentioned in the next chapter. In general, the subject of formal linguistics is concerned with the properties of various classes of languages. Since a formal language is a set of strings, it is meaningful to talk about set-related notions such as the intersections, unions, and complements of languages, each of these constructs being a set of strings and, therefore, a language. Much study has been made of the characteristics or classification of languages formed in these ways from other languages.

Automata play a very important role in the study of languages. Any given automaton can be used to define a set of strings—either those it generates or those it recognizes or accepts—and various classes of languages have been defined by the special kinds of automata that can be used to define these classes (cf. Chapter 10).

9.5 EXAMPLES OF THE DEFINITIONS OF LANGUAGES BY THEIR GRAMMARS

1. Every finite set is a type 3 language. Consider, for example, the English alphabet $\alpha = \{A, B, C, \ldots, Z\}$. This set is the language defined by a grammar

with the following specifications:

> terminal vocabulary: $A, B, C, \ldots, Z$
> initial symbol (the only nonterminal): σ
> productions: $\sigma \to A$, $\sigma \to B$, $\sigma \to C$, $\ldots, \sigma \to Z$

It is clear that $\alpha = \{x \mid \sigma \Rightarrow* x\}$. We can similarly write a grammar of this type for any finite set.

2. The set of binary strings $\{0^n 10^n \mid n \geq 1\}$ is a type 2 language. A defining grammar would be:

> terminal vocabulary: 0, 1
> initial symbol (the only nonterminal): σ
> productions: $\sigma \to 0 \sigma 0$, $\sigma \to 1$

Any string of the form $0^n 10^n$ can be derived by applying the rewriting rule $\sigma \to 0 \sigma 0$ n times followed by one application of $\sigma \to 1$.
The syntax tree representation for a derivation of the string $0^2 10^2$ is

It can be shown (cf. the exercises) that no type 3 grammar could be used to generate this language. The next example concerns a slight generalization of this language and of a language mentioned earlier in this chapter.

3. Let T be any finite alphabet, say $\{a_1, a_2, \ldots, a_n\}$, and let x be any word of T^*. Let x' be the word x written backwards. Then the language $\{x \$ x' \mid x \in T^*\}$, sometimes called a "mirror language," is a type 2 language. This language is defined by the following grammar:

> terminal vocabulary: $\$, a_1, a_2, \ldots, a_n$
> initial symbol (the only nonterminal): σ
> productions: $\sigma \to a_1 \sigma a_1$, $\sigma \to a_2 \sigma a_2$, $\ldots, \sigma \to a_n \sigma a_n$, $\sigma \to \$$

Again it is clear that we can generate any string of the form $x \$ x'$. Since x can be any element of T^*, one possible value for x is the null string Λ, and the generated string $\$$ results from this value of x.

The tree representation for a derivation of $a_3 a_1 a_2 \, \$ \, a_2 a_1 a_3$ is

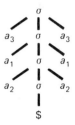

4. The set $\{\, 0^n 1^n 0^n \mid n \geq 1 \,\}$ is a type 1 language. A defining grammar is:

> terminal vocabulary: 0, 1
> nonterminals: σ, a, b
> initial symbol: σ
> productions: $\sigma \to 0\,\sigma\,ab, \ \sigma \to 01b,$
> $\qquad\qquad ba \to ab, \ 1a \to 11,$
> $\qquad\qquad 1b \to 10, \ 0b \to 00$

It is seen that the productions do not have the form required of a type 2 grammar, but they do satisfy the type 1 requirement of not shortening the strings to which they are applied.

We can derive the string $0^3 1^3 0^3$ as follows:

$$
\begin{aligned}
\sigma &\Rightarrow 0\,\sigma\,ab \Rightarrow 00\,\sigma\,abab \\
&\Rightarrow 0001babab \Rightarrow 0001abbab \\
&\Rightarrow 0001ababb \Rightarrow 0001aabbb \\
&\Rightarrow 00011abbb \Rightarrow 000111bbb \\
&\Rightarrow 0001110bb \Rightarrow 00011100b \\
&\Rightarrow 000111000
\end{aligned}
$$

We leave it to the reader to recognize that any string of the form $0^n 1^n 0^n$ can similarly be obtained and that the data manipulation is reminiscent of what occurs in a Turing machine computation. Note that it is not possible to represent a derivation in this case as a tree because the left sides of some of the productions contain *two* elements of the vocabulary.

We shall see that it is not possible to define this particular language by a type 2 or context-free grammar.

5. We look next at an abridged version of a part of the ALGOL 60 report [7] that is concerned with the definition of arithmetic expressions. We define a context-free grammar that generates well-formed arithmetic expressions built up by addition, subtraction, multiplication, division, and exponentia-

tion from the variables x, y, z. The BNF conventions for writing productions will be assumed in the following:

terminal vocabulary: $0, 1, 2, 3, 4, 5, 6, 7, 8, 9, +, -, *, /, (,), \uparrow, x, y, z.$
nonterminals: $<$digit$>$, $<$unsigned number$>$, $<$adding operator$>$,
$\quad\quad\quad\quad\quad\quad$ $<$multiplying operator$>$, $<$term$>$, $<$primary$>$,
$\quad\quad\quad\quad\quad\quad$ $<$factor$>$, $<$variable$>$,
$\quad\quad\quad\quad\quad\quad$ $<$simple arithmetic expression$>$
initial symbol: $<$simple arithmetic expression$>$

In writing the productions of this grammar we shall abbreviate each nonterminal by using its first letter only (no ambiguity results from such abbreviation):

productions:
$<$d$>$ ::= 0 | 1 | 2 | 3 | 4 | 5 | 6 | 7 | 8 | 9, $<$u$>$ ::= $<$d$>$ | $<$u$><$d$>$,
$<$a$>$ ::= + | $-$, $<$m$>$ ::= $*$ | /, $<$v$>$ ::= x | y | z,
$<$p$>$ ::= $<$u$>$ | $<$v$>$ | ($<$s$>$), $<$f$>$ ::= $<$p$>$ | $<$f$>$ $\uparrow$ $<$p$>$,
$<$t$>$ ::= $<$f$>$ | $<$t$><$m$><$f$>$,
$<$s$>$ ::= $<$t$>$ | $<$a$><$t$>$ | $<$s$><$a$><$t$>$

The class of simple arithmetic expressions is the set of terminal strings that can be derived from $<$s$>$ by a sequence of applications of the rewriting rules. We illustrate the derivation of a well-formed arithmetic expression by generating $x \uparrow (6 * (z + y * x))$.

$<$s$>$ $\Rightarrow$ $<$t$>$ $\Rightarrow$ $<$f$>$ $\Rightarrow$ $<$f$>$ $\uparrow$ $<$p$>$ $\Rightarrow$ $<$p$>$ $\uparrow$ $<$p$>$ $\Rightarrow$ $<$v$>$ $\uparrow$ $<$p$>$
$\quad$ $\Rightarrow x \uparrow <$p$>$ $\Rightarrow x \uparrow (<s>$) $\Rightarrow x \uparrow (<t>$) $\Rightarrow x \uparrow (<t><m><f>$)
$\quad$ $\Rightarrow x \uparrow (<f><m><f>$) $\Rightarrow x \uparrow (<p><m><f>$)
$\quad$ $\Rightarrow x \uparrow (<u><m><f>$) $\Rightarrow x \uparrow (<d><m><f>$)
$\quad$ $\Rightarrow x \uparrow (6 <m><f>$) $\Rightarrow x \uparrow (6 * <f>$) $\Rightarrow x \uparrow (6 * <p>$)
$\quad$ $\Rightarrow x \uparrow (6 * (<s>$)) $\Rightarrow x \uparrow (6 * (<s><a><t>$))
$\quad$ $\Rightarrow x \uparrow (6 * (<t><a><t>$)) $\Rightarrow x \uparrow (6 * (<f><a><t>$))
$\quad$ $\Rightarrow x \uparrow (6 * (<p><a><t>$)) $\Rightarrow x \uparrow (6 * (<v><a><t>$))
$\quad$ $\Rightarrow x \uparrow (6 * (z <a><t>$)) $\Rightarrow x \uparrow (6 * (z + <t>$))
$\quad$ $\Rightarrow x \uparrow (6 * (z + <t><m><f>$)) $\Rightarrow x \uparrow (6 * (z + <f><m><f>$))
$\quad$ $\Rightarrow x \uparrow (6 * (z + <p><m><f>$)) $\Rightarrow x \uparrow (6 * (z + <v><m><f>$))
$\quad$ $\Rightarrow x \uparrow (6 * (z + y <m><f>$)) $\Rightarrow x \uparrow (6 * (z + y * <f>$))
$\quad$ $\Rightarrow x \uparrow (6 * (z + y * <p>$)) $\Rightarrow x \uparrow (6 * (z + y * <v>$))
$\quad$ $\Rightarrow x \uparrow (6 * (z + y * x))$

Note that at most steps of this derivation we had a choice of several productions to apply, corresponding to the several nonterminals appearing in the sentential form being transformed. In each case we chose to apply a production to the left-most nonterminal in the string. A derivation formed in this manner is called a *left-most derivation.* If we had selected the right-most nonterminal at each step as the left side of a production, the chain would be a *right-most derivation.*

The syntax representing this derivation is shown in Fig. 9.3. Note that many different derivations give rise to the same tree. For example, we used the direct derivation $<f>\uparrow<p> \Rightarrow <p>\uparrow<p>$. If we had chosen to transform the nonterminal $<p>$ we would have obtained $<f>\uparrow<p> \Rightarrow <f>\uparrow(<s>)$ and we could arrive eventually at the same

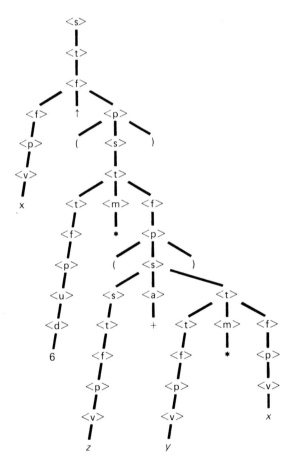

Fig. 9.3   The tree for the derivation of $x\uparrow(6*(z+y*x))$. The leaves, read from left to right, form this string.

final string. Different derivations in this case correspond to different ways in which we might traverse the syntax tree starting at the root. In other words, any particular derivation could be considered a prescription for painting the tree proceeding down from the root, with the restriction that whenever we choose to continue from a particular node N we must simultaneously paint all branches extending from N to its sons.

Observe that the information present in the syntax tree can be used to construct an algorithm to compute the arithmetic expression $x \uparrow (6 * z + y * x))$ when values are assigned to x, y, z. A procedure can be defined to compute the value of each nonterminal node by tracing the tree up from the leaves or terminal nodes. This leads eventually to an algorithm for $<s>$, the root node which represents the entire expression.

If a node $<n>$ has a single son $<c>$ the procedure for that parent will be taken to be the same as that for the son, or $<n> = <c>$. Suppose next that a parent node has several sons. As an example, assume a somewhat simplified grammar that leads to a syntax tree for the expression $z + y * x$ which is a pruned version of the appropriate part of the tree of Fig. 9.3.

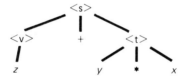

The procedure for $<t>$ will compute the product of y and x, and that for the root node $<s>$ will be the sum of z and $y * x$. If this is the syntax tree for the expression $z + y * x$, which contains no parentheses, it implies that multiplication is to be performed before addition.

This is an example of a *syntax-directed* translation or compilation. In order for this technique to be viable, it is essential that the syntax tree corresponding to a given expression be unique. Otherwise, the interpretation of an expression will be ambiguous. We return later to this important consideration.

In example (5), the sentences of the language are the properly formed arithmetic expressions that can be written with a restricted vocabulary. With a more ambitious grammar we can attempt to define strings which are entire programs. In the full ALGOL report, the starting symbol is taken to be the nonterminal $<program>$, and the class of strings of terminal symbols that can be derived from this initial nonterminal is (almost) the class of properly formed ALGOL programs.

9.6   SYNTAX, SEMANTICS, AND AMBIGUITY

The *syntax* of a natural or of a programming language is the system governing the proper order of words or symbols from its vocabulary in constructing
the sentences of the former or the programs of the latter. Syntax is concerned
largely with form or structure while *semantics* on the other hand is the study
of how meaning is obtained from sentences. We have seen in a somewhat
cursory way that the meaning of English sentences is only partly obtained
from the syntax of a sentence. Here, the problems of the relationship between language and meaning run very deep and, it is thought by some, relate
to the nature of the mind itself, with the study of syntax possibly providing a
key to some mental processes. The boundary between syntax and semantics
is vague, and linguists sometimes differentiate between the *deep structure* of
a sentence which determines its meaning and the *surface structure* that determines its sound.

The United Nations interpreter who translated a fragment of Russian as
"what's on the road, a head?" instead of "what's on the road ahead?" made
an error in surface structure. The well-publicized translation of a comment
by Nikita Khrushchev in 1956 as "we will bury you" instead of "because our
system is better than yours we will survive you" was an error in deep structure.

In any event, while the fundamental significance of any sentence of a
natural language is the meaning that it conveys to a human mind, our
problems in dealing with automata are more straightforward. The semantics
of a program concern the actions that it causes a computer to take when it
executes that program—that is, the algorithm executed after compilation or
interpretation of the program. One might say, by analogy with the linguistics
of natural languages, that two programs that obtain identical results for all
possible inputs have the same "deep structure."

We have seen that a sentence of English can be ambiguous even when it
is well-formed. There are several reasons for this. One possible cause is that
our grammar makes it possible to write down *two* syntax trees for the given
sentence. As we have implied in the preceding, it is the *tree* that is of significance in assigning meaning to a sentence and not a particular derivation of
that sentence.

Suppose, as an example of ambiguity, that we are given the following
fragment of English grammar:

$$
\begin{array}{ll}
S \rightarrow NP\ V\ NP & ADJ \rightarrow failing \\
NP \rightarrow N & NP \rightarrow ADJ\ N \\
N \rightarrow they & N \rightarrow students \\
V \rightarrow are & V \rightarrow are\ failing
\end{array}
$$

(S = sentence, NP = noun phrase, V = verb, N = noun, ADJ = adjective)

> initial symbol: S
> terminals: they, are, failing, students

We can give two syntax trees for the sentence "they are failing students"

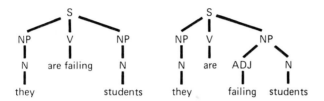

If, then, we are given this sentence without the context in which it appears, it has *two* possible meanings as implied by these two different trees. These two interpretations correspond to whether "they" refers to a group of students or of instructors. It may be possible to remove the ambiguity in a situation of this kind by revising the grammar so that every sentence has a unique syntax tree. (We could, in the given example, decide arbitrarily that "failing" should not be classified as an adjective.) However, this cannot always be done and for some formal languages no grammar can be given that will make all possible sentences unambiguous. Such a language is said to be *inherently ambiguous* (the language $\{0^i 1^j 0^k \mid i = j \text{ OR } j = k\}$ can be

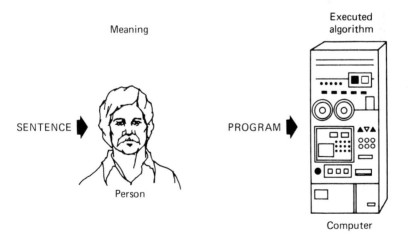

Fig. 9.4 The semantics of natural and programming languages.

shown to be an inherently ambiguous, context-free language; cf. the exercises). In designing programming languages, it is usually desirable, but not necessary, that their grammars be unambiguous and, therefore, lead to unique syntax trees for all well-formed programs. Ambiguous grammars can be used *if* the compiler makes use of additional rules and rejects unwanted extraneous syntax trees, thus leading to a unique tree for each component of the program. Unique syntax trees imply that a unique object program will be obtained as a result of the compilation.

In the case of natural languages, a sentence may be ambiguous even if the syntax tree is unique. Consider the sentence:

the race is furious.

The syntax tree is shown here:

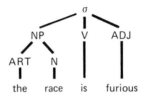

Even though the sentence can be parsed in only one way it has two possible meanings corresponding to two possible meanings of race and of furious. Sentences of natural languages can be ambiguous, as in this case, because the elements of the vocabulary may have more than one meaning. In designing programming languages, this kind of ambiguity is comparatively easy to avoid, but we must take pains to make the definitions of all items of the vocabulary precise and unique. For example, when we stipulate in using FORTRAN that an undeclared variable name beginning with the letter I represents a fixed point variable, we are avoiding an ambiguity, or when rules prevent our using the predefined names of built-in functions as the names of new variables in, say, PL/I this is done to assure that these names are uniquely defined.

As an example of an ambiguous grammar in the definition of a programming language, suppose that we use expressions to conform with a grammar that includes the following productions:

$$\sigma \rightarrow E \qquad\qquad E \rightarrow (E)$$
$$E \rightarrow E * E \qquad\qquad E \rightarrow \text{IDENT}$$
$$E \rightarrow E + \text{E} \qquad \text{IDENT} \rightarrow X \mid Y \mid Z$$

The expression, or sentence of this grammar, $X * Y + Z$ can then be parsed in two different ways (Fig. 9.5).

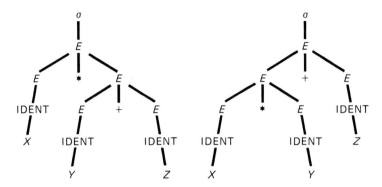

Figure 9.5

This fragment of the defining grammar is ambiguous. The two possible derivations correspond to the two meanings $X * (Y + Z)$ and $(X * Y) + Z$.

The grammar can be made unambiguous in a number of ways. We might, for example, use the productions:

$$\sigma \to E, \quad E \to E + E, \quad E \to F * F,$$
$$F \to \text{IDENT} \quad E \to \text{IDENT}, \quad \text{IDENT} \to X \mid Y \mid Z.$$

The expression $X * Y + Z$ can now be parsed in only one way (Fig. 9.6).

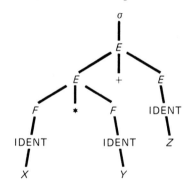

Figure 9.6

This modified grammar assures that multiplications are executed before additions in expressions of this kind. However, since it lacks parentheses, the language it defines is completely inadequate for general expressions involving multiplication and addition. A slight modification of the original grammar that allows parenthetical expressions and is unambiguous is

$$\sigma \to E, \quad E \to (E * E), \quad E \to (E + E),$$
$$E \to \text{IDENT}, \quad \text{IDENT} \to X \mid Y \mid Z.$$

The expression $X \star Y + Z$ is *not* a sentence of the language defined by this grammar. The well-formed expression that is computationally equivalent is $((X \star Y) + Z)$, and this has a unique syntax tree.

9.7 PARSING

To *parse* a given sentence of a natural language is to resolve it into its elements, or different parts of speech. In terms of the Chomsky derivation of the sentences defined by a context-free grammar, to parse a sentence is equivalent to constructing its syntax tree, starting with the leaves. In other words, it is the operation inverse to that of derivation.[1]

Suppose that a programming language is defined by an unambiguous context-free grammar. Given any well-formed expression, statement, or program, to parse that expression, statement, or program is to find the syntax tree that shows its derivation. More generally, our problem can be stated as follows. Given any supposed sentence of a context-free language, we ask (1) is it a well-formed sentence of the language? and (2) if so, what is its syntax tree, i.e., how can it be derived from the initial symbol? This is the problem of parsing, and it is fundamental to the construction of compilers for, as we have seen, the information implicit in the syntax tree is essential to the determination of the semantics of a program. Because of its importance, computer scientists have studied the problem at great length, and a considerable body of literature is devoted to it.

The derivation of a given sentence S of a context-free grammar begins with the initial symbol σ, and the productions of the defining grammar are applied until the sentence, a sequence of terminals, is obtained, $\sigma \Rightarrow_\star S$. To parse a given sentence is to begin with that sentence and apply the inverses of the productions or, as we shall call these inverses, *reductions,* until we obtain σ. (If $\alpha \to \beta$ is a production then $\beta \to \alpha$ is its inverse.) This is equivalent to determining the syntax tree of S. Thus, given a context-free grammar G, to parse a given sentence S of $L(G)$, we take S to be an initial string and assume a set of rewriting rules that are the productions of G with the arrows reversed. If these rules are considered to be the productions of a grammar G' (no longer necessarily a context-free grammar since these reversed rewriting rules may *decrease* the length of a string), a derivation in G', $S \Rightarrow_\star \sigma$, will be the reverse of the derivation in G, $\sigma \Rightarrow_\star S$.

---

[1]   We henceforth assume only context-free grammars with no "null rules", i.e., of the form $\alpha \to \Lambda$, where Λ is the null string. For, any grammar that includes such productions can always be replaced by one without them that defines the same language, except possibly for Λ. (Try to prove this.)

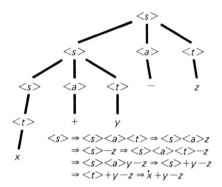

$$<s> \Rightarrow <s><a><t> \Rightarrow <s><a>z$$
$$\Rightarrow <s>-z \Rightarrow <s><a><t>-z$$
$$\Rightarrow <s><a>y-z \Rightarrow <s>+y-z$$
$$\Rightarrow <t>+y-z \Rightarrow \dot{x}+y-z$$

Figure 9.7

We illustrate these notions using the following fragment of a grammar.

terminal vocabulary: $x, y, z, +, -$
nonterminals: $<a>, <s>, <t>$
initial symbol: $<s>$
productions: $<s> \rightarrow <s><a><t>$
  $<a> \rightarrow +$ $<t> \rightarrow x$
  $<a> \rightarrow -$ $<t> \rightarrow y$
  $<s> \rightarrow <t>$ $<t> \rightarrow z$

The sentence $x + y - z$ can be derived from $<s>$. The syntax tree as well as a right-most derivation are shown in Fig. 9.7.

If we start with the string $x + y - z$ with no knowledge of its syntax tree or derivation, its reduction to $<s>$ is a derivation $x + y - z \Rightarrow \ast <s>$ using a grammar G', inverse to G, whose productions are as follows:

$<s><a><t> \rightarrow <s>$
  $+ \rightarrow <a>$ $x \rightarrow <t>$
  $- \rightarrow <a>$ $y \rightarrow <t>$
  $<t> \rightarrow <s>$ $z \rightarrow <t>$

The steps in this reduction are those in the derivation shown above, $<s> \Rightarrow \ast x + y - z$, written in reverse order and with all arrows reversed. In writing the reduction or the parse, we underline that substring at each step which is transformed or reduced in order to produce the next string in the reduction.

$$\underline{x} + y - z \Rightarrow \underline{<t>} + y - z \Rightarrow <s> \underline{+} y - z$$
$$\Rightarrow <s><a>\underline{y} - z \Rightarrow \underline{<s><a><t>} - z$$
$$\Rightarrow <s> \underline{-} z \Rightarrow <s><a>\underline{z}$$
$$\Rightarrow \underline{<s><a><t>} \Rightarrow <s>$$

The successive steps of this parse enable us to build the syntax tree from the bottom up. Starting with the string $x + y - z$ of terminal symbols, we have after the first step,

$$<t>$$
$$x \; + \; y \; - \; z$$

After the fifth step we have

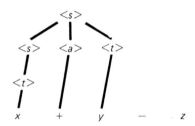

After the last step, the full syntax tree is obtained.

At each step in this parse, which is the inverse of a right-most derivation, a left-most substring is reduced. This substring is called a *handle*. This example illustrates a "left-to-right, bottom-up" parse. Starting with the input string $x + y - z$ we have scanned it from left to right, and the successive reductions enable us to build the syntax tree from the bottom up.

It is helpful to describe this type of parse in graphical terms, referring to the syntax tree. Recall that a subtree is the structure obtained by taking any node together with all nodes and branches that can be reached by traveling down from the given node. In a left-to-right, bottom-up parse the first handle selected for reduction is the string consisting of the terminal nodes of the left-most *minimal* subtree. (A tree is minimal if its leaves are all of level number 1.) If we prune this subtree from the syntax tree (leaving the root of this subtree), the next handle to be reduced is again the string of terminal nodes of the left-most minimal subtree. This continues until the last reduction obtains the root node of the syntax tree. Thus, in the above example the left-most subtree at the first step is the branch from $<t>$ to x. After pruning this branch, the left-most subtree is the branch from $<s>$ to $<t>$, and so forth. Figure 9.8 shows a hypothetical syntax tree and the handles in the order in which they would appear in a left-to-right, bottom-up parse, e.g., the string consisting of the symbols at the three nodes marked 5 would be the handle used in the fifth reduction.

The central problem in a parse of this kind is that of finding the handle

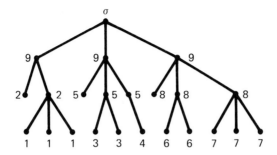

Fig. 9.8 A syntax tree and the handles of a left-to-right, bottom-up parse.

to reduce at each step. In the example we have given there is no difficulty in doing this for when we consider the possible reductions, the rewriting rules of G', we see that every left-hand string that can appear in a reduction is uniquely determined by its first symbol, either $<s>$, $+$, $-$, $<t>$, x, y, or z. But, this need not be the case in general. Consider the following productions of a grammar which defines a subset of the well-formed arithmetic expressions chosen from our earlier ALGOL example. We write the productions in BNF form

$$<s> ::= <s> + <t> \mid <t>$$
$$<t> ::= <p> \mid <t> * <p>$$
$$<p> ::= x \mid y \mid z \mid (<s>)$$

Consider the parsing of the expression $x * y + z$. The syntax tree is shown in Fig. 9.9.

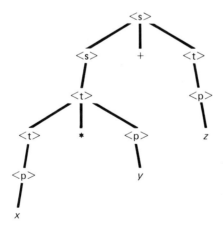

Fig. 9.9 Syntax tree for $x * y + z$.

The first three successive reductions are:

$$x * y + z \Rightarrow <p> * y + z \Rightarrow <t> * y + z \Rightarrow <t> * <p> + z$$

At this point we have a choice of reductions. Should we take the substring $<t>$ as the handle and reduce $<t> * <p> + z$ to $<s> * <p> + z$, or should we take it to be the substring $<t> * <p>$ and reduce $<t> * <p> + z$ to $<s> + z$? Only the latter choice is correct. If we were to use the former reduction we should not be able to proceed further in the parse. We must note that the symbol following $<t>$ is $*$ and realize that we shall run into a blind alley if we reduce $<t>$ to $<s>$. Suppose we attempt to program a parser that scans an input string from left to right and yields the syntax tree in a bottom to top order, as in our manual parse. Then we shall have to build enough intelligence into the program so that, in general, it does not decide on a reduction without looking beyond the first substring it finds that can be reduced.

We have mentioned earlier that any context-free language that does not contain the null string is context sensitive. Such a language is, therefore, a recursive set and a general procedure exists to determine if any given string is a sentence of the language. (If a context-free language includes the null string it is still recursive.) The parsing problem has in this case a straightforward solution. We can write a program that will parse any given sentence of such a language by exhaustively trying all feasible sequences of reductions to determine if the given sentence can be reduced to the initial symbol. We are assured that the procedure will terminate since all rewriting rules are nondecreasing in length (and, therefore, all reductions are nonincreasing). However, this approach might require a prodigious computation, and the problem in practical parsing is not merely to determine how a given sentence can be derived but to do this in an efficient manner.

We have looked briefly at some of the details associated with a particular method of parsing in order to illustrate the kinds of problems that are involved. As we have mentioned, a great deal of work has been done on these problems.

A "top-down" parse constructs the syntax tree from top to bottom. We start with the initial symbol and, in a goal-directed activity, seek to apply the productions of the grammar to derive the given sentence. Consider, for example, using again the grammar of our earlier example, the parsing of $x + y - z$ by this approach. Starting with the initial symbol $<s>$ we have a choice of rewriting rules, either $<s> \rightarrow <s><a><t>$ or $<s> \rightarrow <t>$. If we chose the latter rule, the second production in the derivation would then be chosen to be $<t> \rightarrow x$. Our goal could then not be achieved and we see that $<s> \rightarrow <s><a><t>$ must be used at the first step. By this kind of analysis we could eventually obtain the syntax tree, drawn from the root to the terminal leaves. We shall not pursue further the intricacies of this particular approach.

9.8 SOME USES OF FINITE AUTOMATA IN RECOGNIZING AND PARSING SENTENCES OF CONTEXT-FREE LANGUAGES

The problem of recognizing the sentences of a context-free language is not trivial. However, there is a simple solution for a proper subset of the context-free languages, namely, the class of type 3 languages. We shall first describe this solution, for it illustrates a number of key ideas that find application in more complex situations.

We show that a finite automaton can be defined to accept any type 3 language. In other words, any type 3 language is a regular set. We shall also see that any regular set is a type 3 language and, therefore, that the class of type 3 languages is the same as the class of regular sets.

Consider, by way of example, the type 3 grammar G defined as follows:

> terminal vocabulary: $A, 1$
> nonterminals: σ, x, y
> initial symbol: σ
> productions: $\sigma \rightarrow Ax,\ \sigma \rightarrow Ay,\ x \rightarrow 1\sigma,\ y \rightarrow 1$

This grammar generates the language $L(G)$: $\{(A1)^n \mid n \geq 1\}$.

A nondeterministic finite automaton A that recognizes this set of strings is shown in Fig. 9.10. A accepts precisely those sequences of terminals $A, 1$ that are the sentences of $L(G)$ read from left to right.

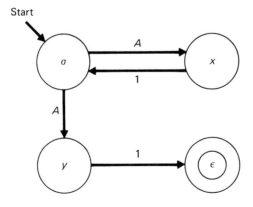

Fig. 9.10 The state transition diagram of A, a nondeterministic automaton that recognizes $L(G)$.

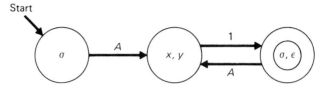

Fig. 9.11   The state transition diagram of A', a deterministic automaton equivalent to A.

Each nonterminal of the vocabulary becomes a state of A. In addition, we shall need a state ε corresponding to the null string. A production of the form $\alpha \to A\beta$ defines a transition in A from state α to state β when the symbol A is read. A production of the form $\alpha \to A$ identifies a transition, when symbol A is read, from state α to the state ε. The grammar of our example does not contain a "null rule," i.e., a production of the form $\alpha \to \varepsilon$. When such a rule appears it is translated into a state transition.

This is tantamount to identifying the state α with the state ε.

The initial symbol σ defines the start state, and the state ε is an acceptance state.

We can use the subset construction to obtain A', a deterministic version of A. This is shown in Fig. 9.11. A' is incompletely defined since it does not include defined responses for those strings *not* accepted by A. Its completion is easily obtained by introducing a new reject state to which transition is made when a string that is not acceptable is read. This completed automaton is shown as A'' in Fig. 9.12.

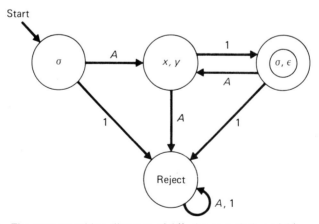

Fig. 9.12   The state transition diagram of A'', the completion of A'.

We observe two things about the automaton A''. First, it provides a simple effective procedure to determine if any given sentence is in $L(G)$. The state transition diagram can be translated directly into a flowchart for a program that recognizes $L(G)$. Each state becomes a decision box with GO TO's based on the next input symbol. Second, it can be used to provide a derivation for any sentence of $L(G)$. Suppose, for example, that in the course of reading a string s a transition is made from one state to another as in the following:

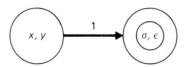

The corresponding production must then be either $x \to 1\,\sigma$ or $y \to 1$ depending on whether another input symbol follows 1 or not. In general, each transition in the chain of state transitions occurring when s is read specifies a set of possible productions to use at that step in the derivation of s. To pick out a correct production from this set we must consider the subsequent symbols of s.

Note that an equivalent grammar for $L(G)$ can be read off from A''. If we identify the state (x, y) with a new nonterminal u and the state (σ, ε) with a nonterminal v, then the grammar whose productions are $\sigma \to Au$, $u \to 1v$, $v \to Au$, $v \to \varepsilon$, is seen to generate the same language as G.

The method for obtaining A, and then A'', can be applied to any type 3 grammar G. To prove that A recognizes the sentences of $L(G)$ it is sufficient to observe that if s is any string accepted by A, the sequence of state transitions leading to an acceptance state defines a sequence of productions of G that, starting with the initial symbol, yields a derivation of s.

Conversely, any sentence in $L(G)$ is accepted by A. The sequence of productions applied in a particular derivation of a sentence s of $L(G)$ defines a path in the state transition diagram of the automaton A. This path leads from the start state σ to an acceptance state. The sentence s is the sequence of terminals that identify the segments in this path.

Thus, the set of sentences accepted by A is precisely the set of sentences in $L(G)$, and, by generalizing our argument, any type 3 language is a regular set.

We can easily prove in similar fashion the converse result, that any regular set is a type 3 language. If we are given a regular set S defined by a finite automaton A with specified start state σ and acceptance states $F_1, F_2, \ldots, F_n$ we can, by reversing the procedure outlined above, obtain a type 3 grammar that defines S. It suffices to illustrate this for a given exam-

Start

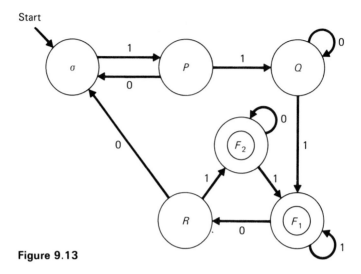

Figure 9.13

ple. Consider the regular set defined by the NDFA B in Fig. 9.13. (B is nondeterministic for no action is specified when it is in state σ and reads a 0.)

We can write down the equivalent grammar G directly from the state transition diagram of B (ε denotes the null string).

> terminal vocabulary: 0, 1
> nonterminals: $\sigma, P, Q, R, F_1, F_2$
> initial symbol: σ
> productions: $\sigma \to 1P$, $P \to 1Q$, $P \to 0\sigma$, $Q \to 0Q$, $Q \to 1F_1$,
> $R \to 0\sigma$, $R \to 1F_2$, $F_1 \to 1F_1$, $F_1 \to 0R$, $F_1 \to \varepsilon$,
> $F_2 \to 0F_2$, $F_2 \to 1F_1$, $F_2 \to \varepsilon$

The method for translating the automaton into the equivalent grammar is seen to be applicable to any given finite automaton. The proof of the equivalence of $L(G)$ and $T(B)$ is based on the same observations we have made in showing that any type 3 language is a regular set. After defining G, any string s in $T(B)$ is seen to be a sentence of $L(G)$, for it can be derived using the sequence of productions of G that corresponds directly to the chain of state transitions as B reads s, starting in state σ and extending to an acceptance state. Similarly, from our earlier remarks, any sentence of $L(G)$ is in $T(B)$.

9.9   THE RECOGNITION OF PREFIXES IN PARSING

We turn next to a possible use of finite automata in coping with a simplified version of a problem that occurs in parsing. Suppose we are given the productions of a grammar G and a string s of terminals, where s is a possible sentence of $L(G)$. We have noted that the key problem at each step in a bottom-up, left to right parse of s is the determination of the handle to reduce at each stage of the parse. Recall that a handle is a string on the right side of a production of the grammar, and that at a given stage in a bottom-up parse it is the left-most such string whose reduction can eventually lead to the initial symbol σ. At each stage in the reduction of s to σ we have an intermediate string, or sentential form. In this kind of parse we must search this intermediate string for the left-most occurrence of a substring which is the right-hand side of a production. Such a substring is a candidate for being a handle; it must also satisfy the requirement that its reduction *can* eventually lead to the initial symbol. This second condition need not be satisfied. Consider, for example, the following grammar G.

> terminal vocabulary: 0, 1
> nonterminals: σ, x
> initial symbol: σ
> productions: $\sigma \to 10x$, $x \to 0\sigma$, $x \to 1$

The syntax tree for the sentence 100101 is:

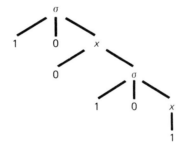

The right-most derivation for this string is

$$\sigma \Rightarrow 10x \Rightarrow 100\sigma \Rightarrow 10010x \Rightarrow 100101$$

If we are given the string 100101 and seek to parse it by a left to right, bottom-up parse, the correct sequence of reductions would be the following (we write $\underset{r}{\Rightarrow}$ to denote a reduction, the application of the reverse of a production of G):

$$100\underline{101} \underset{r}{\Rightarrow} 10\underline{010}x \underset{r}{\Rightarrow} 10\underline{0\sigma} \underset{r}{\Rightarrow} \underline{10x} \underset{r}{\Rightarrow} \sigma$$

The handle at the first step of this parse is the right-most 1, even though either one of the 1's to its left can also be taken as the right-hand side of a production of G. If, for example, we attempt to parse the given string by reducing the left-most 1 at each stage, we would be unable to reach our goal

σ. We would obtain

$$\underline{100101} \Rightarrow x00\underline{101} \Rightarrow x00x\underline{01} \Rightarrow x00x0x$$

and we can go no further in the attempt to parse the given sentence.

We see, therefore, that a certain amount of look-ahead is necessary (as we have also noted in top-down parsing) to decide on the proper sequence of reductions (cf. Section 10.2). However, we shall ignore the substantive problems introduced by this complication and shall consider merely the problem of determining the left-most occurrence of the right side of a production. We shall, however, introduce a small but necessary refinement in this search procedure. Suppose that $\alpha\beta$ and $\alpha\beta\gamma$ are both right-hand sides of a production. In scanning a string $\ldots\alpha\beta\gamma\cdots$ from left to right we should not reduce the substring $\alpha\beta$ immediately after detecting its presence for we must recognize the occurrence of $\alpha\beta\hat{\gamma}$ and consider the possibility of this substring being the handle needed in the parse. Of course neither $\alpha\beta$ nor $\alpha\beta\gamma$ may be the correct choice for reduction. Let us now design a NDFA which will scan a given string from left to right and will recognize occurrences of the right-hand side of a production—with the proviso that if u and uv $(u, v \varepsilon V^*)$ are *both* such right-hand sides we shall recognize the occurrence of uv as well as that of u.

Suppose, for example, that ab, abc, b, bd, bce $(a, b, c, d, e \in V)$ are the right-hand sides of the productions of a grammar G. We shall design a NDFA (specified incompletely in Fig. 9.14) that will read a given string of symbols of V from left to right and will enter a favorable state after reading each symbol *if*, at that point in the scan, the automaton has detected a substring that is the right-hand side of some production.

Each state is identified by the list of possible right-hand sides of which the automaton has read a prefix at that point in the scan. The notation "$a{:}bc$" is used to mean that the prefix a of the possible substring abc has been read when the automaton enters the designated state.

In addition to the state transitions shown there will be a transition from every state to state A on reading a, and to state B on reading b. There will also be transitions from every state back to the start state for any symbol read other than a, b. A transition from one of the acceptance states indicates that we have read past a right-hand side, but not necessarily past a handle.

Our automaton can easily be modified to accept all prefixes of a given sentence while the search for the right-hand side of some production continues, but to reject those prefixes for which the search has gone too far. That is, such a modified automaton will reject those strings where it is certain that it has read beyond the first occurrence of a right-hand side. An accepted prefix for a sentential form in a left-to-right, bottom-up parse is called (in [1])

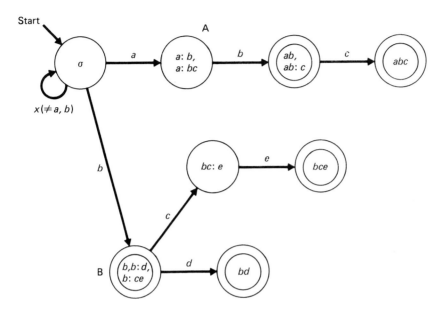

Figure 9.14

a "viable prefix" when the right-hand side is a handle. Such a prefix is characterized by the fact that it does not contain any symbols to the right of a handle.

Clearly, additional actions are called for in deciding on the handle to be reduced at each stage, but our purpose at this point is merely to show that notions of finite automata are useful in coping with some of the problems related to parsing.

9.10 A NECESSARY CONDITION FOR A LANGUAGE WITH SUFFICIENTLY LONG SENTENCES TO BE CONTEXT FREE

We prove the following:

THEOREM: *Any sufficiently long sentence of a context-free language* $L(G)$ *can be written as*

$$s = uvwxy,$$

where $v, x \neq \Lambda$, *so that all strings*

$$s_k = uv^k wx^k y, \ (k \geq 1),$$

are also in $L(G)$.

We shall refer to this theorem as "the *uvwxy* theorem."

Since any infinite language must include sentences that are as long as we please, the theorem can be applied to such languages.

The proof is based on the same idea that we have used earlier (Chapter 8) in proving that any sufficiently long tape that is accepted by a finite automaton A can be written as *usv*, where all of the tapes $\{us^kv \mid k \geq 1\}$ are accepted by A.

We shall assume that the grammar G contains no rewriting rules of the form $A \rightarrow B$ where B is a nonterminal. This is in no way restrictive, for any given context-free grammar can always be modified so that this condition is satisfied (cf. the exercises). In this case the lengths of intermediate strings increase in the course of a derivation, and every nonterminal node in a syntax tree, except possibly for those nodes that are one path segment from a terminal node, will have at least two branches emanating from it.

Suppose we consider the syntax tree for a long sentence s of $L(G)$, shown in Fig. 9.15.

On the assumption that we can choose a sentence (the sequence of terminal leaves) that is arbitrarily long, it must also follow that we can assume a syntax tree that contains a path from the root σ to one of the terminal leaves that is as long as we please. (Suppose this is not the case and that all path lengths are bounded by some number k. Since no production involves more than some number, say m, of symbols on its right-hand side,

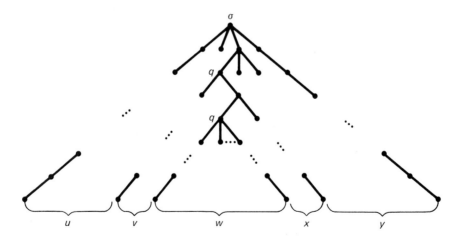

Figure 9.15

the number of leaves in such a tree would then have to be bounded by m^k, and we could not have sentences in $L(G)$ that are longer than this.)

Suppose that p is a path whose length exceeds the number of symbols in the vocabulary V. It follows then that the same symbol, say q, must appear at two of the nodes on the path p. Let us call that node which is closer to the root the "q senior" node and the other the "q junior" node.

Consider the subtrees emanating from each of these two nodes where q appears. As suggested in Fig. 9.15, let the string of leaves in the q junior subtree be w and the string of leaves in the q senior subtree be vwx. The sentence s can then be written as $s = uvwxy$.

Now, a new syntax tree defining another sentence of $L(G)$ can be obtained by placing the subtree from the q senior node at the q junior node, replacing the original subtree at the q junior node. The new sentence thus obtained will be

$$uv^2wx^2y.$$

By replicating this construction any number of times we can obtain a syntax tree for any string of the form

$$uv^kwx^ky, k \geq 1,$$

thus proving the stated theorem.

We can use this result to show that certain languages are not context free. For example, consider the set of strings $\{0^n1^n0^n \mid n \geq 1\}$ that we have shown earlier to be a context-sensitive language. This language is *not* context free. Suppose it were; since this language includes arbitrarily long sentences, the theorem can be applied to it. Assume that $s = 0^m1^m0^m$ is a sentence of the language to which the result applies. Then s can be written as $uvwxy$ so that all strings uv^kwx^ky are also of the form $0^n1^n0^n$ for some n. This, however, is not possible for we can argue as follows. Neither v nor x contains *both* 0's and 1's since the strings v^k, x^k would then not have the requisite structure for $k > 1$. Suppose, therefore, that v includes only 0's. If x includes only 0's, there would not be enough 1's in uv^kwx^ky for $k > 1$. If x includes only 1's, there would not be enough 0's in uv^kwx^ky for $k > 1$. Similarly, v cannot consist only of 1's. It follows, therefore, that this language is not context free.

It is useful to note further that there is some fixed number l such that the length of vwx in the statement of the $uvwxy$ theorem can be assumed to be less than l (i.e., $\mid vwx \mid < l$). This follows from a closer look at the preceding proof. After having chosen a suitably long path from the root to one of the terminal leaves, we can pick the repeating q senior and q junior nodes as close as possible to a terminal leaf. If n is the number of nonterminal symbols in the vocabulary, we can always pick the q senior node so that it is at a distance of not more than $n + 1$ from a terminal leaf. (We must have at least one repetition of a nonterminal in a string of $n + 1$ nonterminals.) With such a choice for the q senior (and corresponding q junior) node, the subtree with root at the q senior node cannot have more than m^{n+1} leaves. We are then assured that $| vwx |$ can be taken to be less than this number.

EXERCISES

9.1 Show that a monoid cannot have *two* distinct identity elements Λ_1, Λ_2.

9.2 What language is generated by the grammar that includes the following productions:

$$\sigma \to \sigma 1, \ \sigma \to \alpha 0, \ \alpha \to 1\alpha 1, \ \alpha \to 0?$$

9.3 What is $L(G)$ if G includes the following productions:

$$\sigma \to 0u, \ \sigma \to 1\sigma, \ u \to 1u1, \ u \to 0?$$

9.4 Show that any type 0 language is a recursively enumerable set.

9.5 A type 1 grammar uses productions $\alpha \to \beta$ satisfying $| \alpha | \leq | \beta |$. Show that a language defined by such a grammar can be defined by a grammar whose productions are all of the form $A\alpha B \to A\beta B$ where A, B are strings of V^*, $| \alpha | = 1$, and β is a nonnull string. (Show that any production of the form $s_1 s_2 \cdots s_m \to t_1 t_2 \cdots t_n$, with $m \leq n$, can be replaced by a set of productions having the requisite form.)

9.6 Show that every type 1 language is a recursive set.

9.7 A "left linear grammar" contains productions of the form $\alpha \to \beta A$ or $\alpha \to A$ where α, β are nonterminals and A is a terminal or the null string. Show that a language defined by such a grammar is a regular set, and conversely.

9.8 Show, by writing the appropriate grammars, that the sets of tapes accepted by the automata of Figs. 8.1, 8.6, 8.11 are in each case a type 3 language.

9.9 Assume the grammar for generating well-formed arithmetic expressions in ALGOL as given in Example (5) of Section 9.5. Construct a syntax tree for the expression

$$(x - y + z) \uparrow ((x + z) * (y - z)).$$

9.10 Show that the set of finite sequences of 0's and 1's in which the number of 1's is a multiple of 3 is a context-free language. Write down a grammar for this language.

9.11 Construct a type 3 grammar that defines FORTRAN integer identifiers (alphanumeric strings of length from one to six and beginning with I, J, K, L, M, or N).

9.12 Show that the complement, with respect to T^*, of the language $\{xx' \mid x \in T^*\}$, where $V = \{\sigma, 0, 1\}$, $T = \{0, 1\}$, is a context-free language.

9.13 Show that the set of finite sequences of 0's and 1's in which the number of 0's is equal to the number of 1's is a context-free language.

9.14 Construct a context-free grammar that generates the class of well-formed parenthetical expressions as these were defined in Section 4.2.

9.15 In Section 2.12 we defined the class of well-formed Boolean expressions. Construct a context-free grammar that generates this class.

9.16 Show that the set of sequences $\{a^n b^n \mid n \geq 1\}$ is a context-free language that is not a regular set and is, therefore, not a type 3 language.

9.17 Show that no infinite subset of the mirror language $\{x \$ x' \mid x \in T^*\}$, where T is some finite alphabet, is a regular set.

9.18 Show that $\{1^{n^2} \mid n \geq 1\}$ is a context-sensitive (type 1) language. Show that it is not context free.

9.19 Show that $\{uu \mid u \, \varepsilon \, V^+\}$ is a context-sensitive language.

9.20 We have seen earlier that the set of finite sequences made up of 0's and 1's where there are a prime number of 1's is not a regular set. Show that this set is not context free. Is it a type 0 language?

9.21 Is the set of postfix strings accepted by a tree automaton (Section 8.13) always a context-free language?

9.22 Show that every recursively enumerable set (type 0 language) on the alphabet $\{0, 1\}$ can be generated by a grammar with not more than two nonterminal symbols.

9.23 Given any phrase structure grammar G, define an algorithm that can be used to determine if $\Lambda \, \varepsilon \, L(G)$.

9.24 How many different meanings can you assign to the sentence "I like her cooking"? Construct a syntax tree for each possible meaning.

9.25 Consider the following statement from some programming language:

$$\text{IF } C_1 \text{ THEN IF } C_2 \text{ THEN } S_1 \text{ ELSE } S_2;$$

where C_1, C_2 denote conditions, and S_1, S_2 are statements.

Show two different ways of interpreting this statement. Devise two different fragments of a grammar corresponding to the two different syntax trees that might be considered for the two different interpretations.

9.26 Show that any given context-free grammar can be replaced by one that includes no productions of the form $A \rightarrow B$, where A, B are nonterminals, and that defines the same language.

9.27 Consider the Turing machine S defined in Chapter 5 to compute the successor function $S(x) = x + 1$. Write down an equivalent phrase structure grammar whose productions will effect the same sequencing of instantaneous descriptions as will S. (The details of the construction are easily extended to show that any recursively enumerable set is a type 0 language.)

9.28 Prove that the language $L = \{0^i 1/0^k \mid i = j \text{ OR } j = k\}$ is an inherently ambiguous context-free language. That is, no grammar can be chosen that provides a unique syntax tree for every sentence in the language.

Sketch of proof (fill in the gaps in the argument):

1. Show that L is context free by writing a grammar that generates L.

2. Let $s = 0^m 1^m 0^{m+m!}$ be a sentence in L with derivation, defined with respect to some grammar G, that is specified by its syntax tree. Let m be chosen so big that we can find in this tree, as in the proof of the $uvwxy$ theorem, a sufficiently long path extending from the root node σ to one of the m leading 0 leaves so that this path includes a repetition of some nonterminal node A. In this case it follows that (a) the $uvwxy$ theorem applies, and (by looking at the tree) (b) u, v contain only 0's, (c) $s_k = uv^k wx^k y$ $(k \geq 1)$ is also in L, and, therefore, x must consist only of 1's, (d) $|v| = |x| = p$, some number less than m, (e) s_k can be written as $0^{m+pk} 1^{m+pk} 0^{m+m!}$, and there is a derivation of the form

$$\sigma \Rightarrow \ast uv^k A x^k y \Rightarrow \ast s_k,$$

where the nonterminal A generates a string (w) of 0's followed by 1's (at least one of each).

3. Apply the symmetric argument to the string $s' = 0^{m+m!} 1^m 0^m$. (Assume that the same m, big enough to satisfy the stated conditions for both s, s', is chosen.) We arrive at the conclusion that a derivation of $s'_k = 0^{m+m!} 1^{m+p'k} 0^{m+p'k} = u'(v')^k w'(x')^k y'$ exists that is of the form

$$\sigma \Rightarrow \ast u'(v')^k B(x')^k y' \Rightarrow \ast s'_k,$$

where y', x' consist only of 0's, v' only of 1's, and the nonterminal B generates a string (w') consisting of 1's followed by 0's.

4. Consider the string $t = 0^{m+m!} 1^{m+m!} 0^{m+m!}$, which is of the form s_k for $k = \dfrac{m!}{p}$, and of the form s'_k for $k = \dfrac{m!}{p'}$. (Why did we pick $m!$ initially?) t has a derivation (and syntax tree) from its s_k structure and also one from its s'_k structure. These two trees must be distinct, for A cannot appear in any subtree whose root is B, and B cannot appear in any subtree whose root is A. Therefore, if the two syntax trees for t were identical, A and B would have to be distinct nodes generating distinct substrings of t. But this is impossible (because of the structures of w, w', t), and, therefore, t has at least two distinct syntax tree derivations. Therefore, any grammar G for L is ambiguous, and L is inherently ambiguous.

REFERENCES

1. Aho, A. V., and J. D. Ullman, *Principles of Compiler Design*. Reading, Massachusetts: Addison-Wesley, 1977.

2. Chomsky, N., "Three Models for the Description of Language." *IRE Trans. Information Theory,* **IT-2,** No. 3 (1956).

3. Chomsky, N., "On Certain Formal Properties of Grammars." *Information and Control,* **2** (1959).

4. Feldman, J. A., "A Formal Semantics for Computer Languages and Its Application in a Compiler-Compiler." *Comm. Assn. Comp. Mach.,* **9,** 1 (January 1966).

5. Knuth, D. E., "The Semantics of Context-Free Languages." *Math. Systems Theory,* **2,** 2 (1968).

6. Lucas, P., P. Lauer, and H. Stigleitner, *Method and Notation for the Formal Definition of Programming Languages.* Tech. Rep. 25.087, IBM Laboratory, Vienna, 1968.

7. Naur, P., ed. "Revised Report on the Algorithmic Language ALGOL 60." *Comm. Assn. Comp. Mach.,* **6,** 1 (January 1963).

8. Steel, T. B., Jr., ed. *Formal Language Description Languages for Computer Programming.* Amsterdam: North-Holland Publishing Company, 1966.

9. Wegner, Peter. "The Vienna Definition Language." *Computing Surveys,* **4,** 1 (March 1972).

10
Formal Languages—Further Relationships With Automata and Programming Languages

In this chapter we describe a number of important, but scattered, results concerning formal languages, their relationships with automata and programming languages, and the semantics of programming languages.

The all-inclusive type 0 languages are the recursively enumerable sets. That is, any language in this class is the set of outputs of some Turing machine. The sentences of such a language can be recognized by a nondeterministic, or by a deterministic, Turing machine. Each of the three other types of languages in the Chomsky hierarchy can be defined in terms of the special characteristics of those restricted automata (that is, machines that are less powerful than the universal Turing machine) that can recognize the sentences of a language in that class. We have already seen that the most restricted class in the hierarchy, the type 3 languages, consists of those sets of finite strings on some alphabet that can be recognized by finite automata. The type 1, or context-sensitive, languages can be recognized by nondeterministic Turing machines whose work tape never exceeds in length some fixed multiple of the length of the input tape. That most important class of all, particularly relevant to the study of programming languages, the context-free or type 2 languages, are recognizable by nondeterministic pushdown automata.

The use of pushdown automata in parsing the sentences of context-free languages provides insight into efficient machine procedures for parsing, or deriving the syntax of, programs. Some special grammars, with restrictions on their rewriting rules, enable the efficient use of a stack during the compiling process in parsing a program written in a language defined by such a grammar. We look briefly at some grammars of this kind and how the syntax derivation might proceed.

ALGOL and most other programming languages are not really context free when they are not subject to certain limitations, such as that on the length of identifiers. But this is only of theoretical interest, and, in a practical sense, these languages can be considered context free.

We look briefly at an unsolvable problem, the Post Correspondence Problem. We show, on the basis of the impossibility of a general solution to the halting problem, that this problem of formal languages has no general effective, or recursive, solution. A number of other important impossibility results for formal languages are consequences of the unsolvability of the Correspondence Problem.

Given any relation, the "transitive closure" of that relation is, loosely speaking, the result of iterating that relation any finite number of times. This mathematical construct plays a significant role, in several different guises, throughout computer science. We look at a particular application of this concept to a problem of formal languages.

It is certainly desirable to do what we can toward proving, in rigorous fashion, the correctness of programs, and some simple mathematical notions provide us with a means of attacking this problem. So far, these results have been quite limited in scope, but they are, nevertheless, of interest. There is the hope that some of these program validation techniques can be automated and thus find much greater applicability.

The last parts of this chapter concern different aspects of semantics, of the assignment of meaning to programs. We consider how the semantics of a program should be defined, and we look at an ambitious formal system, the Vienna Definition Language, for making precise the syntax *and* semantics of programming languages. This technique for definition has been successfully applied to give a precise description of PL/I.

Relevant to the semantics of formal languages we look last at the design of a surprisingly rich language to communicate with remote, intelligent beings in the universe (if there are such). Here, there is no interacting dialogue, and we cannot explain to the receivers of our messages, using some intermediate language (or metalanguage), the semantics of the language in which our messages are written. No Rosetta stone is possible. The meaning must somehow be inferred from the messages themselves. How can this be done? We consider the approach taken by a mathematician who has studied this problem. It is then tempting to speculate on the extent to which a computer might "learn" the semantics of a new language from seeing it used. We do not, however, seriously suggest such an approach in the compiling process.

10.1   THE DEFINITION OF THE LANGUAGES IN THE CHOMSKY HIERARCHY IN TERMS OF CLASSES OF AUTOMATA

We have shown in the preceding chapter that the type 3 languages of the Chomsky hierarchy are the same as the class of regular sets, those sets of strings on a given alphabet that can be recognized by finite automata. We have also noted that the all-inclusive class of the type 0 languages is the same as the class of the recursively enumerable sets, those sets that can be defined as the set of outputs of some Turing machine. A recursively enumerable set is, as we have seen in Chapter 6, not necessarily recursive. Therefore, if to "recognize a given sentence of a language" is taken to mean to "apply a procedure that determines *whether or not* a given sentence is in the language," then the sentences of a type 0 language cannot necessarily be recognized by some Turing machine. However, the word "recognize" is usually taken to have the following broader meaning. A language is said to be recognizable if a procedure exists that can determine that a given sentence is in the language *if* that sentence is in the language; however, if the sentence is not in the language, then the procedure either makes this determination or it makes no determination at all. That is, if the answer to the question of the membership of the sentence in the language is YES, this answer is forthcoming, but we cannot count on any answer at all if it is NO. With this interpretation, the sentences of a type 0 language are recognizable by some Turing machine. It is easy, following our discussion below of the type 1 languages, to design a nondeterministic Turing machine that recognizes the sentences of a given type 0 language. We can then define a deterministic Turing machine (cf. Chapter 6) that performs the same task.

It is, in similar fashion, possible to define the type 1 and type 2 languages in terms of the capabilities of special kinds of automata. Consider a Turing machine with a separate input tape, as described in Chapter 7. Suppose that such a machine is restricted with respect to the length of the work tape that it can use during a computation. If the input tape is of length l, let us assume that the work tape cannot exceed kl in length for some fixed number k, no matter what l is. We can equally well define such a machine to be one that is limited to its input tape in the course of a computation if we assume that $k + 1$ squares are used for each bit in the input argument (i.e., the argument could then appear on the first l squares, and the remaining kl squares could serve as the work tape).

Such a machine, whose work tape is bounded by some linear function of the length of the input tape, is called a *linear bounded automaton* or LBA.

If we consider a Turing machine that is nondeterministic in the sense of Chapter 6, such a nondeterministic LBA is often abbreviated as a NDLBA. It is not difficult to show that the context-sensitive, or type 1, languages are precisely those sets that can be recognized by such NDLBA's. We shall offer a proof of this fact, but only in heuristic fashion.

The type 1 grammars are those that use productions $\alpha \to \beta$ with $|\alpha| \leq |\beta|$. It is possible, based on such a grammar G, to define a nondeterministic machine procedure that will accept all sentences of the language $L(G)$. That is, for any given sentence or sentential form we can execute a procedure on a nondeterministic Turing machine that will scan that string and replace any substring that is a right-hand side β of a production by the left-hand side α of that production. We can define a *set* of machine instructions or quintuples (a "macro" operation) corresponding to each production of the grammar. Such a macro operation will replace the right-hand side of the production to which it corresponds by the left-hand side. Nondeterminism is desirable in this approach for we may have two productions $\alpha_1 \to \beta$, $\alpha_2 \to \beta$, thus needing two sets of quintuples, starting from the same initial ID, that will reduce β to either α_1 or α_2. A string s is accepted if the NDLBA corresponding to the given grammar can follow *some* path that reduces s to the starting symbol σ. Such a path amounts to a parse of s and shows its derivation from σ using the rules of the grammar. (We leave the details of the construction to the exercises.)

So far, of course, our argument applies to any phrase structure grammar. However, the rules of a context-sensitive grammar satisfy the restriction that the length of every left-hand side of a production does not exceed the length of the corresponding right-hand side. This means that the work tape is never longer than the input tape. We can, in fact, use only the input tape segment since the input string cannot be lengthened by the execution of each macro operation.

We are thus led to the conclusion that the sentences of any context-sensitive language can be recognized by a nondeterministic linear-bounded automaton. In this case it suffices to use a NDLBA that does not need more than its input tape segment ($k = 1$) in the course of its calculation.

We turn next to that most important class of languages, the context-free or type 2 languages. The grammar of such a language includes productions of the form $\alpha \to \beta$ where $|\alpha| = 1$. A still more restricted kind of automaton will suffice to recognize such languages.

In Chapter 6 we described a pushdown automaton (PDA). We shall show that the context-free languages can be recognized by nondeterministic pushdown automata (NDPDA). Again, we shall omit many of the technical details necessary to a rigorous demonstration of this fact. As in the preceding discussion we assume a Turing machine with a separate work tape. But now the tape is used as a pushdown, or LIFO, stack. The machine can only read the symbol at the top of the stack. (The symbol read is "popped" from the stack.) When a symbol is written, the stack is pushed down and the new symbol appears under the read head at the top of the stack.

That we can use such a nondeterministic device to recognize the sentences of a context-free language is almost immediate from the representation of the parse of a sentence as a syntax *tree*. We can argue as follows.

As described earlier, consider a bottom-up left-to-right parse, where we reduce a handle at each step to the single symbol that appears on the left-hand side of the appropriate production. Suppose, as in the preceding use of a NDLBA, that we assume a machine with a macro set of machine instructions for each possible reduction of the right-hand side of a production. Since we are assuming a nondeterministic machine we can presume that the machine makes a fortuitous choice of the handle to reduce at each step. The machine can read the input string, storing on the stack the symbols read until it finishes reading a substring that is a handle. It then pops the stack, reading this handle from the top, and replaces it by the (single) symbol to which it reduces. The machine continues reading (nondeterministically) either the stack or the input tape until it identifies the next handle at the top of the stack. Eventually the input string is reduced, if it is a sentence of the language, to the starting symbol. The whole procedure is feasible with a stack machine because $|\alpha| = 1$ when each reduction $\beta \underset{r}{\to} \alpha$ is executed.

Thus, any context-free language can be recognized by a NDPDA. Conversely, any language accepted by a NDPDA can be shown to be context free. We omit the proof, which consists of showing that any computation on such a machine leading to an acceptance state can be described as the reduction of some sentence, using a context-free grammar.

We have shown the following classification:

Languages	*Recognized by*
type 0	Nondeterministic or deterministic Turing machines
type 1	Nondeterministic linear bounded automata
type 2	Nondeterministic pushdown automata
type 3	Finite automata

10.2   SOME RESTRICTED CONTEXT-FREE GRAMMARS THAT ARE OF SPECIAL IMPORTANCE IN PARSING THE SENTENCES, OR PROGRAMS, OF PROGRAMMING LANGUAGES

We have seen that parsing an arbitrary sentence of a context-free language is in general a difficult task. Both a top-down parse (a derivation) and a bottom-up parse (the inverse of a derivation) can easily be described, as we have seen, in terms of nondeterministic procedures. However, there are complications involved in making these procedures deterministic and computable in a practical fashion. This is because of those ambiguous situations that we have noted, where there may be more than one candidate for the application of a production in the course of a top-down parse, or more than one candidate for a reduction in a bottom-up parse. We, therefore, found it necessary to use *nondeterministic* pushdown automata as recognition devices in general for the context-free languages. However, it is desirable to define programming languages by grammars with special properties, not shared by all context-free grammars, that facilitate parsing procedures.

A *deterministic* language is one whose sentences can be recognized by a deterministic pushdown automaton. It can be shown that these languages are precisely the same as those context-free languages whose sentences can be recognized or parsed in a left-to-right scan on a pushdown automaton *if* the parser is permitted to look ahead on the input string some fixed number of symbols to the right. The $LR(k)$ grammars, introduced by Knuth [15], are those in which a look-ahead of at most k symbols is allowed in determining the handle to be reduced at each stage of a left-to-right, bottom-up parse. The union of the $LR(k)$ languages, for all k, can be proved to be the same as the class of deterministic languages. In fact, it can be shown that every deterministic language has an $LR(1)$ grammar, that is, a grammar that defines a language whose sentences can be parsed with a look-ahead of not more than one symbol. It can also be proved that not all context-free languages are deterministic.

The parsing procedure for a given context-free language is often specified by a parsing table, or control table, that defines the behavior of a deterministic pushdown automaton as it reads an arbitrary input sentence of the language. A substantial part of compiling theory is devoted to the study of classes of grammars that are flexible enough to define real programming languages and yet possess properties that are helpful in the compiling process. These grammars often enable a procedure that automates the preparation of an efficient parsing table, given as input the set of productions of a grammar in that class. This table is then a key element of the compiling procedure for all programs written in the given language. An example of a grammar that is useful in this way is one that satisfies the conditions that (i) the right-hand sides of all productions begin with a terminal symbol, and (ii) two different productions having the same left-hand side have right-hand sides starting with different terminal symbols. We illustrate the use of a parsing table in the following example of a grammar that satisfies these two conditions. Our example is taken from the book on *Compiler Design Theory* by Lewis, Rosenkrantz, and Stearns [16].

Suppose that a language is defined by the following grammar G.

terminal vocabulary: a, b
nonterminals: σ, R
initial symbol: σ
productions: (1) $\sigma \to abR$ (2) $\sigma \to bRb\sigma$
               (3) $R \to a$ (4) $R \to bR$

It is readily seen that this grammar satisfies the two stated conditions. For such grammars, a simple algorithm exists to obtain a parsing table.

Such a parsing table for the sentences of $L(G)$ appears in Fig. 10.1. This table governs the actions of a pushdown automaton as it reads an input sentence S, a string of a's and b's, in $L(G)$. In understanding how the table specifies the behavior of the automaton, the reader should keep in mind the diagram of Section 7.6 that shows the configuration of a pushdown automaton. The automaton reads its input tape, containing S, from left to right, with the end of the input string signaled by a special end-of-tape mark ⊣. The automaton can write any one of four symbols $\sigma, R, b, \triangledown$ on its stack. We start with the initial symbol σ at the top of the stack and, below it, a special symbol $\triangledown$ that will mark the bottom of the stack throughout the procedure. At successive time steps, the automaton moves to the right on its input tape, scans the symbol at the top of the stack as well as the new input symbol, and takes certain actions as specified by these two symbols in the table. To "POP" the stack is to move the stack up one symbol, eliminating the symbol that was at the top of the stack before this action is taken. To "ADVANCE" is to move ahead to the next symbol on the input tape. We note from the table in Fig. 10.1 that six different combinations of a particular stack symbol and a particular input symbol will cause the automaton to reject the input sentence, and for one such combination, it will accept this sentence as being in $L(G)$.

Stack symbol	Input symbol		
	a	b	⊣
σ	(1)	(2)	REJECT
R	(3)	(4)	REJECT
b	REJECT	POP& ADVANCE	REJECT
$\triangledown$	REJECT	REJECT	ACCEPT

(1): POP the stack, then write R, b in that order on the stack, ADVANCE.
(2): POP the stack, then write σ, b, R in that order on the stack, ADVANCE.
(3): POP the stack, ADVANCE.
(4): POP the stack, then write R on the stack, ADVANCE.

Fig. 10.1   A parsing table for $L(G)$ (from [16]).

The four actions specified by (1), (2), (3), (4) correspond to the four productions of G, and each describes the corresponding reduction. These actions are taken when the automaton has just read on its input tape the first symbol (a prefix) of the right-hand side of one of the productions of G. The machine replaces the symbol at the top of the stack by the suffix (if there is one), that is, by the symbols that follow the prefix, of that right-hand side. The automaton is thus "remembering" on its stack the remaining symbols it must read before identifying a complete handle. The conditions satisfied by the grammar assure the feasibility of this parsing procedure.

We illustrate the operation of the parser by following the behavior of the automaton as it reads several input strings. The contents of the stack are shown as the automaton reads through the input string.

Input string: *bbbbaba* $\dashv$

Time step:	0	1	2	3	4	5	6	7	8
Symbol read:	*b*	*b*	*b*	*b*	*a*	*b*	*a*	$\dashv$	

Contents of stack when symbol is read:	σ	R	R	R	R	b	σ	b	REJECT
	$\triangledown$	b	b	b	b	σ	$\triangledown$	R	
		σ	σ	σ	σ	$\triangledown$		$\triangledown$	
		$\triangledown$	$\triangledown$	$\triangledown$	$\triangledown$				

Input string: *bbbababa* $\dashv$

Time step:	0	1	2	3	4	5	6	7	8	9
Symbol read:	*b*	*b*	*b*	*a*	*b*	*a*	*b*	*a*	$\dashv$	

Contents of stack when symbol is read:	σ	R	R	R	b	σ	b	R	$\triangledown$	ACCEPT
	$\triangledown$	b	b	b	σ	$\triangledown$	R	$\triangledown$		
		σ	σ	σ	$\triangledown$		$\triangledown$			
		$\triangledown$	$\triangledown$	$\triangledown$						

In all cases, a decision on the input sentence is reached when the end-of-tape mark " $\dashv$ " is read, if not earlier. A left-most top-down parse of an accepted sentence is defined by the sequence of productions corresponding to the actions of the automaton as these actions are executed during the scan of the input string.

An $LL(k)$ grammar is one that defines a language whose sentences can be parsed *top-down* in a left-to-right scan if a look-ahead of up to k symbols is allowed. The grammar of our example is an $LL(0)$ grammar.

A number of different kinds of special context-free grammars that permit efficient top-down or bottom-up parsing of the sentences of their languages have been studied. It is possible to make good use of such grammars for the practical problems associated with the compiling of programming languages. As still another example of a restricted context-free grammar we mention an "operator" grammar. This is one in which no right-hand side of a production contains two adjacent nonterminals.

We shall not go further into these matters in this survey. The interested reader is advised to refer to a number of recent works [1, 2, 8, 10, 11, 16] devoted to compiler design, or to the applications of formal languages, for the further elaboration of these ideas and their applications.

10.3 ALGOL IS NOT CONTEXT FREE

A number of programming languages, including ALGOL, when specified in very general terms, not limited by the requirements of a particular implementation, are *not* context free. We shall show this as a consequence of the *uvwxy* theorem.

First, we show that the language $L = \{zz \mid z \in \Sigma^+\}$, where Σ is any alphabet consisting of at least two symbols, is *not* context free. Our proof is similar to that we used earlier to show that $\{0^n 1^n 0^n \mid n \geq 1\}$ is not context free. Let $\Sigma = \{0, 1\}$ and consider those substrings of L that are of the form $0^n 1^n 0^n 1^n$, $n \geq 1$. Suppose that L is context free. Let n be taken large enough to assure that the *uvwxy* theorem applies to the string $s = 0^n 1^n 0^n 1^n$ ($= uvwxy$), so that all strings of the form $uv^k wx^k y$, $k > 1$, are also of the form zz. Further, let n exceed the length of the substring vwx (cf. the last remark in the discussion of the *uvwxy* theorem in Section 9.10). In this case, neither 0^n nor 1^n can be a substring of vwx, and, therefore, we must have either $vwx = 0^p 1^q$ or $vwx = 1^q 0^p$ for some p, q satisfying $n > p, q \geq 0$. If $vwx = 0^p 1^q$ for $p, q \geq 0$, this substring of s must lie entirely within the left or within the right half of s. But this is impossible, for it is easy to see that the string $uv^2 wx^2 y$ could not then be of the form zz. (If, for example, vwx lies within the left half of s, then the center of the string has shifted left, and the right half of $uv^2 wx^2 y$ must begin with a 1, which is different from the 0 that marks the beginning of the left half; a similar argument indicates that vwx does not lie entirely within the right half of s.)

Therefore, vwx must be of the form $1^q 0^p$, with $p, q > 0$, and the midpoint of s must be situated within vwx. In order for the string $uv^2 wx^2 y$ to be of the form zz, the midpoint must mark the beginning of at least n 0's and the end of at least n 1's. This means that v cannot contain any 0's, x cannot contain any 1's, and they must lie on opposite sides of the midpoint of $uv^2 wx^2 y$. Again, however, $uv^2 wx^2 y$ could not then be of the form zz. Therefore, L is not context free.

We can apply a similar argument to show that $\{\alpha w \beta w \gamma \mid w \varepsilon \Sigma^+\}$, where α, β, γ are fixed words, is not context free. We leave the details to the reader (cf. exercises).

The following set S of ALGOL programs is of this last type and is, therefore, not context free.

$$\{\text{BEGIN INTEGER } w;\ w : = 1;\ \text{END}\}$$

Here, w is any identifier composed from an alphabet of at least two characters, α is the string "BEGINbINTEGERb," β is the string ";b," and γ is the string "b: $= 1;b$END." ("b" denotes the blank.)

Let A be the set of all well-formed ALGOL programs. It can be shown (cf. the exercises) that if A were context free then so would S be context free. We conclude, therefore, that A is not a context-free language.

In general, any programming language that admits arbitrarily long identifiers and requires their declaration before their use is not context free. If, however, the number of identifiers is restricted, as it would be in any real implementation, the language will be context free. (There are other, but similar, reasons for a programming language not to be context free; again, the language will be context free under the restrictions of most real implementations.)

10.4 POST'S CORRESPONDENCE PROBLEM

Consider the following problem, deceptively simple in its statement, but a problem, nevertheless, that we shall show to be impossible of general solution. Suppose we are given two equally long lists of (nonnull) words on some alphabet Σ, where Σ contains at least two symbols. Let the lists be $U = (u_1, u_2, \ldots, u_n)$ and $V = (v_1, v_2, \ldots, v_n)$. We ask, is there some string made up by concatenating words from the first list, say

$$S = u_{i_1} u_{i_2} \cdots u_{i_k},$$

(where each index is in the set $\{1, 2, \ldots, n\}$ and may be repeated) which is the same as the string formed by using in each position the corresponding word of the second list? That is, does there exist such an S satisfying $S = T$ where

$$T = v_{i_1} v_{i_2} \cdots v_{i_k}?$$

Example 1. Let the two given lists of words on the alphabet $\{a, b\}$ be $U = (b, aa, babab)$ and $V = (abb, a, ab)$. Is there some string of u's that matches the string of corresponding v's?

In attempting to construct such a sequence, we must clearly begin with $u_2 = aa$ and $v_2 = a$, these being the only corresponding words that can possibly initiate two matching sequences (since one of two such words must necessarily be a prefix of the other). It is not difficult to continue the attempt to construct two matching sequences, and in this case we actually succeed in doing this by choosing as the successive words that form the two sequences those with indices 2, 1, 3, 1. We obtain

$$aa \mid b \mid babab \mid b$$

from the u's and

$$a \mid abb \mid ab \mid abb$$

from the v's.

Example 2. Let the two given lists be $U = (aaba, abb, bbab)$ and $V = (aab, baab, abba)$. Here, a very little analysis shows that it is not possible to form two matching strings by using corresponding words from the two lists. To see this, assume that such a string existed. Consider the last u_i and its corresponding v_i that appear at the ends of the matching strings. Clearly, only u_2 and v_2 can be considered for this role since they are the only corresponding pair that have the same last symbol. However, they disagree in the next to the last symbol and, therefore, cannot possibly appear at the ends of two matching strings (one of two such terminal words must be a suffix of the other).

We have succeeded in analyzing these simple examples in a quite straightforward fashion. We now ask if there is some general algorithm that can resolve the question of whether such matching strings exist for two given arbitrary lists. Or, in other words, can we write a program that will take as input two arbitrary, but equally long, lists U, V of words and will give as its output result the answer to the question of whether or not two matching strings, made up of the u_i, v_i, exist? Our question, stated in these terms, is another example of a "decision problem" as we have defined this in Chapter 6. Put still another way, and in considerably looser language, can we define some finite bag of tricks that we can use to resolve all problems in this class?

The answer to our question, and perhaps the reader will find it at variance with his or her intuition, is NO. The problem of constructing a general algorithm to make this decision is unsolvable. This problem, known as the Correspondence Problem, was first studied by Post [21] in 1946 and proven by him to have no solution. We shall sketch informally a fairly simple proof of the unsolvability of the problem, along lines suggested by Floyd [4] and Minsky [20]. The proof is based upon the impossibility of a general solution to the halting problem, the key tool in proving impossibility results of this kind. The unsolvability of the Correspondence Problem can be used to show that a number of problems concerning formal languages are effectively unsolvable.

We shall show that *if* there were an algorithmic solution to the Correspondence Problem, it could be used to solve the halting problem for any given Turing machine and given initial instantaneous description. We shall, in fact, use the impossibility result for the simpler version of the halting problem which indicates that there is no effective procedure to determine if an arbitrary Turing machine will eventually stop after starting on a *blank* tape (cf. Exercise 6.6).

To simplify our discussion to some extent, we shall consider the halting problem for a particular Turing machine that starts on a blank tape, and we shall show how the halting problem for this machine can be transformed into an example of the Correspondence Problem. Our methods will, however, be quite general and will be applicable to *any* given Turing machine. Any general algorithmic solution to the Correspondence Problem could then serve to resolve the halting problem for that machine. We shall leave it to the reader to translate our discussion of the problem for a particular machine into one that will apply to the halting problem for an arbitrary machine.

The impossibility of a general solution to the halting problem will then imply that *there is no general solution to the Correspondence Problem.*

There is no loss of generality in assuming that the given machine has an initial state that appears in only one quintuple and that it has a unique stop state. Using devices described in Chapter 5, any given Turing machine could be modified to satisfy these conditions without changing its halting behavior.

Consider, then, the following example of such a machine, with start state q_0 and stop state q_ω.

$$\left\{\begin{array}{ll} q_0\,B\,1\,L\,q_3 & q_2\,1\,1\,L\,q_3 \\ q_1\,B1\,L\,q_3 & q_3\,B\,1\,L\,q_2 \\ q_1\,1\,B\,R\,q_2 & q_3\,1\,1\,R\,q_\omega \\ q_2\,B\,1\,R\,q_1 & - \end{array}\right\} \tag{1}$$

We shall assume the use of end-of-tape marks $*$ flanking the tape segment used during a computation and, therefore, should modify these quintuples and add additional ones to handle these marks, as discussed in Chapter 5. That is, we must shift the symbol $*$ one square to the right if it is encountered on a move of the read head to the right and shift it one square to the left if it is encountered on a move to the left. However, we prefer not to introduce these slight complexities at this point and we assume that the reader could, if required, make these changes, following our earlier discussion.

As we have noted in Chapter 6, the transformation on instantaneous descriptions that is defined by the quintuples (1) can equally well be defined by the rewriting rules of a type 0 grammar. We list below the productions that will define the same computation, for any initial ID, as will (1). Here, we shall include those rules needed to handle the end-of-tape marks. It is, as we have seen, a trivial matter to write down the productions, given the quintuples.

We shall have occasion to reference separately the left- and right-hand sides of these productions and, therefore, we show these as appearing within two lists, L and R.

$$
\begin{array}{cc}
L & R \\
\star q_0 B \to \star q_3 B \, 1 \\
B q_1 B \to q_3 B \, 1 \\
1 q_1 B \to q_3 \, 1 \, 1 \\
\star q_1 B \to \star q_3 B \, 1 \\
q_1 \, 1 \to B q_2 \\
q_1 \star \to q_1 B \star \\
q_2 B \to 1 q_1 \\
q_2 \star \to q_2 B \star
\end{array}
\qquad
\begin{array}{cc}
L & R \\
B q_2 \, 1 \to q_3 B \, 1 \\
1 q_2 \, 1 \to q_3 \, 1 \, 1 \\
\star q_2 \, 1 \to \star q_3 B \, 1 \\
B q_3 B \to q_2 B \, 1 \\
1 q_3 B \to q_2 \, 1 \, 1 \\
\star q_3 B \to \star q_2 B \, 1 \\
q_3 \, 1 \to 1 q_\omega
\end{array}
\qquad (2)
$$

These rules define the following sequence of ID's if the machine starts in state q_0 on a tape that is blank, except for the two end-of-tape marks. The reader can confirm that the transformations of ID's are indeed the same as those accomplished by the machine's quintuples (suitably augmented by those needed to handle the end-of-tape marks).

$$
\begin{aligned}
\star q_0 B \star \to &\; \star q_3 B 1 \star \to \star q_2 B 1 1 \star \to \star 1 q_1 1 1 \star \\
\to &\; \star 1 B q_2 1 \star \to \star 1 q_3 B 1 \star \to \star q_2 1 1 1 \star \to \star q_3 B 1 1 1 \star \quad (3) \\
\to &\; \star q_2 B 1 1 1 1 \star \to \star 1 q_1 1 1 1 1 \star \to \dots
\end{aligned}
$$

It will be desirable for us to impose one further condition on the given machine, even though our example machine does not satisfy this condition. We shall suppose that, before stopping, the machine will erase the tape and derive, as its terminal ID, $\star q_\omega B \star$. Again, there is no loss of generality in assuming this, since any given machine can be modified (using devices of Chapter 5) so that, instead of stopping in its normal stop state, it goes on to erase the tape and finish with the indicated terminal ID.

The crucial step, now, in casting the halting problem as a correspondence problem is to look at (3) as a string of characters, ignoring spaces, and to note that this string can be formed by concatenating in proper order selected elements of a list L of words, *or,* equally well, by concatenating the corresponding elements of a list R of words. The elements of the two lists will be principally the left-hand (list L) sides and right-hand (list R) sides of the productions in (2). It will, however, be necessary to add some matching items to the two lists, as shown in (4) below, in order to take care of the beginning parts of the matching strings, of the ends of the strings if a computation

terminates, and of that tape data at each step that is not involved in the
execution of a quintuple.

$$
\begin{array}{ll}
L & R \\
B & B \\
1 & 1 \\
\star & \star \\
\rightarrow & \rightarrow \\
\star\, q_0 B & \star\, q_0 B \star \rightarrow \star\, q_3 B1 \\
\star\, q_\omega B \star \rightarrow H & H
\end{array}
\tag{4}
$$

To clarify this construction somewhat, we shall show how the sequence
(3) can be formed by concatenating elements of L in the top row shown
below, and by concatenating elements of R in the bottom row.

$$
\begin{array}{l}
L: \star\, q_0 B \star \qquad\quad \star \rightarrow \quad \star\, q_3 B \quad 1 \star \rightarrow \star \quad q_2 B \quad 11 \star \rightarrow \star 1 \quad q_1 1 \quad 1 \\
R: \star\, q_0 B \star \rightarrow \star\, q_3 B1 \star \rightarrow \quad \star\, q_2 B1 \quad 1 \star \rightarrow \star \quad 1q_1 \quad 11 \star \rightarrow \star 1 \quad Bq_2 \quad 1
\end{array}
$$

$$
\begin{array}{l}
L: \star \rightarrow \star 1 \quad Bq_2 1 \quad \star \rightarrow \star \quad 1q_3 B \quad 1 \star \rightarrow \quad \star\, q_2 1 \quad 11 \star \rightarrow \ldots \\
R: \star \rightarrow \star 1 \quad q_3 B1 \quad \star \rightarrow \star \quad q_2 11 \quad 1 \star \rightarrow \quad \star\, q_3 B1 \quad 11 \star \rightarrow \ldots
\end{array}
$$

To see that the same sequence will be generated by concatenating the
indicated elements of the list L as by concatenating the corresponding elements of the list R, we can argue by induction on the number of ID's that
appear up to some specified arrow in the top row. We shall show that, at any
selected arrow, the top row is a prefix of the bottom row, with the latter
containing one more ID than the former (except, as we shall see, for the
string ending in the terminal ID). At the end of the first ID in the top row, the
bottom row is the string of the first two ID's (the first word of the bottom row
was constructed in the list R expressly to satisfy this condition). To continue
the argument by induction, assume that after forming a string of k successive
ID's, $(ID)_1 \rightarrow (ID)_2 \rightarrow \ldots \rightarrow (ID)_k$, the bottom row is the string of $k + 1$
successive ID's, $(ID)_1 \rightarrow (ID)_2 \rightarrow \ldots \rightarrow (ID)_k \rightarrow (ID)_{k+1}$. We must then show
that when $(ID)_{k+1}$ is appended to the top row, its successor $(ID)_{k+2}$ will be
appended to the bottom row. However, this follows from our construction.
The successor $(ID)''$ to any $(ID)'$ is obtained by using the appropriate
rewriting rule of (2) and, therefore, is formed by concatenating those elements of the R list that correspond to the elements of the L list which form
$(ID)'$.

Suppose the machine halts after m steps. Because we have specified the
terminal ID to be $\star\, q_\omega B \star$, the top row will end in $\star\, q_\omega B \star$. Let us add the
fictitious symbols "$\rightarrow H$" to this word to indicate that the halt state has been

reached. Then we have the following strings at the ends of the top and bottom rows, using the last matching pair of the L, R lists

$$\ldots \to (ID)_{m-1} \to \star\, q_\omega B \,\star \to H$$
$$\ldots \to \star\, q_\omega B \,\star \to H.$$

The top row has now caught up with the bottom row, and we have a solution to the correspondence problem for the given L, R lists.

There remains one serious flaw in our analysis before we can conclude that a solution to the correspondence problem for the L, R lists implies a solution to the halting problem for the given machine. That is, there are many unwanted trivial solutions to this correspondence problem for the L, R lists, e.g., $\star 1 \star$ is such a solution. We are really only interested in knowing if the particular solution that describes a computation exists, and, therefore, wish to insure that this be the *only* solution to this correspondence problem. If we can do this, then we can conclude that solving the general correspondence problem is tantamount to solving the general halting problem.

We want, then, the only possible solution to the correspondence problem to be one that begins with $\star\, q_0 B$ from the L list and terminates with $\star\, q_\omega B \,\star \to H$ from the R list. A special trick will assure this and will prevent the occurrence of the extraneous solutions. This device consists of using a new special symbol, say #, and (1) writing every symbol α, except H, that appears in the R list of words as $\#\alpha$, (2) writing every symbol β, except H, that appears in the L list as $\beta\#$, and (3) prefixing the desired starting word of the L list (the *second* word containing q_0) with #, making it $\#\star\#\, q_0 \# B \#$.

Now, any possible matching sequence formed from the two lists *must* begin with the second word in L containing q_0, this being the only word of L that is a prefix of its corresponding word in R.

Further, this construction forces any solution to this correspondence problem to terminate with the word in L that ends in H, this being the only word that agrees in its last position with the corresponding word of R.

Now, we conclude that the solution to this particular correspondence problem can be generalized and implies a general solution to the halting problem. Since the general halting problem is recursively unsolvable, so is the Correspondence Problem.

This result can be used to show that a number of problems concerning the context-free languages are also unsolvable. For example, there is no general procedure to determine whether or not an arbitrary given context-free grammar is ambiguous. Also, the problem of determining if two given context-free languages have any sentences in common has no general solution.

10.5   THE TRANSITIVE CLOSURE OF A RELATION

If R, S are two given relations, we can define the product relation RS as follows.

$$RS = \{(x, y) \mid \exists z[(xRz) \& (zSy)]\}$$

Example. If R is the relation defined by "xRy if and only if $y = x + 2$" and S is the relation defined by "xSy if and only if $y = x + 4$" then $xRSy$ is the relation defined by $y = x + 6$.

We leave it to the exercises to see that the multiplication of relations satisfies the associative law $R(ST) = (RS)T$.

Letting R^2 denote the product RR we have $xR^2y \equiv \exists z[(xRz) \& (zRy)]$. By iterating this construction we can define the relation R^k ($k \geq 2$) by

$$xR^ky \text{ if and only if } \exists z [(xR^{k-1}z) \& (zRy)].$$

It is easy to see, from the associative law, that if $k = m + n$, this definition implies that $R^k = R^m R^n$.

We then define the *transitive closure* R^+ to be the relation defined by the following equation.

$$xR^+ y = xRy \cup xR^2y \cup xR^3y \cup \cdots$$

This notation is taken to mean that the graph of the relation R^+ is the union of the graphs of R^k, $k = 1, 2, \ldots$, or, in other words, that xR^+y if and only if we have xR^ky for some k.

R^+ is not necessarily reflexive, and we often have occasion to make use of a slight modification of R^+ to insure that it be reflexive. We let R^* denote the relation defined by

$$xR^* y \equiv (x = y) \mid (xR^+y).$$

It is then immediate that R^* is reflexive. It is called the *reflexive transitive closure* of R.

We leave it to the exercises to show that R^+ (or R^*) is indeed a transitive relation.

This mathematical construction finds application in a number of places in computer science. We have seen a closely related concept when we defined the function fg^* during the discussion (Section 4.12) of iteration as a substitute for minimalization in the definition of the partial recursive functions. Also, and this is our principal reason for introducing this notion at this point, the derivation relation $t \Rightarrow_* s$ (where the string s is derived from the string t by applying a sequence of productions of some grammar G) is seen to be the reflexive transitive closure of the relation $q \Rightarrow p$ (where the string p is derived from the string q by an application of one of the rewriting rules of G).

The problem of parsing a sentence of a context-free language is, in essence, that of determining an inverse of the transitive closure relation that defines derivations. That is, given a grammar G and a possible sentence $s \in L(G)$ (and, therefore, that we may have $\sigma \Rightarrow* s$), we seek a sequence of reductions that transforms s into σ, $s \underset{r}{\Rightarrow}* \sigma$.

In Chapter 6 we used the notation $ID_i \Rightarrow ID_{i+1}$ to indicate that ID_{i+1} is the instantaneous description that succeeds ID_i as the result of applying some quintuple of a given Turing machine. We wrote $(ID)_1 \Rightarrow* (ID)_n$ to show that the instantaneous description $(ID)_n$ is obtained from an initial instantaneous description $(ID)_1$ as the result of a chain of applications of quintuples. Using the language of this section we recognize that if "$\Rightarrow$" is considered a relation, defined as just stated on instantaneous descriptions, then "$\Rightarrow*$" is the reflexive transitive closure of that relation. More generally, a "computation" on any real machine can be defined in terms of the transitive closure of the relation that describes the succession of machine states, or of machine snapshots. If the relation "$\Rightarrow$" is defined on machine states so that $S_i \Rightarrow S_{i+1}$ means that the state, or snapshot, S_i is succeeded, at the beginning of the next instruction, or perhaps at the beginning of the next machine cycle, by S_{i+1}, then a computation is defined by the reflexive transitive closure $\Rightarrow*$ of $\Rightarrow$, the terminal snapshot S_f being related to the initial snapshot S_0 by $S_0 \Rightarrow* S_f$.

If there are only a finite number of elements in the domain and, also, in the range of a relation R, we can interpret R^+ or R^* in graphical terms. Suppose that there are n possible elements involved in a relation R. We can then represent R by a digraph of n nodes in which a directed path segment extends from node i to node j if and only if iRj (Fig. 10.2).

In the case of a finite relation R, represented in this way, we note that xR^ky if and only if there is a directed path of k segments extending from node x to node y. It follows that xR^+y if and only if there is some directed

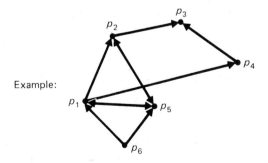

Example:

Fig. 10.2 A relation R defined on the objects $\{p_i \mid i = 1, 2, \ldots, 6\}$. A directed path segment extends from p_i to p_j if and only if p_iRp_j. Thus, p_2Rp_3 and $\neg(p_3Rp_4)$.

path, of any length, extending from node x to node y. In the Appendix to Chapter 3 we considered the computation of the path matrix for any given finite digraph. This path matrix, computed from the adjacency matrix of the digraph corresponding to a given finite relation R, then defines the transitive closure R^+. That is, if the element a_{ij} of the path matrix is 1, then iR^+j. If we make all diagonal elements of the path matrix equal to 1, it becomes the defining matrix for R^*.

10.6   AN APPLICATION OF THE TRANSITIVE CLOSURE OF A RELATION TO A PROBLEM OF FORMAL LANGUAGES

Suppose we are given a grammar G, with vocabulary V and set of productions P, that defines a context-free language $L(G)$. Let α, β be given elements of V. We ask the question: Is there some derivation of the form

$$\alpha \Rightarrow * \ldots \beta \ldots ?$$

That is, is there some derivation, starting with α, that generates a string that includes β? We shall show that the problem can be answered by computing the reflexive transitive closure of a certain relation.

Let us write α BEGETS β if and only if there is some production in P of the form

$$\alpha \rightarrow \ldots \beta \ldots$$

Consider the reflexive transitive closure BEGETS * of BEGETS. We then have that

$$\alpha \text{ BEGETS } * \beta$$

if and only if there is some chain of productions of the form:

$$\alpha \rightarrow \cdots \gamma_1 \cdots, \ \gamma_1 \rightarrow \cdots \gamma_2 \cdots, \ \cdots, \ \gamma_n \rightarrow \cdots \beta \cdots, \text{ or if } \alpha = \beta.$$

Such a sequence clearly implies that there is a derivation of the form

$$\alpha \Rightarrow * \cdots \beta \cdots,$$

or, in other words, that some derivation, starting with α, leads to a string containing β.

Conversely, if such a derivation exists, $\alpha \Rightarrow * \ldots \beta \ldots$, a chain of such productions must exist (look at the parsing tree). That is, we must have α BEGETS * β.

Since the relation BEGETS is defined, for any given grammar, on a finite set, that is on the elements of V, the remarks of the preceding section apply, and it is straightforward to compute the matrix that describes BEGETS *. We illustrate the computation of the reflexive transitive closure in the following.

Example. Consider the following grammar G.

> terminal vocabulary: $0, 1, 2$
> nonterminals: σ, A, B, C
> initial symbol: σ (5)
> productions: $\sigma \to A\sigma \mid A$
> $\qquad\qquad\quad A \to \sigma B \mid 0 \mid 2A0 \mid AA$
> $\qquad\qquad\quad B \to BB \mid BC$
> $\qquad\qquad\quad C \to A \mid 1B \mid 2A$

Compute the matrix that defines the relation α BEGETS $*$ β for any two elements α, β in the vocabulary of G.

The matrix M that defines the relation BEGETS for G is given below. Each row and column of this matrix corresponds to one of the 7 elements of the vocabulary, and a "1" appears in the position whose row is identified by α and column by β if and only if α BEGETS β; otherwise, a "0" appears in that position.

$$
M:\quad
\begin{array}{c}
\\ \sigma \\ A \\ B \\ C \\ 0 \\ 1 \\ 2
\end{array}
\begin{array}{c}
\sigma\ A\ B\ C\ 0\ 1\ 2 \\
\left[
\begin{array}{ccccccc}
1 & 1 & 0 & 0 & 0 & 0 & 0 \\
1 & 1 & 1 & 0 & 1 & 0 & 1 \\
0 & 0 & 1 & 1 & 1 & 0 & 0 \\
0 & 1 & 1 & 0 & 0 & 1 & 1 \\
0 & 0 & 0 & 0 & 0 & 0 & 0 \\
0 & 0 & 0 & 0 & 0 & 0 & 0 \\
0 & 0 & 0 & 0 & 0 & 0 & 0
\end{array}
\right]
\end{array}
$$

We then compute the successive powers of M, using Boolean operations, as in computing the path matrix for a finite graph. We obtain

$$
M^2:\quad
\begin{bmatrix}
1 & 1 & 1 & 0 & 1 & 0 & 1 \\
1 & 1 & 1 & 1 & 1 & 0 & 1 \\
0 & 1 & 1 & 1 & 0 & 1 & 1 \\
1 & 1 & 1 & 1 & 1 & 0 & 1 \\
0 & 0 & 0 & 0 & 0 & 0 & 0 \\
0 & 0 & 0 & 0 & 0 & 0 & 0 \\
0 & 0 & 0 & 0 & 0 & 0 & 0
\end{bmatrix}
\qquad
M^3:\quad
\begin{bmatrix}
1 & 1 & 1 & 1 & 1 & 0 & 1 \\
1 & 1 & 1 & 1 & 1 & 1 & 1 \\
1 & 1 & 1 & 1 & 1 & 1 & 1 \\
1 & 1 & 1 & 1 & 1 & 1 & 1 \\
0 & 0 & 0 & 0 & 0 & 0 & 0 \\
0 & 0 & 0 & 0 & 0 & 0 & 0 \\
0 & 0 & 0 & 0 & 0 & 0 & 0
\end{bmatrix}
$$

$$
M^4 = M^5 = M^6 = M^7:\quad
\begin{bmatrix}
1 & 1 & 1 & 1 & 1 & 1 & 1 \\
1 & 1 & 1 & 1 & 1 & 1 & 1 \\
1 & 1 & 1 & 1 & 1 & 1 & 1 \\
1 & 1 & 1 & 1 & 1 & 1 & 1 \\
0 & 0 & 0 & 0 & 0 & 0 & 0 \\
0 & 0 & 0 & 0 & 0 & 0 & 0 \\
0 & 0 & 0 & 0 & 0 & 0 & 0
\end{bmatrix}
$$

The matrix for BEGETS ***** is then given by $M \cup M^2 \cup \ldots \cup M^7$ with the additional requirement, to insure reflexivity, that all diagonal elements must be 1. We thus obtain the following matrix representation of BEGETS *****.

$$
\begin{array}{c c}
 & \begin{array}{c c c c c c c} \sigma & A & B & C & 0 & 1 & 2 \end{array} \\
\begin{array}{c} \sigma \\ A \\ B \\ C \\ 0 \\ 1 \\ 2 \end{array} &
\left[\begin{array}{c c c c c c c}
1 & 1 & 1 & 1 & 1 & 1 & 1 \\
1 & 1 & 1 & 1 & 1 & 1 & 1 \\
1 & 1 & 1 & 1 & 1 & 1 & 1 \\
1 & 1 & 1 & 1 & 1 & 1 & 1 \\
0 & 0 & 0 & 0 & 1 & 0 & 0 \\
0 & 0 & 0 & 0 & 0 & 1 & 0 \\
0 & 0 & 0 & 0 & 0 & 0 & 1
\end{array} \right]
\end{array}
$$

We can easily read directly from this matrix whether or not any given character α generates, using G, a string that includes a given character β. For example, to see if the terminal 1 appears in some string derived from σ we note that the element in the row for σ and column for 1 is "1" indicating that there *is* such a derivation.

10.7 ON PROVING THE CORRECTNESS OF PROGRAMS

Proper programming technique helps in reducing the occurrence of errors. We have, for example, cited this as a reason for using the structured programming approach. But once a program is written, how can we be certain that it is correct—that it will give the correct answers for *all* admissible input values? The usual debugging procedures involve checking the results for a sampling of possible input values. Such tests can, then, make it highly plausible that a program is correct, but they do not in general provide an unconditional guaranty of correctness under all circumstances. This is strikingly evident in the universal occurrence of error reports and of subsequent program corrections issued after the initial release of just about any complex programming system. It is, therefore, an attractive notion to seek proofs of program correctness that are as rigorous and sure as are good mathematical proofs. It would be nice to be able to assert the correctness of a program with the same certainty with which we assert the truth of, say, the Pythagorean theorem.

A fair amount of effort has gone into the study of possible mathematical proofs of the correct behavior of programs. We look briefly at some of the key ideas implicit in this work.

Any computational procedure at all accomplishes some transformation of input data to output results. Any program step or any set of consecutive program steps in the course of such a procedure can be described in terms of the changes in the state of the machine that result from the execution of these program steps. At any given point in a computation certain assertions can be made about the intermediate computed quantities that have been obtained at that stage in the computation. At the end of a computation, the assertions that can be made about the final results include the criteria for correctness—the statements of those properties that characterize these results if they are correct. As early as 1947, von Neumann and Goldstine [7] described flow-chart procedures, for the definition of computations, with conventions that allowed the inclusion of such nonexecutable assertions at designated points in a flowchart. These assertions could be used to indicate salient properties that the programmer wished to emphasize at selected points in a procedure.

Let us, following the terminology of the relevant literature [5, 9, 19], call a point in a flowchart at which an assertion is made a "cutpoint." Suppose that in a particular computation, viewed as a path through the flowchart, we designate the finite sequence of cutpoints through which the path passes as $C_0, C_1, \ldots, C_n$. (Repetitions of a subsequence of cutpoints will denote the execution of a loop.) Let the corresponding assertions be $A_0, A_1, \ldots, A_n$. Suppose that A_0 is an assertion stating the requisite properties of the input data and that the final assertion A_n describes sufficient conditions for the final results to be correct. Suppose further that we can show that the segment of code between any two successive cutpoint assertions A_i, A_{i+1} is such that if assertions $A_0, A_1, \ldots, A_i$ are assumed true, then assertion A_{i+1} must be true. That is, we are able to show the chain of implications

$$A_0 \to (A_0 \& A_1) \to (A_0 \& A_1 \& A_2) \to \ldots \to (A_0 \& A_1 \& \ldots \& A_n).$$

Invoking the law of the syllogism in logic $[((A \to B) \& (B \to C)) \to (A \to C)]$, this implies that

$$A_0 \to A_n.$$

That is, if the input conditions are satisfied, the final results must be correct.

We illustrate these notions by considering the following program to compute $gcd(M, N)$, the greatest common divisor of two given numbers M, N. Our example is taken from [9]. We give the procedure first, Fig. 10.3, as a flowchart using the basic building blocks of the structured programming technique (SEQUENCE, IF_THEN_ELSE_, DO_WHILE). This is followed by a PL/I program, Fig. 10.4, corresponding to the flowchart description. This program should be intelligible to a programmer who is fluent in any general purpose language. In Fig. 10.3, the cutpoints are accompanied by assertions claimed to be true as a consequence of the program steps executed since the preceding cutpoint.

The procedure we have defined employs three cutpoints with accompanying assertions. The first assertion states a necessary property of the input values M, N; the last assertion states the condition for the output value K to be the correct result. The second assertion, at cut 2, is a consequence of the portion of the algorithm in the DO WHILE loop between cut 1 and cut 2, no matter how many times this loop is executed. We leave it to the reader to prove that $gcd(K, L) = gcd(M, N)$ at cut 2 as a result of either decreasing K by L or decreasing L by K, according to which is the larger. When the DO WHILE condition is no longer satisfied, that is when $K = L$, we reach cut 3. Assuming the assertion at cut 2 *and* the fact that $K = L$, we infer the final assertion, that includes $gcd(M, N) = gcd(K, K) = K$.

The procedure, then, appears to be proved correct. However, there is one additional point that must be considered. That is, how can we be certain that under all circumstances the flow of the computation will reach cut 3, that is, how can we prove that the DO WHILE loop will always terminate? The

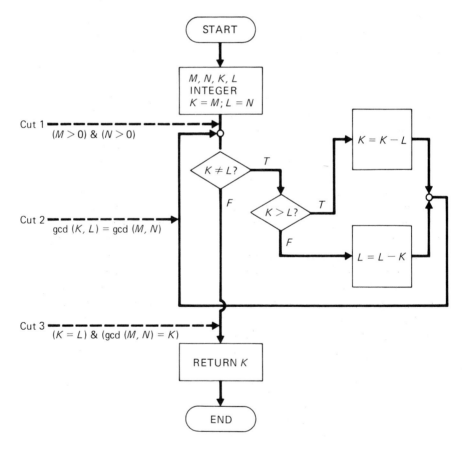

Fig. 10.3 A flowchart description, with cutpoints, of the computation of $gcd(M, N)$.

proof of this fact is not difficult, and we shall not rewrite the assertions to include all the details necessary to the proof. If we denote the successive values of K, L on each pass through the loop as $K^{(i)}, L^{(i)}$ ($i = 0, 1, 2, \ldots$), where $M = K^{(0)}$, $N = L^{(0)}$, then it is immediate that

$$M + N = K^{(0)} + L^{(0)} > K^{(1)} + L^{(1)} > \ldots > K^{(i)} + L^{(i)} > \ldots$$

Since $K^{(i)} + L^{(i)}$ is strictly decreasing and cannot be reduced to zero (why not?), the procedure must terminate after some finite number of steps under all conditions.

Some problems associated with this technique for proving the correctness of programs are:

1. The method of proof we have outlined requires the proper identification of the cutpoint assertions $A_0, A_1, \ldots, A_n$. It is straightforward to give A_0, the conditions satisfied by the input data, and it is also usually easy to write down A_n, the criterion for the correctness of the results. But the problem remains to identify intermediate cutpoints and assertions in a way that will make a proof feasible for the given flowchart description of a computation. In our example, it seemed clear that there should be an additional cutpoint at a completion of the DO WHILE loop. More generally, cutpoints at the end of any loop execution in a given procedure may be appropriate. We shall not pursue further the details of such cutpoint identification. A "backtracking" technique to yield intermediate cutpoint assertions, starting from A_n, can proceed in a rather routine fashion and is described in [19].

2. This technique applies to algorithms whose numeric operands, identified by symbols, are assumed to be represented exactly in the course of a computation—that is, where no roundoff errors contaminate the arithmetic operations. However, such errors are usually, of course, eventually unavoidable in any real machine implementation where words of limited size are used for the representation of numbers (unlike the more abstract implemen-

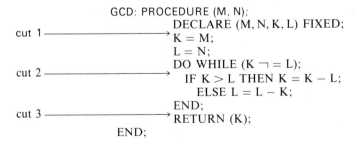

Figure 10.4   A PL/I program for the computation of *gcd(M, N)*.

tation on a growing automaton, such as a Turing machine). This means that in many situations the mathematical conditions satisfied by final results or by intermediate quantities are only approximately satisfied by the computed results. For example, a computed root of an equation is in general only an approximation to that root and thus will *not* satisfy the equation exactly. The situation in many numerical computations is further complicated by the occurrence of truncation errors—those errors resulting from approximating some infinite procedure, such as the summing of an infinite series, by using a finite terminating procedure (such as computing a partial sum in the case of an infinite series). Thus, in general, the assertions will be true only if we consider the *symbolic* representations of the operands and the exact algebraic manipulation of these symbols. They are *not* true for the actual machine-computed quantities unless the assertions include tolerances on the claimed equality of two expressions.

3. A proof of the correctness of an algorithm should include a proof that the algorithm terminates for those input arguments for which we expect results, as we have noted in our example. No general recipe, however, can provide such a proof because of the impossibility of a general solution to the halting problem. Therefore, the best that can be done is to indicate certain guidelines that in many situations will lead to a proof of termination [13, 22]. The *gcd* computation that we have analyzed is a prototype example showing how such a proof of termination might proceed.

Some work has progressed toward developing program validation systems that automate the machinery of proofs, along the above lines, of program correctness [3, 12, 14].

10.8   THE DEFINITION OF SEMANTICS

We have seen how the syntax of a programming language, the set of rules that determine the well-formed programs of that language, can be specified by the set of productions of a context-free grammar. A grammar defined in this way then provides a precise and completely clear definition of the conditions that must be satisfied for any string of characters to constitute a properly written program of that language.

The semantics of a program, however, concerns the *actions* that a computer takes in the course of executing that program. It is, therefore, not possible to define the semantics precisely except in terms of a machine interpretation of the program when it is executed.

Consider, for example, the "program" of a given Turing machine to be its set of quintuples. The "semantics" of such a program is defined precisely in terms of the mapping of instantaneous descriptions into instantaneous descriptions that is defined by the set of quintuples (cf. the discussion in Section 5.10 on the interpretation of the quintuples of a Turing machine in terms of functions on ID's). If, as noted in Section 7.2, we take the ID (rather than a q_i) to be the "state" of the machine, the semantics can be said to be defined in terms of the machine state transitions.

More generally, for any given real machine the semantics of a program is simply defined by the transition function on the machine states (or, using the common jargon, the machine "snapshots") that governs the execution of that program. That is, a sequencing of machine states occurs when the program is executed, and each successor state is determined from its predecessor state by the meaning or interpretation given the program in the course of its machine execution. A machine "computation" can be considered to be the complete sequence of states from the initial (input) state to the terminal (output) state.

10.9 THE VIENNA DEFINITION LANGUAGE

One of the most noteworthy achievements in providing a method for the precise definition of both the syntax and semantics of a programming language is that of a group at the IBM Laboratory in Vienna, in cooperation with other IBM groups at Hursley, England, and Poughkeepsie, New York. The methods for the formal definition of programming languages which they developed during the late 1960s have, in particular, been applied to the definition of PL/I, but the techniques used are of a quite general nature and can be used for the definition of any programming language.

We refer the reader to several expository original papers [17, 18] and to a description of the definition language that has appeared in *Computing Surveys* [23] for a detailed description of the language. We shall, in our survey of these matters, only touch briefly on a few of the key ideas implicit in this work.

The fundamental representation of both programs (syntax) and the machine interpretation of these programs (semantics) is given in terms of tree structures. It is assumed that a parsing tree can be routinely obtained from a program originally given as a character string. The *abstract* syntax refers to the rules that determine membership in the class of tree structures that represent programs, while the specification of the correctly formed character strings that denote programs is called the *concrete* syntax. The latter can be described, as we have noted, by a context-free grammar.

The states of the machine that interprets a program, given by the abstract syntax of a tree structure, are also represented as trees. The objects that represent both programs and machine states are denoted by trees with named branches. A composite object, written as

$$\{<s_1:A_1>, <s_2:A_2>, \cdots, <s_n:A_n>\},$$

can be represented by the tree in Fig. 10.5.

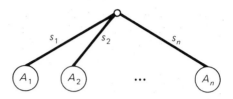

Figure 10.5

The representation is recursive in the sense that each of the $\{A_i\}$ may denote a tree representation of similar kind (a subtree), or it may represent a terminal leaf or "elementary object."

$$e_0^\circ$$

Only branches of the tree and the terminal nodes need have names.
    Thus, a machine instruction such as

$$\text{Inst} = A\ 3, 1600(4, 2)$$

in IBM 360/370 Basic Assembly Language can be represented by the tree in Fig. 10.6.

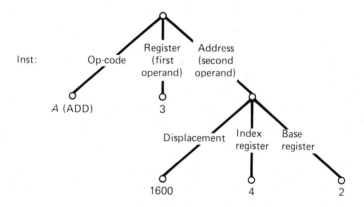

Figure 10.6

The names of the branches serve as selectors, so that in the above example we can write $<\text{op-code:Inst}> = A$, designating the leaf A by the name of the branch leading to it. Similarly, we can write

$$<\text{displacement(address):Inst}> = 1600,$$

where the sequence of branches, or path, leading to the leaf 1600 serves to identify it. In general, any subtree or terminal node can be identified by the sequence of branch names that mark a path leading to the root of that subtree or to that terminal node. To avoid ambiguity, the selectors emanating from any one node are required to be different, but the same selector can occur at different nodes.

The expression − (ALPHA + OMEGA) can be represented by the tree in Fig. 10.7.

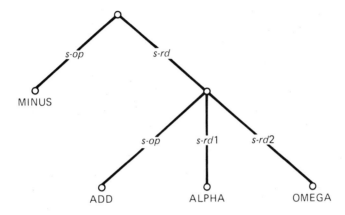

Figure 10.7

The selectors indicate which of the elementary objects, or subexpressions, are operations (*s-op*) or operands (*s-rd*).

The expression $(X + Y) * Z$ can be represented as the tree in Fig. 10.8.

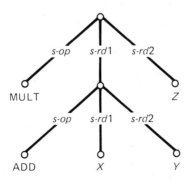

Figure 10.8

The control part of a machine state is also represented as a tree, where each node corresponds to an instruction. Some of these instructions may involve arguments whose assigned values may change during the course of the computation.

A sequence of instructions that, in indented form, might be written as:

$$\text{instr}_1$$
$$\text{instr}_2$$
$$\text{instr}_3$$
$$\text{instr}_4$$
$$\text{instr}_5$$

can be represented as the following tree:

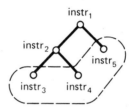

At any given time, any one of the instructions at a terminal leaf, $\{\text{instr}_3, \text{instr}_4, \text{instr}_5\}$, is a candidate for being executed. There are two types of effects that can result from the execution of an instruction. First, the execution at a terminal node may result in a subtree being appended to the tree at that node ("self-replacing" or macro-operation effect). Note that this still preserves the tree structure of the control tree. Second, the execution may have a "value returning" effect where that particular instruction node, and branch leading to it, are deleted from the control tree, and values specified by the instruction are passed to argument places of instructions at predecessor nodes of the control tree.

The execution of a given program then proceeds as a sequencing of control trees, uniquely determined by that program. At any timestep, all the relevant information implicit in a machine computation: the values of all intermediate computed quantities, registers, Boolean variables, the instruction(s) to be next executed, all stored data, etc., can be read off the control tree. The control tree is thus analogous to the instantaneous description of a Turing machine, and the implementation of the program in this manner defines its semantics in unequivocal manner.

10.10 LINCOS, A LANGUAGE FOR COSMIC INTERCOURSE

In 1960 a remarkable book, *LINCOS, Design of a Language for Cosmic Intercourse* [6], by the mathematician H. Freudenthal, was published. At first consideration, this might seem to be a rather unusual title for a publication that appeared within a series devoted to studies in logic and the foundations of mathematics. Some aspects of this work relate to the semantics of formal languages, and we shall briefly discuss some of the key ideas and the provocative questions raised in this study.

"LINCOS" is an abbreviation of the Latin "*lingua cosmica*" for "cosmic language." The author considers the problem of communicating by radio signals with extraterrestrial intelligent beings—"receivers" of our messages about whom we know nothing, but that are assumed to be "human-like" in their thinking processes and in some of their experiences. He sets himself the following problem. How can we communicate sophisticated ideas, related to the human experience, to these receivers of our messages? In fact, he seeks a vehicle that will be adequate to communicate the whole of human knowledge. Supposing that radio signals of various wavelengths and durations are used to encode the basic units from which the words in the vocabulary of the language Lincos are formed, a message will consist of a string of such signals. How, then, can we compose a rich language and, more importantly, *teach* that language to the receivers? The problem is a great deal more formidable than that faced by two humans who do not speak any common language and who try to communicate with each other. In this latter case, speech intensity, facial gestures, pointing at surrounding objects, and so forth, are all available as aids to communication. Or, for that matter, when we teach a small child to talk during the earliest stages of learning a language we must be able to identify freely people, things, and events in his or her immediate surroundings and associate these with basic words of the language. Learning a language when no metalanguage is available for use might seem to be an impossible task without such natural aids.

Here, however, not only can no questions be asked by the learner (i.e., there is no feedback in the learning process), but there is no environment external to the message, at least in the early stages of language usage. (This is not completely true in the case of Lincos. For example, Freudenthal uses radio signals of specified duration to define time intervals. In this case, the signal *is*, to some extent, the thing it represents.) The universe can, in a sense, be considered to be reduced to a string of symbols. Is it possible, within these confines, to teach the intelligent receivers, who probably live in a world very different from ours, a language with a vocabulary that includes words for complex behavioral concepts, apparently far removed from the domain of numbers? Examples of such words within the Lincos vocabulary include "good," "bad," "to wish," "to promise," "decency," and so forth. The author sets no limits on those notions of human experience, cognition, or behavior that might eventually be expressed within the language and taught to the receivers.

It is perhaps noteworthy at this point to recall that our first conscious attempt to communicate with extraterrestrial intelligences was the diagram-

$*$ Ha Inq Ha ⌐

$\wedge n \colon Fn \cdot \leftrightarrow \cdot \vee \ulcorner a . b . c \urcorner \colon a \cup b \cup c . \subset Num \cdot \wedge \cdot a^n + b^n = c^n \colon$

$\wedge \colon \wedge n \colon n \in Pri . \rightarrow \cdot \colon F'n . \leftrightarrow \cdot \vee \ulcorner a . b . c \urcorner \colon a \cup b \cup c . \subset Num \cdot$

$\wedge \cdot \neg . n \, Div \, a \cdot \wedge \cdot \neg . n \, Div \, b \cdot \wedge \cdot \neg . n \, Div \, c \cdot \wedge \cdot a^n + b^n = c^n \colon$

$\wedge \colon G \leftrightarrow \cdot \neg \vee n \colon n - 10 . \in Num \cdot \wedge . Fn$ ⌐

$\rightarrow \colon \neg \vee x \colon x \in Hom . \wedge . Nnc \, x \, Ext . \wedge \cdot Nnc \, x \, Sci . Utr \, G \cdot$

$Tan . \wedge x \colon x \in Hom . \wedge \colon Unq \cdot Sec \, 101 \times 10^{11111} . Ant \cdot Nnc \colon x \, Ext$

$\wedge \, Inq \, x \colon \vee y \colon y \in . Dem^{10} G \cdot$

$\wedge \cdot Nnc \, x \, Sci \colon Utr \cdot y \in . Dem^{10} G$ ⌐ $\cdot \wedge$ ⌐

$\vee x \colon x \in Hom . \wedge \colon Unq \cdot Sec \, 111 \times 10^{11101} . Ant \cdot Nnc \, x \, Ext \colon$

$\frown \colon x \, Dem \cdot \wedge n \colon n - 10 \in Num . \wedge . n < 1100100 \cdot \rightarrow . \neg \, Fn$ ⌐ $\wedge$ ⌐

$\vee x \colon x \in Hom . \wedge . Nnc \, x \, Ext . \wedge \colon PAN \, x \, Dem \cdot$

$\wedge n \colon n - 10 \in Num . \wedge . n < 100110100 \cdot \rightarrow . \neg \, Fn$ ⌐ $\wedge$ ⌐

$\vee x \colon x \in Hom . \wedge . Nnc \, x \, Ext . \wedge \colon PAN \, x \, Dem \cdot$

$\wedge n \colon n \in Pri . \wedge . n \neq 10 . \wedge . n < 10^{11100} \cdot \rightarrow . \neg \, F'n \, *$

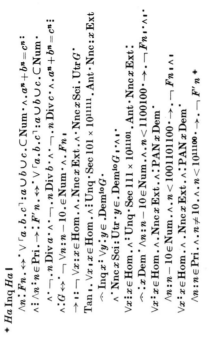

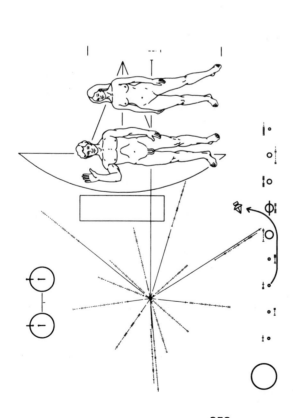

The engraved plate carried aboard Pioneer 10, launched in March, 1972. It contains information on the origin and epoch of the spacecraft, as well as announcing our presence. The Pioneer Plaque was designed by Frank D. Drake, Carl Sagan, and Linda S. Sagan.

A short piece of Lincos text containing a brief history of Fermat's Last Theorem (from Hans Freudenthal, *LINCOS, Design of a Language for Cosmic Intercourse*, Amsterdam: North-Holland Publishing Company, 1960). Reprinted by author's permission.

Fig. 10.9 Two messages for possible ultramundane civilizations—the first already sent, the second a specimen of Lincos text, but written for terrestrial readers.

matic plate (Fig. 10.9) installed in the 1972 Pioneer 10 space probe, and it did *not* consist of a stream of characters. Freudenthal indicates that in his work he is primarily interested in linguistic problems, and he has not paid much attention to communication using pictorial information or television. One might say that he has ignored "two-dimensional" messages as opposed to the "one-dimensional" messages consisting of streams of symbols. He does, however, write that he believes verbal descriptions to be superior to the use of television. He admits the possibility of using television after we succeed in teaching the receiver how to decode television transmitting signals.

How does one make a beginning in this ambitious program to make unworldly creatures worldly wise in our thoughts and ways? Freudenthal begins with mathematics, and this means, consistent with what we have said about the historical and logical development of mathematics, with the natural numbers. It is not difficult to construct starting messages which will signal to the unknown receivers that these messages are not of natural origin. Certainly an initial message such as

$$\bullet \quad \bullet \quad \bullet \quad \bullet \quad \bullet \quad \bullet \text{ and so forth,}$$

representing a sequence of uniform radio signals or "beeps," separated by equal pauses, will not do, since, for example, pulsars emit such signals.

However, a message such as

$$\bullet \mid \bullet \ \bullet \mid \bullet \ \bullet \ \bullet \mid \bullet \ \bullet \ \bullet \ \bullet \mid \bullet \ \bullet \ \bullet \ \bullet \mid \text{ and so forth,}$$

where the vertical bars represent longer equal pauses, should succeed in getting special attention.

The first section of the work, "Mathematics," is devoted to teaching a part of Lincos for communicating basic mathematics and logic. Freudenthal introduces new elements of the vocabulary as these are needed and teaches the semantics of this vocabulary, using what he calls the method of "quasi-general definitions." This is best explained by looking at an example of its use.

The first elements of the mathematical vocabulary that are introduced are the relational symbols of arithmetic $>, <, =$.

">" is defined by sending a large number of messages such as:

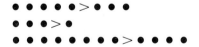

and so forth.

That is, it is expected that the receiver will *infer* the meaning of the word ">" from its repeated usage in a number of examples.

Similarly, the "=" might be defined by a train of messages such as

$$\bullet\ \bullet\ \bullet\ \bullet = \bullet\ \bullet\ \bullet\ \bullet$$
$$\bullet\ \bullet = \bullet\ \bullet$$
$$\bullet\ \bullet\ \bullet\ \bullet\ \bullet\ \bullet = \bullet\ \bullet\ \bullet\ \bullet\ \bullet\ \bullet$$

and so forth.

We leave it to the reader to supply the "texts" to teach the meanings of the "+" and "−" elements of the vocabulary.

Binary notation is defined in obvious fashion

$$\bullet = 1$$
$$\bullet\ \bullet = 10$$
$$\bullet\ \bullet\ \bullet = 11$$
$$\bullet\ \bullet\ \bullet\ \bullet = 100$$
$$\bullet\ \bullet\ \bullet\ \bullet\ \bullet = 101$$
$$\bullet\ \bullet\ \bullet\ \bullet\ \bullet\ \bullet = 110$$

and so forth.

Words that denote variables are introduced by long texts including messages such as

$$100 + a = 100 + a$$
$$100 + a > 10 + a$$
$$100 + a = a + 100$$
$$a + b = b + a$$

and so forth.

Step by step, new elements of the vocabulary are introduced, with their meanings to be inferred from many examples of usage that involve earlier defined words in the vocabulary. Everything rests on the natural numbers.

The author unfolds, along these lines, a substantial portion of elementary mathematics, extending to such topics as the elements of set theory and logic, the rudiments of group theory, of mathematical fields, and so forth. A final version of Lincos might, he indicates, include an exposition of the Calculus, this being a rather straightforward development using the vocabulary and tools introduced in this section. The exposition is quite persuasive of the feasibility of teaching a fully adequate language of mathematics to highly intelligent receivers.

The second part of the development of the language, "Time," is devoted to teaching a vocabulary for time-related concepts. Here, the actual durations of radio signals are used to define units of time. An example of the first series of messages in this section is

$$\mathrm{Dur}\ \overline{\quad\quad} = \mathrm{Sec}\ k.$$

Here, the upper bar denotes a sustained radio signal, and Dur, Sec are new elements of the vocabulary. The symbol "k" is a real number, understandable from its use in the first section on mathematics. This message represents the statement, "The duration of the time signal denoted by $\overline{}$ is k seconds." In this case, the meanings of *two* previously undefined elements (Dur, Sec) of the vocabulary must be inferred from the occurrence of many texts, using signals of varying duration and frequency. (The receiver must realize, or learn, that the frequency of the signal plays no role in the interpretation of the message.)

In this section, a Lincos "clock" is established, much like the built-in clocks of real computers, and the clock is used from this point on to time all Lincos program *events* and to provide a means of referring to them. The vocabulary is enriched to include facilities for referring to the past and the future and such words as "until" and "it happens" are introduced, among others.

The third section is, perhaps, the most interesting of all. It is entitled "Behavior," and here we begin to confront the problem of teaching concepts seemingly far removed from arithmetic. An interesting device to help in this task is employed. The author introduces fictitious (human) characters identified as $Ha, Hb, Hc, \ldots$. Later, the receiver will be told that these are members of the set called *Homo sapiens,* but at this point such clarification is not possible or necessary. He also finds it desirable to introduce a word "Inq" (from the Latin "inquit" for "says") to describe the act of speaking.

A key step at the beginning of this section is the introduction of words to denote "good" (Ben) and "bad" (Mal). Perhaps a look at a bit of Lincos text containing a brief dialogue designed to help the receiver infer the meaning of "good" for the new word "Ben" will be of interest.

$$^{t_1} Ha \operatorname{Inq} Hb \cdot ? \, x.10x = 101^{t_2}:$$
$$Hb \operatorname{Inq} Ha \cdot 101/10^{t_3}:$$
$$Ha \operatorname{Inq} Hb \operatorname{Ben}^{t_4}.$$

This text has been preceded by messages indicating that Ha, Hb are not numbers and Inq is not a member of any set. There has been no previous use of "Ben," and every other vocabulary element in the text has been defined earlier. A superscript small t denotes the clock time at the beginning or end of the event referenced by the position of the t.

The translation should then be clear to our terrestrial reader. "At time t_1, Ha begins asking Hb for the solution to the equation $2x = 5$, finishing his query at time t_2. Hb responds that $x = 5/2$, finishing his statement at time t_3. Ha says 'good.' Time t_4 marks the end of the dialogue."

Many examples of the use of "Ben" are given, and with different "actors" involved in the dialogues. These examples are expected to make clear, if our receiver has the "human-like" qualities we assume, that "Ben" has the meaning of "good" (and not, for example, that of "true"), just as a small child will learn the meaning of a word connoting an abstract idea by hearing it used many times and in different contexts.

Throughout this section the cast of characters engage in continuing dialogues leading to successive extensions of the vocabulary as new concepts are introduced. Words for "exists," "human," "animal," "wishes," "allows," "promises," "enough," "decent" are some of those introduced. Also, the fundamentals of ethics are defined, much as this might be explained to a small child.

The fourth section extends the vocabulary to cope with "Space, Motion, Mass." Much of this proceeds in a highly mathematical fashion, similar to the first section, with an introduction to the definition and salient properties of Euclidean spaces (such as the two- and three-dimensional spaces that one studies in analytic geometry). These new tools enable us to "speak" in Lincos of distances and measurements. Units of length, unlike the units of time defined by the durations of radio signals, are difficult to define. Eventually the "centimeter" is defined in terms of the velocity of light in a vacuum, which is a universal constant. This then makes feasible a description in Lincos, which can be communicated to the receiver, of the approximate physical makeup of humans and of objects of our world.

Two things are of special interest in all of the above. First is the assumption that the receiver will be able to infer the meanings of new words after seeing many examples of their usage in different contexts. Second is the fact that the whole development of the language rests, as does mathematics, on the natural numbers.

The semantics of Lincos are, as we have emphasized, left to the receiver to discern. The language was designed for receivers of "human-like" intelligence, and Freudenthal emphasizes that it was not intended for use with automata. Nevertheless, it is interesting to speculate on the extent to which a computer program might succeed in interpreting the semantics of such a language, as we expect an intelligent receiver to be able to do this. Some parts of this problem, relating especially to the vocabulary of mathematics, can be tackled using ideas from the study of computational complexity that appear in Chapter 11. Suppose, for example, we ask the computer to "infer" the meaning of "$+$" from a number of examples involving binary numbers such as:

$$1 + 1 = 10$$
$$101 + 11 = 1000$$
$$111 + 1101 = 10100$$

$$\vdots$$

There are, of course, many things that the computer might be programmed to do in inferring the meaning of the binary operation "+" from many examples of its use. It could, for example, store the data received for, say, 10,000, input examples in a table. It might, then, interpret the symbol for new arguments not in the table by seeking the result for the closest arguments that do appear in the table.

It is reasonable, however, to assume that the "+" should be taken to mean the *simplest*, in some sense, computer operation that will explain the large number of given examples. That is, we should perhaps program the computer to seek the shortest (suitably defined in terms of space or time) subroutine that will give a result that is consistent with the many examples. Expressed in these terms, the problem becomes one in complexity theory.

The situation is quite analogous to what is involved in those typical questions of intelligence tests that involve writing down the next few numbers of a given sequence. If, say, one is asked to continue the sequence $2, 5, 11, 23, 47, 95, \ldots$, there are an infinite number of formulas that could be used to compute the six given numbers of the sequence and then continue the sequence in an infinite variety of different ways. However, it is, of course, the simplest such rule that is expected.

The reader will recognize that the belief that the simplest explanation is the proper one in these matters is in line with the philosophical principle of Ockham's razor. This enjoiner prescribes economy in the explanation of things. To quote the fourteenth century English philosopher William of Ockham, "What can be done with fewer [assumptions] is done in vain with more."

It is, however, far from clear how we should best approach the problem of assigning meaning, within the computer, to those parts of the vocabulary related to human behavior.

EXERCISES

10.1 Show that the transformation on instantaneous descriptions defined by an arbitrary Turing machine can be defined by a context-sensitive grammar *if* we do not allow the length of tape used, or, that is, the distance between end-of-tape marks, to diminish in the course of a computation. Without such a restriction, it is necessary to use a type 0 grammar to define this mapping on instantaneous descriptions.

10.2 It is not true that a decision procedure exists to determine if an arbitrary sentence is or is not in a given type 0 language $L(G)$. Why not? Show, however, that it is possible to recognize (in the sense in which this word has been used in the text) such a language by a nondeterministic Turing machine. That is, show how, for a given type 0 grammar G, we can easily define such a machine so that *some* computational path will lead to the acceptance of an input sentence s if $s \in L(G)$.

10.3 Define a linear-bounded Turing machine that will recognize the sentences of the language $\{1^n0^n1^n \mid n \geq 1\}$.

10.4 Describe the behavior of a pushdown automaton that recognizes the sentences of the language $\{0^n1^n \mid n \geq 1\}$. Use a table, as in the text, to specify the actions of the automaton.

10.5 Describe a pushdown automaton that will recognize, in one pass through its input tape, the sentences of the language $\{uu' \mid u \varepsilon \{0, 1\}^+\}$, where u' is the string u written backwards.

10.6 Show that every context-free language can be defined by a grammar whose productions are all of the form $A \rightarrow BC$ or $A \rightarrow b$, where A, B, C are nonterminals, and b is a terminal. (A grammar written in this form is said to be in Chomsky normal form.) What does the syntax tree for every sentence in the language then look like?

10.7 If L is a context-free language and S is some subset of L, is S necessarily context free?

10.8 Suppose that $L_1(G_1), L_2(G_2)$ are two context-free languages, defined respectively by grammars G_1, G_2. Show that $L_1 \cup L_2$ is a context-free language.

10.9 Show that the intersection of two context-free languages is not necessarily a context-free language. (*Hint*: Use the fact that $\{0^n1^n0^n \mid n \geq 1\}$ is not a context-free language.)

10.10 Show that the language

$$\{\alpha w \beta w \gamma \mid w \in \Sigma^+\},$$

where the alphabet Σ has at least two symbols, say 0, 1, and α, β, γ are fixed words in Σ^+, is *not* context free. (Use the *uvwxy* theorem.)

10.11 Show that the intersection $C \cap R$ of any context-free (type 2) language C and any regular set R (type 3 language) is a context-free language. Fill in the necessary details in the following outline of a proof.

  Sketch of proof: Suppose that C is defined by the context-free grammar G, with initial symbol σ and vocabulary V, and that R is the set of strings accepted by some finite automaton A ($R = T(A)$). Let $\mathscr{D}$ denote the set of states of A. We shall construct a context-free grammar G', that is based upon G and A. We shall do this in such a way that a derivation, using G', of a sentence s in $C \cap R$ will "monitor" the reading and acceptance of s by A, as well as implying a derivation of s, using G. The vocabulary V' of G' will include the same terminal vocabulary of V, and in addition it will include all words of the form $(q_i S q_j)$ where $q_i, q_j \in \mathscr{D}$ and $S \in V$.

  Replace any production in G of the form

$$\sigma \rightarrow S_1 S_2 \cdots S_n$$

by the *set* of productions

$$(q_0 \sigma q_f) \rightarrow (q_0 S_1 q^{(1)})(q^{(1)} S_2 q^{(2)}) \cdots (q^{(n-1)} S_n q_f)$$

where q_0 is the initial state of A, q_f takes on all possible acceptance states of A, and $q^{(1)}, q^{(2)}, \ldots, q^{(n-1)}$ take on all possible values in $\mathscr{D}$.

Replace every production in G with left-hand side $S \neq \sigma$,

$$S \to S_1 S_2 \cdots S_n,$$

by the *set* of productions of the form

$$(q^{(0)} S q^{(n)}) \to (q^{(0)} S_1 q^{(1)})(q^{(1)} S_2 q^{(2)}) \cdots (q^{(n-1)} S_n q^{(n)})$$

for all possible $q^{(i)} \in \mathcal{Y}$ $(i = 0, 1, \ldots, n)$.

Further, for each terminal τ in V, add the productions

$$(q_i \tau q_j) \to \tau$$

for those pairs of states q_i, q_j satisfying τ: $q_i \to q_j$ in A. (That is, if A is in state q_i and reads τ, it changes to state q_j.)

It is then not difficult to show that $L(G') = C \cap R$, proving the stated result.

10.12 Using the result of the preceding problem, complete the proof of the result cited in the text, that ALGOL is not context free.

We have seen that the set of programs

$$S = \{\text{BEGIN INTEGER } w; \ w := 1; \ \text{END}\}$$

is not context free. Letting ALG denote the set of well-formed ALGOL programs, define a regular set R so that $S = ALG \cap R$. Thus, if ALG were context free so also would S be context free. Hence, ALG is not context free.

10.13 Does Post's Correspondence Problem have a solution for the following pairs of lists?

    a. $U = (ab, ba, aa)$, $V = (abb, aaa, a)$
    b. $U = (x, xx, xyx, yxx)$, $V = (xx, xyx, yxx, xyxx)$.

10.14 We have shown in this chapter that a general solution to the Correspondence Problem would enable us to solve the halting problem for a *particular* Turing machine, and we have implied that our argument could be extended to any machine. Write down all the details needed to cast the given proof in general terms. That is, make the proof of unsolvability rigorous by showing that a general solution of the Correspondence Problem could be used to provide a solution to the halting problem for an *arbitrary* Turing machine starting on a blank tape.

10.15 Show that the Correspondence Problem *is* solvable if the alphabet Σ includes only one symbol.

10.16 We have shown that there is no general algorithmic solution to the Correspondence Problem for lists of words composed from an arbitrary alphabet of more than one symbol. That is, we have seen that there is *some* such alphabet for which the problem is unsolvable. Show that the problem is unsolvable if the alphabet Σ consists of two symbols.

10.17 Show that the multiplication of relations is associative, i.e., if R, S, T are three given relations, then

$$(RS)T = R(ST).$$

(Both sides will be the null set when the multiplication is undefined.)

10.18 Show that the transitive closure R^+ of a relation R is transitive, i.e., if aR^+b and bR^+c, then aR^+c.

10.19 Given a context-free grammar G, let A denote one of the nonterminals in the vocabulary V, and let α be some arbitrary element of V. Consider the problem of determining if a derivation exists of the form

$$A \Rightarrow \ast \; \alpha \cdots .$$

That is, can A be used to derive some string that begins with α? (This relation between A and α is often written as A FIRST $\ast$ α.)

The problem is readily solved by computing the transitive closure of an appropriate relation. Show how this can be done. Apply this result to the grammar (5) in Section 10.6. Determine for every pair of symbols A, α in V whether or not A FIRST $\ast$ α.

10.20 An example of a maze, or labyrinth, is shown below. The problem for such configurations is to find a path, if one exists, from a designated starting chamber S to some "goal" chamber G. In the case of a small maze, as in our example, the problem can be readily solved by visual inspection. This is not true for large mazes.

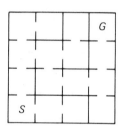

a. Define an appropriate relation R, with finite domain consisting of all the chambers in the maze, so that the existence, or nonexistence, of a solution can be determined by computing the transitive closure $R^\ast$.

b. Describe how to modify the computation of $R^\ast$ so as to solve the problem of the maze, and not merely determine the existence of a solution. That is, show how to compute a path connecting S to G if one exists.

10.21 Represent the following expression as a tree, using the Vienna Definition Language notation.

$$(x + y) + \{[z - (x \ast (y + z))] \div (x - y)\}.$$

REFERENCES

1. Aho, A. V., and J. D. Ullman, *The Theory of Parsing, Translation and Compiling,* Vol. 1: *Parsing,* 1972; Vol. 2: *Compiling,* 1973. Englewood Cliffs, N.J.: Prentice-Hall.

2. Aho, A. V., and J. D. Ullman, *Principles of Compiler Design.* Reading, Massachusetts: Addison-Wesley, 1977.

3. Cooper, D. C., "Programs for Mechanical Program Verification," in *Machine Intelligence.* Eds. B. Meltzer, and D. Michie, Vol. 6. Edinburgh University Press, 1971.

4. Floyd, R. W., *New Proofs and Old Theorems in Logic and Formal Linguistics.* Wakefield, Massachusetts: Computer Associates, Inc., 1964.

5. Floyd, R. W., "Assigning Meanings to Programs." *Proceedings of the Symposium on Applied Mathematics,* **19.** American Mathematical Society, 1967.

6. Freudenthal, H., *LINCOS, Design of a Language for Cosmic Intercourse.* Amsterdam: North-Holland Publishing Company, 1960.

7. Goldstine, H. H., and J. Von Neumann, "Planning and Coding Problems for an Electronic Computing Instrument," 1947, in *Collected Works of John Von Neumann,* Vol. 5. Ed. by A. H. Taub. New York: Pergamon Press, 1963.

8. Gries, D., *Compiler Construction for Digital Computers.* New York: John Wiley, 1971.

9. Hantler, S. L., and J. C. King, "An Introduction to Proving the Correctness of Programs." *Computing Surveys,* **8,** 3 (September 1976).

10. Harrison, M. A., *Introduction to Formal Language Theory.* Reading, Massachusetts: Addison-Wesley, 1978.

11. Hopcroft, J. E., and J. D. Ullman, *Formal Languages and Their Relations to Automata.* Reading, Massachusetts: Addison-Wesley, 1969.

12. Igarashi, S., R. L. London, and D. C. Luckham, *Automatic Program Verification I: Logical Basis and Its Implementation.* Computer Science Report 356. Stanford, California: Stanford University, May 1, 1973.

13. Katz, S. M., and Z. Manna, "A Heuristic Approach to Program Verification." *Third International Joint Conference on Artificial Intelligence.* Stanford, California, August 1973.

14. King, J. C., "A Program Verifier." Ph.D. dissertation, Carnegie-Mellon University, Pittsburgh, Pennsylvania, 1969. Published in the *Proceedings of the International Federation of Information Processing Societies,* 1971.

15. Knuth, D. E., "On the Translation of Languages from Left to Right." *Information and Control,* **8** (1965).

16. Lewis II, P. M., D. J. Rosenkrantz, and R. E. Stearns, *Compiler Design Theory.* Reading, Massachusetts: Addison-Wesley, 1976.

17. Lucas, P., P. Lauer, and H. Stigleitner, *Method and Notation for the Formal Definition of Programming Languages.* Technical Report 25.087, IBM Laboratory. Vienna, 1968.

18. Lucas, P., and K. Walk, "On the Formal Description of PL/I." *Ann. Rev. Automatic Program.,* **6,** 3 (1969).

19. Manna, Z., *Mathematical Theory of Computation.* New York: McGraw-Hill, 1974.

20. Minsky, M. L., *Computation: Finite and Infinite Machines.* Englewood Cliffs, N.J.: Prentice-Hall, 1967.

21. Post, E. L., "A Variant of a Recursively Unsolvable Problem." *Bull. Amer. Math. Soc.,* **52** (1946).

22. Wegbreit, B., "Heuristic Methods for Mechanically Deriving Inductive Assertions." *Third International Joint Conference on Artificial Intelligence.* Stanford, California, August 1973.

23. Wegner, P., "The Vienna Definition Language." *Computing Surveys,* **4,** (March 1972).

11
Studies of Computational Complexity

A principal goal of the study of computational complexity is to learn how to design optimal or most efficient computational procedures for a given problem. No area of computer science is as replete with such a variety of seemingly disjoint topics, and it is perhaps wrong, or at least misleading, to speak of a "theory" of complexity. But there clearly is a common thread running through all of these studies—the concern with defining, assessing, classifying, minimizing the complexity of computation. We shall in this chapter give a number of examples of key results. This is a period of gathering of evidence, and one gets the impression that there is a groping toward a recognition of structure and toward a deeper understanding of the phenomena of computation, with the most powerful results yet to come.

The fundamental notions of the measurement of the extent of "information" are relevant to these studies, and the information content of a finite sequence may be described in terms of the complexity of the smallest finite machine that can write that sequence. One aspect of the complexity of procedures is the complexity of the machines which execute these procedures. We have already noted the use of the state-symbol product to serve as a measure of the complexity of a Turing machine. In other instances, the depth of a machine circuit made up of logical gates determines the time required for some kinds of processing and may be an appropriate measure of complexity.

Some very general measures of complexity can be given in terms of the consumption of some means, or available resource, during a computation, e.g., the total time or the extent of memory used. Such measures satisfy a few simple axioms which are independent of any particular machine on which a computation might be executed. One surprising consequence of this axio-

369

matic formulation is that one cannot expect to be able to optimize the computation of every function. The "Speed-Up Theorem" asserts the existence of a computable function f with the property that for any given program that computes f there is another program that computes f a great deal faster for almost all arguments.

A hierarchy of functions based on a classification of complexity can be achieved in a number of ways. The simplest functions are those that are computable by finite automata. Each class of functions in the Ritchie hierarchy of the "predictably computable" functions includes those functions whose complexity can be computed by a function in the next lower class. The totality of functions so obtained constitute the "elementary arithmetic functions," a proper subset of the primitive recursive functions.

The automata that we have considered are made up of various building blocks that can be described as "fan-in components," organs that have two or more input lines and one output line. A simple argument leads to certain minimal bounds on the time required by a machine made up of such components to compute a given function. In particular, it is possible to establish lower bounds on the time needed for the execution of the arithmetic operations of addition and multiplication. It turns out that the most efficient existing implementations of these operations are close to these lower bounds.

There are a number of examples in computing of "time-space trade-offs," of decreasing the time needed for a computation at the expense of increased use of memory or other physical facilities. Conversely, we can often reduce the physical requirements of a computation at the cost of an increased length of computation.

A "real-time" computation is one, as in certain applications in the real world, where the result is available as soon as the input data is read. The study of such procedures is still another topic of complexity.

Rabin's use of "probabilistic" algorithms admits, for some problems, solution procedures that require far less time than algorithms that are completely deterministic. In these cases a conclusion is reached not to the effect that "the number N has property P" but rather that "the probability is very close to 1 that the number N has property P." These procedures cast a new light on the search for truth in mathematics.

11.1   COMPLEXITY AND SIMPLICITY

complex (Roget): intricate, complicated, perplexed, involved, ravelled, entangled, knotted, inextricable.

We have an intuitive understanding of what it means for a description, a set of instructions, a procedure, an algorithm, a program, a function, a machine, a proof, a theory, a pattern to be complex—to lack simplicity and order. If something is overly complex it not only contains superfluous features, it lacks beauty. In the sciences and in mathematics we tend to consider overly complex theories as being unclean and temporary, not really representative of nature—for we have faith that the closer we get to ultimate truth, the less contrived will our explanations appear. (It should perhaps be mentioned that not everyone concurs that science marches inexorably forward toward ultimate truth, with more elegant and powerful theories, e.g., see Thomas S. Kuhn, *The Structure of Scientific Revolution.*)

In computing, our goals are not only aesthetic, but they are quite practical. We should like ultimately to be able to design programs and machines that are as efficient as possible. In recent years studies of complexity in computer science have taken a great variety of forms, and we shall give a number of examples of these and of results that have been obtained. In some cases, our grappling with the notion of computational complexity provides a new insight into the meaning of complexity in situations that may appear to be far removed from the computer.

If, for example, we say that the pattern

0	1	0	1	0	1
1	0	1	0	1	0
0	1	0	1	0	1
1	0	1	0	1	0
0	1	0	1	0	1
1	0	1	0	1	0

is less "complex" than the pattern

A	C	K	R	B	E
D	U	A	C	K	K
B	A	C	D	U	T
S	S	M	O	J	Y
C	D	E	X	A	U
K	Y	L	Q	A	G

we (probably) mean that the first array can be described very simply, while the second appears to lack order, and thus the only way to describe it completely appears to be to list the elements of the array. If the second array were extended in similar random fashion to, say, 1,000 rows and 1,000 columns, the length of its description would be much greater than the length of the description for a correspondingly larger version of the first array. In computational terms, a much shorter program could be used to print out the first array than would be needed for the second array, especially so if we consider larger versions of these arrays.

When it is said that the often criticized set of instructions for the U.S. federal tax forms are very complex, this may mean, among other things, that a machine language program needed to execute the procedure for the tax computation would contain an exorbitant number of conditional tests and transfer instructions.

If we say that some computable function is more "complex" than another, we expect that more "work" and/or greater resources in some form are needed to obtain the values of the more complex function—perhaps a program that is longer or more complicated in some sense—or a longer computation is needed or one that requires more storage when executed.

A key objective of the structured programming approach is to develop programs that are less complicated (e.g., involve no, or at least fewer, GO TO's), are better structured with a "cleaner" design and, hence, are more easily debugged.

We often speak of a configuration of things having some "order" or "pattern" or "regularity." We may mean in many cases that it is possible to write a short description or, perhaps, to write a simple (short, not too many machine transfers) program that can generate as output a representation of the configuration. If there is no "order," but a completely "random" arrangement prevails, we expect that a complete description enabling someone to copy the configuration would be no shorter than the configuration itself.

11.2 REMARKS ON THE MATHEMATICAL DESCRIPTION OF RATES OF GROWTH

In considering the complexity of problems of computer science we are usually concerned with assessing the tractability of a problem. Is the problem something that requires a lengthy but still manageable solution, or is it something that is hopelessly beyond reach, like the problem of writing the decimal representation of the value of Ackermann's function at $(4, 4)$?

We usually deal with a *class* of problems that involve some parameters, and the complexity of any one problem in the class is a function of these parameters. For example, the time needed to multiply two n-digit numbers clearly depends, if resources are kept fixed, upon the value of n; the bigger n is, the more time will be needed to arrive at the result. Or, the number of arithmetic operations required to find the solutions to a system of n simultaneous linear equations obviously is a function of n. In these cases we may want to indicate how these problems grow in complexity as the defining parameters increase in size.

Suppose that the complexity, measured in some appropriate way, is denoted by y, and the problem statement involves a parameter x. The variation of y with x is best seen from the graph of the function $y = f(x)$.

If the graph showing the functional relationship $y = f(x)$ between two

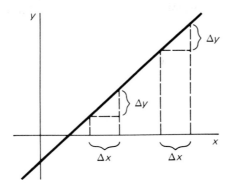

Figure 11.1

variables x, y is a straight line (Fig. 11.1), we say that the dependent variable varies *linearly* with the independent variable. A constant change Δx in x results in a constant change Δy in y, no matter what the value of x.

If y is a polynomial in x, $y = c_1 x^n + c_2 x^{n-1} + \ldots + c_{n+1}$, the graph may take a variety of forms depending upon the values of n and the coefficients. However, we are usually interested in the behavior of problems as the defining parameters become big, and for large x the first term $c_1 x^n$ dominates the expression (since x^n is x times as big as x^{n-1}).

Very rapid growth of y with respect to x occurs when the functional relationship is exponential, i.e., $y = ca^x$. A simple application of the differential calculus shows that this functional relationship is equivalent to saying that y changes at a rate that is proportional to its size. If $a > 1$, y "grows exponentially" (Fig. 11.2a); if $0 < a < 1$, y "decays exponentially" (Fig. 11.2b). A change of Δx in x results in the ordinate y being *multiplied* by the constant factor $a^{\Delta x}$.

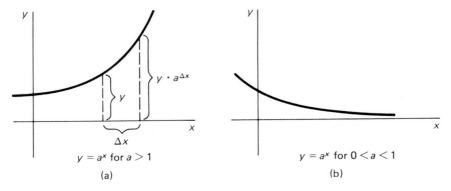

$y = a^x$ for $a > 1$

(a)

$y = a^x$ for $0 < a < 1$

(b)

Figure 11.2

For $a > 1$, the bigger y is, the faster it grows, and for large x the curve is very steep. This kind of growth is characteristic of that of an animal population when there is no limit imposed by restricted space, food supply, predators or other growth limiting factors. This is an example of explosive growth and is in fact descriptive of some of the ongoing physical processes during the explosion of an atomic bomb.

If, for some constant k, the variable y is bounded by kx, i.e., $y < kx$, we often write

$$y = O(x).$$

This is read as "y is of the order of x," or "y is large O of x." In writing this, we are not concerned with the precise mathematical statement of the relationship between y and x but simply wish to indicate that for large x, y grows approximately as x does—that is, the ratio of y to x is bounded. If we write $y = O(\log x)$, a slow growth of y is indicated; y is bounded by some multiple of $\log x$.

If y grows linearly with x this implies that $y = O(x)$. The converse is not true (why not?). Similarly, polynomial growth in y implies that $y = O(x^n)$ for some n, and exponential growth in y implies that $y = O(a^x)$ for some a. Exponential growth is much faster than growth of the order of x^n for any n.

11.3   THE MATHEMATICAL MEASURE OF INFORMATION

Related to the notion of complexity is the concept of the amount of "information" inherent in a message or a configuration. A mathematical theory of information has developed within the last half-century, most notably in the work of Shannon [11]. Among other things, it provides a precise mathematical definition of the measure of information. If we toss a coin, the information implicit in knowing whether the coin falls heads or tails is certainly less than the information in the knowledge of which one of the six possible throws of a die occurs. It is much less than that in knowing the winning number in a lottery of 1,000,000 participants. In each case, the information concerns knowing which event of a set of possible equally likely events has occurred. At the low end of the scale no information at all is included in the knowledge that a two-headed coin falls heads or, in general, in knowing that a particular event has occurred when there is only one possibility for that event.

If there are m equally likely possible configurations of a system, the information implicit in knowing which one of the m configurations occurs should certainly depend upon m, and the larger that m is, the more information is represented by that knowledge. However, we show that it is desirable to use something other than m itself as a measure of this information content.

Consider a message consisting of a single word W_1 chosen from a vocabulary of m words.

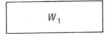

Suppose we couple this word with another word W_2 chosen from a vocabulary of n words, yielding the message $W_1 W_2$

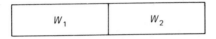

It appears reasonable that the information content of the two-word message $W_1 W_2$ should be the sum of the information contents of the individual words W_1, W_2. However, the number of possible configurations of $W_1 W_2$ is mn not $m + n$. Therefore, we use not the number m of possible configurations as a measure of information content but some function f, to be determined, of m.

It remains to make a suitable choice of the function f. It appears from our considerations that we should have

$$f(mn) = f(m) + f(n). \tag{11.1}$$

Further, if $m > n$ we certainly want

$$f(m) > f(n). \tag{11.2}$$

It can be shown from (11.1), (11.2) that $f(m)$ must be taken as log m to some base b. The smallest amount of nonzero information occurs when there are just two equally likely configurations, or when $m = 2$. It is reasonable to pick a measure of information that gives the value 1 for this fundamental case, the information content of a binary bit. To achieve this we use as base $b = 2$ (i.e., $\log_2 2 = 1$). Thus, we arrive at the definition of the information content implicit in the knowledge of which one of m equally likely configurations occurs as

$$\log_2 m.$$

The information provided by one decimal digit is then

$$\log_2 10 \doteq 3.322.$$

The information in knowing the winning number in a lottery of 1,000,000 numbers is

$$\log_2 1{,}000{,}000 \doteq 19.932.$$

An ASCII character represents an information content of

$$\log_2 256 = 8.$$

Consider the set of all programs of length 30 statements written in 10-statement FORTRAN. If we ignore the fact that not all sequences of 30 statements are equally likely as programs, the information in knowing merely the sequence of statement types that occur in a particular 30-statement program is

$$\log_2 (10^{30}) \doteq 99.658.$$

11.4 THE INFORMATION CONTENT OF A FINITE SEQUENCE

If we are given a string of 1,000,000 zeros, this string can be described very simply (as we have just done) without the necessity of writing it out. Our brief description (as "a string of 1,000,000 zeros") would enable anyone, or a machine, to produce it in its entirety if this were necessary. On the other hand, it is not clear that anything much shorter than the actual string could be used to replace something as complex as the string of characters that constitutes the entire *Encyclopedia Britannica* (we ignore the savings in representation that can be achieved by data compaction devices; in fact, assume that we are looking at an encyclopedia that has already been so encoded).

We concern ourselves with defining the information content, along lines suggested by Kolmogorov [4] and Chaitin [2], of an arbitrary string of characters drawn from some alphabet. The situation is rather different from that which we have considered in the preceding section. There, we assumed that we were given a "message" that was one of a number of equally likely messages, and we wanted to assign a measure to the "information content" implicit in knowing which one of the possible set of message configurations occurs. Here, we are concerned with the "structure" of the message beyond its mere distinctness from other possible messages.

The information content of a sequence S is defined to be the length in bits of the shortest program that can write the sequence S. In defining "shortest program" it is natural to do this in terms of Turing machines so that the shortest program is interpreted as the set of quintuples requiring the fewest number of binary bits to write. We can equally well consider the shortest program in terms of the universal Turing machine U. The "program" would then be the description of that Turing machine T which might be given as input to U and would lead to U writing the sequence S when it simulates T.

A Turing machine that writes out 1,000,000 zeros will be rather small, but a machine that writes out the encyclopedia will have to be about as extensive (in terms of the number of bits required to represent all its quintuples) as the encyclopedia itself.

11.5   COMPLEXITY OF MACHINES

Before looking at a variety of issues related to complexity, we consider some simple examples of appropriate measures of complexity for some machines—for logical circuits, finite automata, and for Turing machines.

In discussing the applications of Boolean algebra and in composing automata from basic building blocks we have used circuits employing logical gates or neurons as basic components. It is reasonable to define the complexity of a machine composed of such organs to be the number of these elementary organs that appear in its construction, this being a measure of the "size" of the machine. On the other hand, the *time* that the machine requires to furnish its output may be more significant to us. In this latter case we could consider a more appropriate measure, preferable to the size of the machine, to be the "depth" of the circuit, where depth is defined as the maximum path length from the input to any organ (i.e., we are looking at the circuit as a digraph with nodes at the gates and path directions conforming to signal flow). The depth is then the time, measured in some unit, required for an electrical signal to reach the organ that is furthest (in number of path segments) from the input. Ignoring feedback, which will depend on the input signals, this would be the greatest time for a signal to pass through the machine from input to output.

Even in this simple example we see that we can emphasize either *space* (i.e., the size of the machine) or *time* (the depth of its circuit). This point will be given additional emphasis in later examples.

The complexity of a finite automaton, with prescribed alphabet, can be defined to be simply the number of its states. Given any finite automaton recognizer we have considered the state minimization problem and noted that we can apply a procedure to obtain an equivalent automaton, i.e., one that recognizes the same set of tapes, with the smallest possible number of states. In this case the problem of finding the simplest (or least complex) automaton is a solvable one. In general, this will not be the case.

The number of states taken alone would not constitute a proper definition of the complexity of a Turing machine for, given any Turing machine of more than two states, it is possible to replace this machine by one that computes the same function and that employs only *two* states (cf. Exercise 6.19 and [12]). The two-state machine will, however, need a larger alphabet than the machine it replaces.

In the discussion of universal Turing machines in Chapter 6, we implicitly made use of a measure of complexity for Turing machines. We made brief reference to the search for the "smallest" universal Turing machine where "smallest" meant the machine having the smallest product $m \times n$ of m, the number of symbols in its alphabet, multiplied by n, the number of its internal states. It is this state-symbol product that is usually taken as a measure of the complexity of a Turing machine (cf. Shannon [12]).

The justification for this definition is based on two facts. First, it seems reasonable that a machine's complexity should be defined so that it is proportional to the number of its internal states and to the size of its alphabet. If the number of states, or if the alphabet is doubled, the "complexity" should be doubled. Second, and perhaps more important, Shannon shows that the state-symbol product stays approximately constant when certain simple transformations of a Turing machine are made to obtain an equivalent machine with either fewer states or with a smaller alphabet. To decrease the size of the alphabet, the number of states must increase; as the number of states decreases, the size of the alphabet must increase. There is a form of tradeoff between states and symbols that keeps the product approximately constant.

We saw in Chapter 5 (cf. Exercise 5.16) that it is possible to replace any machine T that uses an alphabet of m symbols, where $m > 2$, by a machine T' that uses an alphabet of only two symbols. This is done at the expense of increasing the number n of states. Each symbol S_j in the alphabet of T is replaced by a *field* of binary characters. Each quintuple $q_i S_j$ --- in T is replaced by a set of quintuples that manipulates these fields as the original quintuples manipulated the individual symbols before binary encoding. Looking at the details of the coding needed to accomplish this, we can see that, while the alphabet of T' is reduced to two symbols, the number of states of T' is $O(mn)$, i.e., the number of states of T' is less than Kmn for some constant K that holds for all Turing machines. Thus, the state-symbol product for T' is $O(mn)$. Except for a constant multiplication factor, this bound is the same as the state symbol product for T.

Similarly, Shannon shows that a Turing machine T of n states, where $n > 2$, can be replaced by a machine T'' of two states that computes the same function as does T. T'' simulates T. It uses a tape that looks exactly like the tape of T but it records an indication of the state of T by writing special characters on the tape square being scanned and on the square that T would next read. Again, the coding shows that while the number of states is reduced to two, the number of characters in the new alphabet will be $O(mn)$. As before, the state-symbol product stays approximately invariant.

11.6 SOME VARIED PROBLEMS OF COMPLEXITY THEORY

Finding efficient algorithms for a given class of problems.   Much of numerical analysis concerns the search for efficient algorithms to solve mathematical problems. The efficiency of an algorithm is often assessed in terms of the number of arithmetic operations—of additions/subtractions and of multiplications/divisions required to arrive at a satisfactory solution. A more effi-

cient algorithm will involve less computer time for the solution. Depending
on the ratio of a computer's multiply time to its add time, the number of
multiplications/divisions may be much more significant than the number of
additions/subtractions. We mention this area of complexity study because
of its importance, but, strictly speaking, most studies in this area belong to
numerical analysis rather than to the rapidly growing body of recent theoretical results relative to complexity.

As a simple example, consider the evaluation of the quadratic expression

$$ax^2 + bx + c.$$

For given a, b, c, x, this can obviously be evaluated by computing successively

$$x^2, ax^2, bx, ax^2 + bx, (ax^2 + bx) + c.$$

This involves 3 multiplications and 2 additions. Suppose, however, we write
the expression in the equivalent form

$$(ax + b)x + c.$$

This implies as a possible computation:

$$ax, ax + b, (ax + b)x, (ax + b)x + c,$$

and a savings of one multiplication has been obtained.

As a more complex example of a choice of methods, consider the problem of solving a set of simultaneous linear equations. In secondary school
algebra one learns at least one method for doing this, usually the method of
elimination. Let a system of n equations in n unknowns be written:

$$\begin{cases} a_{11}x_1 + a_{12}x_2 + \ldots + a_{1n}x_n = c_1 \\ a_{21}x_1 + a_{22}x_2 + \ldots + a_{2n}x_n = c_2 \\ \quad \vdots \\ a_{n1}x_1 + a_{n2}x_2 + \ldots + a_{nn}x_n = c_n \end{cases} \qquad (1)$$

An efficient elimination scheme might begin by dividing the first equa-
tion by a_{11}, assuming $a_{11} \neq 0$; if $a_{11} = 0$ rearrange the equations. It is in fact
desirable to have a comparatively large coefficient in this "pivotal" position.
Then subtract suitable multiples of the first equation from each of the other
equations to eliminate x_1 from each equation. The result of this first elimination will be $n - 1$ equations in $n - 1$ unknowns. Repeat the procedure to
eliminate x_2, then successively eliminate $x_3, x_4, \ldots, x_{n-1}$. The result of this
"forward" part of the elimination procedure will be a single equation in x_n.
This equation can be solved for x_n. Substituting back in an equation that
involves only x_{n-1}, x_n we can find x_{n-1}, then by repetition $x_{n-2}, x_{n-3}, \ldots, x_1$.
This phase of the procedure is called the "back" solution.

In general, this procedure is quite efficient, and certain variations in the procedure (such as "positioning for size") will improve the accuracy of the solution. A tally of the number of multiplications required for the complete solution gives approximately $1/3\ n^3$.

An alternative method to solve this problem would be to use "Cramer's rule" (usually taught in secondary school courses in "advanced algebra"). This expresses each solution x_i as the quotient of two determinants. Thus, the first unknown x_1 is given by

$$x_1 = \frac{\begin{vmatrix} c_1 & a_{12} & \cdots & a_{1n} \\ c_2 & a_{22} & \cdots & a_{2n} \\ & & \vdots & \\ c_n & a_{n2} & \cdots & a_{nn} \end{vmatrix}}{\begin{vmatrix} a_{11} & a_{12} & \cdots & a_{1n} \\ a_{21} & a_{22} & \cdots & a_{2n} \\ & & \vdots & \\ a_{n1} & a_{n2} & \cdots & a_{nn} \end{vmatrix}}$$

If we were to use this formula to find x_1, with similar expressions for $x_2, x_3, \ldots, x_n$, we might perhaps (naively) attempt to evaluate these determinants in a straightforward manner by expanding them directly from their definition.

A determinant of n rows and n columns, such as the denominator or numerator in the above expression, represents a sum of $n!$ terms. Each term is a product of n factors where these factors include one element from each row and from each column of the determinant with no two elements being from the same row or same column. A typical term is

$$a_{i_1 1}\, a_{i_2 2}\, a_{i_3 3} \cdots a_{i_n n}$$

where no two row subscripts are the same. A sign is attached to each such term determined by the tally of the number of times that a row index i_k precedes a row index $i_{k'}$ that is smaller. If this tally is even, the associated sign is $+$, if it is odd the sign is $-$.

(Thus, the 3rd order determinant

$$\begin{vmatrix} 2 & -3 & 1 \\ 4 & 2 & -2 \\ -1 & 3 & -4 \end{vmatrix}$$

represents the sum:

$$+ (2)(2)(-4) - (2)(3)(-2) - (4)(-3)(-4)$$
$$+ (4)(3)(1) + (-1)(-3)(-2) - (-1)(2)(1) = -44.)$$

The evaluation of a determinant of nth order by this method would involve $(n - 1)n!$ multiplications. The complete solution of n simultaneous linear equations by evaluating determinants in this way would involve approximately $n^2 \cdot n!$ multiplications/divisions. For large n, this number is much bigger than the $1/3 \, n^3$ multiplications required in the elimination procedure. Suppose, for example, we wish to solve a system of 100 linear equations. The elimination method would involve approximately $1/3$ (1,000,000) multiplications/divisions while the naive evaluation of determinants (there are more efficient schemes for computing determinants) and the use of Cramer's rule would involve more than 10^{160} multiplications.

In other words, the elimination method in this problem would be quite feasible on a modern computer, but a misguided use of Cramer's rule along the lines we have described would require more than 3×10^{20} years on a computer capable of multiplying two numbers in a picosecond (10^{-12} second). This time period is 10^{10} times as great as the estimated life of the universe (according to the "big bang" theory).

The moral is that the numerical analyst can be far more important than the speed of the computer in determining the feasibility of problem solution.

In other problems of data processing it may be more appropriate to assess the complexity of procedures by counting not arithmetic operations but other kinds of fundamental operations. For example, it is more appropriate in evaluating a technique for sorting an array of numbers to count the number of comparisons that have to be made rather than by counting non-existent arithmetic operations. We refer the reader to Knuth's encyclopedic coverage of sorting [3] for detailed analyses of a large number of such algorithms.

Strassen's improvement of the procedure for matrix multiplication. We give still another example of a reformulation of a problem solution that provides greater efficiency. This result concerns the operation of matrix multiplication, a fundamental operation that appears in many procedures of numerical analysis. In the appendix to Chapter 3 we reviewed the basic definition of matrix multiplication. In particular, the product of two 2×2 matrices is given by:

$$\begin{pmatrix} a_{11} \, a_{12} \\ a_{21} \, a_{22} \end{pmatrix} \begin{pmatrix} b_{11} \, b_{12} \\ b_{21} \, b_{22} \end{pmatrix} = \begin{pmatrix} a_{11}b_{11} + a_{12}b_{21} & a_{11}b_{12} + a_{12}b_{22} \\ a_{21}b_{11} + a_{22}b_{21} & a_{21}b_{12} + a_{22}b_{22} \end{pmatrix}$$

We see then that the computation of the four elements of the product involves 8 multiplications and 4 additions. The general tally of operations in multiplying two nth order matrices is easily shown, from the formula we have given earlier for the elements of the product matrix, to be n^3 multiplications and $n^2(n - 1)$ additions. As we have remarked, the tally of the number of multiplications is generally far more significant in assessing computational labor than the tally of the number of additions.

At first (or second) glance there does not seem much that one can do to rewrite the expressions for the elements of the 2×2 matrix product so that a savings in arithmetic multiplications can be achieved. However, Strassen [14] gave the surprising result that these four elements can be computed with a total of only 7 multiplications. Although the discovery of this fact is not at all obvious, its verification is quite straightforward.

Compute the following 7 products:

$$c_1 = (a_{11} + a_{22})(b_{11} + b_{22})$$
$$c_2 = (a_{21} + a_{22})b_{11}$$
$$c_3 = a_{11}(b_{12} - b_{22})$$
$$c_4 = a_{22}(-b_{11} + b_{21})$$
$$c_5 = (a_{11} + a_{12})b_{22}$$
$$c_6 = (-a_{11} + a_{21})(b_{11} + b_{12})$$
$$c_7 = (a_{12} - a_{22})(b_{21} + b_{22})$$

The four elements of the product matrix can then be computed using only additions and subtractions of the c's. We leave it to the reader to verify the following simple algebraic identities:

$$\begin{cases} a_{11}b_{11} + a_{12}b_{21} = c_1 + c_4 - c_5 + c_7 \\ a_{21}b_{11} + a_{22}b_{21} = c_2 + c_4 \\ a_{11}b_{12} + a_{12}b_{22} = c_3 + c_5 \\ a_{21}b_{12} + a_{22}b_{22} = c_1 - c_2 + c_3 + c_6 \end{cases}$$

The product matrix is thus computed using a total of 7 multiplications and 18 additions/subtractions. There has been a "tradeoff" of one multiplication for 14 additions/subtractions.

It has been shown by Winograd [17] that at least 7 multiplications are required for the multiplication of 2×2 matrices. Thus, the Strassen algorithm is optimal for this problem so far as the number of arithmetic multiplications is concerned.

The Strassen result, in minimizing the number of arithmetic multiplications, has not been extended to larger matrices, but it is easy to show from the result for 2×2 matrices that two matrices of order n can be multiplied with $O(n^{\log_2 7})$ arithmetic multiplications.

Lower bounds, average complexity, upper bounds.   We can consider several kinds of statements that might be made concerning the complexity or difficulty or "cost" of a computation. Suppose we have a class of problems where the "size" of a particular problem is given by the value of a parameter n

(such as the problem of solving a system of n simultaneous linear equations). The following kinds of assertions about the complexity of the solution procedure can be made, where $K(n)$ is some function of n.

1. complexity $\leq K(n)$
2. average complexity for all problems of size $n = K(n)$
3. complexity $\geq K(n)$

In (3) we are indicating the existence of some lower bound on the use of time or space, and any search for an algorithm that improves on this lower bound would be fruitless. We shall see an example of this in the sequel where we cite Winograd's results on the least time needed for the execution of arithmetic addition and multiplication. Once such a result is established, it implies the optimality of an algorithm that achieves this minimum time.

We often wish to know the *average* complexity of a solution procedure, as in (2). For example, the time needed for most procedures to sort a given file will depend on the initial ordering of that file. If the given file is already in sorted order it will take (for some procedures) very little time to recognize that no reordering is necessary. The time for execution of the procedure will increase for different input data to that needed to handle some worse case. Some assessment of the average time may be made, and this determines the average cost of this application when it is done many times. As another example, we might consider the variable time needed to multiply two binary numbers if a machine algorithm is used which exploits the presence of zeros in the multiplier (e.g., to multiply 11010111 by 10000010 we need only add 11010111 × 2 to 11010111 × 2^7). The average time for such a multiplication procedure depends on the average number of 1's to be expected in the multiplier.

In many cases we may be able to determine upper bounds on the cost of a computation, as in (1). For example, we can find a given element in an ordered list of n elements by making no more than $\lceil \log_2 n \rceil$ comparisons (by binary search) although we may conceivably succeed in finding the given element at the very first comparison.

"device dependence" of complexity. The time (or perhaps "space" in the of the storage used) required to do some tasks will depend in part on automaton on which these tasks are carried out. As examples, we have in Chapter 10 the use of several kinds of automata with different e-handling capabilities for problems related to formal languages.

hough we have seen that any computation that can be performed by a ape Turing machine can equally well be performed by a one-tape Tur achine, it is true that a multitape machine may be able to perform som s in significantly less time. Similarly, a two-way finite automaton (i.e., with read tape backwards capability) is not able to perform any task that some machine restricted to forward tape reading cannot do, but it can do some tasks with far fewer internal states.

A variety of machine characteristics, both abstract and real, will affect the time, or length of the program, or amount of storage needed to accomplish various procedures. By way of example these include: multiple tapes, tapes with multiple read heads, two-way tape reading, multidimensional tapes, nondeterminism, push-down stacks, two-way stacks, the repertoire of built-in instructions, random access memories, associative memories, and so forth.

However, some statements about complexity can be made that are "device independent," and this is described in the next several sections.

Included among the variety of possible machine characteristics is the facility to perform "parallel processing," i.e., to execute several subprocedures simultaneously. This may have a marked effect on the total time needed for a task. For example, consider the problem of computing the product $C = A \times B$ of two nth order matrices, $A = \{a_{ij}\}$, $B = \{b_{ij}\}$. Each element c_{ij} of the product matrix is found by the formula

$$c_{ij} = a_{i1}b_{1j} + a_{i2}b_{2j} + \ldots + a_{in}b_{nj}.$$

The n terms that sum to c_{ij} are independent of each other, and if we could put n processors to work simultaneously, each of them could compute a different one of these products $a_{ik}b_{kj}$ $(k = 1, 2, \ldots, n)$. These n computations could then all be done in the time for one multiplication, and this would cut down the total time for the computation of the elements of the product matrix by a factor of $1/n$ if we ignore the time needed for additions.

A number of important problems of numerical analysis have been investigated with a view to casting the solution procedures in a form that will allow parallelism to be exploited.

11.7 AN AXIOMATIC, MACHINE INDEPENDENT APPROACH TO THE DEFINITION OF THE COMPLEXITY OF THE PARTIALLY COMPUTABLE FUNCTIONS

M. Blum has made a notable contribution [1] to the formal study of th complexity of the partially computable functions. He has enunciated a fe simple axioms that many appropriate measures of complexity should parently satisfy, and he has shown some interesting and surprising co quences of these axioms.

Given any partially computable function $\varphi(n)$, consider such po measures of complexity as the number of steps needed on some mach compute this function for given argument n, or the amount of memory is used, or the number of machine language transfer operations executed. Either each of these measures increases as the computation proceeds or, as in the use of memory, if usage remains fixed while the computation continues beyond some designated point, we can conclude (cf. below) that the computation must be interminable. If and when the computation terminates, each of these measures will have some definite value.

All of these are examples of what Blum calls "step counting functions," and each can be considered to be a measure of the use of some means, or available resource, in the computing process, of the consumption of time, of space, of transfer operations, respectively, in the three examples cited. Such a measure, which we shall denote by $\Phi(n)$, is, like $\varphi(n)$, a function of the input argument n. It possesses the following properties.

Axioms: 1. The measure $\Phi(n)$ is defined for any argument n for which $\varphi(n)$ is defined.
2. We can effectively determine if the measure $\Phi(n)$ is equal to any given value m for given input argument n (i.e., we can effectively determine if $\Phi(n) = m$).

We then abstract from the special cases and say that any function that satisfies these two axioms is a "step counting function," or is a complexity measure. Any measure of the use of some means in the computing process satisfies the axioms.

For example, the total number of machine steps executed by any machine that computes $\varphi(n)$ is a function of n that clearly satisfies the axioms. With respect to (1), the number of steps is defined if the machine computing $\varphi(n)$ eventually halts, i.e., if $\varphi(n)$ is defined. Second, by monitoring the computation of $\varphi(n)$ on the given machine, we can determine if the total number of steps needed for the computation is equal to any given number m, and thus (2) is also satisfied.

The number of transfer operations during a computation on a stored program machine also satisfies the axioms. (1) is clearly satisfied, and (2) is also satisfied for any machine with a finite high-speed store. To see this second point, note that we can, as before, monitor the computation of $\varphi(n)$. The number of machine transfer operations executed must strictly increase as the computation proceeds, with only a limited number of steps being possible between consecutive transfer operations. That is, the maximum number of instructions that can be held in the high speed store is the maximum number of instructions that can be executed sequentially without executing a transfer instruction.

The number of memory accesses occurring in a computation similarly satisfies the two axioms. (1) is obvious. With respect to (2), note that, as with the transfer operations, we can monitor a computation to determine, for given m, if the program has accessed precisely m words of memory by the time the computation stops. We can do this because either the memory usage strictly increases as the computation proceeds or, if it stays stationary, the machine must eventually loop (any machine with fixed memory acts like a finite automaton). The monitoring program can recognize when this occurs.

Any function $\Phi_{\varphi(n)}$ corresponding to a given partially computable function $\varphi(n)$ can be considered a complexity measure for $\varphi(n)$ if it satisfies axioms (1), (2). Such abstract complexity measures possess some interesting properties that we shall illustrate below. These properties will hold for *any* measure of the use of some means in the computing process, and will be independent of any particular machine or particular program that might be used to evaluate a given partially computable function. For this reason, this theory is said to be machine independent.

Before we leave the axioms, however, we remark that they are not necessarily satisfied by *all* possible measures of complexity that might appear to be intuitively acceptable. For example, any measure that behaves like the *work* done by some physical machine in a computing process would not necessarily satisfy the axioms. Axiom (1) will hold, but axiom (2) would not be satisfied, there being in general no effective procedure to determine if the work done by some physical computing machine by the time it stops (if it stops) will be equal to some prescribed value. For example, if a one-pound weight is repeatedly raised and lowered one foot, at the surface of the earth, the work done after any number of repetitions would be zero. In such a situation, if we are given the work done in a physical process (more generally in any "conservative" field), it is not possible to determine if that process terminates or not. If we were to attach measures of "work," including possibly negative as well as positive measures, to such events as the state transitions that occur in a Turing machine computation, this would not necessarily satisfy the axioms. Such a measure would not behave like those measures that represent the use of some means in the computational process.

However, there are a number of very reasonable measures, as we have seen, that do satisfy the axioms and that, therefore, lead to certain conclusions we next describe.

11.8   THE SPEED-UP THEOREM

Certain remarkable consequences can be proved for complexity measures that satisfy the axioms.

We have cited as one practical goal in the study of complexity that of finding the most efficient algorithm or machine to perform some task. One of Blum's theorems indicates that if "most efficient" means "least complex," then our goal cannot be achieved in general. It is not possible to determine for an arbitrary computable function $\varphi(n)$ a machine or program that will, for almost all arguments n (this means all but some finite number of arguments), compute $\varphi(n)$ in the least number of steps. More generally, we cannot hope to minimize any complexity measure that satisfies the axioms we have given.

The speed-up theorem provides an example of a total computable function f that takes on the value 0 or 1 for each argument and has the following surprising property. If Z_f is a program or a machine that computes f, there exists another program or machine Z'_f that for most arguments computes f in far fewer steps. Specifically, if $\Phi_f(n)$ is the complexity measure computed for the machine Z_f that computes f and $\Phi'_f(n)$ is the complexity measure for machine Z'_f then a special case of the speed-up theorem implies that

$$\Phi_f(n) > 2^{\Phi'_f(n)}$$

A second application of the theorem implies that there is a machine Z''_f that computes $\varphi(n)$ much faster than Z'_f in that

$$\Phi'_f(n) > 2^{\Phi''_f(n)}.$$

By repetition we obtain a never-ending sequence of machines $Z_f, Z'_f, Z''_f, Z'''_f, \ldots$ where the complexity of the computation of f for each machine in the chain is exponentially greater, for most arguments, than the complexity of the computation on the next machine in the sequence!

$$\Phi_f(n) > 2^{\Phi'_f(n)} > 2^{2^{\Phi''_f(n)}} > 2^{2^{2^{\Phi'''_f(n)}}} > \ldots$$

There is then no machine Z that computes f with an associated complexity measure that is minimal.

We omit the proof of the speed-up theorem, which appears in [1].

11.9 FUNCTIONS COMPUTABLE BY FINITE AUTOMATA

We shall look more closely at a question we have touched upon briefly in Chapter 8. What functions can a finite automaton compute? In a sense, these are the simplest possible functions of all from the point of view of computational complexity, for a finite automaton transducer can always be designed to complete its output immediately upon finishing its scanning of the input data. It follows from our earlier discussion (Chapter 7) that we can take as the model of a finite automaton a Turing machine that can move over its tape in only one direction. We might equally well assume, as an alternative model, a machine with three tapes, a read-only input tape that moves in only one direction, a fixed size "working storage" tape, and a write-only output tape. The bound on the length of this working storage tape is assumed to be fixed for *all* possible values of the input data. Any such Turing machine can always be described as a conventional finite automaton whose "states" include the (finite number of) possible configurations of its working storage tape.

Let F denote the class of functions $\{f(x)\}$, where x is an n-tuple, that can be computed by a finite automaton. We have seen that this class must be quite restricted, for it does not even include the product function $f(x, y) = xy$. However, we have seen that we can compute the sum $x + y$ with such a restricted machine. We shall show, more generally, that the class F includes the three basic functions of the class of primitive recursive functions, and that it is "closed" under certain operations.

A finite (i.e., fixed size working tape) Turing machine can compute each of the basic functions: $N(x) = 0$, $S(x) = x + 1$, $U_i^{(n)}(x_1, x_2, \ldots, x_n) = x_i$. This is seen by simply observing that in all three cases the Turing machines we designed earlier for the computation of these functions make use of a fixed portion of tape (actually 0 squares or 1 square) in excess of that needed for the input data.

Further, the class F is "closed" under composition, i.e., if $f(y)$ is computable by a finite machine and $g(x)$ is computable by a finite machine, then $h(x) = f(g(x))$ is computable by a finite machine. We shall sketch the simple proof of this fact.

Suppose then that $f(y)$ is computable on a Turing machine Z_1 whose working tape is limited to M squares, and that $g(x)$ is computable on a Turing machine Z_2 whose working tape is limited to N squares. We leave it to the reader to see, using the results of Chapter 5, that we can define a Turing machine Z_3 that behaves as does Z_2 on given input data until Z_2 is ready to write its first output symbol. Z_3 then starts simulating Z_1, using Z_2's first output symbol as Z_1's first input symbol. When the simulated Z_1 is ready for its next input symbol, Z_3 returns to simulating the behavior of Z_2. Z_3 continues to alternate between the behavior of Z_2 and of Z_1. Its final output will be the output that Z_1 would have obtained after starting with an input tape that contains the output of Z_2. It is evident that a working tape limited in size to $M + N$ will suffice for Z_3. This result is easily generalized to cover the case where y is an m-tuple and x is an n-tuple, and where each argument y_i in $f(y_1, y_2, \ldots, y_m)$ is replaced by a function $g_i(x_1, x_2, \ldots, x_n)$ in the class F.

We can similarly show that F is closed under the operation of addition. That is, if $f(x)$ and $g(x)$ are computable on Turing machines using finite working tapes, then the function $h(x) = f(x) + g(x)$ is computable on such a machine. We leave the details of the proof to the reader.

It follows from these facts that any constant function $f(x) = C$, where C is some constant, is computable on a finite machine. For example, the function $f(x) = 4$ is obtained by composition and addition as $f(x) = S(N(x)) + S(N(x)) + S(N(x)) + S(N(x))$, or by a composition alone as $S(S(S(S(N(x)))))$. More generally, any linear function of n arguments $f(x_1, x_2, \ldots, x_n) = c_1 x_1 + c_2 x_2 + \ldots + c_n x_n$ is obtainable by addition and is thus computable on a finite machine.

11.10 PREDICTABLE COMPLEXITY—THE RITCHIE HIERARCHY OF THE ELEMENTARY ARITHMETIC FUNCTIONS

The class F of functions computable by finite automata consists of those functions that can be computed in the least possible time and using a fixed size working storage (in fact, we have noted that *all* working storage can be dispensed with by modifying a machine so that its internal states represent the finite number of possible configurations of a fixed size working storage). The value of a function computed on such a machine is available as soon as the input has been scanned.

Let us consider the "complexity" of a function computed on a Turing machine to be the total amount of tape, used in the course of a computation, that is in excess of that needed to contain the input data and that needed for the output. As noted in the preceding section, we might, to delineate this classification of storage usage more clearly, envisage a three-tape machine, one input tape that can be read only, one tape for working storage, and one tape for output that can only be written on (Fig. 11.3). We omit listing the superficial details involved in specifying completely the behavior of such a machine. The complexity of a computation is then defined as the maximum size of the working storage tape that is needed during a computation. Intuitively, this seems preferable to having the complexity depend also upon the size of the input or output representations, but only having it depend upon what is involved in transforming the one into the other. We might take as a "real" computing model of this situation a computer configuration that

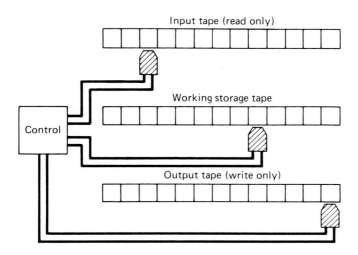

Figure 11.3

employs only a card reader for input (read only) and only a printer for output (write only). The rest of storage would then compare to the work tape.

If a function $f(x)$ can be computed on a machine Z that employs, for all input arguments x, no more than $M(x)$ squares of working storage tape, a bound can also be determined on the number of steps required for the computation. This follows from the fact that only a fixed number, dependent on $M(x)$, of "instantaneous descriptions" can appear without the occurrence of a repetition. Once a description is repeated this signifies an endless loop. Therefore, any bona fide computation is restricted to a sequence of descriptions containing no repetitions. These descriptions can neglect the contents of the output tape, for this tape cannot be read and so does not influence the course of a computation.

The functions of class F can then be said to have zero complexity, and in anticipation of a hierarchy of function classes of increasing complexity we shall write $F = F_0$. In [10] R. Ritchie introduces more complex functions by defining the class F_1 to be those functions whose complexity is bounded by a function in class F_0. F_1 includes F_0 since the complexity of any function in F_0 is bounded by a constant, and the functions $f(x) = k$ (where k is any constant) are in F_0. Unlike [10] we shall in the following discussion assume machines that employ a unary notational scheme throughout.

The product function $f(x, y) = xy$, while not in F_0, is in F_1. The working storage tape for a 3-tape machine that computes xy need only contain a copy of the multiplier, say y. Assuming unary notation, a copy of the multiplicand x must be written as output for every unit in the multiplier. We leave the details of the construction to the reader. A bound on the working storage is then $\varphi(x, y) = y$, and this is a function in F_0.

Similarly, we can show that the function $f_1(x) = 2^x$ is in F_1 but that the function $f_2(x) = 2^{2^x}$ is *not* in F_1 (cf. Exercises).

We define F_2 in turn to be the class of functions with complexity measure bounded by a function in F_1 and, continuing, we are led to an infinite chain of function classes

$$F_0 \subset F_1 \subset F_2 \subset \ldots$$

In each case we define F_i, $i = 1, 2, \ldots$, to be the class of functions computable by machines that use a working storage tape that is bounded by a function in F_{i-1}. The totality of these "predictably complex" functions $\bigcup_{i=1}^{\infty} F_i$ comprise the class of so-called "elementary" functions. It can be shown that they form a proper subset of the primitive recursive functions. Notice the peculiar meaning of the "predictability" of complexity for these functions. For example, if a function $g(x)$ is in F_2, we know that the "predictor" of the "predictor" of the complexity of the computation of $g(x)$ is computable by a finite automaton.

F_i is in every case a *proper* subset of F_{i+1}, for we can show that if the function $f_i(x)$, $i = 1, 2, \ldots$, is defined by

$$\begin{cases} f_1(x) = 2^x \\ f_{k+1}(x) = 2^{f_k(x)} \end{cases}$$

then $f_{i+1}(x)$ is in the class F_{i+1} but is *not* in the class F_i.

11.11   THE USE OF "FAN-IN" COMPONENTS IN A CIRCUIT AND WINOGRAD'S MINIMAL BOUNDS FOR ADDITION AND MULTIPLICATION

The speed of the fundamental arithmetic operations is, as we have noted, of great importance in assessing the capabilities of any high speed computer. Therefore, considerable thought has gone into the design of efficient circuits to implement these operations. But no matter how clever we are in building adders or multipliers, how can we be sure that some significant improvement might not yet be made through the use of an ingenious scheme that has escaped discovery? If the arithmetic operations are accomplished through use of the kinds of components that we have discussed earlier, we do now know that the most advanced circuits currently in use *are* close to being optimal in executing these operations in a time interval that is near an absolute theoretical minimum. We shall briefly outline by example some of the considerations underlying the relevant theory which is due principally to S. Winograd [15, 16].

We have noted that the time for an operation to be performed by a logical circuit composed of fundamental organs such as the AND, the OR, the MAJORITY organ, the NOR, and so forth depends upon the maximum time for a signal to pass through the circuit. This in turn depends upon the depth of the circuit or the maximum number of components in any path from entry to exit of the circuit.

Let us suppose that we make use of components such as the AND, OR, NOR, NAND, DELAY organs, or whatever, in building a logical circuit that realizes a given Boolean function. We shall, however, assume that every possible gate in the circuit has no more than two inputs and has precisely one output so that we rule out for the moment the use of such devices as a MAJORITY organ. We further suppose, as earlier, that a clock governs the actions in the circuit and specifies a time $t = 0, 1, 2, \ldots$. The input signals are assumed to stay constant at each time step, and there is a unit time delay involved for a signal to pass through any single gate. In connecting these various components, lines can split, but they cannot merge. What can we say about the minimal depth, and in consequence the minimal time, for any logical circuit, no matter how it is composed, to compute a given Boolean function?

We shall, by way of example, consider a Boolean function of 9 variables. The complete truth table for such a function includes $2^9 = 512$ rows. Suppose that the fragment of a truth table in Fig. 11.4 applies to a particular function F of 9 Boolean variables $X_1, X_2, \ldots, X_9$.

X_1	X_2	X_3	X_4	X_5	X_6	X_7	X_8	X_9	F
				⋮					
(0)	1	1	0	1	1	1	0	1	0
(1)	1	1	0	1	1	1	0	1	1
				⋮					
0	(0)	0	1	1	0	1	1	0	0
0	(1)	0	1	1	0	1	1	0	1
				⋮					
1	1	(0)	0	1	1	1	0	1	1
1	1	(1)	0	1	1	1	0	1	0
				⋮					
0	1	1	(0)	0	1	0	0	0	1
0	1	1	(1)	0	1	0	0	0	0
				⋮					
0	0	1	0	(0)	0	0	1	1	0
0	0	1	0	(1)	0	0	1	1	1
				⋮					
1	0	0	1	0	(0)	1	0	1	1
1	0	0	1	0	(1)	1	0	1	0
				⋮					
0	1	1	0	1	1	(0)	0	0	1
0	1	1	0	1	1	(1)	0	0	0
				⋮					
0	1	1	1	0	1	0	(0)	1	0
0	1	1	1	0	1	0	(1)	1	1
				⋮					
1	0	1	1	0	0	1	1	(0)	1
1	0	1	1	0	0	1	1	(1)	0
				⋮					

Figure 11.4

We can draw the following conclusions from this portion of the truth table. F *must* depend upon the value of X_1 for we see that the first two rows contain identical values for $X_2, X_3, \ldots, X_9$ and that F assumes the value 0 if $X_1 = 0$ and the value 1 if $X_1 = 1$. Clearly then, X_1 plays a necessary role in determining the value of F. Similarly, inspecting each additional pair of rows, F must depend upon each of $X_2, X_3, \ldots, X_9$. This means that in any logical circuit that realizes the function F there must be some path from each of the input arguments $X_1, X_2, \ldots, X_9$ to the single output line for F (Fig. 11.5).

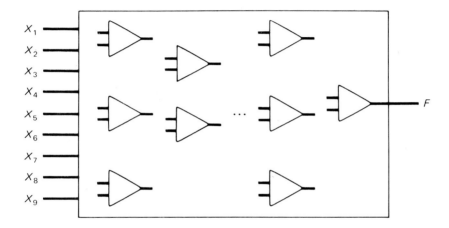

Figure 11.5

Lines can split but not merge in passing through the box. At each time step we can at most cut down by half the number of new path segments involved in the transmission of signals through the box. Therefore, a depth of at least four and an interval of at least four time steps will be necessary for the nine input lines to be joined to the single output line. We can be certain that, using "fan-in" components with no more than two inputs and with precisely one output, *no* possible circuit design can involve a depth of less than four. Thus, if we denote by t_F the time required to compute F we must have

$$t_F \geq 4.$$

We have determined, by this simple argument, a lower bound on the time needed to compute F. There is no assurance, at least from this argument, that we can achieve this lower bound, but it is not possible to compute F in less than four time units.

If we had shown that the output value of F depended upon signals being transmitted from k input lines, the depth t_F of the circuit would have been at least $\lceil \log_2 k \rceil$. (With each time step we can at most halve the number of lines continuing through the circuit; therefore, if the depth is t then $k/2^t \leq 1$, implying $t \geq \lceil \log_2 k \rceil$.) This would be the minimum possible time for any circuit for F. If we had considered fan-in components with r inputs and one output,

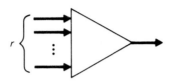

the minimal depth of the circuit would have been $\lceil \log_r k \rceil$.

In [15, 16] Winograd considers circuits made up of such components and in which each line can carry an arbitrary number $d\,(> 1)$ of distinct signals. He establishes certain general results and in particular derives lower limits on the feasible times for addition and multiplication using such circuits.

We give a further example from Spira [13] that illustrates the use of these fundamental ideas in analyzing multiplication.

Consider a circuit to implement the multiplication of two 8-bit integers x, y. Assume that the input values for x, y are represented on 16 lines, 8 of which carry the binary representation of x, and 8 of which represent y. Each input and output line is assumed to have two possible states corresponding to the 0, 1 bits needed in binary representation. The 16-bit product xy is represented on 16 output lines.

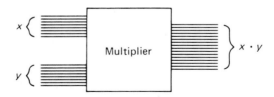

We show that the 8th bit (from the right) of the product xy depends upon every bit position, and therefore every input line, in x and in y. For example, let

$$x_0 = \overbrace{\cdots 0 \cdots}^{k \text{ bits}}, \quad x_1 = \overbrace{\cdots 1 \cdots}^{k \text{ bits}}$$

be two 8-bit numbers that differ only in the kth position (from the right). If $y = 2^{8-k}$, the products $x_0 y$, $x_1 y$ are given by

$$x_0 y = \cdots\cdots 0 \cdots\cdots$$
$$x_1 y = \cdots\cdots 1 \cdots\cdots$$

The 8th bits of these two products differ although the only difference between x_0 and x_1 is in the kth bit position. Since this position can be any one of the 16 bit positions in x or y, it follows that the 8th output line must depend upon *all* 16 input lines.

Therefore, the depth of any circuit implementation of xy is at least 4 (i.e., $\log_2 16$).

If different representation codes are used for the input and the output, this bound can be reduced. Suppose that the input and output numbers are represented by the exponents of the successive primes when these numbers are written in factored form as a product of primes. For example, we write the number 126 as

$$126 = 2^1 \cdot 3^2 \cdot 5^0 \cdot 7^1$$

and then encode 126 by the string of exponents $(1, 2, 0, 1)$ corresponding to the first four primes $2, 3, 5, 7$. (This notation has been suggested as a device for reducing multiplication time—at the expense of increasing addition time.)

Multiplication can be speeded up when the factors and the result are represented in this manner. For example, if we consider the computation of the product of 126 and 70, we have

$$70 = 2^1 \cdot 3^0 \cdot 5^1 \cdot 7^1$$

and therefore,

$$126 \times 70 = 2^2 \cdot 3^2 \cdot 5^1 \cdot 7^2.$$

The point is that the computation of the four exponents $(2, 2, 1, 2)$ that represent the product can proceed in parallel. Each exponent (of $2, 3, 5, 7$ respectively) can be computed at the same time and independently of each other. This shows up in a reduced lower bound on the time required for multiplication.

Consider the output lines needed to represent the exponent of 2 in the product. The value of this part of the output depends only upon the exponents of 2 in the inputs x and y. Since x, y are 8-bit numbers, the biggest possible exponent of 2 in the factored forms of these numbers is 7 (the maximum number of consecutive 0's on the right end of an 8-bit number). Therefore, 3 bits are needed for the binary representations of this exponent in each of the two inputs x, y. Therefore, each of the output lines needed to represent the exponent of 2 in the product xy depends upon at most 6 input lines, and the depth of a circuit that computes this part of the output has a lower bound of $\lceil \log_2 6 \rceil$ which is less than the lower bound we derived assuming ordinary binary notation. The exponents of the primes other than 2 are limited to a smaller range and the worst restriction follows from the result that we have obtained.

Winograd has also given specific schemes for addition and multiplication that obtain the sum or the product in times that are very close to the theoretical lower bound.

11.12   TIME AND SPACE TRADEOFFS

There are many situations in computing where the time required for some procedure can be reduced at the cost of increasing the "space," interpreted as the use of physical facilities during the execution of the procedure. Conversely, the physical facilities used can often be reduced at the expense of using more time. We cite some examples.

Perhaps most obvious is the possibility of obtaining the value of a function by table look-up after storing tabulated function values for a number of arguments, as opposed to computing the function from some analytical expression. This often reduces substantially the time required. Students of trigonometry still learn to apply logarithms and use the trigonometric functions for the solution of problems by referring to printed tables, with the possible use of interpolation. However, the availability of cheap pocket calculators that include very efficient built-in procedures to compute directly the trigonometric, logarithmic and exponential functions will surely change the way these applications of trigonometry are taught. In general, the relative times for table look-up accompanied by interpolation and that for the computation of some analytical expression must be carefully assessed. Sometimes a cleverly designed and efficient algorithm may require less time than that required to obtain the function value by a table look-up procedure, and the time-space tradeoff cannot be realized in this manner.

As somewhat of a generalization of the above situation, we mention the frequent tradeoff that is possible between program size and execution time. There are innumerable situations where a "quick and dirty" solution to a problem can be easily implemented at the expense of increasing run time. As a trivial example we mention the search for some key in an ordered file of fixed length records in direct access memory where the keys for successive records appear in increasing order. A simple way to do this would of course be to search sequentially through the file, starting with the smallest key, until the required key is found. The programming of a binary search would be somewhat more complicated but would result in a substantial saving in the average execution time.

More generally, a program can often be written compactly in a higher level language, but execution time can be reduced by efficient programming directly in machine or assembly language.

In the case of machines, a circuit can often be made faster, that is, the depth can be decreased, by using more components or, in other words, by increasing the size of the machine. Circuits that employ fan-in elements with r inputs, as we have used these in discussing the fundamental limits on add and multiply time, might perhaps be made faster by using elements with larger values of r.

We have noted, with reference to the complexity of Turing machines, the possible tradeoff between the size of a machine's alphabet and the number of internal states it employs, with the product of these two factors remaining approximately constant. This is also a form of tradeoff between space and time. The number of internal states is an indication of the size of the machine, and the number of symbols in the machine's alphabet relates to the number of steps required in a computation. If, for example, the symbols were encoded by binary fields, the time for the equivalent two-symbol machine would obviously be lengthened with the necessity to read binary fields instead of single symbols.

In the real world of computing many procedures can be shortened by increasing physical facilities such as memory size or number of tape units. For example, a sorting procedure that employs an n-way merge using n magnetic tapes will, in general, take less time the larger n is—or the larger the high speed memory that is available for internal sorting, the faster will be the sorting procedure for large files.

Analogously, in the domain of the theoretical, Turing machines with more than one tape or with more than one read head can perform some procedures faster than machines with only one tape and one read head. It can, for example, be shown that in general a one-tape Turing machine may require $O(n^2)$ steps to simulate n steps on a 2-tape machine, but a 2-tape machine can always simulate n steps of a k-tape machine in $O(n \log n)$ steps. A related theorem shows that there are sets of sequences that can be recognized by a Turing machine employing two tapes in n steps, where n is the length of the input sequence, while no one-tape machine will recognize these sequences in n steps. (Cf. Section 11.14, "Real-time" Computations.)

Recall that a "palindrome" is a sequence of symbols that reads the same backwards as well as forwards, such as the string MADAM. No Turing machine with a single input tape and single read head can recognize such sequences in "real time," i.e., in the time required to read the sequence. The machine must move back and forth between the two ends of the tape to recognize its structure. It is, on the other hand, a simple matter to see that a machine with two movable read heads located at either end of the input tape can, by seesawing control back and forth between the two heads, recognize a palindrome in the time required to scan the input tape. Again, the time is reduced with the use of some greater physical facility.

11.13   PROBABILISTIC ALGORITHMS

Some remarkable recent results of Rabin [9] and others have given a possible new form to the nature of mathematical proof. Certain statements concerning the natural numbers may require an inordinate amount of labor in order to demonstrate their truth or falsity. But in some of these situations we may be able to prove comparatively easily that the *probability* is exceedingly close to 1 that the given statement is true (or false). Such a result would not be a rigorous demonstration of truth or falsity, but if we can show that there is less than one chance in, say, 10^{10} that a given statement is false, this might be considered, for all practical purposes, to be tantamount to a demonstration of the truth of that statement.

We have described a decision procedure as an effective procedure, or algorithm, that can be used to determine the truth or falsity of any one of some class of statements. When such a procedure exists, we can unequivocally reach a conclusion that a given statement (e.g., "11,586 and 23,425 have no common divisors") is true or false. By admitting probabilistic procedures in algorithms we may, in some instances, not be able to arrive at a definite conclusion such as "the number n possesses property P"; however, we may reach a conclusion that "the probability is greater than $1 - \varepsilon$ that the number n possesses property P," where ε is a very small number. We shall see that in some instances the complexity of a problem solution, in terms of the time required, can be markedly reduced by admitting such a probabilistic procedure.

A straightforward, simplistic procedure to determine if a given number N is prime might be based on searching for possible divisors of N by trying all prime numbers up to $\sqrt{N}$ in magnitude. This would involve a formidable amount of computation if N is very large, say of the order of 2^{400}. An assessment of the number of primes less than $\sqrt{N}$ can be made using the "prime number theorem" of algebra. This theorem implies that for very large values of n the number of primes less than n is approximately $\dfrac{n}{\log n}$, where $\log n$ is the natural logarithm of n. This means that the number of primes less than $\sqrt{N}$ if $N = 2^{400}$ is about $\dfrac{2^{200}}{200 \log 2} \approx 10^{58}$. To divide N by each of these primes would take about 10^{49} seconds on a machine capable of performing a division in one nanosecond. This time exceeds the estimated life of the universe by a multiplicative factor of at least 10^{30}. There is clearly no hope, at least with such a naive method, of determining if an arbitrary number of this magnitude is prime. We can, it is true, apply more efficient procedures than the one we have described, but even with these methods the problem of determining the primeness of an arbitrary number of the order of 2^{200} is intractable. (There are theorems that enable practical tests for the primeness of numbers of a particular form, and these have been used for a number as large as $2^{19,937} - 1$, but these methods do not work for an arbitrary given number.)

Rabin has suggested attacking the problem of determining if a large number N is prime by exploiting the fact that if N is composite more than half of the numbers less than N will satisfy a certain easily verifiable condition, and if N is prime *no* number less than N will satisfy this condition. Suppose we then pick at random numbers less than N and check to see if they satisfy the condition that assures that N is composite. A number satisfying this condition is called by Rabin a "witness" to the compositeness of N. If N is composite it follows from what we have stated that the probability is at least $1/2$ that an arbitrarily selected number smaller than N is a witness to this composite character of N. If we pick at random k numbers smaller than N and none of these is a witness to the compositeness of N, then the probability is less than $\frac{1}{2^k}$ that N is composite. That is, the probability is greater than $1 - \frac{1}{2^k}$ that N is prime.

If b is any natural number smaller than N, then N must be composite if

    1. $b^{N-1} \not\equiv 1 \pmod{N}$ *or* if

    2. $N - 1$ is a multiple of some power of 2, say
      $N - 1 = m2^i$, and $1 < gcd(b^m - 1, N) < N$.

This result is due to G. Miller [8].

(1) or (2) then specifies the condition $W(b)$ that b be a witness to the compositeness of N. The computational verification of $W(b)$ can proceed in a very efficient manner since the modular arithmetic that is required can be done without using greatly extended precision arithmetic (i.e., in all multiplications we need only the excess over a multiple of N; in all divisions by N we need only the remainder).

Rabin and Pratt [9] ran some experiments using an algorithm based on this probabilistic approach. They looked for the largest prime below 2^{400}, testing each successive number by looking for witnesses of compositeness.

Within one minute they found that all numbers were composite down to $2^{400}-593$. This last number was tested more than 100 times with all trial numbers failing the test to be a witness to its compositeness.

There is, then, less than one chance in 2^{100} that $2^{400}-593$ is composite, or, in other words, the probability that $2^{400}-593$ is prime is better than 99.99999999999999999999999999999%. Who would not be willing to accept these odds as being firmly indicative of the primeness of this number?

In fact, assume that some *nonprobabilistic* algorithm were used to test the primeness of some number, and that the execution of this algorithm required one minute of computer time. In order for us to have more confidence in the result obtained than in the result we have cited for $2^{400}-593$, the procedure would have to be executed on a computer with a mean error-free path (the expected time between machine errors) of more than 100,-000,000,000,000 times the life of the universe (assuming the life of the universe to be 30×10^9 years).

The probabilistic method for the problem of primality is very effective because of the abundance of the "witnesses" to compositeness. If only one randomly selected number fails to satisfy the condition for the compositeness of a number N, we already know that the probability is greater than $1/2$ that N is prime. In [9] Rabin suggests that a similar approach may be useful in the verification of some classes of programs or subroutines. The usual testing of a program involves its trial on varied input data. However, those instances of input data that pinpoint certain possible errors in the program may be rare, and many bugs may be very elusive. (Witness the many months needed for the verification of a large operating system.) If it is possible to increase substantially the "witnesses" to the incorrectness of a program by using different tests or input data, then a few tests might assure the correctness of a program with a high probability.

11.14   "REAL-TIME" COMPUTATIONS

We have noted earlier that a finite automaton provides its result for given input as soon as that input string has been scanned. Such processing is then an example of a real-time computation, a computation which requires no additional time beyond that needed to read the input data. This is analogous to those real life situations where the input data characterizing some ongoing process is used to modify that process, as in process control or other computer-monitored systems. We have seen, however, that the class of computations that can be performed on a finite automaton is quite restricted.

Yamada [18] has enlarged the scope of real-time computations by considering a somewhat restricted use of a machine. He introduces the notion of a function being "countable" in real-time in the following sense. Suppose that a given total function $f(x)$ is strictly increasing, that is

$$f(0) < f(1) < f(2) < \ldots$$

We then describe the following procedure for the computation of the numbers in the range of $f(x)$. Assume that a machine receives as input a string of 1's and that it emits as output on each reading of an input bit either a 0 or a 1, determined as follows. Consider at time t the number of 1's read to that point (this number is t if the input stream is made up entirely of 1's). If this number is in the range of $f(x)$, the machine emits an output of 1; otherwise it gives a 0. (To accommodate the possibility that $f(0) = 0$ we might modify the definition in trivial manner so that the output of 1 is emitted after reading $t + 1$ 1's.) With such a machine procedure we can always be sure of determining in time t if the number t is in the range of $f(x)$. In other words, we can decide in time t if t is a member of the recursively enumerable set $\{x \mid \exists y(f(y) = x)\}$. Using some of our earlier terminology we are able to compute in real-time the characteristic function of the range of $f(x)$.

Since $f(x)$ is strictly increasing we can find its value for any given argument k by counting the number of time steps until the $k + 1$st output of 1 is emitted.

In [18] real-time computability is defined with reference to the class of multitape Turing machines. In counting the tapes we consider only "work" tapes, assuming that the special forms of input and output do not require dedicated tapes for their representation. Any function $f(x)$ that is strictly increasing from some point k_0 on and for which a multitape Turing machine exists that can recognize, in the manner we have described, the numbers in the range of $f(x)$, for $x \geq k_0$, is said to be real-time countable. A number of properties of this class of real-time countable functions can be proved in fairly straightforward manner. These include the following:

1. Any polynomial function $p(x)$ with integral coefficients and positive leading coefficient is real-time countable. (Such a function is strictly increasing from some point on.)

2. If $f(x), g(x)$ are real-time countable functions, then so are

$$f(x) + g(x), \ \sum_{i=1}^{x} f(i), \ f(x) \cdot g(x), \ \prod_{i=1}^{x} f(i), \ f(g(x)), \ f(x)^{g(x)}.$$

These properties, and a number of others, of the members of this class can be proven by constructing in each case a multitape Turing machine that will compute in real-time the function asserted to be in the class of real-time countable functions.

We illustrate some of the ideas involved by looking at the real-time computation of the polynomial $p(x) = x^2$. If we tabulate this function together with the successive differences between functional values we obtain the following table.

x	p(x)	$\Delta p(x)$	$\Delta^2 p(x)$
1	1		
2	4	3	
3	9	5	2
4	16	7	2
5	25	9	2

Every entry in the column headed $\Delta p(x)$ is obtained by taking the difference between the number in that row (to its left) of the column headed $p(x)$ and the corresponding number in the preceding row (i.e., $\Delta p(x) = p(x) - p(x-1)$). The numbers in the column headed $\Delta^2 p(x)$ are obtained by taking the differences of the numbers in the column headed $\Delta p(x)$ (i.e., $\Delta^2 p(x) = \Delta p(x) - \Delta p(x-1)$). We note that the last column includes the constant entry 2. It can be easily shown that if any polynomial of the nth degree is tabulated in such a "difference" table, the nth differences $\Delta^n p(x)$ will be constant.

The difference table for $p(x) = x^2$ implies a means of computing this function for succeeding values of x. Knowing that the differences in the $\Delta^2 p(x)$ column are constant, we can write down the next row of the table from right to left as follows:

$$6 \parallel \quad 36 \quad | \quad 11 \quad | 2$$
$$(25 + 11) \quad (9 + 2)$$

We thus obtain the value $p(6) = 36$ and can continue the table to any desired argument.

This scheme provides a clue to the real-time computation of $p(x) = x^2$. Using a Turing machine with two tapes our objective will be to write on these two tapes the successive values of $p(x)$ and of $\Delta p(x)$. Assume, for example, that a 1 has been emitted after a string of 25 input 1's, recognizing that $25 = p(x)$ for $x = 5$. Suppose that at this instant the contents of the two tapes t_1, t_2 are $t_1 : 25$, $t_2 : 9$, and that the read-write heads for t_1, t_2 are in each case over the right-most 1. We design this two-tape machine so that on each succeeding 1 of the input stream we move left on tape t_2, reading a 1 and simultaneously writing a 1 on tape t_1. This continues until t_2 is completely read. On each of the next two input 1's we write a 1 on both t_2 and t_1. When the last of these input 1's is read, a recognition output 1 is emitted, t_1 will contain 36, and t_2 will contain 11. The machine has thus recognized 36 as being the value of $p(x)$ for $x = 6$. We then repeat the procedure, but now read t_2 to the right, continuing to alternate the motion of t_2 between successive recognition output 1's. We omit the details necessary to a complete definition of the machine.

The procedure can be generalized to handle the real-time computation of any nth degree polynomial using a Turing machine with n tapes.

11.15 ON THE RANDOMNESS OF FINITE SEQUENCES

We have earlier alluded very briefly to a possible criterion for the "randomness" of a given finite sequence of characters drawn from some alphabet. That is, the extent of randomness, or of being patternless, might be defined in terms of the length of the shortest program required to write that sequence. Recall that this was also suggested as a measure of the information content or of the complexity of a finite sequence. We elaborate somewhat on this very important notion.

Certainly any sequence can be written by a program that is about the same length as that sequence, for we can always take the sequence itself as part of an input program, and then the machine need only copy it. However, a sequence that is far from being random, such as the string 010101 ... taken to any length, is clearly computable with a very short program because of its great regularity.

By a simple counting argument, we can show that most long sequences require long programs to write them. In other words most long sequences have high information content, or are very complex. We can make our definitions here more precise by considering the computation of binary sequences on a universal Turing machine employing a binary alphabet. This removes the ambiguousness in our definition relative to the particular machine that computes a sequence. Consider all binary sequences of length n. There are 2^n of these, and we can easily estimate how many of these sequences can be defined by programs of length $n/2$ bits or less. Since a program for a universal Turing machine *is* a string of bits, a bound on the number of programs is given by the number of sequences of binary bits of length $n/2$ or less, that is, by

$$1 + 2 + 2^2 + \ldots + 2^{n/2} = 2^{(n/2)+1} - 1.$$

Therefore, the proportion of n-bit sequences that can *not* be defined by programs of length $n/2$ or less is at least

$$\frac{2^n - 2^{(n/2)+1} + 1}{2^n} = 1 - \frac{1}{2^{\frac{n}{2}-1}} + \frac{1}{2^n}$$

which is very close to 1 for large values of n.

Therefore, most long sequences require long programs to compute them, and these sequences have considerable "randomness."

This definition of the randomness of a finite sequence in terms of the length of the program required to write that sequence makes precise a notion that had been rather vague in previous statistical studies that did not take into account the effective computability of sequences. Recall (Section 7.7) that there are an infinite number of possible tests of randomness of binary sequences of arbitrary length n (about half of the bits should be 1's, the number of occurrences of 1001 should, for large n, be about $n/16$, a 1 should follow a 0 about as often as it follows a 1, and so forth). Therefore, it is not possible to verify that any given binary sequence is random by applying a fixed number of tests, independent of the length n of the sequence being tested. By such statistical verification we can only conclude that a given sequence appears to be random, but no complete assurance is possible in general.

In [7], Per Martin-Löf proves that sequences requiring long programs to produce them, that is, sequences with high information content, satisfy all conceivable statistical properties of randomness.

11.16   AN UNSOLVED PROBLEM, IS $\mathscr{P} = \mathscr{N}\mathscr{P}$?

There are many important unsolved problems in the study of complexity, but one in particular has attracted very widespread attention and is even occasionally listed among the most significant unsolved problems of mathematics.

In seeking practical methods for the solution of applied problems it is important that the number of steps required for a solution not grow exponentially with the size of the problem, for we have seen that this kind of growth in complexity quickly puts problems beyond our reach. We would much prefer a procedure where the length of a computation is bounded by a polynomial in terms of the length of the input data. In fact, for a solution to be really practical we should like such a bound on the number of steps to be a polynomial of small degree, say, not exceeding 5. Optimally, it should be of degree 1 in which case the problem has linear complexity.

The class of languages, or class of sets of strings, whose sentences or strings are recognizable on a Turing machine in polynomial time (that is, the time is bounded by a polynomial in x where x is the length of an input string) is designated as $\mathscr{P}$. It can be shown that if a k-tape ($k > 1$) Turing machine recognizes the sentences of a language L in polynomial time, then there exists a one-tape machine that will also recognize L in polynomial (but of higher degree) time. There appears to be a fundamental invariance about a language being a member of the class $\mathscr{P}$—in the sense that, to a large extent, membership in this class is independent of the particular characteristics of the machine that might be used as a recognition device.

We can, as we have noted in Chapter 6, consider a nondeterministic Turing machine as a recognition device for any set of strings. The class of languages that can be recognized on a nondeterministic Turing machine in polynomial time is designated as $\mathcal{NP}$. It is immediate that $\mathcal{P} \subset \mathcal{NP}$, but as of this writing it is not known if every language recognizable on a nondeterministic machine in polynomial time is recognizable on a deterministic Turing machine in polynomial time, that is, it is not known if $\mathcal{P} = \mathcal{NP}$.

We can also consider the class of languages whose sentences can be recognized in polynomial *space;* that is, the amount of tape used in a recognition procedure is bounded by a polynomial in x, the length of the input string. It is easy to see that the class of polynomial time languages is contained in the class of polynomial space languages. It is, however, presently unknown whether or not these two classes are equal [6].

EXERCISES

11.1 We have defined the information content of a sequence S to be the length in bits of the shortest program that can write the sequence S. Show that the fraction of the 2^n binary sequences s of length n that have an information content $I(s) \leq n - k$ is at most 2^{-k+1}.

11.2 Consider the 7-state Turing machine defined in Chapter 5 to compute the function $U_2^{(3)}(x_1, x_2, x_3) = x_2$. Show, by actual construction, that this machine can be replaced by an equivalent 2-state machine, but with an increased alphabet, that computes the same function. (Use the halting convention suggested in Exercise 6.19.)

11.3 Suppose that a given Turing machine Z (1) has m possible states and uses an alphabet of n characters and (2) employs a tape whose length is bounded during the course of a computation by the number $k + l$, where k is the number of squares needed for the input and l is the additional "work space." Give an upper bound on the number of steps in a computation on Z if we know that the machine never goes into an endless loop.

11.4 Compute the number of comparisons needed in using the well-known "bubble" sort to put a given sequence of numbers $a_1, a_2, \ldots, a_n$ in increasing order. In this method a_{n-1} is first compared with a_n and the two numbers are interchanged if a_n is smaller. Then a_{n-2} is compared with the number in the $n - 1$st position, and the smaller of the two is put in the $n - 2$nd position. These successive comparisons and possible interchanges are continued up to the first position. At the end of this first pass the smallest number in the array will have "bubbled" to the top or to the first position. Then the procedure is repeated with the remaining $n - 1$ numbers to put the second smallest number in the second position, and so forth until the whole array has been sorted.

What can be said about the number of interchanges needed during the complete sort?

11.5 Consider the solution of a system of n simultaneous linear equations by the method of elimination using multiplication and subtraction. Given the system (1) described in Section 11.6, we can eliminate x_1 from the first two equations by multiplying the first equation by a_{21}, the second equation by a_{11} and subtracting the second equation from the first. This yields an equation in $x_2, x_3, \ldots, x_n$. This is done repeatedly to reduce the n equations in n unknowns to a system of $n-1$ equations in $n-1$ unknowns, then to $n-2$ equations in $n-2$ unknowns, and so forth through the "forward" part of the solution. Then the back solution is applied to obtain all the unknowns.

Tally the number of multiplications/divisions and of additions/subtractions needed in a complete (forward and back) solution of such a system of n equations.

(The identity of Section 4.11, $\sum_{i=1}^{n} i^2 = (n)(n+1)(2n+1)/6$, will be useful.)

As implied in the text, how can a significant saving in computational labor be easily achieved?

11.6 The Gauss-Seidel method for solving simultaneous linear equations is an iterative method that converges to the correct solution under certain special conditions. As in the preceding problem, assume the system (1) described in the text. Starting with some initial approximation, a sequence of successive approximations $x_1^{(k)}, x_2^{(k)}, \ldots, x_n^{(k)}$ to the solutions $x_1, x_2, \ldots, x_n$ is obtained by using the ith equation to obtain a new approximation to the ith unknown. That is, the $k+1$st approximation to x_1, designated as $x_1^{(k+1)}$ is obtained by solving the first equation

$$a_{11}x_1^{(k+1)} + a_{12}x_2^{(k)} + a_{13}x_3^{(k)} + \ldots + a_{1n}x_n^{(k)} = c_1$$

The $k+1$st approximation to x_2 is then obtained by solving the second equation

$$a_{21}x_1^{(k+1)} + a_{22}x_2^{(k+1)} + a_{23}x_3^{(k)} + \ldots + a_{2n}x_n^{(k)} = c_2$$

for $x_2^{(k+1)}$, and so forth.

One complete sweep through the equations yields a new set of approximations to all the x_i, $i = 1, 2, \ldots, n$.

How many iterations using the Gauss-Seidel method are equivalent in computational labor to the solution of the system of equations by the method of elimination described in the preceding problem?

11.7 Consider the characteristic function $f(n)$ for the set of palindromes: $f(n) = 1$ if n is a palindrome, $f(n) = 0$ otherwise. (A palindrome is a finite sequence that reads the same backwards as forwards.) Given some Turing machine Z that computes $f(n)$ by seesawing between the two ends of the tape and comparing elements, show that there corresponds to Z another machine Z' that computes $f(n)$ in about half as many steps for infinitely many arguments n.

11.8 Assume that $f(x) \in F$, $g(x) \in F$, where F is the class of functions computable by finite machines (assume a Turing machine with a fixed-size work tape, a "read only" input tape and a "write only" output tape). Show that if $h(x) = f(x) + g(x)$ then $h(x) \in F$, i.e., this class of functions is "closed" under addition.

11.9 Show that the function $f_1(x) = 2^x$ is in the class F_1 of the Ritchie hierarchy, but the function $f_2(x) = 2^{2^x}$ is not in F_1.

11.10 Using fan-in components with two inputs, what is the minimum possible number of time steps needed to compute the even parity bit for 9 given input bits $X_1, X_2, \ldots, X_9$?

11.11 Show that if $f(x), g(x)$ are real-time countable functions then so are $f(x) + g(x)$ and $f(x) \cdot g(x)$.

11.12 Show that any language whose sentences can be recognized in polynomial time is recognizable in polynomial space.

REFERENCES

1. Blum, M., "A Machine-Independent Theory of the Complexity of Recursive Functions." *J. Assn. Comp. Mach.,* **14** (April 1967).

2. Chaitin, G. J., "On the Length of Programs for Computing Finite Binary Sequences." *J. Assn. Comp. Mach.,* **13** (October 1966).

3. Knuth, D. E., *Sorting and Searching* (Vol. 3 of *The Art of Programming*). Reading, Massachusetts: Addison-Wesley, 1973.

4. Kolmogorov, A. N., "Three Approaches to the Quantitative Definition of Information." (Translation) *Intern. J. Comp. Math.,* **2** (1968).

5. Lewis, H. R., and C. H. Papadimitrou, "The Efficiency of Algorithms." *Scientific American,* **238,** 1 (January 1978).

6. Machtey, M., and P. Young, *An Introduction to the General Theory of Algorithms.* New York: Elsevier North-Holland, 1978.

7. Martin-Löf, P., "The Definition of Random Sequences." *Information and Control,* **9** (1966).

8. Miller, G. L., "Riemann's Hypothesis and a Test for Primality." *Proceedings of the Seventh Annual Association for Computing Machinery, Symposium on the Theory of Computing,* 1975.

9. Rabin, M. O., "Probabilistic Algorithms." *Algorithms and Complexity, New Directions and Recent Trends.* Ed. by J. F. Traub. New York: Academic Press, 1976.

10. Ritchie, R. W., "Classes of Predictably Computable Functions." *Trans. Amer. Math. Soc.,* **106** (1963).

11. Shannon, C. E., "A Mathematical Theory of Communication." *The Bell System Tech. J.,* **27** (1948).

12. Shannon, C. E., "A Universal Turing Machine with Two Internal States." *Automata Studies.* Ed. by C. E. Shannon and J. McCarthy. Princeton, New Jersey: Princeton University Press, 1956.

13. Spira, P. M., "The Time Required for Group Multiplication." *J. Assn. Comp. Mach.,* **16** (1969).

14. Strassen, V., "Gaussian Elimination Is Not Optimal." *Numer. Math.,* **13** (1969).

15. Winograd, S., "On the Time Required to Perform Addition." *J. Assn. Comp. Mach.,* **12** (April 1965).
16. Winograd, S., "On the Time Required to Perform Multiplication." *J. Assn. Comp. Mach.,* **14** (October 1967).
17. Winograd, S., "On the Number of Multiplications Necessary to Compute Certain Functions." *Comm. Pure and Appl. Math.,* **23** (1970).
18. Yamada, H., "Real-Time Computation and Recursive Functions Not Real-Time Computable." *IRE Trans. Electronic Comp.,* EC-11, No. 66 (December 1962).

12
Restatement and Summary of the Influence of Mathematical Ideas on Computing—Perspective, Comments

This chapter is a summary of some of the principal ways in which mathematical ideas have influenced programming and computing. Conversely, we make mention of the impact of computing on mathematics, for the relation between mathematics and computing is a symbiotic one. As we have noted earlier, the restriction to effective, or constructive, methods leads to the very significant development of constructive mathematics. Beyond this, the computer has been used as a powerful aid in some mathematical investigations. We illustrate this with a brief description of the recent solution, in which the computer played a key role, of the famous hitherto unsolved problem, the four-color theorem.

These close ties with mathematics are of no surprise. As we have repeatedly emphasized, the computer is fundamentally a mathematical machine, no matter how far removed from mathematics some of its applications may appear to be. The objects we manipulate are always represented as natural numbers, and all the operations we perform are arithmetic ones.

Much of computer science can be thought of as a part of mathematics, with modern works in the theories of automata and formal languages being essentially within the domain of algebra. These subjects are not merely fertile areas for the application of existing mathematical techniques; rather, they enable insight into new mathematical objects and structures.

Keeping pace with the explosive engineering developments in computing has been a rapid development of the theoretical parts of computer science. Automata theory and formal linguistics have already enabled a marked improvement in the efficiency of compiler development. It is hoped that similar significant results in the optimization of algorithms and programs and in program verification will also be achieved.

12.1   FUNDAMENTAL NOTIONS AND A QUICK SURVEY OF SOME SELECTED HISTORICAL DEVELOPMENTS

The early history of mathematics *is* the early history of digital computing. As we have noted, the natural numbers are fundamental to mathematics and, of course, computing has no meaning without them.

It took some millennia before Man could learn to count to 31 with the fingers of one hand and not just up to 5. The idea underlying positional, or "place value," notation, that a symbolic string using two or more distinct symbols can represent information in part through the ordering or the positions of the symbols in the string, is a quite sophisticated concept. The string "387" can be assigned a meaning determined by the relative positions of the symbols 3, 8, 7 and not just by the collection of these digits. Such an abstract idea would surely not have occurred readily to the early shepherd who might have maintained a tally of the number of sheep in his flock by keeping a similar number of stones in a pouch (an example of unary notation). The difference between representing the size of such a flock by, say, the string 11010 as opposed to 26 stones represents a great intellectual leap. (Recall the etymology of the word "calculate," which comes from the Latin word "calculus" for "stone" or "pebble.")

The Babylonians employed a positional notation using base 60. The need for a special symbol for zero apparently first appeared in using this notation because of the necessity to mark a "zero place." It seems that at first the spacing of the digits was used for this purpose (as we might write the decimal number 305 as 3 5), but this was ambiguous and later a special symbol was used to mark the absence of a positive digit in a particular position.

The definition of the arithmetic operations and their facile implementation took many centuries. The Romans used a notation that was partly positional (the C in MC has a different meaning from the C in CM, but the two X's in CXX have the same significance). Impeded by this clumsy notation, they found arithmetic done by symbolic manipulation to be a ponderous task, and the abacus was an essential tool for the efficient execution of the arithmetic operations.

We have noted the early use of the word "algorithm" to describe the symbolic manipulation schemes for performing the arithmetic operations on numbers written in positional notation and the consequent use of the word to include, more generally, arbitrary schemes for manipulating strings of symbols.

It might appear at first sight that much of the mathematics of the ancient Greeks, in particular that part related to geometry (as we have seen this illustrated in the study of Euclidean geometry), is concerned with continuous entities that require graphic representation, and so perhaps is not relevant to computing. However, the recasting of geometry by Descartes into the form that we now call analytic geometry puts the fundamental notions in the domain of the real numbers and operations on such numbers. Beyond this the recent successful attempts [7, 8], in the spirit of artificial intelligence, to solve problems of elementary geometry by devising algorithms that simulate solution procedures used by students of geometry, and, in addition, the development of an algorithmic decision procedure [15] for problems of elementary geometry both indicate that one should not hastily conclude that the computer is irrelevant to any mathematical pursuit.

The great seventeenth century German mathematician and philosopher Leibnitz apparently first recognized the possible fruitful role of a binary notation in a calculus for dealing with logical operations. He suggested several versions of such a calculus that were similar to Boolean algebra. Much later, the nineteenth century saw the development, within a progression of computing devices, of automata for the solution of logical problems. These machines manipulated symbolic strings that did not just represent numbers.

As we have pointed out earlier, it was a confluence of a number of mathematical developments together with the technological development of efficient electronic switching devices that led to the modern computer.

12.2 PEANO'S AXIOMS

Because of the vital role of the natural numbers, we look briefly at the axioms that underlie a formal development of the laws of arithmetic. Near the end of the nineteenth century the Italian mathematician G. Peano characterized the natural numbers by the following postulates.

1. If n is a natural number, then it has a successor, i.e., the successor function $S(n)$ is defined for any natural number n.

2. If $S(m) = S(n)$, then $m = n$, i.e., if two numbers have the same successor, they are equal.

3. There is a unique natural number, call it 1, that is not the successor of any number.

4. If a set R of natural numbers includes 1 and includes $S(n)$ whenever it includes n, then R includes all the natural numbers.

Postulate (4) is called the principle of finite induction, and, as we have seen earlier, it is closely related to recursion. When a function is defined by recursion it is the principle of induction that assures that the function is well-defined. Suppose, for example, that we are given, as the definition of the function $r(x)$ by primitive recursion, the two equations:

$$\begin{cases} r(0) = k \\ r(x + 1) = g(x, r(x)) \end{cases}$$

If we let R be the set of numbers for which the function $r(x)$ is defined, the principle of finite induction assures that R includes *all* numbers. To see this, note that the first equation indicates that 0 is in R, and the second equation implies that whenever n is in the set R then its successor $n + 1$ is in R. The first application of the second equation shows that 1 is in R, and we conclude from postulate (4) that R includes all natural numbers. That is, the function $r(x)$ is defined for all natural numbers.

We see the significance of recursion, or of the related notion of induction, at the very roots of mathematics.

12.3 COMPUTABILITY

We have noted that both Post and Turing sought to base their explanations of effective computation (via their machines) on a rudimentary understanding of what takes place in the brain. We remark further on the differences between their approach in formalizing the notion of effective computability and that of Church's theory of the partial recursive functions. In the theory of recursive functions we dealt with *functions* as the fundamental objects. Certain basic functions were given as members of the class of partial recursive functions, and certain combining operations were defined. These operations generate new functions in the class from functions already known to be in the class. In the Turing machine approach, we spelled out the allowable *elemental steps* that could be used in a machine procedure to compute an arbitrary function in the class of computable functions. We saw that the two approaches were equivalent and, therefore, either one would be suitable in defining the class of computable functions.

In [13] H. Rogers gives a quotation from a talk that Post gave at a meeting of the American Mathematical Society in 1944: "Indeed, if general recursive function is the formal equivalent of effective calculability, its formulation may play a role in the history of combinatory mathematics second only to that of the formulation of the concept of natural number."

After more than forty years since the formulation of the recursive functions it is not clear that the overwhelming importance of this concept, as predicted by Post, has been proven. However, it is of great importance, and perhaps it is premature to make any final judgment of the significance that Post seemed to attribute to it. Certainly, if the omnipresent role of the computer in our society could be offered as supportive evidence for his statement, there would be no question about the correctness of his forecast.

12.4 THE NATURE OF MODERN MATHEMATICS —
ABSTRACTION AND AXIOMATIZATION

Modern mathematics is characterized by great abstraction and by the use of the axiomatic approach. Rarely do pictures appear in papers in the research journals. The degree of abstraction is so great that the reading audience that feels comfortable in the rarefied atmosphere of most papers on the frontiers of research is quite small, usually restricted to a limited number of specialists in the field of the paper.

Mathematical structures are defined in abstract terms by (1) starting with undefined basic symbolic expressions to represent the fundamental objects of a system, (2) giving a formal listing of the properties of the objects of the system, and (3) enunciating the axioms of the system. Compare this with our earlier discussion of "formal systems" in Chapter 2. The axiomatic approach plays a key role in this development. The theorems of a "deep" theory are often surprising, or at least not obvious, consequences of simple axioms.

There is a continual attempt to generalize, with the goal of achieving greater simplicity, and of determining the basic underlying structure of a system, by reducing the necessary assumptions of a theory. When this is done, the results obtained are applicable to any situation where an interpretation may be given to the basic terms in such a way that the axioms still express true statements when these new interpretations are used.

These ideas prevail in all of modern mathematics, and, in particular, they are greatly emphasized in algebra. However, even the reader with modest mathematical experience that does not extend beyond the elementary calculus has seen a number of instances in elementary mathematics where this approach appears.

Perhaps the very first abstraction we see in mathematics, the use of symbols for the natural numbers, portends what is to come. In elementary algebra the use of a symbol such as x to represent an unknown and the use of expressions formed from x are abstractions. At first glance, Euclidean plane geometry may not seem, with its reliance on diagrams, to be a good example of abstraction, but it is a model of the axiomatic approach, and of course the lines and points with which we deal are idealized entities—only represented in approximate fashion in diagrams. (Points have no dimensions, lines have no width.) The pictures, however, can be dispensed with, and the degree of abstraction extended with the recasting of Euclidean geometry in the form of analytic, or coordinate, geometry. The basic entities are then real numbers, and points are identified by pairs (in the plane) of numbers. A "metric" or "distance" function is defined (the distance between the points (x_1, y_1) and (x_2, y_2) is $\sqrt{(x_1 - x_2)^2 + (y_1 - y_2)^2}$), and all geometric properties can be expressed in terms of the properties of pairs of numbers in a "space" of such pairs.

The extension of the natural numbers to include zero, the negative integers, rational numbers, the real numbers, the "imaginary" numbers illustrates the continual process in mathematics of idealizing and generalizing. The very name of the imaginary numbers gives striking emphasis to the abstractness of these objects and the difficulty of gaining widespread acceptance, at first, of these constructs. There is an enormous conceptual gulf between the "3" represented by some primitive human holding up three fingers and the number $3\sqrt{-1}$.

There is one great advantage that comes out of the axiomatic approach and of dealing with abstract quantities in symbolic terms. That is a sharpness and clarity that is often lacking in other intellectual pursuits. Sometimes our intuition leads us, in our first attempts to grapple with ideas that are radically new, to use methods that are fuzzy and more reminiscent of philosophy than of mathematics—such as in Leibnitz's handling of infinitesimals in the calculus. However, such methods are often justified by later developments in which the key ideas are made more precise and the early methods are validated—such as the justification of the use of infinitesimals by more rigorous expositions of the calculus or, better, by A. Robinson's model theory [12].

Many of the topics of computer science have been described in the literature in abstract terms with a deemphasis on the "real" world of computing that provided the original motivation for these studies. For example, we have described a finite automaton as a fixed size, deterministic, synchronous, finite state machine. A far more precise description in abstract terms is often given as follows.

A finite automaton (sequential machine) is a sextuple $(\Sigma, \Sigma', Q, f, g, s)$ where:

Σ, the input alphabet, and Σ', the output alphabet, are finite sets of symbols,

Q is the set of states,

f is a function, $f: \Sigma \times Q \to Q$, called the "state transition function" that associates to every ordered pair of a symbol σ of the input alphabet Σ and a (present) state q of Q a (next) state q' in Q,

g is a function $g: \Sigma \times Q \to \Sigma'$, the "output function," that associates to every ordered pair of a symbol σ of Σ and a state q in Q an output symbol σ' in Σ',

$s(\in Q)$ is a distinguished state (the start state).

To the uninitiated, this definition of an automaton as a sextuple of sets and functions will seem quite remote from the image we initially had in mind in thinking of a finite automaton. Where are the machine, the tape, the read/write head, the clock? But, with careful consideration, it is seen that this abstract definition provides everything essential to understanding the information transforming properties of a sequential machine—the input and output alphabets, the list of internal states and the functions that determine the next state and the output symbol as each input symbol is read. All other "machine" considerations are superfluous to understanding the behavior of such a finite automaton.

When couched in terms like these, computer science becomes a part of mathematics. The problems of the "real" world of computing serve to motivate the abstract formulation of the structures with which we deal, but once this is done we are often in domains that can be considered a part of algebra rather than of electrical engineering. It is no surprise that recursive function theory is a part of mathematics, but it was probably not expected that automata theory would reach the present stage where it is rapidly being integrated into modern algebra.

As we have indicated, much of mathematics involves the search for structure, for a perspective that unifies and often explains phenomena that apparently lie in disparate fields. We have seen a number of examples of this search for structure in computer science, with varying success in finding such structure.

Successful attempts at identifying structure include the definitions of the classes of the primitive recursive and the partial recursive functions, the classification by type of the languages defined by phrase structure grammars, the classification of the elementary functions by a complexity hierarchy such as the Ritchie hierarchy, and many other such results. Some areas, such as the totality of results in complexity studies, may seem at present to be rather chaotic. The collection of various isolated phenomena and results are far from being explainable by a unified theory. In this respect the situation may be likened to a frequently occurring one in the physical sciences. For example, the problem of explaining the structure of matter has led, since the time of the ancient Greeks, to theories of atomic structure, including notably the Bohr theory, and these have imparted considerable order to a very complex situation. However, although several successful theories are very useful in explaining many regularities and in predicting a variety of physical phenomena, no single comprehensive theory can explain all recent physical experimental results in a unified way. As we learn more about the unexpectedly varied types of elementary particles, the original theories seem to be oversimplifications, and the search for a unifying structure and theory continues. More and more observational data are being obtained from physical experiments, and this is necessary to the formulation of more successful theories. Analogous to this situation, we are, in computing, going through a period of extensive gathering of evidence. There are a great number of partial theoretical results and considerable empirical data on computer-related phenomena. Although there cannot be any guarantees, many believe that more powerful, comprehensive theories will be forthcoming and that these theories will find wide application to the "real" world of computing.

12.5   THE INFLUENCE OF COMPUTING ON MATHEMATICS

Much of mathematics, especially the "classical" mathematics that preceded the highly abstract corpus of a large part of modern mathematics, was developed in order to cope with the problems of the real world, especially those of physics and astronomy. Newton's exposition of the Calculus in his great work, *Philosophiae Naturalis Principia Mathematica,* was the elaboration of a tool that was needed to analyze the problems of mechanics.

In considering those new problems introduced by the computer and the mathematical developments that these have sparked, the most obvious influence is on applied mathematics, especially numerical analysis. The availability of the high speed computer has motivated very considerable work in the development of efficient algorithms for the solution of a great variety of problems. "Finite," or "discrete," mathematics is the study of the properties of finite sets and is usually considered to include the "combinatorial" mathematics to which we alluded in the appendix of Chapter 3. This area of mathematics has received a great deal of attention in recent years and is very relevant to computer applications. Because of this, it seems likely that the basic mathematical training given computer science students in the universities will include more work in this mathematics of the discrete with, perhaps, a reduced emphasis on the study of the Calculus, that is, on the mathematics of the continuous. Education in the Calculus itself is becoming more "computerized" with a number of pedagogical experiments under way in developing courses where the student uses the computer in part as an experimental tool with which to investigate the properties of functions. This is akin to the use of the computer to conduct simulated physical experiments (cf. Chapter 1).

The influence of the computer may be seen strikingly in looking at modern books on logic. The classical works in this area, written, say, a century or more ago, clearly belonged more to philosophy than to mathematics, with an emphasis on Aristotelian logic. In the first half of the twentieth century, following on the work of Frege, Peano, Russell and Whitehead, and others, a highly mathematical development of formal logic took place. Very recent books on mathematical logic often include extensive treatments of decision and proof methods with detailed coverage of those algorithmic or computational procedures that are significant in these studies.

Perhaps of greatest interest, however, in considering the influence of computing on mathematics, is the use of the computer to assist in the discovery or proof of difficult theorems. There are examples of computer-aided proofs of some previously unproven theorems of algebra, but these are somewhat technical. However, we can see a simply expressed, and yet spectacular, example of such computer-aided mathematical proof in the recently obtained proof of the four-color theorem, which we next describe.

12.6   THE FOUR-COLOR THEOREM

Mathematics is replete with unsolved problems, but most of these require too technical a description to be understood by the layman. There are, however, some notable exceptions, problems whose statements can be given in the simplest terms but which, nevertheless, have defied solution for many years. Some problems in this class (such as the ruler and compass constructions involving the trisection of the angle, the squaring of the circle, and the duplication of the cube) have been proved impossible of solution, and in these cases the problems are effectively dispatched by these rigorous proofs of impossibility. Other problems, like Fermat's last theorem, cited earlier, have resisted all attacks for many generations.

One of the best-known problems of this last kind is the four-color problem, first proposed in 1852 by Francis Guthrie, a young graduate of University College London, and not solved for 124 years. The problem consists of showing that any map drawn in the plane can be colored with not more than four colors so that every two countries sharing a common border (assumed to be a line, not a point) are distinguished by coloring them with two different colors.

The statement of the problem is deceptively simple and does not reflect its difficulty. The problem is usually considered to be within the domain of topology, that branch of mathematics that concerns the study of certain properties of geometric configurations (properties that remain invariant under any deformation unaccompanied by tearing or other discontinuity). However, the great arsenal of existing mathematical results have not provided an easy solution to the problem. Surprisingly, some corresponding problems for maps drawn on some more complex surfaces than the plane were solved much earlier and more easily (it can be shown, for example, that seven colors suffice to color any map drawn on the surface of a torus—a doughnut-shaped surface). The seemingly simpler problem for the plane could not be breeched until 1976, when it was solved by Appel and Haken. A very readable account outlining their solution is given by them in [3]. It is remarkable that the key ideas of their successful attack are fully comprehensible to the layman. As we shall see, the computer played a vital role in their proof.

That at *least* four colors are needed to color an arbitrary map is easily seen from the diagram of Fig. 12.1.

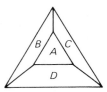

Fig. 12.1   A map requiring four colors.

Since each of the four regions A, B, C, D touches the other three, it is not possible to color this map with fewer than four colors.

In 1879 a purported proof of the four-color conjecture was given by an English barrister and amateur mathematician, Alfred Bray Kempe. His paper contained a fundamental error; however, it did include most of the basic ideas that eventually led to a correct proof. Kempe introduced one simplification by showing that if the theorem is proved true for what he called "normal" maps, then it must be true for arbitrarily drawn maps. A normal map is one in which (1) no country completely surrounds another country and (2) no more than three countries meet at a single point. It is not difficult to show that the result for normal maps implies the result for maps not restricted in this manner. In the following discussion, all maps will be understood to be normal maps.

The successful proof of Appel and Haken is an application of the method of reductio ad absurdum, as was the attempt of Kempe. Assume that there exists some map that requires *five* colors. Among such maps there must then be one that contains the smallest number of countries. Call such a map a minimal "five-chromatic map." It must then be possible to color with only four colors any map that has fewer countries than a minimal five-chromatic map. If we succeed in showing that a map with fewer countries than a minimal five-chromatic map requires *five* colors, a contradiction will have been reached, and the assumption that some map requires five colors must be wrong.

Every map can be analyzed by the kinds of "configurations" that appear locally within it. For example, some possible local configurations involving just a few countries are shown in Fig. 12.2.

These represent respectively countries with precisely two, three, four, and five neighbors. Each configuration is assumed to be a part of some larger map. The dotted line outer boundaries indicate that the part of the map lying outside this "locality" is unspecified.

The authors then show that there exists a set of configurations that are "unavoidable" in the sense that every five-chromatic map must contain locally at least one configuration in the set—and, further, that these unavoidable configurations are all "reducible," meaning that whenever a configuration in the set appears as part of a five-chromatic map it is possible to reduce the number of countries in the map so that it still requires five colors.

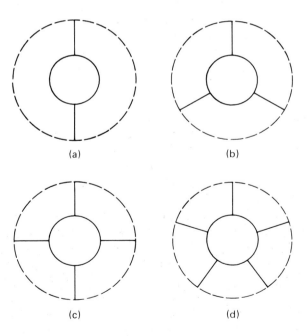

(a)   (b)

(c)   (d)

Fig. 12.2 A set of four unavoidable configurations.

The existence of such an unavoidable, reducible set of configurations proves the four-color hypothesis. For, *no* minimal five-chromatic map can exist. If it did it would have to contain at least one configuration in the unavoidable set. Since this configuration would also be reducible, the given map could be reduced to one with fewer countries and still requiring five colors. Therefore, *no* minimal five-chromatic map exists, and every map can be colored with not more than four colors.

Kempe had attempted a proof along these lines, but he had erred in identifying a set of unavoidable, reducible configurations. He correctly showed that the configurations of Fig. 12.2 comprise an unavoidable set. Every five-chromatic map must contain at least one country with precisely two, three, four, or five neighbors. However, his proof that the five-neighbor case (d) was reducible was defective. This error in his proof was pointed out some eleven years after its original publication.

The problem of representing maps within the computer is solved, and a reformulation of the problem that is key to its solution is obtained, by using the "dual" of a map. The dual is an example of an undirected, connected graph. Every map can be replaced as follows by a set of nodes and path segments connecting these nodes. Each country in a given map is replaced by a single point with a color associated with that point. If two countries share a common border a line is drawn between the two points corresponding to these two countries. It is as though we replaced each country by a point representing its capital and then drew a connecting road between the two capitals of neighboring countries, with that road cutting across their common boundary. Thus, the dual graph for the map of Fig. 12.1 is shown in Fig. 12.3.

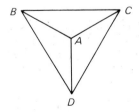

Fig. 12.3 The dual of the map of Fig. 12.1.

Given such a connected graph the four-color problem is now to show that, using no more than four colors, we can attach a color to every node so that connected nodes have distinct colors.

Such dual maps can be represented in the computer using several techniques, including that of the connectivity matrix, as we have seen earlier.

Some quite ingenious, but elementary, methods were used by Appel and Haken to generate an unavoidable set of reducible configurations. However, such a correct set is far more extensive than the four configurations wrongly assumed by Kempe and it includes some 1,500 possible arrangements of countries. The generation of this set of configurations, including the demonstration that they are unavoidable and reducible, involves a substantial computational effort. The methods used to show that large (many countries) configurations are reducible require the analysis of a very large number of details, and it is not possible to execute these procedures without the aid of a high speed computer. Some 1,200 hours on three different computers were used in arriving at the complete solution. This time included computer experiments to perfect some of the key ideas involved in the proof. The authors point out that it is not even possible to check the correctness of their proof without the aid of a computer. They indicate that some mathematicians are rather dismayed by the unavoidable use of the computer in arriving at the solution.

Of great interest is the fact that the computer was used for experimental purposes in developing strategies in the search for an unavoidable set of configurations. Further, it began to give unexpected results. We quote from [3].

> At this point the program, which had been absorbing our ideas and improvements for two years, began to surprise us. When we had hand-checked the analyses produced by the early versions of the program, we were always able to predict their course, but now the computer was acting like a chess-playing machine. It was working out compound strategies based on all the tricks it had been taught, and the new approaches were often much cleverer than those we would have tried. In a sense the program was demonstrating superiority not only in the mechanical parts of the task but in some intellectual areas as well.

The four-color theorem appears to be an ideal example of a theorem that requires such a long proof that it is beyond the reach of ordinary methods. (It is, of course, quite possible that someone will yet discover a short proof of this theorem.) In mathematics there is a premium attached to short, elegant proofs—but there is no assurance that such proofs exist for all interesting theorems. In fact, one of the consequences of the results of Gödel (cf. Chapter 6) and others on the incompleteness of nontrivial mathematical systems is that there are theorems in such systems that can be stated rather compactly but which require prodigiously long proofs. It is possible that a number of important theorems can only be proved with the aid of the computer—that conventional proofs for such theorems might require far more than one person's lifetime simply to write down by manual means.

As still another variant of computer-assisted methods we mention again the notion of a "probabilistic" proof, as in our discussion in Chapter 11 of Rabin's work on probabilistic algorithms. In those instances where such a method is applicable we are able to show in reasonable time that the probability is very high that a certain statement is true. When this probability is exceedingly close to 1, we might consider such a "proof" as being tantamount to a certainty.

These computer-aided approaches have opened up new possibilities in the search for truth in mathematics.

12.7 A CHECKLIST OF SOME KEY RELEVANT MATHEMATICAL IDEAS

By way of review and of emphasis, we briefly list some of the mathematical notions that we have seen to be significant in the art of programming.

- The concept and the key role of function, including functions of higher order; the consequent need in designing programming languages for facilities for the definition of functions and of subroutines.

- The role of logic and of Boolean algebra, both in the design of computers and as a programming tool; the need for the inclusion of logical operations in programming languages.

- The set theory ideas that have influenced the design of programming languages such as SETL.

- The proof of the adequacy of a proposed set of programming facilities, of order codes or of schema such as the structured programming approach, by showing that these suffice, given unlimited space and time, to compute an arbitrary recursive function.

- The essential roles of the operations of composition, recursion, and minimalization in computing an arbitrary computable function; the need for programming facilities to handle these operations, in particular the universal role and great importance of recursion.

- The format used in the description of mathematical structures, such as formal systems, as a model for the rigorous description of programming languages.

- The use of the theory of finite automata and of formal languages in compiler design.

Our list is not intended to be complete but rather to emphasize some of the more important ideas upon which we have dwelt. Recall also that we have in this work largely ignored computer *applications* and that in consequence we have not included the plethora of mathematical results relevant to the full use of the computer.

12.8   GENERAL REMARKS, THE CHRONOLOGY OF EVENTS

We have seen that the relationship of mathematics to computing is far from being only that of donor to donee. Computing is influencing mathematics in several ways apart from the practical one of the changing nature of employment opportunities for those with mathematical inclinations. The computer is not merely a tool that can be used to advantage in some mathematical investigations. Of perhaps greater importance, the constructive approach, as we have emphasized in the appendix to Chapter 1, is having an impact on mathematics that cannot yet be fully assessed.

The growth of the subject matter in such subjects as automata theory during the last several decades has been surprising. What was only a few years ago a highly esoteric subject with few practitioners has proliferated considerably with, as one evidence of this, a significant production rate of new Ph.D. dissertations written in this area. In 1956, E. F. Moore, one of the pioneers in this field, published a paper "Gedanken Experiments on Sequential Machines." Some fifteen years later he mentioned that at the time he wrote his article he had thought that his paper (of some 30 pages) included most of what was worth saying about finite automata. He had in no way foreseen the astonishing development that was to take place in the following years. Undoubtedly much of this work has been motivated in part by the increasingly dominant role that the computer plays in the sciences and in our society at large.

Perhaps nowhere in the practice of computing has a mathematical approach had a greater impact on a subject than in the study of compiling. Original efforts along these lines, as evidenced, say, by the early work on the first FORTRAN compiler, described in a 1957 paper by its authors [4], included a number of ingenious ad hoc procedures (cf. also [14]), with no reference to the theory of automata or of formal languages. Compare this with the highly mathematical exposition in a number of recent books on compiler design [1, 2, 9, 10]. A quite formalistic approach is now both feasible and desirable, and nowhere is the transition of programming from art to science made more evident. One result of this more formal, disciplined approach in handling some of the problems of compiling is a sharp reduction in the programming effort needed to implement a compiler.

In some respects, perhaps because it is a "frontier" science, a more relaxed approach appears in some communications within the computer sciences than in some of the older sciences. Fragmented and partial results, occasionally more heuristic than profound, sometimes appear in the literature, and these would never be accepted for publication in some of the more staid journals of mathematics. Articles that mainly give promise of future results, rather than describe substantial accomplishments, and bearing titles like "Toward a Theory of _____" appear on occasion. This may not be surprising in view of the comparative newness of the subject matter and the brief period during which the search for structure has gone on.

We close this discussion by emphasizing again that all of computer science concerns, in essence, the study of the manipulation of symbols. (Recall the salient characteristics of Turing machines, automata, and formal languages.) We could also have begun the study of mathematics by describing the natural numbers as symbolic strings and then defining the arithmetic operations in terms of symbolic manipulation. All of mathematics could subsequently be unfolded in formal terms (the language of mathematics), where we manipulate symbolic strings using unambiguous rules (effective procedures), that we hope reflect some underlying structure.

The application of computing is limited only by the extent to which such symbolic representation and manipulation can mirror reality. In fact, the only precise way in which we can describe reality is by assuming such representation in symbolic terms. Of course, however, something is lost in mapping some structures into the natural numbers or into symbols. A string of bits that is an encoding of Beethoven's *Pastoral* Symphony or of Michelangelo's *David* might, it is true, contain enough information to enable one to reconstitute these works of art, but that which is significant in their structure would not be recognizable. No one would applaud on seeing such a bit string.

APPENDIX
THE INFLUENCE OF MODERN ALGEBRA

A number of "pure" mathematicians, most notably S. Eilenberg, have recognized the algebraic character of much of automata theory and of formal linguistics, and a major effort is under way to reformulate large parts of these areas of computer science in algebraic terms. It is clear that this approach results in more succinct demonstrations of existing theorems, and it is hoped that the new perspective and clarity of mathematical structure so obtained will lead to important new discoveries. To give the reader some taste of this formulation in algebraic terms we briefly describe an algebraic category and show how to describe in these terms the class of finite automata and a class of machines that realize the partial recursive functions.

   This kind of mathematics has been described (by some mathematicians) as "abstract nonsense," but the fruitful perspective that it seems to provide in considering the applied problems of computer science indicates that this criticism is too harsh.

   Our discussion follows that given in [5].

12.9 COMPUTER SCIENCE AND ALGEBRA

The search for greater order and clearer structure in the computer sciences has led a number of research workers to cast many of the problems of automata theory, computability, and linguistics in algebraic terms. In particular, the perspective offered by categorical algebra is very useful. This branch of algebra is a recently developed subject that has been successfully applied to the study of the structure of a number of mathematical systems. The central ideas are fertile in that they often relate developments in quite disparate mathematical fields. Thus, the theory provides a substantial unifying force that is often antithetical to the great profusion of modern mathematics. The notions involved are at times suggestive of new results or of interesting problems, and the tools, techniques, and vocabulary of the theory often permit compact and elegant expositions of earlier obtained mathematical results. It is not unreasonable, therefore, to expect that a language and perspective that are so productive in describing and guiding the development of large portions of mathematics should be equally useful in automata theory, computability, and formal linguistics.

   A major effort in recasting much of the subject matter of computer science in algebraic terms is described in the books on *Automata, Languages, and Machines* by S. Eilenberg [6].

   To give the reader some appreciation of an algebraic orientation in studying parts of computer science we shall briefly describe categorical algebra, and we shall define a finite automaton in these terms.

   Category theory concerns objects that are often taken to be sets and generalized mappings or "morphisms" between pairs of these objects. As MacLane has observed [11], "Each type of mathematical system gives rise to a corresponding category, whose objects are the systems of that type and whose morphisms are the maps of such systems. Put differently, this approach suggests that whenever a new type of mathematical system is defined, one should simultaneously define the morphisms of that system." Many of the structures of the mathematical computer sciences allow expression within this framework. We give here only the most fundamental notions of category theory.

Definition of "category." A category $\mathscr{C}$ is a given collection of objects, $A, B, C, \ldots$, and for each ordered pair of these objects a given set (possibly empty) of "maps" or "morphisms." We write $f: A \rightarrow B$ or $A \xrightarrow{f} B$ to denote a morphism associated with the ordered pair (A, B). The name "map" suggests that the early consideration of these structures actually concerned mappings from a set A into a set B. We even call A the "domain" of f and B the "codomain" or "range" of f. However, a key point is that morphisms, while they satisfy the basic properties of mappings, are generalizations of them. They are not necessarily mappings or functions, and various other interpretations may be appropriate in those parts of automata theory to which these ideas have been applied.

The axioms satisfied by the objects and morphisms of a category are the following:

1. Composition of Morphisms: If $f: A \rightarrow B$ and $g: B \rightarrow C$ then a unique morphism $h: A \rightarrow C$ is determined and we write $h = gf$. We can represent this situation pictorially as

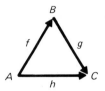

The fact that $h = gf$ is expressed by saying that this diagram "commutes" (i.e., the two paths from A to C identify equivalent morphisms). Note the implied order in the writing of "gf." This stems from functional notation where $(gf)(x)$ is generally taken to be the result of applying the function f to x followed by applying the function g to this result.

2. Associativity of Composition: The multiplication of morphisms, defined in (1), is associative, i.e., $f(gh) = (fg)h$ whenever fg and gh are defined.

3. Identity Morphisms: Associated with every object A is a morphism $I_A: A \rightarrow A$ that satisfies $fI_A = f$ for every morphism $f: A \rightarrow B$, and satisfies $I_A g = g$ for every $g: B \rightarrow A$. It is easily shown that I_A is necessarily unique.

If, for a given morphism $f: A \rightarrow B$, there exists a morphism $g: B \rightarrow A$ so that $gf = I_A$ and $fg = I_B$, f is said to be invertible, and its inverse is g. The inverse, if it exists, can be shown to be unique. Two objects A, B are said to be *equivalent* if there exists an invertible $f: A \rightarrow B$. An invertible morphism is sometimes called an isomorphism.

If a category has just one object, then any pair of morphisms can be multiplied and by axioms (1), (2), (3) these morphisms constitute a monoid. (Cf. Section 9.3)

As an example, the family of all sets together with functions defined between them form a category generally identified as *Ens*. In many categories that are studied the objects may be a number of different kinds of mathematical structures.

Given a category $\mathscr{A}$ we may denote by hom $\mathscr{A}$ the class of morphisms in $\mathscr{A}$. For two given objects A, B in $\mathscr{A}$, hom(A, B) denotes the class of morphisms whose domain is A and codomain is B, i.e.,

$$\text{hom}(A, B) = \{f \mid f: A \rightarrow B\}.$$

In looking at any particular system of automata theory, be it a machine or a class of machines or a class of functions, and so forth, we can interpret that system as a category if we identify a class of objects and a class of morphisms so that the axioms (1), (2), (3) are satisfied. Sometimes there are several ways of doing this, and one approach may be more rewarding than another—leading to more interesting questions and a more useful perspective. On occasion a system may only in the most trivial way be considered a category, with little apparently gained from such identification. As we have pointed out, if only one object is identified in the class of objects, we are dealing with a monoid, and it does not seem reasonable to expect any "rich" development or new insight to be provided by such a perspective in this case.

To illustrate these notions, we shall describe a finite automaton from this point of view.

A Finite Automaton as a Category.   Consider a finite automaton $\mathscr{A}$ with states $S = \{s_0, s_1, \ldots, s_{n-1}\}$ and associated alphabet $\Sigma = \{\sigma_1, \sigma_2, \ldots, \sigma_p\}$. Let s_0 be the "start state," and, using the notation of Chapter 8, designate by $S_F = \{s_i \mid i \in F\}$ the subset of "favorable" final states. A state transition function $M: S \times \Sigma \rightarrow S$ is defined and, as usual, the behavior of A consists of "recognizing" or "accepting" a set of tapes or strings of symbols drawn from Σ (i.e., elements of the free monoid Σ^* that includes as identity the null tape Λ). We can, in fact, conforming to customary usage, define the *behavior* of $\mathscr{A}$, written as behavior ($\mathscr{A}$), to be this set of accepted tapes.

We can consider $\mathscr{A}$ to be a category by taking its objects to be the states S, and, as the morphisms of $\mathscr{A}$, we define hom(s_i, s_j) to be the set of tapes which transform s_i into s_j. Thus, in the state transition graph, illustrated in Fig. 12.4, of a typical automaton $\mathscr{A}$ with alphabet 0, 1, start state s_0 and acceptance state s_4, hom(s_i, s_j) consists of all labeled paths beginning at s_i and continuing to s_j, $(i, j \in \{0, 1, 2, 3, 4\})$.

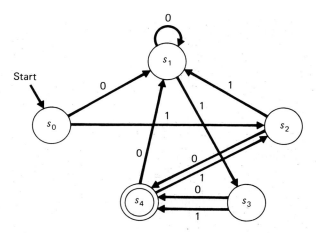

Figure 12.4

It is clear then that in general the set of accessible states, or states that the automaton can reach after starting in state s_0, is $\{s_j \mid \hom(s_0, s_j) \neq \Phi\}$ where Φ is the null set. We also note that behavior $(\mathscr{A}) = \bigcup_{f \in F} \hom(s_0, s_f)$.

The composition of morphisms is, of course, defined by concatenation. If $f: s_i \rightarrow s_j$ and $g: s_j \rightarrow s_k$ then $h = gf$ is by definition the tape consisting of f with g catenated in the obvious way (if $f = \sigma_1^{(1)} \sigma_2^{(1)} \cdots \sigma_p^{(1)}$ and $g = \sigma_1^{(2)} \sigma_2^{(2)} \cdots \sigma_q^{(2)}$, then $gf = \sigma_1^{(1)} \sigma_2^{(1)} \cdots \sigma_p^{(1)} \sigma_1^{(2)} \cdots \sigma_q^{(2)}$).

Composition of morphisms is clearly associative, and the identity morphism for each object (state) is taken to be the null tape Λ.

We remark that $\hom(s_i, s_j)$, a subset of Σ^*, is called an *event* and the notion of the automaton's being "strongly connected" is that $\hom(s_i, s_j)$ is never empty. The identical notion appears in category theory.

12.10 CATEGORIES OF MACHINES

In some unpublished work of Eilenberg and Elgot, a physical realization of the category of recursive functions is defined that is helpful in describing the structure of machines with specified behavior. We summarize some of their work below.

An "object" in such an interpretation is a k-tuple of lines corresponding to a k-tuple of natural numbers. A "line" is understood as a potential carrier of signals representing the integers. At any given time a single line may contain no information or it may, by its configuration, represent a particular integer. A "morphism" is a "black box" which transforms an incoming k-tuple into an outgoing m-tuple (Fig. 12.5) and we write $f: [k] \to [m]$.

Figure 12.5

A few fundamental morphisms and combining operations for morphisms suffice to describe the structure of a machine with any specified behavior, corresponding to the computation of a partial recursive function. These include the following.

1. Composition. If $f: [k] \to [m]$, $g: [m] \to [n]$ then there exists a unique $h: [k] \to [n]$ such that $h = gf$.

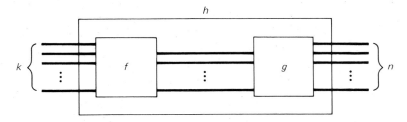

This is seen to be the categorical composition of morphisms.

2. Mapping Functions. $f: [m] \to [n]$.

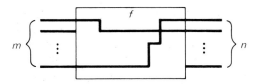

Every output line comes from only one input line, i.e., lines can split but not merge in passing through the box.

3. The direct sum operation, which associates with $f: [m] \rightarrow [p]$, $g: [n] \rightarrow [q]$ the morphism $f \oplus g: [m + n] \rightarrow [p + q]$ as implied by the following diagram.

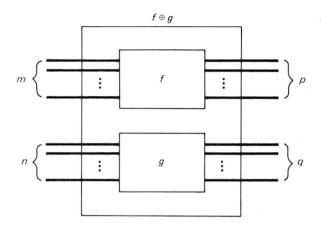

4. The operation of iteration, which associates with morphisms $f: [r] \rightarrow [r]$, $g: [r] \rightarrow [r]$ the morphism gf^* corresponding to the function defined in Section 4.12. We can represent this schematically as

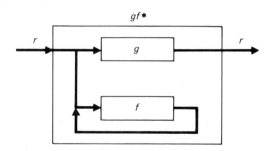

Here r represents a bundle of r lines.

With these "building blocks" it can be shown that a machine realization for any partial recursive function can be given.

REFERENCES

1. Aho, A. V., and J. D. Ullman, *The Theory of Parsing, Translation and Compiling,* Vol. 1: *Parsing,* 1972; Vol. 2: *Compiling,* 1973. Englewood Cliffs, N.J.: Prentice-Hall.

2. Aho, A. V., and J. D. Ullman, *Principles of Compiler Design.* Reading, Massachusetts: Addison-Wesley, 1977.

3. Appel, K., and W. Haken, "The Solution of the Four-Color-Map Problem." *Scientific American,* **237,** 4 (October 1977).

4. Backus, J. W., et al., "The FORTRAN Automatic Coding System." *Proceedings of the Western Joint Computer Conference,* **11** (1957). Reprinted in S. Rosen, ed. *Programming Systems and Languages.* New York: McGraw-Hill, 1967.

5. Beckman, F. S., *Categorical Notions and Duality in Automata Theory.* IBM Res. Rep. RC 2977, July 28, 1970.

6. Eilenberg, S., *Automata, Languages, and Machines.* New York: Academic Press, Vol. A, 1974; Vol. B, 1977.

7. Gelernter, H., "Realization of a Geometry Theorem-Proving Machine." *Proceedings of the International Conference on Information Processing.* Paris: UNESCO House, 1959. Reprinted in E. Feigenbaum, and J. Feldman, eds., *Computers and Thought.* New York: McGraw-Hill, 1963.

8. Gelernter, H., J. Hansen, and D. Loveland, "Empirical Explorations of the Geometry Theorem-Proving Machine." *Proceedings of the Western Joint Computer Conference,* **17** (1960). Reprinted in E. Feigenbaum, and J. Feldman, eds., *Computers and Thought.* New York: McGraw-Hill, 1963.

9. Gries, D. *Compiler Construction for Digital Computers.* New York: John Wiley, 1971.

10. Lewis II, P. M., D. J. Rosenkrantz, and R. E. Stearns, *Compiler Design Theory.* Reading, Massachusetts: Addison-Wesley, 1976.

11. MacLane, S., "Categorical Algebra." *Bull. Amer. Math. Soc.,* **71** (1965).

12. Robinson, A., *Non-Standard Analysis.* Amsterdam: North-Holland Publishing Company, 1966.

13. Rogers, H., Jr., "The Present Theory of Turing Machine Computability." *J. Soc. Industr. Appl. Math.,* **7,** 1 (March 1959).

14. Sheridan, P. B., "The Arithmetic Translator-Compiler of the IBM FORTRAN Automatic Coding System." *Comm. Assn. Comp. Mach.,* **2** (February 1959).

15. Tarski, A., *A Decision Method for Elementary Algebra and Geometry.* Berkeley, California: University of California Press, 1951.

Index

Index

Dedekind, R., 21
deep structure, 306
depth of a machine circuit, 369, 377, 393, 397
delay element, 78, 238
delimiters, 296
De Morgan's laws, 66, 82
denumerable, 90
derivation, 297, 344
   left-most, 304
   right-most, 304, 311
Descartes, R., 85, 411
determinant, 380
deterministic language, 334
deterministic procedures, 27
diagonalization, 92–94, 211
difference table, 402
digitize, 15
digraph, 100, 223, 345, 346
Dijkstra, E. W., 143, 150
disjoint sets, 81
disjunction (OR), 55
disjunctive normal form, 62, 78, 97
distributive law, 81
"double-line" trick, 242
doubly recursive, 124, 125
"do while", 131, 145, 150
dual automaton, 269, 275
dual of a map, 420
Dunham, C., 194, 217

effective computability, 1, 9, 115, 130, 151, 152, 174, 228, 412
effective procedures, 1, 2, 17, 152, 228
   in physics, 26, 224
effectively calculable, 9
Eilenberg, S., 137, 138, 150, 200, 424, 425, 428, 431
elementary arithmetic functions, 370
Elgot, C., 137, 138, 150, 428
elimination, 379, 406
ELIZA, 251
encoding of graphs, 107
enumerable, 90
equality of sets, 81
equivalence relation, 43

Euclidean geometry, 51, 142, 362, 411, 413, 414
event, 428
exclusive OR, 66, 76
exponential growth, 373, 374

fan-in components, 370, 391–397
feedback, 220, 243–246
Fermat's last theorem, 215, 358, 417
file, 88
   inverted, 88
finite automata, 202, 219, 227, 228, 246, 255–285
   as acceptors, 255
   defined as categories, 427, 428
   how they are described, 256
   dual of a finite automaton, 269, 275
   functions computed by, 264–267, 370, 387–389
   input alphabet, 256, 257, 414
   nondeterministic, 267–271
   notation, 268, 269
   output alphabet, 256, 415
   with read tape backwards capability, 276–279, 383, 384
   as recognizers, 228, 261
   sequential machines, 229, 246
   use in parsing sentences of context-free languages, 315–321
finite mathematics, 416
finitely performable procedures, 4
FIRST, 366
floor, 128
flowcharts, 143–147, 349
Floyd, R. W. 339, 367
formal languages, 182, 205, 227, 255, 287–363, 410
formal systems, 9, 19, 47, 49, 142, 213, 290
   axioms of, 50, 60
FORTRAN, 175, 308, 324, 376, 423
four-color problem, 417–422
Frege, G., 417
Freudenthal, H., 356–358, 367
full adder, 77, 78